African American History

Lisbeth Gant-Britton

HOLT, RINEHART AND WINSTON

A Harcourt Education Company

Orlando • **Austin** • New York • San Diego • London

Author

Dr. Lisbeth Gant-Britton

Dr. Lisbeth Gant-Britton is currently the Student Affairs Officer of the Afro-American Studies Program at the University of California, Los Angeles (UCLA), where she co-administers the undergraduate and graduate programs. Formerly the Marlene Crandell Francis Professor of the Humanities in the English Department at Kalamazoo College in Kalamazoo, Michigan, she has also taught African American history and culture at UCLA and at the USC Film School, among other universities.

Dr. Gant-Britton has taught courses in African American Studies, American literature, ethnic literature, contemporary fiction, and the novel. She has written extensively on subjects including female writers of color in science fiction and fantasy. Her work on African American history has been recognized by the Los Angeles mayor's office with a special commendation for its contribution to racial understanding through education.

Cover photos (top to bottom): Tuskegee Airmen (Bettmann/CORBIS), Maya Angelou (AP/Wide World Photos), Harriet Tubman (CORBIS), George Washington Carver (George Washington Carver Stamp Design ©1997 United States Postal Service. All Rights Reserved. Used with Permission.), Frederick Douglass (Onondaga Historical Association, #1998.1.21.171B), Martin Luther King Jr. (Time & Life Pictures/Getty Images)

Back cover (top to bottom): Rosa Parks (AP/Wide World Photos), Mae Jemison (NASA), Charles Drew (Alfred Eisenstaedt/Time Life Pictures/Getty Images)

ISBN 978-0-03-096954-6

ISBN 0-03-096954-9

1 2 3 4 5 6 7 8 032 10 08 09 08 07

Program Advisors

Educational Reviewers

Vannetta Bailey-Iddrisu
Miami-Dade County Public Schools
    and Miami Dade College
Miami, Florida

Lawrence D. Broughton
Proviso East High School
Maywood, Illinois

John R. Doyle
Administrative Director, Curriculum
    and Instruction, Social Sciences
Miami-Dade County Public Schools
Miami, Florida

Calvin D. Freeman
Durham School of the Arts
Durham, North Carolina

Kevin A. Gideon
Bolton High School
Arlington, Tennessee

Jason Matthew Hayes
Dobie Middle School
Austin, Texas

Jacquelin S. McCord
Social Science Manager
Department of High School
    Curriculum and Instruction
Chicago, Illinois

Valerie Miller
Detroit Public Schools
Detroit, Michigan

Lance A. Robert
St. Bernard High School
Playa del Rey, California

Sherrilyn Scott
Miami-Dade County
    Public Schools, Supervisor
Miami, Florida

Gloria P. Simmons, M.S.W.
Executive Director
Miami-Dade County Public Schools,
    Office of Diversity Compliance
Miami, Florida

Rev. Abraham J. Thomas
African American Advisory Committee
Miami, Florida

Alvesta Britt Walker
Miami-Dade County Public Schools
Miami, Florida

Partnership Consultants

Barbara Andrews
Director of Curatorial Services,
    National Civil Rights Museum
Memphis, Tennessee

Dr. Thomas C. Battle
Director, Moorland-Spingarn
    Research Center, Howard University
Washington, D.C.

Sylvia Cyrus-Albritton
Executive Director, Association
    for the Study of African American
    Life and History
Washington, D.C.

Dr. John E. Fleming
National President, Association for the
    Study of African American Life and
    History
Cincinnati, Ohio

Contents

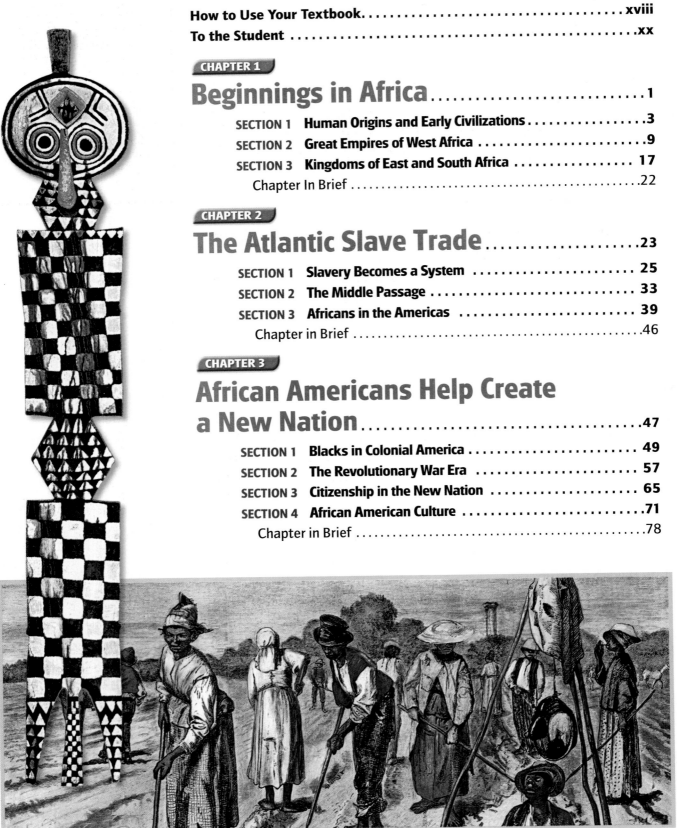

The Granger Collection, New York

CAUTION!! COLORED PEOPLE OF BOSTON, ONE & ALL, You are hereby respectfully CAUTIONED and advised, to avoid conversing with the Watchmen and Police Officers of Boston, For since the recent ORDER OF THE MAYOR & ALDERMEN, they are empowered to act as KIDNAPPERS AND Slave Catchers, And they have already been actually employed in KIDNAPPING, CATCHING, AND KEEPING SLAVES. Therefore, if you value your LIBERTY, and the Welfare of the Fugitives among you, Shun them in every possible manner, as so many HOUNDS on the track of the most unfortunate of your race. Keep a Sharp Look Out for KIDNAPPERS, and have TOP EYE open. APRIL 24, 1851.

The Granger Collection, New York

Features

Applying What You've Learned

Apply your knowledge of important events, issues, and people in African American history.

As You Read

Take notes on key points from each section with helpful graphic organizers.

Building Social Studies Skills

Learn, practice, and apply key critical thinking and social studies skills.

PRIMARY SOURCES

Examine key documents, speeches, images, and other primary sources that tell the story of African American history.

HISTORY'S VOICES

"The new Negro, through the Universal Negro Improvement Association, is speaking for himself. The new Negro is saying to the world: 'There can be no abiding peace until we are fully emancipated.'"

—Marcus Garvey, Speech in Washington D.C., 1921

FACES OF HISTORY

Meet the people who have made history and learn about their lives.

Charts, Graphs, and Info Graphics

Analyze information presented visually to learn more about history.

Maps

Interpret maps to see where important events happened and to analyze how geography influenced African American history.

Primary Sources

Relive history through eyewitness accounts, literature, and documents.

ASSOCIATION FOR THE STUDY OF AFRICAN AMERICAN LIFE AND HISTORY

ASALH
"Founders of Black History Month"

Holt, Rinehart and Winston is collaborating with the oldest and most prestigious organization dedicated to the study of African American history—the **Association for the Study of African American Life and History, Inc.**, (ASALH). Founded in 1915 by Dr. Carter G. Woodson, the mission of ASALH is "to promote research, preserve, interpret, and disseminate information about Black life, history, and culture to the global community."

THE FATHER OF BLACK HISTORY

Dr. Carter G. Woodson, the "Father of Black History," founded ASALH in 1915 as the Study of Negro Life and History. Woodson strongly believed that educating the public about the contributions made by African Americans to U.S. history and culture would transform race relations and empower African Americans. Working toward this end, Woodson directed ASALH until his death in 1950. Woodson also published more than 20 books on black history.

Dr. Carter G. Woodson

BLACK HISTORY MONTH

Today, from its headquarters in Washington, D.C., ASALH strives to fulfill Woodson's vision. Every year ASALH sets the theme for the national Black History Month. This tradition dates back to 1926, when Woodson instituted a "Negro History Week" to bring attention to the contributions of African Americans. Woodson chose the second week of February to honor the birthdays of President Abraham Lincoln and famed abolitionist Frederick Douglass. In 1976 the nation celebrated its first official Black History Month. Today ASALH provides information and support for its annual Black History Month theme with the *Woodson Review* and other instructional materials.

ASALH celebrates and promotes African American history and culture.

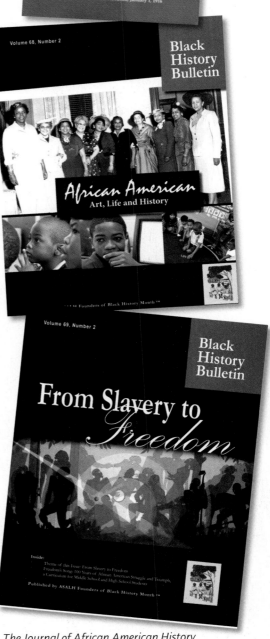

PROMOTING AFRICAN AMERICAN HISTORY

In 1916, recognizing that the struggles and achievements of African Americans were often ignored or misrepresented, ASALH launched *The Journal of Negro History*, now called the *Journal of African American History*. Today the *Journal of African American History* continues to be the premier outlet for prominent scholars publishing in the field of African American history.

ASALH also publishes the *Black History Bulletin*. First published in 1937, the *Black History Bulletin*, formerly the *Negro History Bulletin*, is a widely circulating publication geared toward meeting the needs of primary and secondary educators. This innovative publication provides teachers access to current research in African American history along with exciting teaching strategies and lesson plans that conform to national history standards.

go.hrw.com
Program Home Page
Keyword: SAAH STUDENT

ASALH's *Black History Bulletin* provides educators with instructional strategies and lessons plans for teaching African American history.

The Journal of African American History and the *Black History Bulletin* help promote the study and teaching of African American history.

HOWARD UNIVERSITY'S
MOORLAND-SPINGARN RESEARCH CENTER

Holt, Rinehart and Winston is proud to partner with **Howard University's Moorland-Spingarn Research Center**, home to one of the largest collections of materials chronicling the history and culture of people of African descent. The center is dedicated to preserving, protecting, and providing access to a range of resources that trace the black experience in Africa, the Americas, and other parts of the world.

Students and scholars can browse the vast collection of materials at the Moorland-Spingarn Research Center.

THE BEGINNING

The Moorland-Spingarn Research Center is located at Howard University in Washington, D.C. Founded in 1867, Howard University is one of the nation's leading comprehensive academic and research institutions. A predominantly African American university, Howard is known for its emphasis on leadership and diversity. The university, which offers more than 120 areas of study leading to undergraduate, graduate, and professional degrees, attracts top students from around the nation and the world.

The history of the Moorland-Spingarn Research Center officially began in 1914 when Jesse Moorland, a Washington, D.C., minister, donated his extensive library to Howard University. The true origins of the research center, however, date back to the founding of Howard University. Shortly after the university was chartered, a committee was assembled to select books for the library. Among the library's first titles were books on Africa and books and photographs from the personal collection of General Oliver Otis Howard, a founder of Howard University and a great supporter of the library. Others contributed books and materials on slavery, the abolitionist movement, and the Civil War.

Mod Mekkawi, Director, University Libraries at Howard University

Howard University emphasizes leadership and diversity.

Ceremonial Oba mask

Space shuttle pilot Colonel Frederick Drew Gregory carried this Spingarn Medal (shown below) into space.

THE COLLECTION

Today, the Moorland-Spingarn Research Center has one of the world's largest collections devoted to black history and culture. The center's library boasts more than 200,000 books and tens of thousands of newspapers and journals. The center's manuscript division holds a wealth of primary source documents, including more than 1,000 oral histories, 15,000 sound recordings, nearly 2,000 film and video recordings, 3,000 sheets of music, and more than 100,000 prints, photo graphs, maps, and other graphic images.

The Moorland-Spingarn Research Center is also a treasure trove of artifacts. The center's vast holdings include a rare seventeenth-century map of Africa; an eighteenth-century ceremonial Oba mask, carved of ivory, from the Kingdom of Benin; slavery deeds of sale; reward posters for runaway slaves; an early photograph of abolitionist Frederick Douglass; a World War II poster featuring a Tuskegee airman; Black Panther Party posters from the 1960s; and memorabilia from the twentieth anniversary of the March on Washington.

THE CONNECTION

Together with the Moorland-Spingarn Research Center, Holt presents **Connecting to Our Past**. This exciting new online feature brings African American history and culture to life through rarely seen artifacts from the collection at Howard University's Moorland-Spingarn Research Center.

go.hrw.com
Program Home Page
Keyword: SAAH STUDENT

World War II poster featuring a Tuskegee airman

Museum exhibits (left to right): African American protests; one of many lunch-counter sit-ins; a freedom-ride bus

NATIONAL CIVIL RIGHTS MUSEUM

Holt, Rinehart and Winston proudly partners with the **National Civil Rights Museum** to bring you *Holt African American History*. The primary mission of the National Civil Rights Museum is to document the history of the American civil rights movement. Established at the historic Lorraine Motel in Memphis, Tennessee, the Museum aims to advance the legacy of the civil rights movement by inspiring ongoing participation in civil and human rights movements worldwide.

A wreath marks the balcony where Dr. Martin Luther King Jr. was assassinated.

THE LORRAINE MOTEL

In April 1968 Dr. Martin Luther King Jr. traveled to Memphis, Tennessee, to lend his support to the city's striking sanitation workers. As was his custom when visiting Memphis, King was a guest at the Lorraine Motel. On April 4, he stepped out of Room 306 and onto the motel's balcony. Minutes later, he was shot dead by an assassin's bullet. King's death was a tragic blow to the U.S. civil rights movement, but African Americans and many others continued to press for the equal rights that were guaranteed to them under the U.S. Constitution. Today the National Civil Rights Museum is located at the site of the historic Lorraine Motel.

Exhibits (left to right): Memphis, Tennessee, sanitation workers' strike; Rosa Parks refusing to give up her seat; the March on Washington

THE MUSEUM

On September 28, 1991, after nearly a decade of planning, the Lorraine Motel opened its doors to visitors as the National Civil Rights Museum. Today the Museum serves as a memorial for Dr. King and as a testament to the spirit of the U.S. civil rights movement.

Through a series of interactive exhibits, the Museum chronicles the struggle of African Americans to gain freedom and equality from the slavery period to the present. Exhibits transport visitors back in time to key moments in the civil rights movement—to the day that Rosa Parks refused to relinquish her seat, sparking the Montgomery, Alabama, bus boycott; to a student sit-in demonstration at a lunch counter reminiscent of Greensboro, North Carolina; to the burned shell of a freedom-ride Greyhound bus; to the re-creation of the room Dr. King occupied at the Lorraine Motel on the evening of his death.

EDUCATIONAL PROGRAMS

The educational focus of the National Civil Rights Museum is designed to increase awareness and promote active participation in the ongoing struggle for civil and human rights throughout the world. To accomplish this goal, the Museum's educational programs and initiatives utilize the histories contained in the permanent exhibitions as a springboard for learning. Web site programming—including expanded oral history excerpts, biographies, brain teaser exercises, and resource guides—help enhance and stimulate an atmosphere for learning and citizenship engagement. Public Forum events

present unique opportunities for the public to learn from world leaders about the transformative power individuals have to affect change.

Since opening its doors, the focus of the National Civil Rights Museum has included a global mission to recognize and advocate for civil and human rights movements worldwide. Toward this end, the Museum annually bestows two Freedom Awards, one national and one international, to people who have contributed significantly in the struggle for equality, justice, and freedom for the world's people.

For more information on the National Civil Rights Museum, please visit **www.civilrightsmuseum.org**.

go.hrw.com
Program Home Page
Keyword: SAAH STUDENT

Experience the civil rights movement as you visit the many exhibits in the museum.

xvii

How to Use Your Textbook

Holt African American History features a new and exciting WorkText design that allows you to make the book your very own. Use the graphic organizers, activities, and other pieces to enhance your understanding of African American history.

Student WorkText

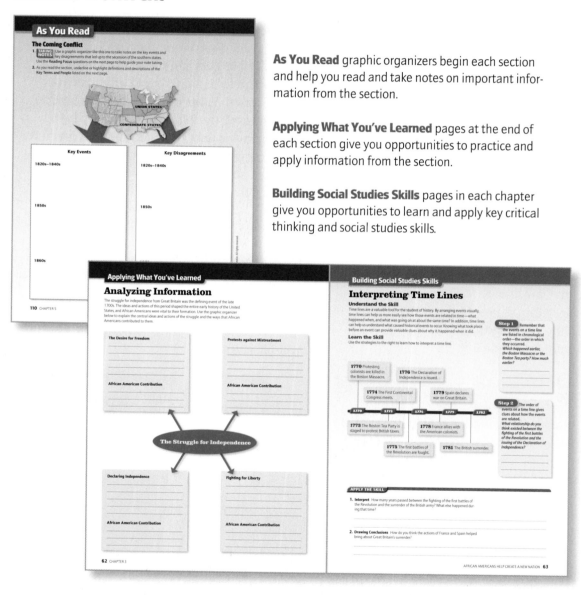

As You Read graphic organizers begin each section and help you read and take notes on important information from the section.

Applying What You've Learned pages at the end of each section give you opportunities to practice and apply information from the section.

Building Social Studies Skills pages in each chapter give you opportunities to learn and apply key critical thinking and social studies skills.

Chapter

Chapter Openers include an Expressing Your Opinion writing feature that allows you to take a stand on important issues that relate to African American history.

Chapter in Brief pages summarize key points to remember from each section in the chapter and provide easy-to-find links to the online program.

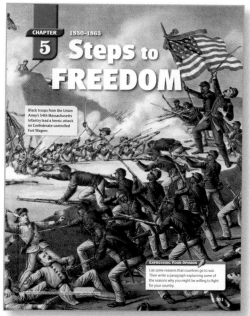

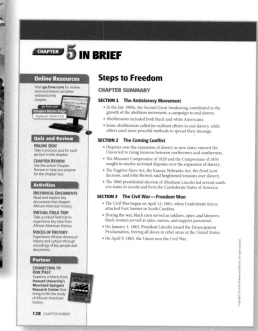

Section

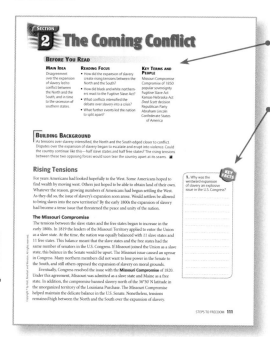

The section's **Main Idea statement**, **Focus Questions**, and **Key Terms and People** appear at the beginning of each section and help guide your note taking.

Key Facts features help you to focus on important details from the section.

Reading Check Questions provide frequent opportunities to review and assess your understanding.

Section Assessments help you check your understanding of the main ideas or key terms and people in each section. There is also assessment practice online.

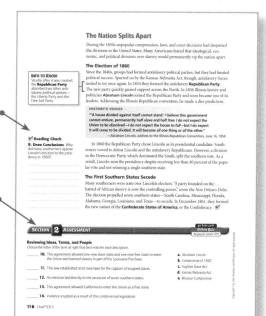

HOW TO USE YOUR TEXTBOOK **xix**

To the Student

Every February, in schools across the United States, students and teachers celebrate Black History Month. We owe this national tradition and, more importantly, the study of African American history to Dr. Carter G. Woodson, who in 1926 introduced "Negro History Week." Dr. Woodson was deeply disturbed by how black people were ignored in the history books of his day. Absent from the official record were the great civilizations of Africa, the determined will of black Americans to survive the most dire of circumstances, as well as the collective and individual contributions of African Americans to our nation's culture and history. In response, Woodson took on the challenge of writing these stories into United States history.

Following in Woodson's footsteps, *Holt African American History* aims to tell a complete history of black America. The story begins in ancient Africa and travels through the Atlantic slave trade to colonial America and the building of a new nation. From there, the story continues to touch upon the experiences and achievements of African Americans in their heroic struggle for freedom—the Civil War, Reconstruction, segregation and the Jim Crow Era, two world wars, the Harlem Renaissance, the Great Depression, desegregation, and the Civil Rights and Black Power movements. In the book's final chapters, you will read about African American social, political, and cultural life in the United States today, as well as the goals that black leaders have set for the future.

In telling these stories, *Holt African American History* intends to walk again in Woodson's footsteps by showing that the history of African Americans is part of the story of all Americans. The legacy of slavery, segregation, and the Civil Rights movement is a legacy that shapes the experiences of all Americans. Moreover, from their earliest appearance in North America, people of African descent have influenced all aspects of American culture—from food, clothing, music, literature, and the arts to science, business, leadership, and even the meaning of democracy. In short, this is a history that runs wide and deep, shaping the very core of our nation's character. This is our past and your story. Remember it and pass it on.

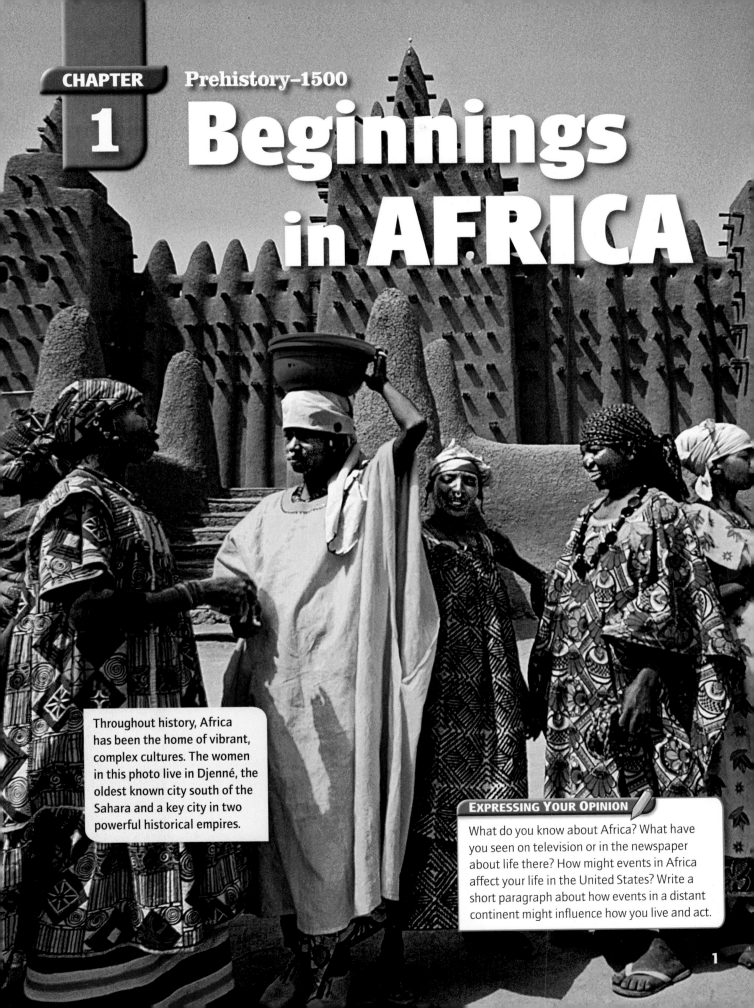

Beginnings in AFRICA

Throughout history, Africa has been the home of vibrant, complex cultures. The women in this photo live in Djenné, the oldest known city south of the Sahara and a key city in two powerful historical empires.

EXPRESSING YOUR OPINION

What do you know about Africa? What have you seen on television or in the newspaper about life there? How might events in Africa affect your life in the United States? Write a short paragraph about how events in a distant continent might influence how you live and act.

1

As You Read

Human Origins and Early Civilizations

1. **TAKING NOTES** Use a graphic organizer like this one to take notes on human origins in Africa, civilization in Egypt, and the kingdom of Kush. Use the **Reading Focus** questions on the next page to help guide your note taking.

2. As you read the section, underline or highlight definitions and descriptions of the **Key Terms** listed on the next page.

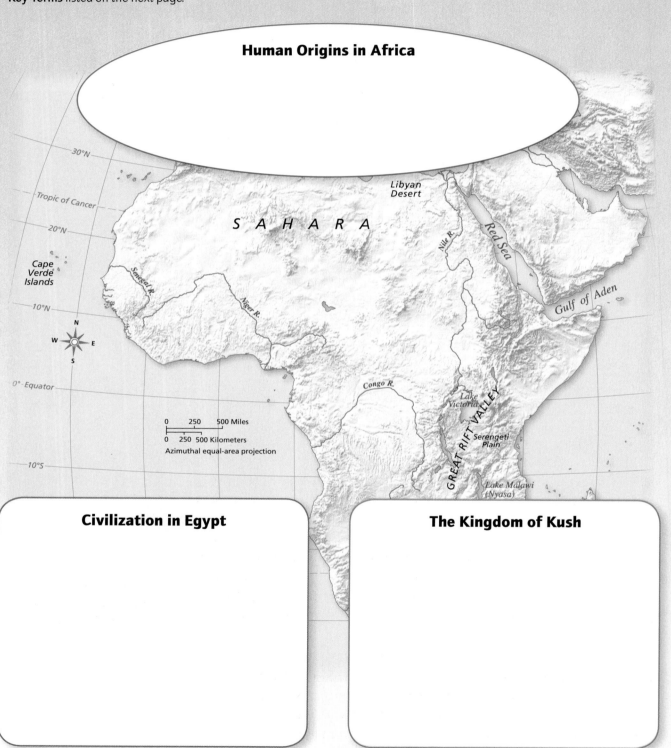

Human Origins in Africa

Civilization in Egypt

The Kingdom of Kush

Human Origins and Early Civilizations

BEFORE YOU READ

MAIN IDEA

Africa was home to some of the world's earliest known humans and to several advanced civilizations.

READING FOCUS

- What do scientists know about humanity's origins in Africa?
- What were some accomplishments of the ancient Egyptians?
- How was the ancient kingdom of Kush influenced by Egypt?

KEY TERMS

hominids
domestication
pharaoh
dynasties
hieroglyphics
Nubia
Meroë

BUILDING BACKGROUND

It is not possible to fully understand African American history without first gaining a basic understanding of its roots in Africa. Therefore, before we can begin our study of the contributions African Americans have made to the United States, we must briefly study the history of the African continent. ◼

Human Origins in Africa

Human history began in Africa. The first ancestors of modern humans appeared in East Africa about 3 million years ago. Because they were not identical to modern humans, scholars generally refer to these early ancestors as **hominids**, a generic term for human or humanlike beings that walk on two feet. Early hominids learned valuable skills that enabled them to survive, such as how to make stone tools and how to control fire.

Scientists are not sure exactly when or where the first modern humans lived. Many think that they first appeared in East Africa about 200,000 years ago. Scientists call these early humans *Homo sapiens*, or "wise man." Every person alive today belongs to the species *Homo sapiens*.

For thousands of years, humans lived as hunters and gatherers. They hunted animals such as deer and bison and scavenged for edible plants. Eventually, however, human beings learned how to grow their own food by planting crops and raising animals. Before long, they learned how to change plants and animals to make them more useful, a process called **domestication**. The domestication of plants and animals allowed larger societies, or civilizations, to develop and prosper.

With the discovery of domestication, people settled down and formed societies. These societies developed cultures with languages, religions, and art. Over hundreds of thousands of years people migrated all over the world. It was in Africa, however, that some of the ancient world's most advanced civilizations developed. Some of these civilizations left behind huge monuments and thorough records; others did not. But they all played prominent roles in shaping later cultures and ideas. ✔

✔**Reading Check**

1. Interpret Why can Africa be called the birthplace of human history?

Ancient Egypt

Nestled along the mighty Nile River in northeast Africa, Egypt was the home of one of the greatest civilizations in world history. One of the world's earliest advanced societies, Egypt flourished around 2500 BC, long before ancient Rome was even a tiny village of farmers and shepherds.

Ancient Egypt developed into a powerful state for one main reason—its location. The Nile valley was tremendously fertile; seasonal river floods covered nearby fields with rich layers of soil. Thus, the people of the Nile region found it easy to grow food, which gave them plenty of time to spend on other pursuits, such as improving their society.

KEY FACTS

2. Why was the Nile River important to life in ancient Egypt?

A Mighty Kingdom

One reason for Egypt's prosperity was its strong central government. Egypt's government was headed by a ruler called the **pharaoh**. Egypt's pharaohs were revered; in fact, people saw them as gods on Earth. As a result, pharaohs had nearly unlimited power, but they also had tremendous responsibilities. To help rule, the pharaoh surrounded himself with thousands of officials and priests, all assisted by slaves.

To organize their studies of ancient Egypt, historians have divided ancient Egypt's pharaohs into **dynasties**, or ruling families. All together, 28 dynasties ruled during Egypt's 1,500-year history. These dynasties were then organized into long periods called the Old, Middle, and New Kingdoms.

Egypt's pharaohs were very clever when it came to running their government. For example, in order to collect taxes, they ordered officials to take the world's first known census, or official count of the population. The early census takers counted up to four million Egyptian people at one time. This was probably more than the population of all the rest of the African continent put together.

Egyptian Achievements

Though their government was huge and well organized, the ancient Egyptians are better known for their other achievements, especially their tombs. When early pharaohs died, they were buried in gigantic pyramids, masterworks of ancient engineering. Later pharaohs were buried in elaborate temples that were no less impressive than the earlier pyramids. The builders of these temples were among the first people in all of world history to use stone columns as support for their structures, an innovation that was later copied by other civilizations.

Inside Egyptian tombs, entire walls were covered with writing in a form called **hieroglyphics**, which used intricate combinations of pictures and symbols to represent objects and ideas. Egyptian hieroglyphics was one of the world's first writing systems, and it helped shape the writing of many later cultures.

Around 450 BC—long after Egypt's height—a famous Greek scholar and traveler, Herodotus, traveled to Egypt. In writing about his journey, he expressed amazement at the many achievements of the Egyptians, including their sophisticated and accurate calendars, systems of record keeping, and mathematics. He called the Egyptians "the best historians of any nation of which I have had experience." He was awestruck at the precise written account of no fewer than 330 monarchs. Herodotus left Egypt amazed at its civilization and its people.

VIRTUAL FIELD TRIP

Go online to experience a virtual field trip to key sites in Africa.

go.hrw.com

Chapter Activity

Keyword: SAAH CH1

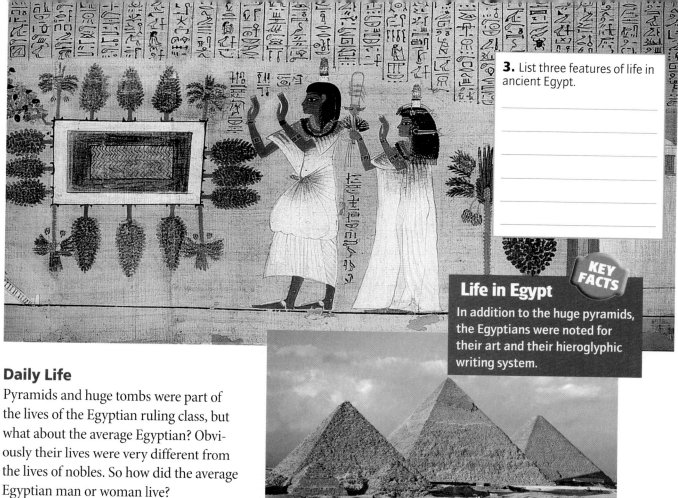

3. List three features of life in ancient Egypt.

KEY FACTS

Life in Egypt

In addition to the huge pyramids, the Egyptians were noted for their art and their hieroglyphic writing system.

Daily Life

Pyramids and huge tombs were part of the lives of the Egyptian ruling class, but what about the average Egyptian? Obviously their lives were very different from the lives of nobles. So how did the average Egyptian man or woman live?

The vast majority of Egyptians were farmers, toiling in the fields to grow enough food to survive. During the Nile's flood season, when most of the land was covered with water and couldn't be plowed, many farmers were forced to work on major building projects, such as the pyramids. Together with their families, the farmers were moved to settlements near the work project, where they were fed and housed until the project was finished.

For those ordinary Egyptians who longed to be something other than farmers, the most common path to career advancement was to learn how to write. A few skilled writers had the chance to become scribes and join Egypt's bureaucracy, the network of clerks, tax gatherers, and other officials who helped run the government. As in most ancient civilizations, such opportunities were limited to men; though Egyptian women had the right to sign contracts and own property, they did not enjoy the same privileges as men did. ✔

✔ **Reading Check**
4. Identify What were the major achievements of the ancient Egyptians?

Ancient Kush

Though Egypt is the best known of Africa's early civilizations, it was not the only one. South of Egypt, along the great bend of the middle Nile River, was a region known to the Egyptians as **Nubia**, a name meaning "land of the blacks." Nubia was home to another advanced civilization, Kush, with which Egypt had a very complicated—and constantly changing—relationship.

Egypt and Kush

Early in their history, the Egyptians traded with the Kushites for goods such as ivory and ebony, a very dark wood. Skilled traders, the Kushites had obtained these goods from Africans who lived farther south. Eventually, however, the Egyptians decided they were not content to simply trade with Kush. In the 1500s BC, Egyptian troops conquered most of Nubia, including Kush. During this period, the Egyptians introduced many elements of their culture, such as clothing styles and pyramid building, into Kush.

By 750 BC, though, Egypt was in decline. The Kushites, tired of centuries of Egyptian rule, decided to turn the tables. After a fierce invasion and years of heavy fighting, the Kushites took over Egypt and made one of their rulers the new pharaoh. Kush then ruled Egypt for several centuries.

Kushite Achievements

Late in its history, Kush's civilization was centered on its capital, the city of **Meroë**, located just north of present-day Khartoum, the capital of Sudan. The city was a great trading center. Gold, ivory, ebony, leopard skins, and ostrich feathers flowed north through Meroë. Traders also carried goods east to parts of the Red Sea and then to India and China. Traders also went east, into central Africa. In addition, Meroë was the center of Kush's most famous industry—iron working. Iron from Kush was traded to distant locations in return for luxury goods.

Like the Egyptians, the Kushites developed their own form of writing, one which has remained undeciphered to the present day. They also built huge brick buildings, small pyramids, and fine temples, and made beautiful pottery.

Over time, Kush attracted the interest of outsiders. A Roman army attacked Kush in 23 BC, but failed to conquer it. Later, desert people began to attack Kush. Meroë was finally destroyed in AD 350 by the rival state of Aksum, located in the northern highlands of present-day Ethiopia. Kushite civilization had dominated the middle Nile region for nearly 2,000 years. In the process, it created its own Egyptian-Nubian culture, a culture which influenced the people of the region for generations. ✔

✔ Reading Check

5. Describe How did the relationship between Egypt and Kush change over time?

_____

_____

_____

_____

_____

_____

SECTION 1 ASSESSMENT

go.hrw.com
Online Quiz
Keyword: SAAH HP1

Reviewing Ideas, Terms, and People

Choose the letter of the term at right that best matches each description.

_____ **6.** This system of writing invented by the ancient Egyptians used pictures and symbols instead of words.

_____ **7.** This city was the capital and center of the ancient Kushite civilization.

_____ **8.** These ruling families are used by historians to organize the study of Egyptian history.

_____ **9.** This generic term refers to a human or humanlike being that walks on two feet.

_____ **10.** This region south of Egypt was home to an advanced civilization.

_____ **11.** This was the name given to the ruler of Egypt.

a. pharaoh

b. Meroë

c. Nubia

d. dynasties

e. hieroglyphics

f. hominids

Interpreting Maps

Understand the Skill

Maps are flat representations of the world and can be of many types. Political maps show a region's major political features, such as countries and their borders, capitals, and other major cities. Physical maps show an area's elevation and natural features, such as mountain ranges, plains, deserts, rivers, and oceans. Historical maps show information about the past. Many of the maps in this book are historical maps. Special-purpose maps focus on one special topic, such as climate, resources, or population. By interpreting maps, historians can learn how geography has affected people and events in the past.

Learn the Skill

The map shown here combines environmental information about Africa with historical information. Use the strategies listed to learn how to interpret maps.

1. Read the map's title, distance scale, and legend, if provided. These items provide basic information about the map's subject and content.

2. Read the map's labels carefully to identify content in the map.

3. Note any colors, patterns, and symbols used on the map. Use the map's legend to identify what each color, pattern, and symbol means.

4. Note the size and shape of features and the location of places in relation to other places.

5. Use information from the map to draw conclusions.

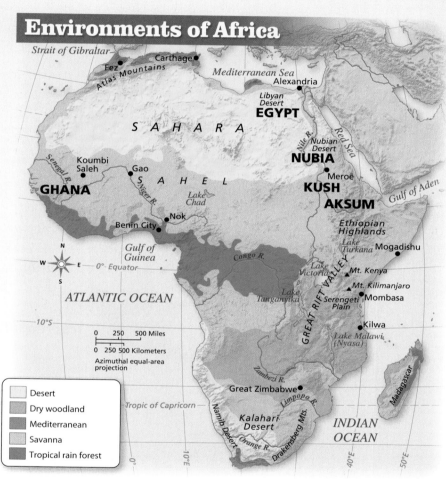

Environments of Africa

APPLY THE SKILL

1. **Analyze** What relationship does the map show between early settlement patterns in Africa and the location of rivers?

_____

_____

2. **Locate** Where was Egypt located in relation to Kush?

_____

_____

Great Empires of West Africa

1. **TAKING NOTES** Use a graphic organizer like this one to take notes on the empires of West Africa and traditional African culture. Use the **Reading Focus** questions on the next page to help guide your note taking.

2. As you read the section, underline or highlight definitions and descriptions of the **Key Terms and People** listed on the next page.

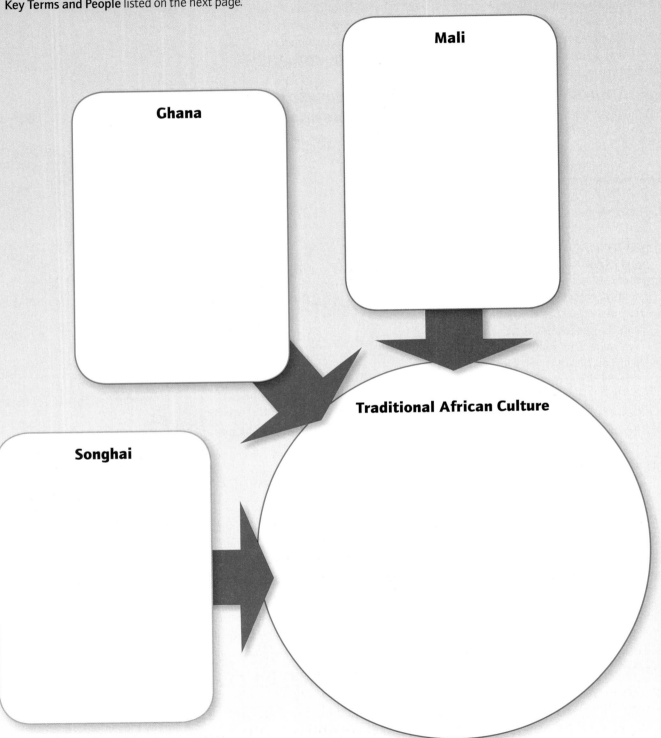

Ghana

Mali

Songhai

Traditional African Culture

2 Great Empires of West Africa

BEFORE YOU READ

MAIN IDEA

Three powerful empires that grew rich from trade were established in West Africa.

READING FOCUS

- How did trade contribute to the growth of Ghana?
- What were the significant achievements of Mali?
- How did Songahi become a powerful empire?
- Why do modern historians study traditional African culture?

KEY TERMS AND PEOPLE

sub-Saharan Africa
Mansa Musa
oral history
extended family
age-sets
animism
griots

BUILDING BACKGROUND

After Egypt and Kush, the next African civilizations that came to the attention of other parts of the world were the fabulously wealthy kingdoms of West Africa. Separated from Egypt by the vast Sahara Desert, practically an ocean of sand and wasteland, these kingdoms grew in total isolation from the civilizations of northern Africa. ◼

Ghana

For centuries, merchants from North Africa had crossed the Sahara in search of valuable products like gold and slaves. These products could only be found south of the desert in the region known as **sub-Saharan Africa**, which includes all of Africa south of the Sahara. Through this trade, the people of sub-Saharan West Africa grew wealthy and built powerful empires. They were Ghana, Mali, and Songhai.

Trade

Thanks to its location on the southern edge of the Sahara, ancient Ghana—not to be confused with the modern nation of Ghana, which is farther south—quickly gained fame as a trading center. From the north, merchants sent camel caravans laden with expensive <u>commodities</u> Africans south of the Sahara could not produce themselves, including copper, horses, and luxury goods. They also brought salt, which was in short supply south of the desert and thus was very valuable. In Ghana, they traded their goods for gold, which was mined to the south, as well as ivory and slaves.

By taxing all trade in their kingdom, Ghana's rulers grew rich enough to support a powerful army. Ghana's kings protected their livelihood by keeping the location of West Africa's gold mines a closely guarded secret.

From about 700 to 1000 Ghana was at the height of its power. The people of Ghana conquered several neighboring kingdoms, enslaved some captured peoples, and forced others to pay them tribute in exchange for their freedom.

INFO TO KNOW
Both Ghana and Mali are the names of countries in Africa today, but they are not located in the same places as the ancient empires with those names.

ACADEMIC VOCABULARY
1. Use the context, or surrounding words in the sentence, to write a definition of the word **commodities**.

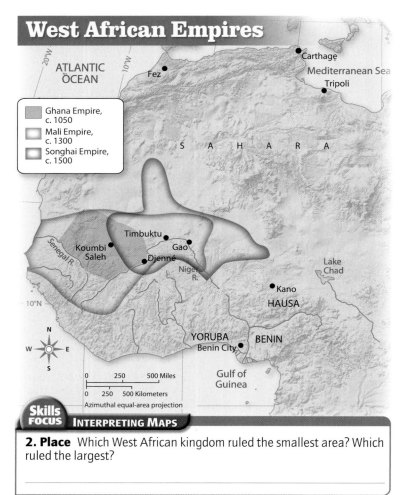

West African Empires

ATLANTIC OCEAN

- Ghana Empire, c. 1050
- Mali Empire, c. 1300
- Songhai Empire, c. 1500

SAHARA

Carthage
Mediterranean Sea
Tripoli
Fez

Timbuktu
Koumbi Saleh
Gao
Djenné
Niger R.
Senegal R.
Lake Chad
Kano
HAUSA
YORUBA
Benin City
BENIN
Gulf of Guinea

0   250   500 Miles
0   250   500 Kilometers
Azimuthal equal-area projection

Skills FOCUS   INTERPRETING MAPS

2. Place Which West African kingdom ruled the smallest area? Which ruled the largest?

✔ **Reading Check**

3. Identify How did Ghana's rulers grow rich and powerful?

Wealth and Splendor

Over time, Ghana became so wealthy that it was known in other parts of the world as the "kingdom of gold." Visitors and writers from Europe and the Middle East marveled over the luxury with which its rulers were surrounded:

HISTORY'S VOICES

"The King [wears] necklaces round his neck and bracelets on his forearms and he puts on a high cap decorated with gold and wrapped in a turban of fine cotton. He holds an audience in a domed pavilion around which stand ten horses covered with gold-embroidered materials . . . on his right, are the sons of the vassal kings of his country, wearing splendid garments and their hair plaited with gold."

"At the door of the pavilion are dogs of excellent pedigree. Round their necks they wear collars of gold and silver, studded with a number of balls of the same metals."

—Abu Abdullah al-Bakri, *The Book of Routes and Kingdoms,* 1068

Ghana's kings were respected not only for their wealth and power, but they were also worshipped as gods. People also worshipped the spirit of the Niger River.

Ghana's Fall

As in Egypt, ancient Ghana's wealth and fame eventually attracted fierce invaders. Their constant attacks wreaked havoc on Ghana's agricultural system and eventually scared off many of the merchants who came to do business. Over time traders and merchants alike began to move out of Ghana into other kingdoms. With the loss of their trade, Ghana grew weak and unable to hold its empire together. After about 700 years of glory, Ghana collapsed. ✔

Mali

A new empire, Mali, soon arose to take Ghana's place. Mali began as a small kingdom within Ghana. After Ghana collapsed, however, Mali gained control of the caravan routes that crossed the Sahara. With these caravan routes came wealth and power, and Mali became the leading power in West Africa.

Mansa Musa

In all of Mali's long and prosperous history, one emperor, or *mansa*, stands out. He was **Mansa Musa**, and his reign in Mali from 1307 to 1337 is known for the peace and security that prevailed. An Arab scholar of the day called him "the most powerful, the richest, the most fortunate, the most feared by his enemies, and the most able to do good to those around him."

Mansa Musa, who was a devout Muslim, is perhaps best remembered for his famous pilgrimage to the holy city of Mecca. In 1324, taking with him thousands of slaves, Mansa Musa began a great trek across the Sahara to Mecca. The entire trip is said to have taken the better part of a year, including travel there and back. Like heads of state today, Mansa Musa visited the leaders of countries along the way. He lavished gifts upon those he visited, pouring huge amounts of gold into the economies of cities like Cairo, Egypt. Indeed, some historians have estimated that Mansa Musa's trip caused the price of gold to drop greatly due to the quantity of the metal that the Malians brought.

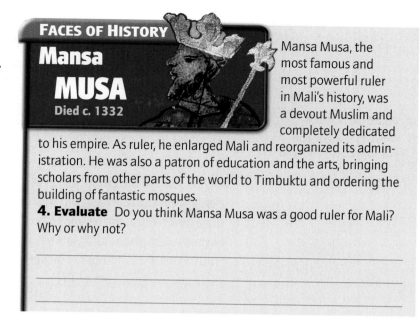

FACES OF HISTORY

Mansa
MUSA
Died c. 1332

Mansa Musa, the most famous and most powerful ruler in Mali's history, was a devout Muslim and completely dedicated to his empire. As ruler, he enlarged Mali and reorganized its administration. He was also a patron of education and the arts, bringing scholars from other parts of the world to Timbuktu and ordering the building of fantastic mosques.

4. Evaluate Do you think Mansa Musa was a good ruler for Mali? Why or why not?

_____

_____

_____

Achievements

As ruler of Mali, Mansa Musa put great emphasis on education. He built great universities for religion and law in the cities of Timbuktu and Djenné. These centers of learning gained fame throughout the Muslim world. Indeed, books in Arabic became one of the hottest items on the trans-Saharan trade routes. Scholars from all over Africa, the Middle East, and Europe came to Mali to study.

Mansa Musa also worked to spread Islam through his empire. He built mosques, or Muslim houses of worship, in many cities and helped convert thousands of people to the religion. In addition, by making his famous pilgrimage, Mansa Musa brought knowledge of the wealth and power of Mali to people from distant lands. ✔

✔ **Reading Check**
5. Describe What were the main achievements of the rulers of Mali?

_____

_____

_____

_____

Songhai

Just as ancient Mali sprang from part of the Ghana empire, the next West African empire, Songhai, developed from the Mali empire. In 1325 Mansa Musa had conquered the Songhai people and their capital city of Gao. For about 50 years, Songhai was part of Mali. Then, Songhai cast out the Malians and won back its independence.

Growth

In 1464, King Sunni Ali Ber came to power and began the expansion that would make Songhai a major empire. Sunni Ali, a brilliant strategist, was one of the first African kings to equip his army with horses. He also built a navy, made up of warriors in large canoes who patrolled the Niger River. Sunni Ali was also a skilled politician, for 28 years maintaining an alliance between the two major factions in his empire. On the one side were rural farmers and fishermen who worshipped traditional Songhai gods; on the other were the townspeople who were mainly Muslim.

During Sunni Ali's reign Songhai conquered much of Mali's former territory. The empire of Songhai continued to grow until its three main cities—Gao, Timbuktu, and Djenné—had populations of up to 40,000 people each. Philosophy, medicine, and law flourished.

Decline

In the mid-1500s, several states Songhai had conquered began to reassert their independence. Thus weakened, Songhai was soon defeated by an army of Spaniards and Moroccans. The last great West African empire was no more. Trade routes shifted farther west, to the Atlantic coast.

The reason for the shift in trade routes was the arrival of Europeans in West Africa. In the 1400s Portuguese explorers sailed south along the West African coast, building forts and trading centers where they bought ivory, gold, cotton, pepper, and slaves. Most of the Europeans' business was conducted with the people of the city of Benin, near the mouth of the Niger River, who profited greatly from this trade. With their new wealth, the people of Benin built a splendid capital city that became one of the busiest places in West Africa. They also created art that is still admired worldwide. What they did not do, however, was build a political empire to rival Ghana, Mali, and Songhai. ✔

✔ **Reading Check**

6. Identify Cause and Effect What led to the decline of Songhai?

_____

_____

_____

_____

Traditional West African Culture

Although the empires of West Africa had great power and tremendous wealth, we know relatively little about what life was like for anyone but the ruling classes. What little we do know comes from the writings of people who visited the empires. This is because the civilizations of West Africa, advanced though they were, did not have written languages.

In addition to visitors' accounts, historians and anthropologists have been able to learn about life in West Africa through two means. One is studying **oral history**, a spoken record of past events passed down from generation to generation. The people of West Africa have a centuries-long oral history, accounts of the great deeds and customs of their ancestors. In addition, historians and anthropologists can learn about the past by studying West African traditions that are still practiced in the region today. Among the traditions that people today study are forms of village and family life, religion, and the arts.

African Arts

Left: A traditional West African wooden mask. Right: People gather to perform traditional dances and listen to a griot's stories.

Village and Family Life

A typical early West African family was an **extended family**. It usually included the father, mother, children, and close relatives in one household. West African society expected each person to be loyal to his or her family. In some areas people also became part of **age-sets**, groups, usually of men, born within a few years of each other who formed special bonds. Women, too, sometimes formed age-sets.

Within a family or age-set, each person had specific tasks. Men hunted, farmed, and raised livestock. Women farmed, collected firewood, ground grain, carried water, and cared for children.

Religion

Religion was another central feature of village life. Many West Africans believed that their ancestors' spirits stayed nearby when they died. To honor these spirits, families marked places as sacred by putting specially carved statues there. They also offered food to their ancestors. Another common West African belief was **animism**—the belief that bodies of water, animals, trees, and other natural objects have spirits.

The Arts

West African art flourished in many forms. For example, they made beautifully detailed carvings from wood and bronze. They also created fantastic masks that were worn as part of religious ceremonies.

The performing arts were also important in West African society. Music and dance were common in rituals and ceremonies. In addition, the crucial task of remembering and telling West Africa's history was entrusted to storytellers called **griots**. They were highly respected in their communities because they helped keep history alive for each new generation. Many griots even served as advisers to kings. Even today, the griot tradition is alive in West Africa. Modern griots tell both traditional and contemporary stories to entertain audiences worldwide. In addition, some griots, like Youssou N'Dour from Senegal, are internationally known singers. ✔

KEY FACTS

7. Write one to two sentences summarizing the traditional culture of early West Africa.

✔ **Reading Check**

8. Summarize Why do modern historians study traditional ways of life in West Africa?

SECTION 2 ASSESSMENT

go.hrw.com
Online Quiz
Keyword: SAAH HP1

Reviewing Ideas, Terms, and People

9. Describe What role does oral history play in modern studies of life in West Africa?

10. Identify For what were the empires of West Africa best known outside of the region? How did Mansa Musa contribute to this view of West Africa?

11. Compare and Contrast What was one way in which the empires of Ghana and Mali were similar? What was one way in which they were different?

Creating a Museum Exhibit

Imagine that you are helping choose items for a museum exhibit focusing on early West African empires and traditional culture. Use your notes from this section to help you identify objects that reflect key aspects of the empires or culture of early West Africa. Objects might include documents, clothing, jewelry, trade items, religious items, or recordings of oral histories. Then limit your list to six objects. Below, describe each object and briefly explain why you chose to include it in your exhibit.

Object: _____
_____
_____

Reason to Include: _____
_____
_____

Object: _____
_____
_____

Reason to Include: _____
_____
_____

Object: _____
_____
_____

Reason to Include: _____
_____
_____

Object: _____
_____
_____

Reason to Include: _____
_____
_____

Object: _____
_____
_____

Reason to Include: _____
_____
_____

Object: _____
_____
_____

Reason to Include: _____
_____
_____

ASSESS YOUR KNOWLEDGE

1. **Find the Main Idea** Based on the objects you selected, what theme might describe your museum exhibit?

_____

_____

2. **Analyze** What would you title your museum exhibit, and why?

_____

_____

Writing a Historical Interview

Imagine that you are a time-traveling reporter for a history cable channel. Your assignment is to interview a leader from one of the early West African empires. Use your notes from this section to identify key leaders and facts about their achievements and empires. Then select one leader and write three interview questions and answers for that person. The answers to the questions can be creative but should accurately reflect historical facts.

Interview with: _____

Question: _____
_____

Answer: _____
_____
_____
_____
_____

Question: _____
_____

Answer: _____
_____
_____
_____
_____

Question: _____
_____

Answer: _____
_____

ASSESS YOUR KNOWLEDGE

1. Find the Main Idea Why is the leader you selected considered a significant person in African history?

_____

_____

2. Make Judgments What is your opinion of this leader, and why?

_____

_____

Kingdoms of East and South Africa

1. **TAKING NOTES** Use a graphic organizer like this one to take notes on trade in East Africa and the kingdoms of central and southern Africa. Use the **Reading Focus** questions on the next page to help guide your note taking.

2. As you read the section, underline or highlight definitions and descriptions of the **Key Terms** listed on the next page.

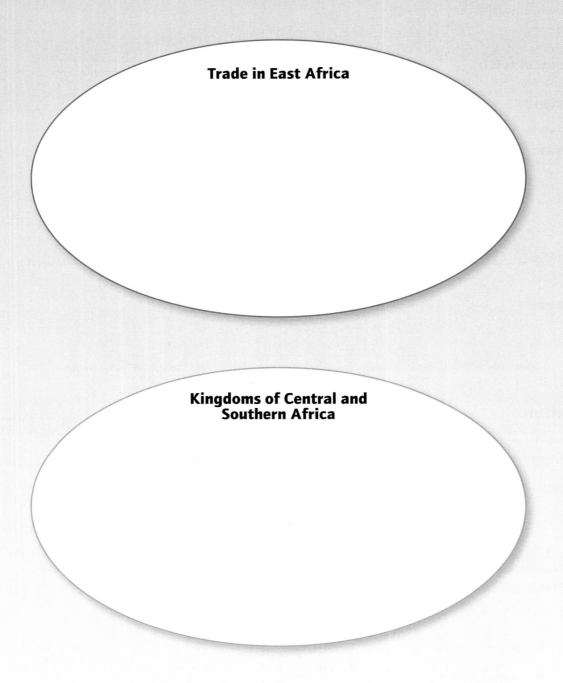

Trade in East Africa

Kingdoms of Central and Southern Africa

Kingdoms of East and South Africa

BEFORE YOU READ

MAIN IDEA

Powerful trading societies emerged in East, Central, and South Africa.

READING FOCUS

- How did Arabs influence the culture and trade of East Africa?

- How were the kingdoms of central and southern African organized?

KEY TERMS

Swahili
Bantu Migrations

BUILDING BACKGROUND

Just as the West African kingdoms became rich through trade, so too did other civilizations to the east and south. Along the eastern and southern coasts of Africa, other advanced cultures grew up that based their success on trade. These cultures left behind a legacy that is still felt in the region today. ◼

East Africa

Along the eastern coast of Africa, far to the south of the Nubian kingdoms of Kush and Aksum, another cluster of powerful African civilizations arose. East Africa—which you may remember is considered the birthplace of the first hominids—is a land of stunning geography. Broad, flat savannahs, or grasslands, give way to deep valleys and majestic mountains. Roaming over these savannahs are the wild animals commonly associated with Africa, including lions, elephants, and rhinoceroses.

To the east of East Africa is the Indian Ocean, across which lie the Middle East and India. As early as the 900s sailors from Persia—modern Iran—had reached East Africa and made contact with the people living there. One result of this contact was the beginning of long-term trade with people in other lands.

Trade with Other Lands

Like West Africa, East Africa was home to a prosperous and profitable trade. Unlike in the west, however, where most trade was conducted with other Africans, traders in the east dealt with people from other continents. Middle Eastern and Asian traders came to Africa in search of many goods, including ivory and exotic animals, but what they were most often looking for was slaves. Slaves from East Africa were shipped across the Indian Ocean to work in communities throughout Asia.

In exchange for African goods and slaves, traders and travelers brought expensive products to the region. As contact between the groups increased, new foods were introduced into Africa as well. For instance, Malaysian travelers brought Africa the banana, the yam, and certain kinds of coconuts. These new foods proved to be extremely well suited to East Africa's climate, and they quickly became staples in the diets of the people who lived there.

1. Use the context, or surrounding words in the sentence, to write a definition of the word **intermediaries**.

Arab traders began flocking to East Africa in large numbers between 1000 and 1300. These Arab trade representatives married local women and set up small trading settlements along the coast. They became <u>intermediaries</u> with other traders from African societies in the interior. They were also on hand to service the ships that sailed the Indian Ocean. Traders exchanged Arab axes, glass, and wheat for African ivory, tortoise shells, cinnamon, rhinoceros horns, and palm oil.

They also traded a great deal of Chinese porcelain. Remnants have been found from as early as the seventh-century Tang dynasty to the thirteenth-century Song Dynasty. And we have evidence that as early as the 900s the Chinese depended on East African ivory for making ceremonial objects as large as the ornately carved chairs on which they carried their kings and queens.

Rise of Powerful Kingdoms

By the year 100 Middle Eastern and Asian ships routinely traded along the East African coast as far south as present-day Tanzania. From records left by the crews of these ships, we know that several powerful states had developed in East Africa by that time. For example, one traveler, a Greek Egyptian, published a small handbook in that year in which he explained that the East African region was called Azania, and he mentioned cities with exotic names like Rhapta. This book noted that the men were of very great stature and that each place within Azania had its own ruler.

Later, in 915, the Arab traveler and historian al-Masudi described an East African kingdom called Zanj which exported leopard skins, which they also used to make clothing and saddles. In addition, they exported tortoise shells and ivory for making implements like combs. According to al-Masudi, the king of the Zanj was known as the Waklimi, or supreme lord, and was known for his fairness and integrity:

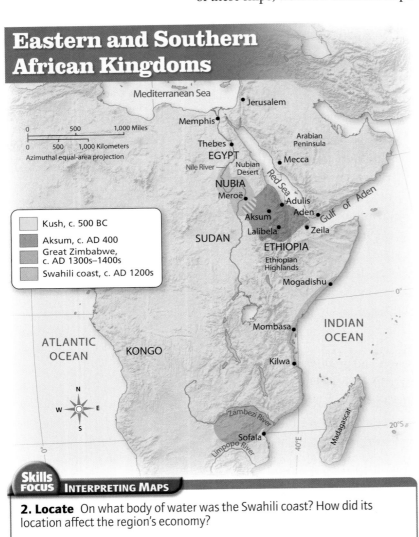

Eastern and Southern African Kingdoms

Mediterranean Sea

0   500   1,000 Miles
0   500   1,000 Kilometers
Azimuthal equal-area projection

Jerusalem
Memphis
Thebes
EGYPT
Nile River
Nubian Desert
NUBIA
Meroë
Arabian Peninsula
Mecca
Red Sea
Adulis
Aksum
Aden
Gulf of Aden
Lalibela
Zeila
SUDAN
ETHIOPIA
Ethiopian Highlands
Mogadishu

Kush, c. 500 BC
Aksum, c. AD 400
Great Zimbabwe, c. AD 1300s–1400s
Swahili coast, c. AD 1200s

ATLANTIC OCEAN
KONGO

INDIAN OCEAN

Mombasa
Kilwa

0°

Zambezi River
Madagascar
20°S
Sofala
Limpopo River
40°E

N W E S

Skills FOCUS INTERPRETING MAPS

2. Locate On what body of water was the Swahili coast? How did its location affect the region's economy?

HISTORY'S VOICES

They give this title to their sovereign because he has been chosen to govern them justly. If he becomes tyrannical or strayed from the truth he is killed and his seed excluded from the throne for ever, for they claim that in thus conducting himself he ceases to be the son of the Master, that is to say of the king of heaven and earth.

—Ali al-Masudi, *Meadows of Gold and Mines of Gems*, c. 916

Swahili Culture

The trading cities in which Africans had most of their contact with Asians and Arabs were located on what was known as the Swahili coast. (The word *Swahili* is Arabic for "coasts.") The region's inhabitants were a Bantu-speaking people who farmed the coastal lands, fished the ocean waters, and traded with foreign visitors. Over time, the people developed a unique **Swahili** culture that blended elements of African and Arab life.

The most obvious example of this cultural blending was the introduction of Arabic words into the Swahili language. Through centuries of trade, Swahili speakers adopted thousands of words from Arabic and incorporated them into their language. Many Swahili speakers also adopted the Arabic alphabet as a means of writing their language, as previously Swahili had not had a written form.

The Arabs also introduced new ideas into Swahili culture. For example, most Africans before had thought of land as being owned by the community as a whole, with everybody profiting. The Arabs, on the other hand, brought with them the notion of individual land ownership. In addition, the Arabs brought the religion of Islam with them, a religion that gained great influence in Swahili culture. Within a few hundred years Islam had spread throughout much of East Africa and from there into other parts of the continent as well.

Because of the Arabs' influence, Swahili customs changed as well. For example, the dress of the Swahili people changed. Where people had once worn skins or grass clothing, they now wore imported cloth. If you were in style, you wore long skirts and robes of cotton or silk. Clothing also became much more modest, since Islam encourages people to dress and act in a modest fashion.

Although one central Swahili empire never emerged, this civilization spread for over 1,000 miles from present-day Somalia southward to Mozambique. By the 1300s the famed Moroccan scholar Ibn Battutah, who had already traveled to India and China, had praised the Swahili city of Kilwa. He called it one of the most beautiful and best-constructed towns in the world. ✔

Kingdoms of Central and Southern Africa

Mighty African kingdoms arose in central and southern Africa too. The cultures that developed in these areas had, on the whole, less contact with people from other parts of the world than did the people of West and East Africa. As a result, we generally know less about their cultures, because the people had no writing systems and there were fewer visitors to record details about life in these civilizations.

The Kongo Kingdom

People have been farming the fertile lands that lie along the Congo River since about AD 800. By 1400 small states governed by kings had emerged in this area. One was the kingdom of Kongo, centered near the mouth of the Congo River.

By 1500 the king of Kongo ruled over a huge area with an excellent structure of government. There were provincial governors. There were judges. And other administrators regulated local disputes, as well as tax and trade matters. Beginning in the 1480s, Kongo traded heavily with the Portuguese.

KEY FACTS

3. Underline or highlight elements of the Swahili culture that developed along the East African coast. What cultures did the **Swahili** culture combine?

_____

_____

_____

_____

✔ **Reading Check**
4. Draw Conclusions Why was trade so central to East African cultures?

_____

_____

_____

_____

The Bantu Migrations

Over the centuries, parts of central Africa became more and more populated due to the settled trading and farming ways of life. Because of this growing population, many African people picked up stakes and began moving south. These travelers came from different ethnic groups. However, they mostly spoke related languages that belong to a family linguists call the Bantu languages. As a result, the people are often called the Bantu, and their movement out of Central Africa into other parts of the continent is known as the **Bantu Migrations**.

Great Zimbabwe

One of the greatest Bantu kingdoms arose in southern Africa by the late 1400s. Called Zimbabwe, it was centered on a settlement known as Great Zimbabwe. A city of between 10,000 and 20,000 people, Great Zimbabwe was a major trading center. The city takes its name from the word *zimbabwe*, a Shona term for the court or house of a chief. Most zimbabwes consisted of small clusters of stone buildings set atop a hill. Great Zimbabwe is much larger, and it included religious structures in addition to royal residences. Surrounding them were homes for common people.

The most famous structure in Great Zimbabwe is probably the Great Enclosure, a massive wall historians think may have surrounded a school. In some places more than 32 feet tall and 17 feet thick, the wall is a masterpiece of architecture and design. The stones in the wall were carved with intricate geometrical patterns.

As you have read, Africa was a continent of movement and change, the home of advanced and dynamic civilizations. By the late 1400s, however, a series of events began that led to drastic, and often catastrophic, changes in Africa. At about that time, Europeans began to make their way south along the African coast. In search of new opportunities for trade, they found them. Unfortunately, one of the products they found to trade was people. Over the next few centuries, millions of Africans were ripped from their homes and carried against their will to distant lands, where they were forced to work in thankless, miserable jobs. The slave trade marked one of the saddest times in all of human history. You will read more about that dismal period in the next chapter. ✔

✔ **Reading Check**
5. Contrast How did the cultures of Southern Africa differ from those of East Africa?

_____

_____

_____

_____

_____

SECTION 3 ASSESSMENT

go.hrw.com
Online Quiz
Keyword: SAAH HP1

Reviewing Ideas, Terms, and People

6. Describe What was the city of Great Zimbabwe like?

_____

_____

7. Explain What led to the development of Swahili culture?

_____

_____

8. Elaborate How did contact with other cultures lead to major changes in Africa?

_____

_____

_____

Writing a Travelogue

Imagine that you are a traveler who visited Africa during the time period covered in this section. Write a travelogue—an account of a trip—that describes your visit to either the region of the East African Trading Centers or to Central and Southern Africa. Use your notes from this section to gather key facts about the region you selected. Then use the form below to write your travelogue. Your travelogue should be creative and include descriptive information about the region, such as its people, government, trade, structures, and culture.

My Travels in _____

_____

_____

_____

_____

_____

_____

_____

_____

_____

_____

_____

_____

_____

_____

_____

_____

_____

ASSESS YOUR KNOWLEDGE

1. **Analyze** What do you think is the most interesting feature or aspect of the region you selected for your travelogue? Explain your answer.

_____

_____

2. **Contrast** How did the civilization(s) of the region you selected differ from the civilization(s) of the other African region covered in this section?

_____

_____

Visit **go.hrw.com** for review and enrichment activities related to this chapter.

go.hrw.com

Chapter Home Page

Keyword: SAAH CH1

Quiz and Review

ONLINE QUIZ
Take a practice quiz for each section in this chapter.

CHAPTER REVIEW
Use the online Chapter Review to help you prepare for the chapter test.

Activities

HISTORICAL DOCUMENTS
Read and explore key documents that shaped African American history.

VIRTUAL FIELD TRIP
Take a virtual field trip to experience key sites from African American history.

VOICES OF HISTORY
Experience African American history and culture through recordings of key people and documents.

Partner

CONNECTING TO OUR PAST
Examine artifacts from **Howard University's Moorland-Spingarn Research Center** that bring to life the study of African American history.

Beginnings in Africa

CHAPTER SUMMARY

SECTION 1   Human Origins and Early Civilizations

- The world's first humans developed and lived in Africa.
- Ancient Egypt, located along the Nile River in North Africa, was home to one of the most highly advanced civilizations of the ancient world.
- South of Egypt, the kingdom of Kush also formed a highly advanced society.

SECTION 2   Great Empires of West Africa

- Ghana, the first great empire to develop in West Africa, grew extremely rich by controlling trade in salt and gold.
- Mali, which ruled West Africa after Ghana, was also a powerful empire, largely because of its gifted rulers.
- Songhai, the last of the great West African empires, had a powerful military and great centers of learning and culture.
- To learn about the history of West Africa, historians depend on oral histories and on studies of traditional life in the region.

SECTION 3   Kingdoms of East and South Africa

- In East Africa, traditional African customs blended with Arabic and other influences to form a unique culture.
- The Bantu peoples who lived in Central and South Africa formed several large and powerful kingdoms.

2 The Atlantic SLAVE TRADE

This 1846 painting depicts slaves aboard the Spanish slave ship *Albanoz* shortly after the British navy captured the ship and freed the captives aboard.

EXPRESSING YOUR OPINION

Over a period of about four centuries, many millions of Africans were shipped to the Americas and forced into slavery. Write a paragraph explaining whether or not you think such a devastating event could happen today.

Slave Ship: Albanoz, by Lt. Francis Meinell, 1846/The Granger Collection, New York

Slavery Becomes a System

1. **TAKING NOTES** Use a graphic organizer like this one to take notes on the institution of slavery, Africa and the slave trade, and the European trade for slaves. Use the **Reading Focus** questions on the next page to help guide your note taking.

2. As you read the section, underline or highlight definitions and descriptions of the **Key Terms and People** listed on the next page.

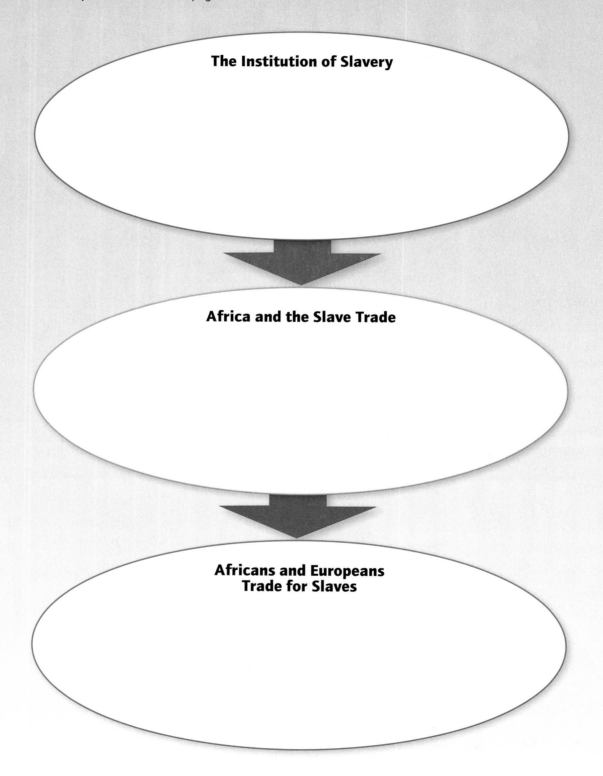

The Institution of Slavery

Africa and the Slave Trade

Africans and Europeans Trade for Slaves

Slavery Becomes a System

BEFORE YOU READ

MAIN IDEA

Slavery, which has been practiced around the world for thousands of years, has a long history in Africa.

READING FOCUS

- What was slavery like in ancient times?
- How did the arrival of Europeans in Africa affect the slave trade?
- Why were Europeans eager for slaves from Africa?

KEY TERMS AND PEOPLE

manual labor
manumission
Prince Henry the Navigator
plantations
Atlantic slave trade

BUILDING BACKGROUND

Africa's great wealth eventually attracted the attention of other civilizations around the world. Soon there was a growing demand for trade with the empires of gold-rich West Africa. Among the leaders of this new trade were Europeans, who found another valuable trade good in Africa—slaves. ▰

The Institution of Slavery

Europeans were not the first people to own slaves. In fact, thousands of years before Europeans first bought and sold African slaves, countless other societies had relied on slavery—the practice of owning individuals for use as labor.

Slavery's Origins

Although historians do not know exactly when slavery first began, we do know that it has existed for many thousands of years. The practice of slavery was common all around the world in ancient times. For example, people in ancient China, Egypt, and Rome often owned slaves. Ancient Babylon's Code of Hammurabi, the oldest known code of law, even includes specific laws regarding the treatment of slaves. Societies in Africa and Europe also practiced slavery, as did the Muslim empires in Asia and some Native American groups in North and South America.

No matter where slavery was practiced, slaves almost always served the same function—labor. Most societies used slaves for **manual labor**, or physical work done by hand. Slaves were often a vital form of cheap labor for societies. For example, the Maya in Central America put slaves to work tending crops and building temples, pyramids, and other structures. Slave labor was tremendously valuable in ancient Rome, where slaves worked on farms, in mines, and on construction projects.

Slaves performed a number of other jobs as well. For example, in many civilizations slaves were skilled workers, such as musicians, weavers, or carpenters. Muslim rulers often trained male slaves to serve as professional soldiers in their armies. In ancient Rome educated slaves served as teachers, while others were featured in the theater and in gladiator competitions.

> **KEY FACTS**
>
> **1.** What purpose did slaves serve in most civilizations?
>
> _____
> _____
> _____
> _____
> _____
> _____

The Treatment of Slaves

In all societies, slaves were considered the property of their owners. However, the ways in which they were treated varied greatly. For example, children born to slaves in Africa generally could not be sold away from their families by their owners. In China slave owners were free to sell the children of their slaves, separating them from their families. Some cultures took steps to regulate the treatment of slaves. Several societies had laws protecting slaves from excessive cruelty. In ancient Athens, as a Greek historian reported, striking a slave was against the law.

Skills FOCUS | **IDENTIFYING POINTS OF VIEW**

2. What is the author's point of view?

_____

_____

_____

_____

_____

HISTORY'S VOICES

"The license [freedom] allowed to slaves and foreigners at Athens is extreme, and a blow to them is forbidden there, nor will a slave make way for you! I shall tell you why this is the custom of the country. If it were legal for a slave or a foreigner or a freedman to be beaten by a free man, you would often have taken the Athenian for a slave, and struck him, for the poor there do not dress better than the slaves and the foreigners!"

—Xenophon, *On the Polity of the Athenians,* c. 424 BC

Unlike slavery in later years, ancient slavery was not based on race. Slaves came from a wide range of backgrounds and cultures. Most slaves in ancient times were captured in war. Conquering armies often imprisoned men, women, and children and took them as slaves. Other times, people accused of crimes were punished by being sold into slavery. Still others were born to parents who were slaves or were sold into slavery to pay off a debt. Once enslaved, these people were considered the property of their owner and could be resold or given away as the owner wished.

Slavery in the Ancient World **KEY FACTS**

3. Use the space provided to list characteristics of slavery in ancient societies.

_____

_____

_____

_____

_____

_____

_____

_____

_____

_____

The slaves here are making preparations for a banquet.

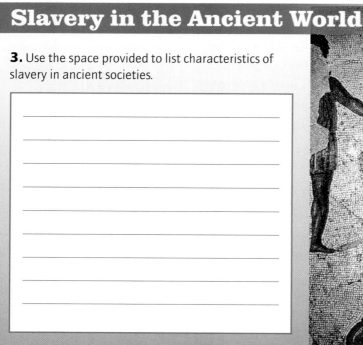

▶ Slaves like those in this Roman mosaic often worked as household servants.

In ancient times it was not uncommon for an owner to free his or her slaves. This act, known as **manumission**, was practiced in many societies around the world. Several societies taught that freeing a slave was an honorable act. For example, the Qur'an—the Muslim holy book—promotes the idea of manumitting, or freeing, slaves. In some societies, slaveholders would free their slaves after years of dedicated service. For example, upon their deaths many Roman slaveholders would use their last will and testaments to grant their slaves freedom. ✔

✔ **Reading Check**
4. Draw Conclusions Why might many ancient societies have practiced slavery?

Africa and the Slave Trade

As you have read, people all around the world—from Asia to the Americas—practiced slavery in ancient times. Like other peoples around the world, Africans were no strangers to slavery. However, contact with Europeans greatly expanded the African slave trade.

Slavery in Africa

By the beginning of the modern age, the institution of slavery had existed in Africa for many centuries. Small African kingdoms and powerful empires alike practiced slavery. For example, the small kingdoms of Kanem and Bornu in Central Africa raided nearby lands in search of slaves. Likewise, the Egyptians and the Nubians in North Africa sought slaves from among the peoples to their south.

Beginning in the AD 600s, Muslims first entered Africa. As they did so, they began to expand the African slave trade. Muslim merchants often captured Africans in raids or purchased them from local rulers and sold them as slaves. African slaves were traded throughout the Muslim world, where the ownership of slaves was a sign of wealth. Most slaves in the Muslim world were traditionally of African descent. They often served as household servants or agricultural workers. Some African slaves were also used as crew members aboard trade ships or as pearl divers in the Persian Gulf. Muslim merchants exported slaves beyond the Muslim world as part of their trade with the rest of Asia. African slaves were sold as far away as India, Southeast Asia, and China. Historians estimate that as many as 18 million slaves were exchanged by Muslim traders between AD 650 and 1905.

INFO TO KNOW
Muslims in Africa had been engaged in the slave trade for more than 600 years before the arrival of European slave traders.

European Contact with Africa

Although Muslim merchants developed an active slave trade throughout much of Asia and Africa, that trade did not involve most of Europe. After the collapse of the Roman Empire in AD 476, Europeans had little contact with other civilizations and were isolated from the outside world. By the 1100s, however, the countries of Europe were ready to end their isolation and enter world trade.

During the 1400s and 1500s Europe experienced a period of great discovery. Interest in trade and adventure led people throughout Europe to set off on voyages of exploration. Europeans wanted to explore the world for many reasons. Some were looking for exciting adventures and fame. Others hoped to spread Christianity to new parts of the world. Many other Europeans hoped to gain great wealth from trade. The lure of spices, jewels, and silks encouraged merchants to launch trade expeditions. As European interest in exploration and trade grew, so too did their interest in Africa.

For many years, Europeans had heard of the great wealth of African kingdoms. Stories of fantastic riches were often told—tales of vast gold mines in West Africa and wealthy African kings such as Mali's Mansa Musa. European access to this gold, however, had long been blocked by powerful Muslim kingdoms in North Africa. By the early 1400s leaders of the European kingdom of Portugal had grown determined to find a way to reach gold-rich Africa.

Portugal took the early lead in exploration due to the efforts of **Prince Henry the Navigator**. The Portuguese prince had a great passion for exploration. He gathered some of Europe's best sailors, astronomers, and mapmakers and sent expeditions into the Atlantic Ocean. He soon grew convinced that his crews could find an overseas route to Asia by sailing south around Africa. At the same time, Prince Henry reasoned, if his men could gain access to West African gold, he could use that wealth to finance future explorations. By 1420 Portuguese expeditions had begun exploring Africa's western coast in search of a route around the continent. The Portuguese soon established trade with African societies in the region. At first they traded for African goods such as gold dust and salt. Beginning in the mid-1400s, however, the Portuguese set their sights on an even more valuable trade good—slaves. ✔

✔ **Reading Check**
5. Recall Why were European explorers initially interested in Africa?

Africans and Europeans Trade for Slaves

As Portuguese sailors and merchants began trading with African kingdoms, they quickly discovered that they could earn great wealth by selling African captives as slaves in European markets. The European settlement of the Americas in the 1500s would eventually cause the demand for slaves to skyrocket.

The Portuguese Trade in Slaves

Portuguese merchants were among the first Europeans to take part in the trade in African slaves. In 1444 the first large-scale shipment of African slaves arrived in Portugal. The shipment, which included some 235 North Africans abducted by the Portuguese, soon triggered more interest in African slaves. Portuguese planters on islands in the Atlantic Ocean were eager for a source of cheap labor for their farms. Wealthy Europeans also sought African slaves for use as domestic servants. By 1550 as many as 50,000 African slaves had been imported to Europe.

As the demand for slave labor increased, the Portuguese changed their methods for obtaining slaves. Early on, Portuguese merchants raided villages in search of captives. When this practice

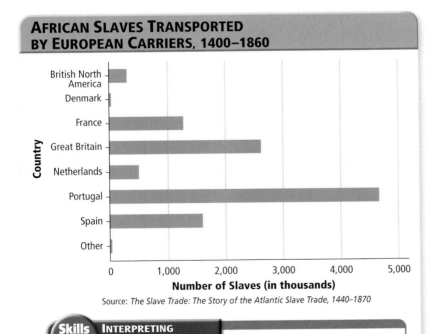

AFRICAN SLAVES TRANSPORTED BY EUROPEAN CARRIERS, 1400–1860

Source: *The Slave Trade: The Story of the Atlantic Slave Trade, 1440–1870*

Skills FOCUS **INTERPRETING GRAPHS**

6. About how many more slaves did Portugal transport than did France?

proved too difficult and time-consuming, they instead turned to trade. Portuguese merchants traded European goods like horses, cloth, or grain to local African rulers in return for their prisoners of war, who were sold into slavery. Soon European traders acquired most slaves in this manner. By the end of the 1400s the Portuguese had established treaties with African kings all along the Atlantic coast and had begun establishing ports on Africa's eastern coast.

Europeans Send Slaves to the Americas

The importation of African slaves to Europe was a minor, but profitable, enterprise. In the 1400s the countries of Europe had no great demand for cheap manual labor. As Spain, Portugal, and other European empires expanded into the Americas in the 1500s, however, the demand for slave labor slowly soared.

Beginning in 1492 Christopher Columbus's voyages set off a wave of European colonization in the Americas. Explorers were immediately attracted by the wealth of natural resources they found in this "New World." They quickly realized that valuable deposits of gold and silver, as well as crops like sugarcane and tobacco, could bring them great riches. Soon European colonists established mines and huge farms, called **plantations**, to take advantage of the region's vast natural resources.

These mines and plantations, however, required enormous amounts of labor to collect and process raw materials. Initially, Europeans used Native Americans as a source of forced labor. Growing resistance to the enslavement of native peoples and the rapidly decreasing native population soon forced Europeans to look elsewhere for a labor force. Their solution was to use African slaves. Unlike Native Americans, African slaves were less likely to succumb to European diseases or to successfully hide after escaping. In addition, African slaves were already familiar with European farming methods and had worked as reliable laborers in Europe for many years.

As early as 1502, Spanish colonists in the Americas imported the first black slaves to the Caribbean. The numbers of African slaves was small at first, but the ever-growing demand for laborers gradually led to an active trade in slaves from Africa to the Americas, a system known as the **Atlantic slave trade**. ✔

✔ Reading Check

7. Explain Why did Europeans look to African slaves as a source of labor in the New World?

SECTION 1 ASSESSMENT

go.hrw.com
Online Quiz
Keyword: SAAH HP2

Reviewing Ideas, Terms, and People

8. Recall How did most people become slaves in ancient times?

9. Compare and Contrast How was the Muslim slave trade in Africa similar to and different from Portugal's Atlantic slave trade?

10. Elaborate Why do you think that slavery has been so common throughout history?

Preparing an Oral Presentation

You have been asked to prepare an informative presentation on the history of slavery in ancient times. Use the information in the section along with at least two other sources to prepare for your oral presentation. Be sure to include examples and visuals that will hold your audience's attention. Use the space provided below to outline the key points and examples you will use in your presentation.

I. Introduction

   A.

   B.

II. History of Slavery

   A.

   B.

   C.

III. Treatment of Slaves

   A.

   B.

   C.

IV. Conclusion

   A.

   B.

ASSESS YOUR KNOWLEDGE

1. Analyze What visuals might enhance your presentation? At what point in your presentation could you use them?

2. Draw Conclusions Why might examples be an important part of an oral presentation?

Identifying Points of View

Understand the Skill

Historical documents such as journals, political cartoons, letters, and news articles often reflect the period and culture in which they were created. Many historical documents reflect their creator's point of view. A **point of view** is a person's outlook or attitude toward a topic or person. Identifying and understanding points of view are a key part of interpreting history.

Learn the Skill

Use the strategies at right to analyze points of view.

> But what heart could be so hard as not to be pierced with piteous feeling to see that company? For some kept their heads low and their faces bathed in tears, looking one upon another; others stood groaning very dolorously [miserably], looking up to the height of heaven, fixing their eyes upon it, crying out loudly, as if asking help from the Father of Nature; others struck their faces with the palms of their hands, throwing themselves at full length upon the ground; others made their lamentations in the manner of a dirge [mournful song], after the custom of their country . . . But to increase their sufferings still more, there now arrived those who had charge of the division of the captives, and who began to separate one from another . . . then was it needful to part fathers from sons, husbands from wives, brothers from brothers. No respect was shown either to friends or relations, but each fell where his lot took him.
>
> O powerful fortune . . . do thou at least put before the eyes of that miserable race some understanding of matters to come; that they may receive some consolation in the midst of their great sorrow.
>
> —Gomes Eannes de Zurara describes the first shipment of African slaves to arrive in Portugal, *Chronicle of the Discovery and Conquest of Guinea*, 1468

Step 1 Identify information about the author and the time in which the source was created. This information can give you hints about the author's attitude. *What can you tell about the author of this document?*

_____

_____

_____

_____

Step 2 Analyze the main points the author is attempting to convey. Understanding the author's point might indicate his or her point of view. *What point is the author attempting to make?*

_____

_____

_____

_____

Step 3 Identify emotional language or imagery. Emotional language may indicate a writer's point of view toward his or her subject. *Underline or highlight emotional language in the document.*

APPLY THE SKILL

1. **Identify Points of View** What is the author's point of view?

_____

_____

2. **Analyze** What specific information provides clues about the author's point of view?

_____

_____

As You Read

The Middle Passage

1. **TAKING NOTES** Use a graphic organizer like this one to take notes on the triangular trade, the journey to the Americas, and the effects of the slave trade. Use the **Reading Focus** questions on the next page to guide your note taking.

2. As you read the section, underline or highlight definitions and descriptions of the **Key Terms and People** listed on the next page.

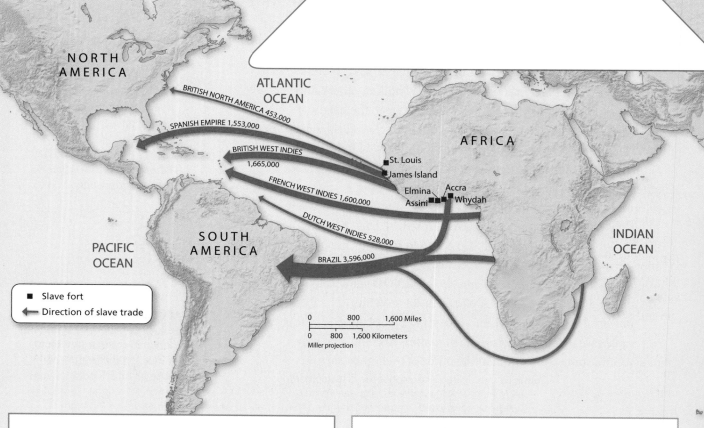

Triangular Trade

NORTH AMERICA

ATLANTIC OCEAN

AFRICA

BRITISH NORTH AMERICA 453,000

SPANISH EMPIRE 1,553,000

BRITISH WEST INDIES 1,665,000

FRENCH WEST INDIES 1,600,000

St. Louis
James Island
Elmina   Accra
Assini   Whydah

DUTCH WEST INDIES 528,000

PACIFIC OCEAN

SOUTH AMERICA

BRAZIL 3,596,000

INDIAN OCEAN

■ Slave fort
← Direction of slave trade

0   800   1,600 Miles
0   800   1,600 Kilometers
Miller projection

The Journey to the Americas

Effects of the Slave Trade

The Middle Passage

BEFORE YOU READ

MAIN IDEA
African slaves were transported by the millions to the Americas.

READING FOCUS
- What role did the slave trade play in the triangular trade?
- What difficulties did captives face on the Middle Passage?
- What were some of the results of the slave trade?

KEY TERMS AND PEOPLE
triangular trade
Middle Passage
Olaudah Equiano
slavers
African diaspora

BUILDING BACKGROUND
The Atlantic slave trade was a key part of an active international trade between the Old World and the New World. Key to this trade system was the traffic of African slaves across the Atlantic Ocean—a tragic journey known as the Middle Passage. ▪

Triangular Trade

As you have read, African slaves were first sent to the Americas in small numbers beginning in the early 1500s. Soon, however, the spread of mines and plantations throughout the Americas created a growing demand for slave labor. As a result, more and more African slaves were imported to Spanish colonies, such as Hispaniola and Cuba in the Caribbean, and to Brazil, Portugal's major colony in South America. By the end of the 1500s the Atlantic slave trade had become an <u>integral</u> part of the international trade system.

Other European powers soon joined Portugal and Spain in the Atlantic slave trade. By the mid-1600s England, France, and the Netherlands were also engaged in the slave trade. Like Spain and Portugal, these countries imported slaves to the Americas to work on plantations. By the mid-1700s British merchants dominated the Atlantic slave trade, importing an estimated 2.5 million slaves to the Americas between 1701 and 1800.

The traffic of slaves between the Old World and the New World was part of a complex system of trade. Because trade routes across the Atlantic Ocean often formed a triangular pattern, this trade system came to be called the triangular trade. The **triangular trade** featured the exchange of goods and slaves between Europe, Africa, and the Americas.

The triangular trade used a number of different trade routes. In one common route, European merchants exchanged manufactured goods, such as guns and alcohol, for African slaves. These merchants then transported the slaves on the infamous Middle Passage across the Atlantic Ocean to various locations in the Americas. There, merchants traded slaves for raw materials, such as sugar, molasses, and lumber, which they transported back to Europe, where the materials might be used to make manufactured goods. ✔

ACADEMIC VOCABULARY
1. Use the context, or surrounding words in the sentence, to write a definition of the term **integral**.

✔ Reading Check
2. Identify What was the triangular trade?

KEY FACTS

The Journey to the Americas

The most profitable leg of the triangular trade was the infamous **Middle Passage**, the journey on which captives were transported from Africa to the Americas. Millions of Africans were captured, enslaved, and sent on the Middle Passage to a life of exhausting labor in the Americas.

Capture and Enslavement

The search for slaves typically began on the West African coast, where the vast majority of slaves were shipped to the Americas. In general, European slave traders did not capture African slaves directly. Instead, they visited the many trading posts that dotted the Atlantic coast. At the trading posts, traders obtained slaves from local middlemen. These middlemen traveled into the African interior to acquire captives from local rulers, who sold prisoners of war and criminals into slavery. In return, the rulers received a variety of goods, including cloth, weapons, liquor, and beads.

After the exchange, captives were chained and marched—sometimes hundreds of miles—to coastal trading posts like Gorée Island, in what is today Senegal, and Elmina in modern-day Ghana. Once there, captives were held in miserable conditions in cells and prisons to await their selection by slave traders.

PRIMARY SOURCES

Olaudah Equiano Describes His Enslavement

In 1789 former slave Olaudah Equiano published *The Interesting Narrative of the Life of Olaudah Equiano,* an account of his life as a slave. In this passage, Equiano describes his capture in West Africa and his initial reaction upon boarding a slave ship bound for the Americas.

The first object which saluted my eyes when I arrived on the coast was the sea, and a slave ship, which was then riding at anchor, and waiting for its cargo. These filled me with astonishment, which was soon converted into terror when I was carried on board . . . Indeed, such were the horrors of my views and fears at the moment, that, if ten thousand worlds had been my own I would have freely parted with them all to have exchanged my condition with that of the meanest slave in my own country. When I looked round the ship too and saw a large furnace of copper boiling, and a multitude of black people of every description chained together, everyone of their countenances [faces] expressing dejection and sorrow, I no longer doubted of my fate; and quite overpowered with horror and anguish, I fell motionless on the deck and fainted.

Skills FOCUS **ANALYZING PRIMARY SOURCES**

4. Identify Points of View What is Equiano's point of view? What parts of the passage indicate that to you?

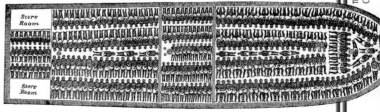

▲ **This 1858 diagram illustrates how slaves were crowded aboard a typical slave ship.**

Slave traders would then examine the captives, looking for healthy men and women who might make good laborers. Because they could perform heavy labor, strong, young men were often in high demand. One African, **Olaudah Equiano**, was captured and sold into slavery at the age of 11. Equiano later wrote about his capture and life as a slave. Branded and shackled, these young captives were transferred aboard **slavers**, or slave ships, and sent to face the horrors of the Middle Passage.

The Middle Passage

Once aboard the slave ships, African captives faced a frightening and difficult trip to the Americas. The voyage on the Middle Passage could take from three to six weeks to complete. During the journey captives were crowded together in cramped quarters below the ship's deck. To maximize the number of slaves they transported—and therefore their profit—many ship captains packed aboard as many slaves as they could. One British slaver, the *Brookes*, was designed to hold 451 captives. However, according to reports, it was known to carry as many as 600 slaves.

Captives aboard slavers experienced horrible conditions. Chained together in pairs, slaves had little room to move. They were often forced to lie on their backs in unsanitary conditions. Although slaves occasionally received exercise and fresh air above deck, they were confined for much of the voyage. As a result, disease and malnutrition were common. So harsh was the Middle Passage that some 10 to 20 percent of all captives did not survive the voyage.

Slaves often took steps to escape captivity aboard slave ships. For many, death was preferable to slavery. Some captives jumped overboard. Others simply refused to eat. One slave described the plan to escape devised by his shipmates.

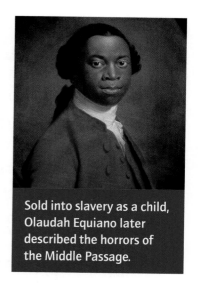

Sold into slavery as a child, Olaudah Equiano later described the horrors of the Middle Passage.

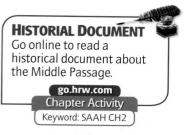

HISTORIAL DOCUMENT
Go online to read a historical document about the Middle Passage.

go.hrw.com
Chapter Activity
Keyword: SAAH CH2

HISTORY'S VOICES

"When we found ourselves at last taken away, death was more preferable than life; and a plan was concerted [developed] amongst us, that we might burn and blow up the ship, and to perish all together in the flames."

Ottobah Cugoano, *Narrative of the Enslavement of Ottobah Cugoano*, 1787

Other captives fought for their freedom. Many accounts tell of uprisings aboard slave ships. In 1730 slaves aboard a ship bound for Newport, Rhode Island, rebelled. After gaining control of the ship, the captives managed to sail back to Africa. Most slaves who rebelled, however, were not so fortunate. Most uprisings aboard slavers were unsuccessful. Slaves were generally subdued and placed back into captivity. ✔

Effects of the Slave Trade

For more than 400 years the Atlantic slave trade stole Africans away from their homelands and forced them into slavery in the Americas. This forced migration had a lasting and profound impact on both Africa and the Americas.

Impact on Africa

There is no doubt that the Atlantic slave trade had a devastating effect on Africa. The greatest impact was the human cost. Historians estimate that 10 to 12 million Africans were shipped to the Americas as part of the slave trade. Some estimates are even higher.

✔ **Reading Check**
5. Describe What were conditions like on the Middle Passage?

_____

_____

_____

_____

_____

DISTRIBUTION OF SLAVES IN THE ATLANTIC SLAVE TRADE

Region	Slaves Bought
Brazil	3,596,000
British Caribbean	1,665,000
British North America	453,000
Dutch Caribbean	528,000
French Caribbean	1,600,000
Spanish America	1,553,000

Source: *Trans-Atlantic Slave Trade Database*

Skills FOCUS ANALYZING INFORMATION

6. According to the chart, about how many slaves were bought in the Atlantic slave trade?

_____

✔ **Reading Check**

7. Summarize How were African kingdoms affected by the Atlantic slave trade?

_____

_____

_____

_____

_____

Countless more died marching to the coast, being crammed aboard slave ships, or resisting enslavement. In addition, slavery deprived millions of people of their freedom.

African kingdoms suffered tremendously. Entire communities were devastated by the loss of their people to slavery. Wars became common among rival African kingdoms and groups as each tried to win captives for the slave trade. This depletion of the population and constant warfare damaged many communities for years. As huge portions of the population in some places were enslaved, valuable members of the community were taken away. African kingdoms also suffered economically because they grew dependent on European goods gained through the slave trade.

Impact on the Americas

The impact of the Atlantic slave trade was not so dire in the Americas. In fact, slaves played a vital role in the settlement of many areas. Millions of slaves were brought to the Americas, particularly to Brazil and the Caribbean, where the majority of African slaves were shipped.

Slavery also benefited the Americas economically. African slaves filled the need for labor on plantations and in mines. Their labor helped strengthen the economies of many colonies. For example, colonies in the Caribbean relied on slaves to provide labor for the highly profitable sugar industry.

Another result of the slave trade was the spread of African culture and traditions around the world. Due to their forced migration, Africans and their descendants were scattered throughout the Americas. This scattering of Africans is called the **African diaspora**. The African diaspora eventually led to the spread of African culture—including music, art, and religion—throughout the world. ✔

SECTION 2 ASSESSMENT

go.hrw.com
Online Quiz
Keyword: SAAH HP2

Reviewing Ideas, Terms, and People

8. Recall What goods were exchanged in the triangular trade system?

_____

_____

9. Explain Why did slave traders seek out young, healthy individuals as slaves?

_____

_____

10. Make Judgments What do you think was the most tragic effect of the Atlantic slave trade? Why?

_____

_____

Working with Maps

The map below illustrates several common routes in the triangular trade system. Use information from the section, as well as outside sources, to identify the different items that were transported along these various routes. Write your answers in the corresponding arrows on the map.

Triangular Trade Routes

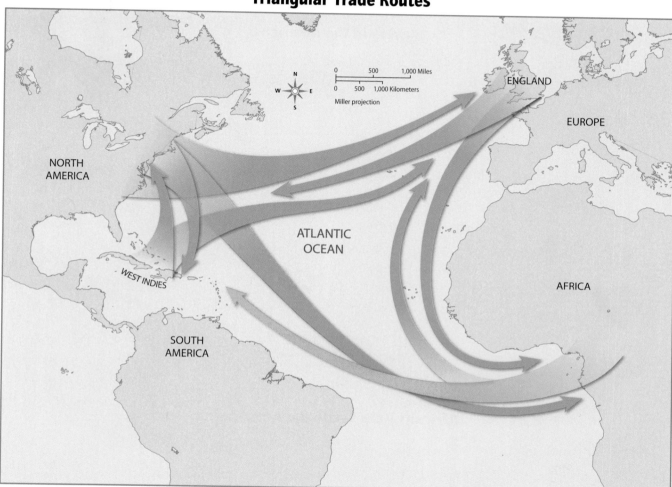

ASSESS YOUR KNOWLEDGE

1. **Identify** What is the significance of the yellow arrow? What was exchanged on this portion of the triangular trade?

_____

_____

2. **Draw Conclusions** In the triangular trade system, Europe received the greatest amount and variety of goods. What might explain this situation?

_____

_____

Africans in the Americas

1. **TAKING NOTES** Use a graphic organizer like this one to take notes on slavery in the Americas and ways that Africans helped settle the Americas. Use the **Reading Focus** questions on the next page to guide your note taking.

2. As you read the section, underline or highlight definitions and descriptions of the **Key Terms and People** listed on the next page.

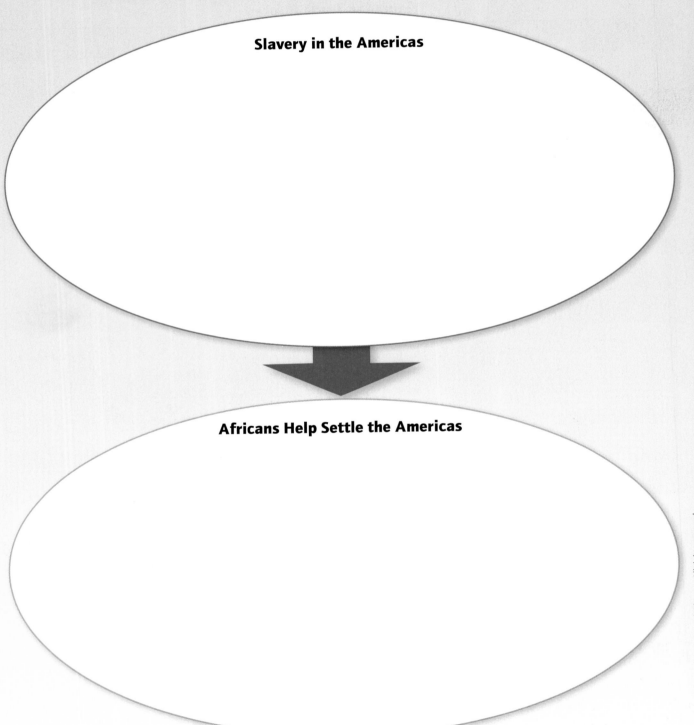

Slavery in the Americas

Africans Help Settle the Americas

Africans in the Americas

MAIN IDEA

After arriving in the New World, blacks made many contributions to the settlement of the Americas.

READING FOCUS

- What different jobs did African slaves perform in the New World?
- What role did Africans play in settling the Americas?

KEY TERMS AND PEOPLE

cash crops
overseers
Maroons
Estevanico
Jean Baptist Point du Sable

BUILDING BACKGROUND

For slaves who survived the treacherous journey known as the Middle Passage, the difficulties were far from over. As they arrived in the Americas, they were often sold to the highest bidder. Thousands of miles away from their homelands, they were forced to start new lives as slaves. ◼

Slavery in the Americas

As you have read, Europeans hoped to take advantage of the rich natural resources they found in the Americas. The lack of a significant native labor force, however, led them to import slaves. Soon Europeans were bringing thousands of African slaves each year to work on plantations in the Caribbean and in South and North America.

The Caribbean

One of the primary destinations of slaves in the Americas was the islands of the Caribbean. Spain, England, France, and other European powers established colonies throughout the Caribbean. Hoping to make a fortune, colonists set up huge plantations to grow cash crops that they could sell in Europe. **Cash crops** are agricultural products that are produced primarily for profit. Tobacco, cotton, and some sugarcane were grown as cash crops in the Caribbean. To provide a labor force for the plantations, colonists imported African slaves and temporary laborers.

In the 1640s the introduction of a large-scale sugar industry dramatically changed life in the Caribbean. Sugar plantations required great amounts of manual labor to plant, harvest, and process sugarcane. To meet this demand, Europeans brought more and more slaves to the islands. For example, when the first sugar plantations began in Barbados in the early 1640s, some 6,000 slaves worked on the island. By 1682 the number of slaves had increased to 46,000. An estimated 4 million African slaves were eventually sent to the Caribbean.

Life for Caribbean slaves was difficult. Most slaves lived on sugar plantations, where the work was demanding and dangerous. Slaves often worked 10 to 18 hours per day with little rest. Colonists employed **overseers** to manage and direct the work of slaves on the plantations. Overseers often relied on violence to demand more labor from slaves. Slaves faced other difficulties as well, including exhaustion, disease, and a lack of food and medical care.

INFO TO KNOW

Spanish priest Bartolomé de Las Casas called for the use of African slaves in order to end mistreatment of Native Americans in the Caribbean. He eventually changed his mind, however, and called for an end to African slavery as well.

▶ **Slaves faced difficult conditions on sugar plantations in the Caribbean.**

ACADEMIC VOCABULARY

1. Use the context, or surrounding words in the sentence, to write a definition of the term **implemented**.

_____

_____

_____

_____

Throughout the 1600s and 1700s Caribbean planters imported more and more slaves. As a result, slaves soon outnumbered colonists on many islands. Slaves in Jamaica outnumbered white colonists five to one in the late 1600s. By 1789 almost 90 percent of the population of the French colony of Saint-Domingue, in modern-day Haiti, was enslaved. To keep slaves in line, colonial governments <u>implemented</u> laws that called for harsh punishments, including whipping, burning, and hanging.

Despite violent punishments, Caribbean slaves did try to resist their captivity. One common way of resisting slavery was to escape. Some runaway slaves, known as **Maroons**, escaped to isolated areas where they joined with other fugitives or with native peoples. Maroon communities developed in Jamaica, Haiti, and Cuba. African slaves also resisted slavery by rebelling. In general, slave revolts in the Caribbean were unsuccessful. However, a 1791 uprising in Saint-Domingue resulted in a full-scale revolution and eventually brought about an end to slavery there.

Mainland Latin America

In addition to the islands of the Caribbean, a key destination of African slaves was mainland Latin America. Spanish and Portuguese colonies on the mainland received an estimated 45 percent of all slaves imported to the Americas. As in the Caribbean, a growing demand for labor led to the importation of African slaves in mainland colonies such as Mexico, Peru, and Brazil. Because there were not enough Europeans willing to live in these new outposts and do the backbreaking work of clearing and settling the land, Spanish and Portuguese colonists brought millions of African slaves to help work the mines, ranches, and plantations. In Brazil, for example, the rise of sugar plantations in the 1540s and the discovery of gold in the 1690s led to dramatic increases in the number of African slaves sent to the colony.

INFO TO KNOW
Native to the Americas, the cacao tree produces valuable beans used to make cocoa and chocolate.

African slaves sent to mainland Latin America worked at a variety of jobs. Most worked on the region's many sugar, coffee, and cacao plantations. African slaves labored in the copper and silver mines of Peru and Mexico and the gold mines of Brazil. They also served as cattle ranchers, loggers, and fishers. In addition, they worked in large urban districts as domestic servants, merchants, and skilled workers.

Throughout much of Mexico and Central and South America, laws were passed to protect slaves. The Spanish legal code granted slaves the right to marry and discouraged the breakup of slave families. The Catholic Church also helped by encouraging slave owners to free their slaves. In addition, slaves were free to learn to read and write and to purchase their freedom if their owners agreed. Other laws protected slaves from physical abuse; however, these laws were often ignored or unenforced. Despite these laws, African slaves still faced difficult lives. They were often overworked and mistreated, as were slaves in the Caribbean.

To escape the misery of slavery, many slaves ran away. Hoping to escape recapture, they often hid in the mountains and forests and occasionally developed Maroon communities. One group of escaped slaves established a town for free blacks near what is now Veracruz, Mexico, in 1608. In 1630 Maroons established the Republic of Palmares in northeastern Brazil. Populated by as many as 20,000 escaped slaves and free blacks, the Republic of Palmares existed for 67 years before it was conquered by Portuguese troops.

British North America

Like other European colonizers, the British also imported African slaves to their colonies in North America. Colonists in British North America, however, imported a much smaller number of slaves than did colonists in the Caribbean or mainland Latin America. Historians estimate that 6 percent—some 600,000 or so—of the slaves transported to the Americas went to the North American colonies.

African laborers arrived in England's North American colonies as early as 1619, when a group of about 20 slaves were sold in Jamestown, Virginia. These first Africans in North America were not lifelong slaves, however. Likely because they were Christians, they earned their freedom after a number of years of service.

Temporary workers like the first Africans were not unusual in the British colonies. Initially, North American colonists relied heavily on indentured servants, temporary laborers who agreed to work a set number of years in exchange for passage to North America. Both black and white workers signed on as indentured servants.

KEY FACTS

2. How did laws regulate the lives of slaves in each region of the Americas?

Caribbean

Latin America

North America

Selling Slaves

Slaves brought to British North America were often put up for auction at local slave markets. These posters advertise slaves for sale in the British colonies in North America.

Skills FOCUS ANALYZING VISUALS

3. What terms do these posters use to attract buyers?

They served as plantation labor, domestic servants, and skilled workers. Because of this labor system, the demand for slaves was low, and few slaves worked in the colonies at first. For example, only 150 slaves were working in Virginia by 1640.

Over time, however, colonists grew less satisfied with temporary laborers. One reason for the colonists' dissatisfaction was that indentured servants were not a permanent labor force. Workers left their jobs once their period of service ended, forcing their employers to find new workers. In addition, indentured servants sometimes ran away and proved difficult to locate. By the late 1600s the number of available European workers began to decline. This shortage forced colonists to look elsewhere for labor. Soon they were importing more slaves than ever before.

As the number of African slaves in the North American colonies rose, colonial governments passed laws regulating slavery. In 1641 Massachusetts became the first colony to legalize slavery, and by the 1700s slavery was firmly established in all the British colonies. New laws established that slaves would serve for life and that the children of female slaves would be enslaved as well. As in the other regions of the Americas, legal codes set restrictions on slaves, such as forbidding them to carry weapons or to travel without the permission of their owners. The basis for American slavery had begun. ✔

✔ **Reading Check**
4. Contrast How did slavery in British North America differ from other regions?

Africans Help Settle the Americas

In addition to performing vital labor in the New World, Africans helped settle the Americas in other ways. People of African descent were instrumental in exploring and settling the Americas and contributing to the region's culture.

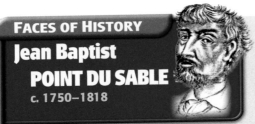

FACES OF HISTORY

Jean Baptist POINT DU SABLE
c. 1750–1818

The Granger Collection, New York

Adventure and an opportunity to earn great wealth likely attracted Jean Baptist Point du Sable to the Great Lakes. The son of an African slave and a French merchant, Point du Sable grew up in Haiti before moving north.

After traveling throughout the Great Lakes region, Point du Sable eventually settled near the mouth of the Chicago River in the 1780s. There, he built a home and a trading post and earned a reputation as an honest merchant. Point du Sable's friendly relations with Native Americans and his skill as a trader brought him success. His small trading post became a thriving business. Although he and his family later left the area, Point du Sable is remembered as the founder of the frontier settlement that would eventually become Chicago, Illinois.

5. Analyze What qualities led to Point du Sable's success?

Exploration and Settlement

There is no doubt that skilled Africans played important roles on many European expeditions to the New World. Africans—both slave and free—took part in numerous explorations throughout the Americas. Black slaves accompanied Vasco Núñez de Balboa in 1513 as he crossed the Isthmus of Panama and discovered the Pacific Ocean. Records also indicate that Spanish conquistador Hernán Cortés included African slaves with his crew when he conquered the Aztecs in Mexico in 1519. In fact, one black member of Cortés's expedition is credited with planting and harvesting the first wheat crop in the Americas.

Other blacks gained fame as explorers and conquerors of the New World. African slave **Estevanico** was one of four men to cross what is now the southwestern United States and northern Mexico. A talented guide, Estevanico later served on an expedition into present-day New Mexico. Other blacks helped in the conquest of the Americas. West African slave Juan Valiente served as a Spanish conquistador in the Americas. With the permission of his owner, he helped defeat native peoples in modern-day Chile and Peru. The Spanish government rewarded Valiente with a valuable estate and slaves of his own.

People of African descent also helped settle what would one day become the United States. One of those individuals was **Jean Baptist Point du Sable**, a native of Haiti, who founded the first permanent settlement in the area that is now Chicago, Illinois. In addition, free blacks helped settle many colonies, including Louisiana, Virginia, and North Carolina. In the late 1600s African slaves were instrumental in the development of profitable rice crops in what would become South Carolina.

African Culture in the Americas

Africans in the New World also played a crucial role in the development of American culture. Once in the Americas, slaves often continued to practice African traditions and customs, perhaps as a way of coping with their life as slaves. Over time, many of these traditions blended with European and native culture to create a new and unique American culture. In Brazil, for example, Angolan slaves introduced capoeira, a blend of dance and martial arts, that is still practiced today. Slaves also introduced African musical instruments, such as the marimba, the banjo, and various types of drums. Slaves brought African foods to the Americas. For example, Creole food from New Orleans is a blend of African, Caribbean, and European cooking.

Africans influenced religion and language in the New World as well. Throughout the Caribbean and elsewhere, slaves blended African religious beliefs with Christian beliefs. In addition, slaves shaped language in the Americas. They often mixed words from their native African languages with the European languages of their owners. An example of this is the mix of African languages and French that took place in Haiti and Louisiana. The unique blending of African and European cultures contributed to the great cultural diversity that exists throughout the Americas to this day. ✔

VIRTUAL FIELD TRIP
Go online to experience a virtual field trip to key sites from the Atlantic slave trade.

go.hrw.com
Chapter Activity
Keyword: SAAH CH2

✔ **Reading Check**

6. Explain How did Africans help explore and settle the Americas?

SECTION 3 ASSESSMENT

go.hrw.com
Online Quiz
Keyword: SAAH HP2

Reviewing Ideas, Terms, and People

7. Identify What were overseers?

8. Draw Conclusions Why might Maroon communities have existed in the mountains and other isolated areas in the Americas?

9. Evaluate What African cultural contribution in the Americas do you think was most significant? Why?

Comparing and Contrasting

As you just read, Europeans introduced African slaves to many different regions of the Americas. Use the Venn diagram below to compare and contrast the conditions slaves faced in the various regions of the Americas. Be sure to include specific examples whenever possible.

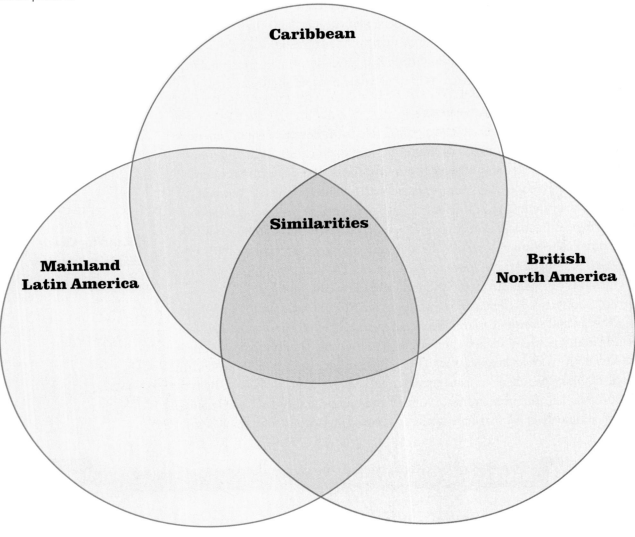

Caribbean

Similarities

Mainland Latin America

British North America

ASSESS YOUR KNOWLEDGE

1. **Compare and Contrast** In what ways was the treatment of African slaves in all three regions similar? In what ways was it different?

   _____

   _____

2. **Evaluate** In which region do you think slaves were treated best? Explain your answer.

   _____

   _____

Writing a Letter

Imagine that you are a traveler on a journey through the Americas in the early 1700s. As you travel throughout South America, the Caribbean, and North America, you are struck by the differences among the slaves in the various regions. Write a letter to a friend back home in which you explain the differences that exist among slaves in the Americas. Be sure to provide specific examples to make your point.

Quiz and Review

ONLINE QUIZ
Take a practice quiz for each section in this chapter.

CHAPTER REVIEW
Use the online Chapter Review to help you prepare for the chapter test.

Activities

HISTORICAL DOCUMENTS
Read and explore key documents that shaped African American history.

VIRTUAL FIELD TRIP
Take a virtual field trip to experience key sites from African American history.

VOICES OF HISTORY
Experience African American history and culture through recordings of key people and documents.

Partner

CONNECTING TO OUR PAST
Examine artifacts from **Howard University's Moorland-Spingarn Research Center** that bring to life the study of African American history.

MOORLAND SPINGARN RESEARCH CENTER

The Atlantic Slave Trade

CHAPTER SUMMARY

SECTION 1 Slavery Becomes a System

- The institution of slavery has existed around the world since ancient times.
- Before the arrival of Europeans in Africa, slavery had been practiced there by different African societies and by Muslim traders.
- European traders established a thriving slave trade in Africa.

SECTION 2 The Middle Passage

- The Atlantic slave trade was part of an extensive international trade system known as the triangular trade.
- Africans were captured and sent on the Middle Passage for the journey into slavery in the Americas.
- The slave trade had lasting effects on both Africa and the Americas.

SECTION 3 Africans in the Americas

- African captives faced difficult lives as slaves in the Americas.
- In addition to performing labor, Africans helped explore and settle the Americas and made many contributions to the region's culture.

African Americans
Help Create
A NEW NATION

During the American Revolution, African Americans took part in several key battles. This image depicts the Battle of Bunker Hill, fought in 1775.

Engraving of the Battle of Bunker Hill, 1800s/The Granger Collection, New York

EXPRESSING YOUR OPINION

If you were helping to create a new nation, what rights would you want to guarantee the people who lived there? Write a preamble, or introduction, to a constitution in which you identify the rights you want to protect.

Blacks in Colonial America

1. **TAKING NOTES** Use a graphic organizer like this one to take notes on the southern, middle, and New England colonies. Use the **Reading Focus** questions on the next page to help guide your note taking.

2. As you read the section, underline or highlight definitions and descriptions of the **Key Terms** listed on the next page.

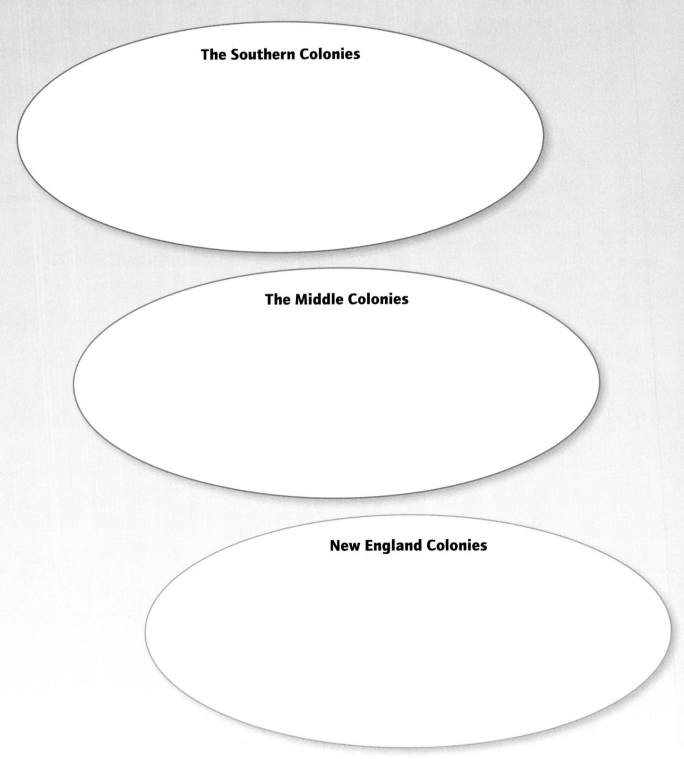

The Southern Colonies

The Middle Colonies

New England Colonies

Blacks in Colonial America

BEFORE YOU READ

MAIN IDEA

Despite protests, slavery existed in some form in all of the English colonies in North America, though slaves were treated differently in various regions.

READING FOCUS

- Why was slavery central to the economy of the southern colonies?
- What roles did slaves play in the middle colonies?
- How were slaves treated in the New England colonies?

KEY TERMS

southern colonies
indigo
middle colonies
indentured servant
New England colonies

BUILDING BACKGROUND

To understand the role of African Americans, both slave and free, in the development of the United States, we have to remember that the country began as a cluster of English colonies. By 1700 these colonies could be divided into three groups characterized more by regional differences than by similarities. As a result, the accomplishments and treatment of African Americans varied dramatically according to the region in which they lived. In all regions, however, America's development as a country was clearly due in part to African Americans' forced labor. ■

The Southern Colonies

As you read in the previous chapter, the first African servants were brought to what is now the United States—then a group of English colonies—in the early 1600s. By the end of that century, nearly all Africans who arrived in the colonies were enslaved. Slavery existed in all of the colonies in some form, but the lives and treatment of slaves varied widely from place to place.

Slavery took hold most firmly in the **southern colonies**—North Carolina, South Carolina, Maryland, Virginia, and Georgia. By 1708 Virginia alone was importing 1,000 slaves each year. Shortly after the colony's creation, South Carolina had a larger black population than white. By 1760 three slaves existed for every two free settlers in that colony.

The Plantation System

Why were there so many slaves in the South? The answer is economics. Because of its rich land, the South became the site of many large, profitable estates called plantations. Plantation owners made their money by growing a single, valuable crop that could demand high prices in England or other countries in Europe. They sold various goods, including crops such as tobacco, rice, and cotton and a dark blue dye called **indigo**. Slaves provided the often backbreaking labor needed to grow these crops. In a sense, slaves were the backbone of the entire southern colonial economy.

KEY FACTS

1. Why were slaves central to the plantation system?

Without slaves, the South's entire economy would have collapsed, as one Virginia planter noted in a letter to his brother:

HISTORY'S VOICES

"To live in Virginia without slaves is morally impossible. Before our troubles, you could not hire a servant or slave for love or money, so that, unless robust enough to cut wood, to go to mill, to work at the hoe, etc., you must starve."

—Peter Fontaine, Letter to Moses Fontaine, 1757

As the demand for their crops grew, planters hurried to buy more land, which required more slaves to work. This vicious cycle prevented the freeing of slaves and kept the institution of slavery strong in the South for many years.

Slaves on Plantations

A single large plantation in one of the southern colonies might have hundreds of slaves working on it. In many cases, these slaves were treated like beasts of burden. Some were flogged, or whipped, mercilessly to make them work in the fields from sunrise to sunset, with only one short break for lunch, six days a week. Many died from exhaustion and malnutrition. After a hard day's work, the slaves slept in tiny cabins, many of which were crammed to capacity with people. Some southern slaves were not allowed to wear shoes except in the winter.

Slaves working in the fields were supervised by overseers, some of whom were quick to whip slaves who slowed down in their work. In addition, strict rules governed the behavior of slaves on plantations. For example, a slave was not allowed to leave a plantation without written permission from his or her owner. Slaves who broke the rules could be whipped, branded, or punished in some other terrible way.

Not every plantation owner treated slaves so cruelly, though. Some southern planters saw themselves as father figures for their slaves. These slave owners tended to view their slaves almost as children, incapable of living on their own. Though slaves on plantations owned by such men were not beaten, they were still forced to work long hours every day in the fields and had no personal freedom.

Slave Auction
African slaves newly arrived in the southern colonies were sold in public auctions.

The Granger Collection, New York

Slaves on Smaller Southern Farms

Although it is the image most commonly associated with the South, it is not true that everyone there lived on plantations. The majority of farms in the South were small family operations. Only about 10 percent of the South's people lived on plantations, though that 10 percent owned 90 percent of the region's wealth.

Slavery, however, was not confined just to plantations. Even small southern farms had slaves. Most farmers owned only a few slaves, perhaps one or two. The farm owners often worked side by side in the fields with their slaves, sharing in their labor. As a result, these farm owners did not usually treat their slaves as poorly as large plantation owners did.

Slave Revolts

Slaves themselves also sometimes took action against their masters. As early as the 1660s, slaves in Virginia had begun planning revolts. Many of these plans were discovered before any revolts occurred, but others actually took place, and a number of slaveholders were killed. On at least two occasions, slaves rebelled and took over slave ships before they even reached America.

As a result of these revolts, southern planters began to fear being outnumbered by slaves. Some tried to restrict or ban the entry of new slaves into their colonies. The planters did not want to do away with slavery, but they wanted to control the number of new slaves coming into their areas. British officials refused to stop importing slaves, however, because the slave trade was too profitable for them. ✔

The Middle Colonies

The **middle colonies** were those that lay between the southern colonies and the New England colonies farther north. They included Delaware, Pennsylvania, New Jersey, and New York. Slavery was permitted in all of the middle colonies, but it was never as central to the economy there as it was in the South.

Slaves and Indentured Servants

Because the economies of the middle colonies were based more on trade and manufacturing than on agriculture, there were no plantations for slaves to work on. Many slaves worked in construction, literally helping build the nation's largest cities. Others toiled in factories, in lumber camps, or in similar places. In some cities, especially New York City, a number of highly skilled slaves had been trained in certain crafts. A skilled slave in the big city could find a job as a

- mason, a person who shaped and placed stone for building
- shipwright, a person who built ships
- goldsmith, a person who shaped and worked gold for jewelry
- glazier, a person who shaped and placed glass in windows

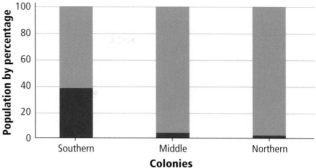

AFRICAN AMERICAN POPULATIONS, 1750

■ Percentage white population ■ Percentage black population

Source: *Historical Statistics of the United States*

Skills FOCUS INTERPRETING GRAPHS

3. In which region was the percentage of African American residents highest? Why?

_____

✔ **Reading Check**

4. Explain Why did slavery take such a firm hold in the southern colonies?

_____

_____

_____

_____

_____

▲ **In 2003 the bodies of 427 African slaves that had been discovered in a Manhattan graveyard were reburied in a special ceremony.**

Rather than buy slaves, business owners in the middle colonies sought other sources of labor. For example, much of the middle colonies' need for manual labor—especially early in the colonies' history—was fulfilled by indentured servants. An **indentured servant** was a person who agreed to work for a certain period of time in exchange for passage to a colony and a place to stay when he or she arrived. After that period was over, the servant was freed.

One reason that indentured servants were used as laborers more often than slaves was that many people in the middle colonies objected to the idea of slavery. This was especially true among the Quakers and Mennonites, two religious groups prominent in Pennsylvania. Members of both groups published works criticizing slavery as an evil institution and tried to persuade other settlers in Pennsylvania that owning other people, regardless of their skin color, was against God's laws.

In 1688 a group of Quakers in Germantown, Pennsylvania, declared their views in what is usually considered to be the first official protest against slavery in North America. The residents of Germantown, recently arrived in the colonies from Germany, were appalled at the thought that Christians owned slaves. Although their protest had little widespread effect on slavery, it did set a precedent for other Quaker and German settlements. No resident of a German religious settlement—including both Quaker and Mennonite settlements—ever took part in slavery, and few other German settlers did either.

Treatment of Slaves

Although many people think that only slaves in the South were treated poorly by their owners, this is not true. Slaves in the middle colonies were subject to terrible treatment as well. Highly skilled slaves might avoid this rough treatment, but those who worked in construction and in factories were not spared.

The extent of the poor treatment slaves experienced in the middle colonies can best be seen through a fairly recent discovery. In 1991 workers in Manhattan laying the foundation for a new skyscraper unearthed the remains of an old graveyard that dates back to the 1700s. Historians called in to investigate the discovery found that the graves belonged to more than 400 African slaves who had been put to work on early buildings in the area.

Fascinated by the discovery, the historians sent the slaves' bones to Howard University in Washington, D.C., for further investigation. Forensic examinations of the remains showed that many of the slaves had literally been worked to death. Years of brutal labor had left them with deformed muscles and broken bones. In addition, the fact that many of the skeletons found in the graveyard belonged to children—many less than six months old—suggested that the slaves had lived in terrible conditions that resulted in short lives.

One of the bodies found in the New York graveyard was particularly fascinating to historians. The body belonged to a woman in her 40s who was buried wearing a belt of beads and shells. In West Africa in the 1700s, only members of royal families were allowed to own even a single one of these types of beads, and the woman buried in New York wore more than 100! From this evidence, historians have assumed that the woman may have been a local noblewoman who was kidnapped, shipped across the ocean, and put to work until she died. ✔

HISTORIAL DOCUMENT
Go Online to read a historical document from the Germantown protest.
go.hrw.com
Chapter Activity
Keyword: SAAH CH3

✔ **Reading Check**
5. Summarize Why were there fewer slaves in the middle colonies than in the South?

_____

_____

_____

_____

_____

New England Colonies

The northernmost English colonies were Connecticut, Rhode Island, Massachusetts, and New Hampshire. Together, they were called the **New England colonies**. Compared to the middle and southern colonies, slavery was less common in the North. Slaves in New England were sometimes put to work building houses and other structures, mostly in cities. Although many restrictions were placed on their activities, slaves here nonetheless had more rights than slaves in other regions. For example, they were often allowed to gather at each other's homes to socialize. In some places slaves were also allowed to participate in certain community events. In some parts of New England, slaves were even allowed to hold elections for kings and governors. Though these positions had no power, they did give the chosen slave prestige among the area's slaves.

As in the middle colonies, many New Englanders considered slavery to be immoral and protested against it. For example, the famous Massachusetts Puritan minister Cotton Mather argued in the late 1600s—in contrast to many other preachers of the day—that Africans were people just like Europeans who deserved to be freed and that to refuse to free slaves was unchristian.

HISTORY'S VOICES

"You have yourselves renounced *Christianity*, if you do not receive that faithful saying of it, and most awful one: *every one of us shall give account of himself to God.* But then remember, that one article of your account will be this: You had poor Negroes under you, and you expected and exacted revenues of profit from them . . . Vain dreamer; canst thou suppose that the *Negroes* are made for nothing but only to serve thy pleasures, or that they owe no homage to their *Maker*?"

—Cotton Mather, "An Essay to Excite and Assist the Good Work," 1689

Although many northerners objected to slavery and slaves in the North were, on the whole, treated better than in the South, slavery remained an evil institution. Some slaveholders still worked their slaves harshly and limited their rights. In addition, many northern business owners were active participants in the slave trade, helping to transport and sell captured Africans to planters in the southern and middle colonies. ✔

✔ Reading Check

6. Analyze What criticisms did New Englanders level against the institution of slavery?

_____

_____

_____

SECTION **1** **ASSESSMENT**

go.hrw.com
Online Quiz
Keyword: SAAH HP3

Reviewing Ideas, Terms, and People

7. Identify In which region of the English colonies were slaves treated the most harshly? How were they treated there?

_____

_____

8. Compare and Contrast How were the lives of slaves in the northern and southern colonies similar? How were they different?

_____

_____

9. Elaborate What were the results of early slave revolts in the English colonies?

_____

_____

Writing to Compare

Travelers between the British colonies were constantly struck by differences in lifestyles and attitudes in different regions. Among the most noticeable differences were the position and treatment of slaves in various colonies. Imagine that you are a traveler visiting an acquaintance in a distant colony. Write a journal entry that describes how you have seen slaves treated in the place you are visiting and how that treatment differs from what you are used to seeing at home.

Date: _____

Drawing Conclusions

Read the document below, which outlines one group of colonists' views on slavery.
Then answer the questions that follow.

"These are the reasons why we are against the buying and selling of human beings: How fearful and worried do many Europeans feel at sea when they see a strange ship. They are afraid that it might be a Turkish ship and that they will be taken and sold as slaves in Turkey. Now, is slavery here any better than in Turkey? Rather it is worse when practiced by those people who say they are Christians. We believe that most Negroes are brought here against their will, and that many of them are stolen.

Now, because they are black, we cannot agree that people are freer to own them as slaves than to own white slaves. There is a saying that we should do unto others as we would have others do unto us, no matter what their social class, their background, or color. And those who steal or rob other human beings, and those who buy or purchase them, are they not all alike?"

ASSESS YOUR KNOWLEDGE

1. Summarize What is the position argued by the writers of this passage?

_____

_____

2. Draw Conclusions Do you think this document was more likely written by
northerners or southerners? Why?

_____

_____

3. Infer What do you think the religious beliefs of the passage's writers were?
Why do you think so?

_____

_____

As You Read

The Revolutionary War Era

1. **TAKING NOTES** Use a graphic organizer like this one to take notes on the dispute with Great Britain, calls for freedom, and African Americans in the revolution. Use the **Reading Focus** questions on the next page to help guide your note taking.

2. As you read the section, underline or highlight definitions and descriptions of the **Key Terms and People** listed on the next page.

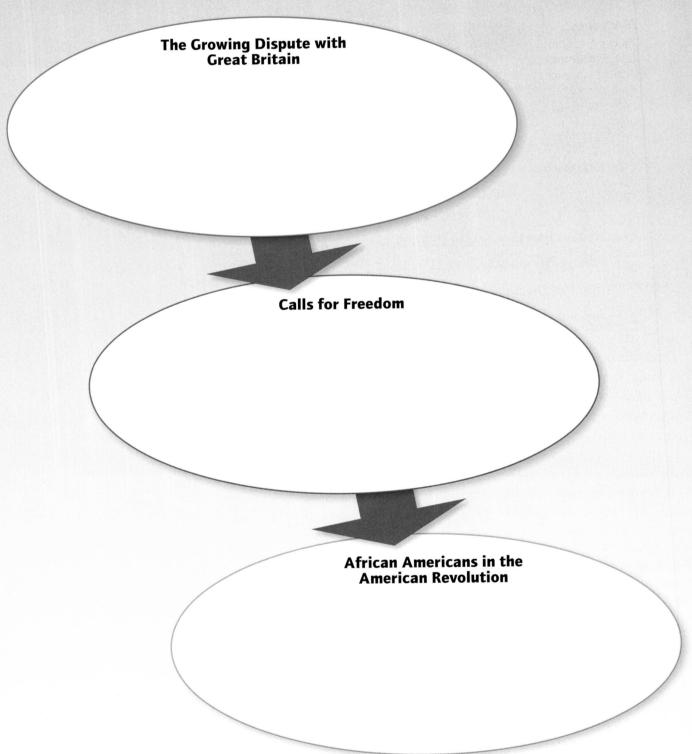

The Growing Dispute with Great Britain

Calls for Freedom

African Americans in the American Revolution

2 The Revolutionary War Era

BEFORE YOU READ

MAIN IDEA

African Americans played major roles in the struggle for American independence from Great Britain, a struggle that led many Americans to call for an end to slavery.

READING FOCUS

- What caused the growing dispute between Great Britain and its American colonies?
- What freedoms did Americans call for in the late 1700s?
- What roles did African Americans play in the American Revolution?

KEY TERMS AND PEOPLE

Navigation Acts
French and Indian War
boycott
Boston Massacre
Crispus Attucks
Revolutionary War
Declaration of
    Independence

BUILDING BACKGROUND

As African American slaves toiled to help the American colonies grow, so did the British colonies toil to keep the British Empire growing. Over time, however, resentment arose in the American colonies toward the mother country. Before long, the colonists rose up in rebellion and declared their independence from Great Britain. ◼

The Growing Dispute with Great Britain

The conflict between the American colonists and the British government grew out of several factors. Many of these factors were economic. Great Britain had originally established its American colonies primarily as a way to get rich. Thus, the British Crown constantly sought ways to draw as much money as possible out of the colonies. For example, it passed laws called the **Navigation Acts** that required all goods being shipped to or from the colonies to be transported on British ships. In addition, the acts demanded that all goods being shipped to the colonies pass through Britain first so they could be taxed. Many colonists did not like these regulations, which made goods more expensive, but they could do little to protest against the king.

The French and Indian War

Although the colonies had been created largely to make money, they also cost the British a great deal. For example, the British fought an expensive war against the French in North America between 1754 and 1763 called the **French and Indian War**. Eventually, the British won the war and drove the French almost completely out of North America. The victory also resulted in Canada becoming a British colony.

However, the victory in the French and Indian War was very expensive for the British. Among other costs, the British now had a much larger empire in North America, and they needed to pay administrators to run it and soldiers to defend it. In order to increase their revenue to pay these new expenses, the British turned their financial attention to the colonies.

FACES OF HISTORY

Crispus ATTUCKS

c. 1723–1770

Among those who died in the Boston Massacre was a 47-year-old black man named Crispus Attucks. Little is known with any certainty about Attucks's life. A crew member on whaling ships, Attucks was known to resent the presence of British soldiers in the colonies. In part, this resentment stemmed from fear that he would be impressed into, or forced to serve in, the British navy.

Some colonists thought of Attucks and his band of revolutionaries as rabble. But many Bostonians, including some of the city's leading citizens, honored him and his compatriots for bravery. Samuel Adams publicly defended Attucks in letters to the *Boston Gazette*. His supporters were impressed that a former slave, one who had not enjoyed freedom his whole life, had spoken out for the freedom of other people.

1. Draw Conclusions Why do you think many Americans consider Crispus Attucks a hero?

_____

_____

_____

VIRTUAL FIELD TRIP

Go online to experience a virtual field trip to key sites from the creation of the nation.

go.hrw.com
Chapter Activity
Keyword: SAAH CH3

✔ Reading Check

2. Summarize Why did the colonists come to resent the British government?

_____

_____

_____

_____

_____

New Laws

As part of their efforts to increase revenue, the British created new taxes. Laws such as the Sugar Act and the Stamp Act set taxes on certain products. The Sugar Act taxed sugar and molasses brought to the colonies from the West Indies. It was especially unpopular in the North, where molasses was used to make rum for export. The Stamp Act required colonists to buy government stamps for all documents, including contracts, licenses, newspapers, almanacs, and playing cards. This act was particularly upsetting to colonists, who began protesting loudly against it. For example, some colonists chose to **boycott**, or refuse to buy, British goods such as fabric. Their boycotts hurt sales and resulted in less profit for the British merchants. The boycotts, however, were largely ignored by the British government, and the act remained in force.

Protests

Some groups of colonists considered the presence of British troops in the colonies a direct threat to their safety. Among them was the Patriot leader Samuel Adams, who declared, "I look upon them [British soldiers] as foreign enemies." Driven by their dislike of the British, these colonists took more active approaches to protest the British than simple boycotts.

One active protest against the British presence in the colonies led to the **Boston Massacre** of March 5, 1770. The massacre began simply enough, when a single British guard got into an argument with a colonist and struck him. Soon, a crowd of rowdy colonists gathered and began pelting the soldier with snowballs and taunting him. More soldiers arrived, and in the confusion that followed they fired into the crowd, killing five people. Among those killed was an African American sailor named **Crispus Attucks**, whose death became a symbol of revolution.

More protests followed. In 1773 a group of colonists staged the Boston Tea Party to protest a new tax on tea. Dressed as Native Americans, they stormed onto a British tea ship, ripped open more than 300 chests of tea, and dumped them overboard. The furious British responded with even stricter laws intended to restore order in the colonies. But their plans backfired. The new laws only stirred up even more resistance to British rule. ✔

Calls for Freedom

Over time, the colonists' protests against the British led many people to call for freedom. By freedom, they did not mean only the independence of the colonies from England. Some people at this time also called for an end to slavery.

The Outbreak of War

The question of slavery also played a role in the First Continental Congress of 1774. Called to unify the colonies in their protests against the British, the First Continental Congress also led to a temporary ban on the importing of slaves. Although it may seem to be a positive move in the fight against slavery, this ban really was not. Instead, the refusal to buy slaves was seen as a way to hurt British merchants.

Shortly after the First Continental Congress ended, the **Revolutionary War**, the fight for independence from Great Britain, began. In April 1775 colonists fought off British soldiers in two Massachusetts towns, Lexington and Concord. Shortly afterward, the Second Continental Congress was convened. One of its first actions was the creation of armed forces that could be used to fight the British.

The Declaration of Independence

Once war broke out, many colonial leaders felt it was time to officially declare independence from Great Britain. The result of this decision was the writing of the **Declaration of Independence** by Thomas Jefferson in 1776. The Declaration stated that all people were equal and had the rights to life, liberty, and the pursuit of happiness. Because King George III had violated the colonists' rights, they were entitled to rebel against him.

Jefferson's first draft of the Declaration of Independence included another reason that the colonists should rebel against George III—he was responsible for slavery in the colonies. However, Jefferson's vocal opposition to slavery angered many of his fellow southerners, who refused to approve the Declaration while the passage was included. As a result, the criticism of slavery was removed from the Declaration, and the document was sent to King George.

Growing Opposition to Slavery

At the same time as colonists were actively protesting against the British, some began to protest against slavery as well. These colonists realized that it made no sense to fight for their freedom even as they stripped slaves of their own freedom.

PRIMARY SOURCES

Jefferson's Original Draft of the Declaration of Independence

Thomas Jefferson's first draft of the Declaration of Independence included a strong protest against slavery as one of the justifications for the colonies' rebellion against England. Expressed in the passage below, this sentiment did not appear in the final version of the document.

"He has waged cruel war against human nature itself, violating its most sacred rights of life and liberty in the persons of a distant people who never offended him, captivating and carrying them into slavery in another hemisphere, or to incur miserable death in their transportation thither. This piratical warfare, the opprobrium [disgrace] of infidel powers, is the warfare of the Christian king of Great Britain. Determined to keep open a market where men should be bought and sold, he has prostituted his negative for suppressing every legislative attempt to prohibit or to restrain this execrable [contemptible] commerce."

Skills Focus ANALYZING PRIMARY SOURCES

3. Interpret How does Jefferson suggest that the king's support of slavery justifies revolution?

Sally HEMINGS
1773–1835

Although Thomas Jefferson wrote eloquently against the king on the subject of slavery, he was himself a slave owner. On his estate of Monticello in Virginia, Jefferson owned about 600 slaves. Among them was a young woman named Sally Hemings, who served as the maid and lady-in-waiting to Jefferson's daughters. Because of her close relationship with the Jefferson family, we know more about Hemings's life than we do about most slaves' lives. For example, we know that she had six children over the course of her life. Even during their lifetimes, rumors circulated that Jefferson was the father of some, if not all, of her children. Though we can never be certain, DNA tests in the 1990s suggest that a member of the Jefferson family was the father of at least one of Hemings's sons.

4. Elaborate How might modern technology affect Sally Hemings's life story?

_____

_____

_____

Speakers such as pamphlet writer Thomas Paine and inventor Benjamin Franklin spoke in favor of banning slavery, helping shift people's views. Influential Boston attorney James Otis, leader of many anti-British protests, did likewise.

HISTORY'S VOICES

"Can any logical inference in favor of slavery be drawn from a flat nose, a long or a short face? Nothing better can be said in favor of a trade that is the most shocking violation of the law of nature, has a direct tendency to diminish the idea of the inestimable value of liberty, and makes every dealer in it a tyrant."

—James Otis, *The Rights of the British Colonies Asserted and Proved*, 1763

Despite the eloquent protests of Otis and others in favor of eliminating slavery, though, little changed for most African Americans in the colonies. ✔

African Americans in the American Revolution

When the Revolutionary War broke out, a number of African Americans volunteered to take part in the fighting. However, many colonists, mainly in the South, were scared stiff at the prospect of arming slaves. They issued orders excusing African Americans from bearing arms. Still, many white northerners argued that if slaves were to fight for America's freedom, they should earn their own freedom at war's end.

African American Patriots

In the early years of the war, the Americans suffered many setbacks. Clearly, the few thousand rebels who had volunteered to fight would not be able to win on their own. Some officers began to eye the large number of black men available to serve.

Virginia began to allow free black men to enlist in the army by 1775. The next year, General George Washington announced that he would accept into his army black soldiers with previous military service. In 1777 Congress officially authorized states to recruit black soldiers, either slave or free, to fight in the war. After that, several states, including Massachusetts and Rhode Island, began actively recruiting black troops.

Not all black soldiers in the war were there entirely by choice. Some were slaves who had been sent by their owners to fight in their places; the owners preferred risking their slaves to risking their own necks. Other black soldiers were free black men who had been hired to fight in the place of others. The majority of black soldiers, however, were in the war in search of one dream—freedom. Many state governments promised to free from slavery any slave who fought in the Revolutionary War, and so slaves had enlisted by the hundreds.

✔ **Reading Check**
5. Sequence What steps did the colonists take in declaring their independence?

_____

_____

_____

_____

_____

_____

KEY FACTS

6. Underline the reasons why so many African Americans fought on the side of the Americans in the Revolutionary War.

Historians estimate that however they were recruited, as many as one-quarter of the soldiers who fought for the Patriots were black. About 5 percent of the American troops in the Battle of Bunker Hill were black, including Peter Salem, who shot down British major Pitcairn, <u>rallying</u> the Americans into action. James Armistead, a black spy in the Continental Army, provided information that enabled the American troops to defeat the British at the final battle of the war, the Battle of Yorktown. Many other blacks also distinguished themselves in battle.

Black Soldiers in the British Army

The British also recruited black soldiers. As some state governments did, British governor Lord Dunsmore promised freedom to any slave who ran away and reached the British army. Tens of thousands of slaves took advantage of his offer, leaving farms and plantations in droves and flocking to the British lines.

Of those slaves who fled to the British, some—perhaps about 1,000, according to some historians—took up arms and fought against the Patriots, either on land or at sea. Far more, as many as 20,000 African Americans, contributed to the British war effort in other ways. They served as nurses, cooks, and general laborers.

After the War

The Revolutionary War continued for eight years. Finally, after a major victory by the Americans at Yorktown in 1781, the British agreed to surrender. With the signing of the Treaty of Paris on September 3, 1783, the Revolution came to an end. No longer colonists of Britain, the Americans had won their freedom.

As brilliantly as African Americans had contributed on the battlefield, so too did many call out for freedom at the war's end. They felt that they had earned their freedom with their efforts during the war. Southern slave owners, however, were determined to maintain the slave system. Despite the American victory, for most of the country's 680,000 African Americans *freedom* was just a word. ✔

ACADEMIC VOCABULARY
7. Use the context, or surrounding words in the sentence, to write a definition of **rallying**.

_____

_____

_____

✔ **Reading Check**
8. Explain How did both the Patriots and the British try to win the support of slaves?

_____

_____

_____

SECTION 2 ASSESSMENT

go.hrw.com
Online Quiz
Keyword: SAAH HP3

Reviewing Ideas, Terms, and People

9. Describe What roles did African Americans play in the American Revolution?

_____

_____

10. Identify Cause and Effect Why did Thomas Jefferson remove his antislavery passage from the Declaration of Independence?

_____

_____

11. Develop What was the link between the call for independence and the call for the freeing of slaves?

_____

_____

Analyzing Information

The struggle for independence from Great Britain was the defining event of the late 1700s. The ideas and actions of this period shaped the entire early history of the United States, and African Americans were vital to their formation. Use the graphic organizer below to explain the central ideas and actions of the struggle and the ways that African Americans contributed to them.

The Desire for Freedom

_____

_____

_____

_____

African American Contribution

_____

_____

_____

Protests against Mistreatment

_____

_____

_____

_____

African American Contribution

_____

_____

_____

The Struggle for Independence

Declaring Independence

_____

_____

_____

_____

African American Contribution

_____

_____

_____

Fighting for Liberty

_____

_____

_____

_____

African American Contribution

_____

_____

_____

Interpreting Time Lines

Understand the Skill

Time lines are a valuable tool for the student of history. By arranging events visually, time lines can help us more easily see how those events are related in time—what happened when, and what was going on at about the same time? In addition, time lines can help us understand what caused historical events to occur. Knowing what took place before an event can provide valuable clues about why it happened when it did.

Learn the Skill

Use the strategies to the right to learn how to interpret a time line.

Step 1 Remember that the events on a time line are listed in chronological order—the order in which they occurred.
Which happened earlier, the Boston Massacre or the Boston Tea party? How much earlier?

_____

_____

_____

1770 Protesting colonists are killed in the Boston Massacre.

1776 The Declaration of Independence is issued.

1774 The First Continental Congress meets.

1779 Spain declares war on Great Britain.

| 1770 | 1773 | 1776 | 1779 | 1782 |

1773 The Boston Tea Party is staged to protest British taxes.

1778 France allies with the American colonists.

1775 The first battles of the Revolution are fought.

1781 The British surrender.

Step 2 The order of events on a time line gives clues about how the events are related.
What relationship do you think existed between the fighting of the first battles of the Revolution and the issuing of the Declaration of Independence?

_____

_____

_____

APPLY THE SKILL

1. **Interpret** How many years passed between the fighting of the first battles of the Revolution and the surrender of the British army? What else happened during that time?

_____

_____

2. **Drawing Conclusions** How do you think the actions of France and Spain helped bring about Great Britain's surrender?

_____

_____

As You Read

Citizenship in the New Nation

1. **TAKING NOTES** Use a graphic organizer like this one to take notes on changing attitudes toward African Americans, free blacks, and slavery and the Constitution. Use the **Reading Focus** questions on the next page to help guide your note taking.

2. As you read the section, underline or highlight definitions and descriptions of the **Key Terms and People** listed on the next page.

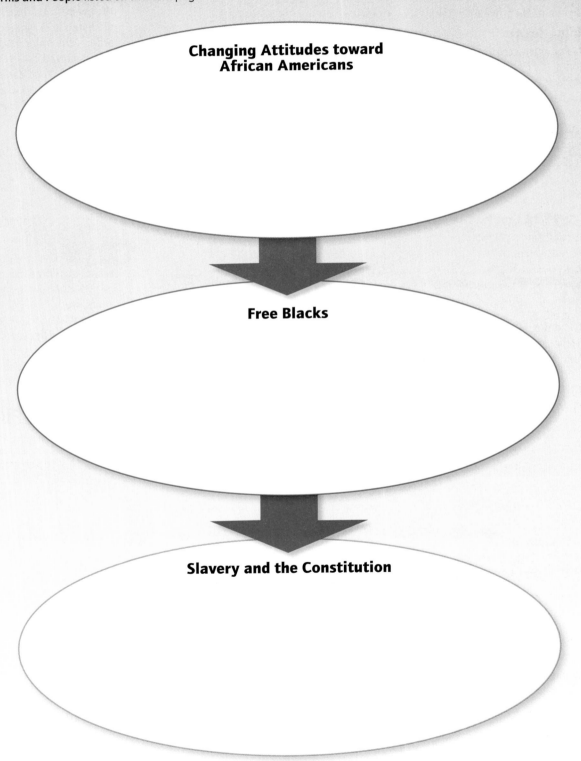

Changing Attitudes toward African Americans

Free Blacks

Slavery and the Constitution

BEFORE YOU READ

MAIN IDEA

Debates over the morality of slavery and opportunities for free blacks were major issues in the years after the American Revolution.

READING FOCUS

- How did people's attitudes toward African Americans change after the American Revolution?
- What opportunities were available in free black communities?
- How was the question of slavery addressed in the writing of the Constitution?

KEY TERMS AND PEOPLE

antislavery societies
Benjamin Rush
Anthony Benezet
emancipation
free blacks
Paul Cuffe
Three-Fifths Compromise

BUILDING BACKGROUND

By the time George Washington became the first president in 1789, the country's population had reached about 3.5 million. Of that population, about 730,000 people—nearly 20 percent—were black. With the signing of the Constitution and the creation of a new government, black people in the North gained new rights and privileges. In the South, however, the institution of slavery continued, and black people were not considered citizens at all. ■

Changing Attitudes toward African Americans

Following the American Revolution, a new government took shape in the United States. The basis of this government was the state. Each state wrote a constitution and created its own system of government. Loosely tying the states together was a document called the Articles of Confederation. Under the Articles, however, the federal government was very weak. Most power rested with the states.

Even as this new government was forming, some Americans began to work for changes in society. Inspired by the passion for liberty, these Americans hoped to improve the lives of many people, including African Americans.

Antislavery Sentiments

One effect of the Revolution was a renewed call for an end to slavery. Although many northerners had called for the banning of slavery even before the war, many more joined in the call now. In part, this renewal was the result of the freeing of slaves who had fought in the Revolution. In most states, slaves who had joined the army to fight against the British were freed at the end of the war. Opponents of slavery thought that if these slaves could be freed, surely all others could as well.

Quakers had formed the first **antislavery societies,** or groups devoted to the elimination of slavery, in the United States in 1775. After the Revolutionary War, many more such societies were created.

> **Skills FOCUS** **INTERPRETING TIME LINES**
>
> **1.** In the space below, list dates and events you could include on a time line of this period.

Slavery in the Early Republic

Examine the maps below and, in the space provided, describe how the issue of slavery was divided along regional lines.

BRITISH CANADA

NEW HAMPSHIRE (1783)
VERMONT (1777)
MASSACHUSETTS (1783)
NEW YORK (1799)
RHODE ISLAND (1784)
PENNSYLVANIA (1780)
CONNECTICUT (1784)
NEW JERSEY (1804)
DELAWARE
MARYLAND
NORTHWEST TERRITORY (1787)
VIRGINIA
KENTUCKY TERRITORY
TENNESSEE TERRITORY
NORTH CAROLINA
SOUTH CAROLINA
MISSISSIPPI TERRITORY
GEORGIA
SPANISH FLORIDA

Lake Superior
Lake Michigan
Lake Huron
Lake Ontario
Lake Erie
Ohio River
Mississippi River
Gulf of Mexico
ATLANTIC OCEAN

40°N
80°W
30°N

0   200   400 Miles
0   200   400 Kilometers
Albers equal-area projection

- Slavery outlawed by federal law
- Slavery banned by state law
- Gradual emancipation
- Slavery legal
- (1787) Year slavery outlawed

Skills FOCUS   INTERPRETING MAPS

2. Evaluate How was slavery divided by region?

_____

_____

_____

✔ **Reading Check**

3. Summarize How did feelings about slavery change after the American Revolution?

_____

_____

_____

Some antislavery societies were led by influential figures. One group in New York, for example, was headed by John Jay, who later became the first chief justice of the United States. Although all antislavery societies wanted to put an end to slavery, they worked toward achieving that goal in different ways. Some published antislavery writings, hoping to change the minds of people who still supported slavery, while others tried to end slavery by moving African Americans out of their states.

Antislavery groups and individuals worked tirelessly for an end to slavery. Two prominent figures in the antislavery fight were **Benjamin Rush**, a signer of the Declaration of Independence, and **Anthony Benezet**, a Protestant leader from Philadelphia. Both men had been active in the fight against slavery for years, but after the Revolution their efforts increased even more. Rush and Benezet wrote passionately in favor of freeing slaves from their bonds.

Northern States Ban Slavery

The efforts of antislavery activists started to pay off when states in the North began to outlaw slavery. In 1780, for example, Pennsylvania approved a constitution with instructions for the eventual abolition of slavery. The same year, Massachusetts issued a new constitution that stated "all men are born free and equal." In 1783 in a trial brought about by escaped slave Quock Walker, judges in Massachusetts ruled that this statement applied to slaves in addition to people who had been born free, so slavery would soon disappear in the state. Over the next few years, several more northern states banned slavery as well. As you can see on the map on this page, slavery had essentially been abolished in the North by 1800.

Although no southern states banned slavery in the 1780s, some did take small steps in that direction. States like Virginia and North Carolina included in their constitutions new laws that made emancipating their slaves easier for slaveholders. **Emancipation** is the process of being freed from bondage.

Congress also got involved in the fight against slavery in the 1780s. In 1787 it passed the Northwest Ordinance, a set of laws written to govern the settlement of the Northwest Territory. This territory, newly added to the United States, was located west of the original American colonies, to the north and west of the Ohio River. The Northwest Ordinance prohibited anyone in the territory to own slaves or other involuntary servants. Opponents of slavery considered this law a major victory. ✔

Free Blacks

Despite the prevalence of slavery, not all African Americans in the new United States were slaves. Even before the end of slavery, there were also substantial communities of free African Americans, both in the North and in the South. African Americans who were not slaves were commonly referred to as **free blacks**.

Becoming Free

Free blacks had gained their freedom in many ways. Some were soldiers who had won freedom in the Revolutionary War. Others had been released from slavery by their owners or by state law. Still others had bought their freedom, often at great cost.

A significant number of African Americans had not been granted their freedom at all but had escaped by running away from their owners. Scholars estimate that about 1,000 slaves ran away to the Caribbean or other regions each year.

Free Black Communities

Most free blacks lived in rural communities and worked in agriculture. While most free black communities were in the South, some northern cities had large black populations. In fact, Boston was the only major city in the United States in 1790 that could boast an entirely free black population: none of the more than 750 blacks who lived in Boston were slaves.

Even free blacks had few rights. They were not allowed to vote, and many white people considered them inferior. As a result, their opportunities were limited.

However, some free blacks made their own opportunities. One such person was **Paul Cuffe**, a black Boston shipper. During the Revolution, Cuffe had become a sailor. By 1780 he owned several ships and a thriving business. Cuffe wanted to use his money to help other black citizens, so he hatched a plan to bring free blacks back to Africa to live. However, high costs made his plans impractical. ✔

HISTORIAL DOCUMENT
Go online to to read a historical document from the free blacks of Boston.

go.hrw.com
Chapter Activity
Keyword: SAAH CH3

✔ **Reading Check**
4. Elaborate What made life difficult for free blacks in the early United States?

Slavery and the Constitution

By 1787 many American leaders had decided that the Articles of Confederation had to be completely revised. They believed the country needed a more powerful national government. As a result, delegates from the states met in 1787 for the Constitutional Convention.

The process of writing the new U.S. Constitution would prove to be a long one, filled with debates over many sticky issues. Among the issues that featured heavily in these debates was slavery.

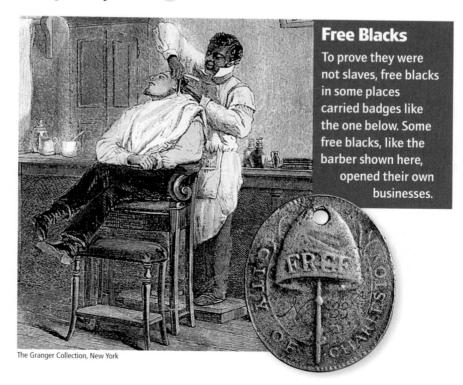

The Granger Collection, New York

Free Blacks

To prove they were not slaves, free blacks in some places carried badges like the one below. Some free blacks, like the barber shown here, opened their own businesses.

The Question of Importing Slaves

Many delegates to the Constitutional Convention wanted to end the importing of new slaves to the United States. Some southern delegates loudly announced that they would not support any document that forbade the slave trade, whereas other delegates—including many from southern states—wanted to include the ban in the Constitution. In the end, the delegates compromised. As it was written, the Constitution did not protect the slave trade forever but guaranteed that it could continue for 20 more years.

The Question of Representation

As fierce as the debate over the importing of slaves was, it was overshadowed by the question of the representation of slaves. Under the new Constitution, each state's representation in Congress would be determined in part by its population. While the delegates were working out the details of this plan, the question arose as to whether slaves would be counted as part of a state's population.

Northerners, who for the most part did not own slaves, argued that slaveholders considered their slaves to be property, not people, so slaves should not be counted. Meanwhile, southern states wanted to count their slaves, because doing so would result in larger populations and thus more representation in Congress.

In the end, the delegates were unable to agree to a plan that made everyone happy. What they settled on is called the **Three-Fifths Compromise**. It stated that every five slaves in a state would be counted as three people. In other words, each slave counted as three-fifths of a person. In this way, southern states got some additional representation from their slaves, but not as much as they wanted.

Reactions to the Constitution

The states finally ratified, or approved, the Constitution in 1790. Although most people were satisfied with the new government it created, some were not. Antislavery groups and free blacks were among the least satisfied. For example, they disliked a clause that required runaway slaves to be returned to their owners. Many were unhappy that the Constitution did not ban slavery outright. ✔

INFO TO KNOW
The Three-Fifths Compromise remained in effect until 1865, when the Thirteenth Amendment canceled it.

✔ **Reading Check**

5. Explain Why were many African Americans dissatisfied with the Constitution?

_____

_____

_____

---

go.hrw.com
Online Quiz
Keyword: SAAH HP3

Reviewing Ideas, Terms, and People

6. Describe For what efforts are Benjamin Rush and Anthony Benezet remembered?

_____

_____

7. Identify Cause and Effect What led to the Three-Fifths Compromise? What effects did the compromise have in the United States?

_____

_____

8. Elaborate Why were most free black communities located in the South?

_____

_____

Copyright © by Holt, Rinehart and Winston. All rights reserved.

Creating a Political Cartoon

By combining humor and satire with visual appeal, political cartoons can serve as powerful ways to express opinions and make points. For centuries, cartoonists have used their work to comment on social practices and changes that they have witnessed. In the space below, draw a political cartoon about one of the topics discussed in this section. Remember that your cartoon should express a clear position or make a meaningful comment on your chosen topic.

ASSESS YOUR KNOWLEDGE

1. **Support a Position** What event did you choose for your political cartoon? Why did you choose that event?

_____

_____

2. **Elaborate** How do you think your opinion today might be different from the opinions of people who lived in the 1790s? Explain your answer.

_____

_____

As You Read

African American Culture

1. **TAKING NOTES** Use a graphic organizer like this one to take notes on African American culture, religion, schools, and achievements. Use the **Reading Focus** questions on the next page to help guide your note taking.

2. As you read the section, underline or highlight definitions and descriptions of the **Key Terms and People** listed on the next page.

The Role of Religion

Keeping African Culture Alive

African American Achievements

African American Schools

BEFORE YOU READ

MAIN IDEA
The African Americans of the period following the American Revolution created a unique culture that blended traditions from Africa with new ideas.

READING FOCUS
- How did black Americans manage to keep African culture alive?
- What role did religion play in African American culture?
- What led to the creation of African American schools?
- What were some advances made by African Americans?

KEY TERMS AND PEOPLE
creole
Richard Allen
Phillis Wheatley
Benjamin Banneker

BUILDING BACKGROUND
Whether enslaved on plantations or living in free black communities, African Americans formed a distinct culture in the years after the Revolution. Inspired by their African roots and shaped by their experiences in America, this culture became a key influence in the lives and expectations of African American citizens. ■

Keeping African Culture Alive

Many black customs in the early United States were, in part, continuations of older African customs. However, some plantation owners were alarmed by the practice of African customs, as they feared such practices could inspire slaves to fight for their freedom. As a result, the owners refused to allow slaves to behave as they wanted.

To keep their African culture alive, then, most African Americans had to seem docile and obedient in public. But in secret, they actively maintained many customs. Some, when given the chance to make quilts, for example, wove designs from their countries of origin. Many slaves also continued to sing and dance the way their ancestors had in Africa. For example, many slaves took part in vigorous juba dancing, accompanied by, among other instruments, a banjo. The banjo is similar to several types of stringed African instruments.

Even African words and names survived the brutality of slavery. Have you heard of a tote bag? The word *tote* probably developed from a Bantu word brought to America by slaves. In some places, more than a few words have survived through the centuries. For example, the Gullah people of South Carolina and Georgia still speak a **creole**, or combined, language that blends English with words from several African languages. The Gullah people were brought to the South from the areas of modern Senegal, Gambia, and Sierra Leone, and their culture shares many similarities with cultures of people who live in that part of Africa today. The Gullah also make many of the same foods as their African relatives, and they still tell many of the same types of stories. ✔

✔ Reading Check
1. Identify What were some of the aspects of African culture kept alive in the United States?

_____

_____

_____

Mary Evans Picture Library

The Role of Religion

Most African slaves in America were converted to Christianity. Many attended church services with their owners and their families.

The Role of Religion

Religion is a powerful force in many people's lives. Religion guides how people act, what they do, and how they think. For many white southerners, religion was even seen as a way to justify slavery.

Christianity and Slavery

In the 1600s and 1700s many Christians used arguments from the Bible to justify the owning of slaves. One common justification they used was a passage from the book of Genesis, which read, "Cursed be Canaan; lowest of slaves shall he be to his brothers" (Gen. 9:25 NRSV). During this time, Christians believed that Canaan—one of Noah's grandchildren—had later moved to Africa and that all black Africans were his descendants. Therefore, they argued, the Bible justified the keeping of black slaves by white people, the descendants of Canaan's uncles and cousins.

Not all white Christians supported this interpretation of the Bible. Many thought that owning slaves was immoral and unchristian. They pointed to biblical passages that called on Christians to love all people and to treat each other compassionately. Within some Christian churches, heated debates over the issue of slavery flared up throughout the 1700s.

Baptism of Slaves

Despite raging arguments over the justification of slavery, nearly all colonists felt that those slaves who were brought to the Americas should be baptized as Christians. In most cases, these baptisms took place even before the slaves were taken from Africa. Once they arrived in the colonies, slaves were forbidden to practice their former religions, which included not only traditional African religions but also Islam. The children of slaves born in the colonies were generally raised as Christians from birth. By the late 1700s most slaves were Christians, at least in name.

Some slave owners were wary of giving their slaves too much religious education, however. They did not want their slaves to learn too much about the Bible, because some of its passages concerned slavery and freedom. For example, the Bible tells how the Hebrew people escaped slavery in Egypt. How could slave owners explain the Hebrews fleeing from oppression when black people were supposed to be content with their own oppression?

Because most southern plantation owners were outnumbered by their slaves, they were reluctant to let slaves gather in large groups, even for prayer meetings. Uneasy and fearful, they could never be sure if their slaves were using the time to plan revolts. Such planning, in fact, did happen, as we will see later.

African American Churches

Although white slave owners prohibited slaves from practicing any non-Christian religions, they also did not want black people worshiping in their churches. Before the early 1800s there were a few churches, mostly in the North, where African Americans might be allowed to worship. But even then, they had to sit in a special

---

INFO TO KNOW

Most but not all African Americans today are still Christians. The figures below list the African American membership of some religious denominations.

Protestant	**30.9 million**
Baptist	15.7 million
Methodist	7.6 million
Other	7.6 million
Catholic	**2 million**
Muslim	**250,000**
Jewish	**30,000**
Other	**2.6 million**

2. Use the statistics above to create a pie graph showing the distribution of African American religion today.

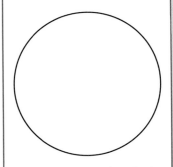

Source: African American Desk Reference, Encyclopedia of African Amercian Society

balcony, away from the white parishioners. One black American Revolutionary war hero, Lemuel Haynes, even became a pastor to white Christians in Vermont. But he was definitely an exception.

Denied access to white churches, black people formed their own congregations. In the South, for example, black people started independent Baptist churches. The earliest was in Silver Bluff, South Carolina, around 1773. Eventually, black churches from other denominations were established in the North as well as the South. The largest such church, the African Methodist Episcopal (AME) Church, grew out of a church founded by **Richard Allen** in 1787. Allen and other ministers, along with their congregations, would form the core of important black freedom efforts.

The AME was the first of many churches formed to deal with the spiritual needs of the African American community. Today, there are many such churches. These black churches, as they are called, are usually Protestant Christian and spend much of their time and energy dealing with social issues that affect black Americans. ✔

✔ **Reading Check**
3. Identify Cause and Effect
Why did African Americans form their own churches?

African American Schools

Many African Americans felt that the best way to improve their lives was to gain a strong education. As a result, many black parents sought education for their children. However, most white schools would not allow black children to enroll.

Since they could not get their children into white schools, some well-to-do black citizens decided to establish schools of their own. One such citizen was Paul Cuffe, the Boston shipper who had been a proponent of the colonization movement. He built a school so that his children and other black youngsters might be educated. Another school builder was Primus Hall, an African American resident of Boston. When black students could not enroll in public schools, Hall allowed them to meet in his home to study with a white teacher. In 1790 the black citizens of Boston sought permission from the city to build a separate school for black children. They were denied, but they built the school anyway. It operated for several years until the first government school for black children was built in 1820.

Some white people helped. In the North, several Quaker schools accepted black students. Even in the South, a handful of white teachers agreed to teach African Americans to read and write. For example, in Charleston, South Carolina, Alexander Garden set up a school for slaves in 1743. Its schoolmasters were two young black slaves. The school was a great success, educating up to 60 slaves at a time. The school continued in operation until 1764.

As time went on, however, white southerners grew even more fearful of education for blacks. State legislatures passed more and more laws that banned teaching blacks to read and write. Still, the thirst of African Americans to gain an education would continue. The first black men to graduate from college in America were John B. Russwurm and Edward Jones. In 1826 Russwurm received his degree from Bowdoin College in Maine, as did Jones from Amherst College in Massachusetts. Other black men would go on to receive degrees from universities in Europe. ✔

▲ **Boston's Abiel Smith School was one of the first built just for black students.**

✔ **Reading Check**
4. Elaborate Why do you think many whites wanted to limit education for black students?

Phillis Wheatley's Poetry

Phillis Wheatley never forgot that she had been stolen from her African home. In a poem she wrote to the Earl of Dartmouth in 1773, Wheatley explained how her life and experiences as a slave had inspired her works.

"Should you, my lord, while you peruse my song,
Wonder from whence my love of Freedom sprung,
Whence flow these wishes for the common good,
By feeling hearts alone best understood,
I, young in life, by seeming cruel fate
Was snatch'd from Afric's fancy'd happy seat:
What pangs excruciating must molest,
What sorrows labour in my parent's breast?
Steel'd was the soul and by no misery mov'd
That from a father seiz'd his babe belov'd:
Such, such my case. And can I then but pray
Others may never feel tyrannic sway?"

Skills FOCUS **ANALYZING PRIMARY SOURCES**

5. Summarize On the lines below, explain Wheatley's poem in your own words.

_____

_____

_____

_____

African American Achievements

African Americans of the early United States made great achievements in many fields. Some of their achievements helped shape the society and culture of the new nation.

Literature

Many African American writers of the Revolutionary War period left behind works that are still read and admired today. A slave named Lucy Terry was the first known African American poet. Her one surviving poem tells of a massacre of local residents near Deerfield, Massachusetts, in 1746.

Phillis Wheatley, a young slave woman of Boston, was actually the first African American poet to have her works published. Wheatley had learned to read and write English after being kidnapped in Africa and brought to America around 1760. She was taught by the wife and daughter of her wealthy master, John Wheatley. Her first poem was published around 1767, and she became a sensation in society. Wheatley's first book of poetry was published in London in 1773. Hailed as a work of genius, Wheatley's book would be reprinted many times. After returning to America, Wheatley wrote another poem, this one praising George Washington. On February 28, 1776, Washington wrote to Wheatley to thank her for the poem and praise her for her talents.

Science and Medicine

African Americans also made great advances in the fields of science and medicine in the years after the American Revolution. Perhaps the greatest black scientist of the time was **Benjamin Banneker**. He was born free, though his father and grandfather had been slaves. As a child, Banneker received a good education at a Quaker school that taught both black and white children. Primarily interested in math and science, Banneker became skilled in engineering and in astronomy.

Among Benjamin Banneker's accomplishments was the publication of his annual almanacs, which listed the dates of various events, such as solar and lunar eclipses. These almanacs won praise from such well-known figures as Thomas Jefferson, as well as many scholars throughout Europe to whom Jefferson showed his copies. Banneker is perhaps best remembered, though, because he was later chosen to help survey the location of the nation's new capital built in the late 1700s, Washington, D.C.

One of Banneker's skilled contemporaries was James Durham, the first black doctor in the United States. Born into slavery, Durham learned the basics of medicine from his owner, a doctor. Later, Durham was sold to a doctor in the French city of New Orleans, with whom he finished his training. Eventually, Durham was able to buy his freedom and—after relocating to Philadelphia—he set up a successful medical practice of his own. ✔

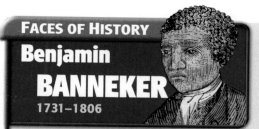

FACES OF HISTORY
Benjamin BANNEKER
1731–1806

Inventor, astronomer, surveyor, and writer Benjamin Banneker was known from a young age for his intelligence and cleverness. At age 30, he amazed everyone by building a working clock from wooden materials. Among those who were impressed by the clock was the owner of a local mill, who invited Banneker to study the inner workings of the mill's machinery. In addition, the mill owner loaned him several books about math and science. Banneker not only read and mastered the content of the books but even found errors the authors had made! It is little wonder that he eventually became known as one of the best minds of his generation.

6. Evaluate Which of Banneker's achievements do you find most impressive? Why?

_____

_____

_____

✔ **Reading Check**

7. Develop What advantages did Phillis Wheatley, Benjamin Banneker, and James Durham have over most blacks?

_____

_____

_____

SECTION 4 ASSESSMENT

go.hrw.com
Online Quiz
Keyword: SAAH HP3

Reviewing Ideas, Terms, and People

8. Identify What were some elements of African culture that shaped black life in the United States?

_____

_____

9. Summarize How did religion help African Americans develop their own culture?

_____

_____

10. Evaluate Which of the African Americans discussed in this section do you think made the most important achievements? Why do you think so?

_____

_____

Analyzing Changes

Two of the most important influences on early African American society were religion and education, both of which changed profoundly in the years immediately following independence. Use the graphic organizer below to examine how religion and education changed and how those changes affected society.

Religion

Before Independence

_____
_____
_____
_____
_____
_____

After Independence

_____
_____
_____
_____
_____
_____

Education

Before Independence

_____
_____
_____
_____
_____
_____

After Independence

_____
_____
_____
_____
_____
_____

ASSESS YOUR KNOWLEDGE

1. Describe What role did religion play in African American society?

_____

2. Explain How did changes in education lead to new opportunities for African Americans?

_____

_____

Writing a Biographical Sketch

African Americans in the 1780s and 1790s made many significant contributions to American society. Choose one prominent figure from this period—either one discussed in this section or another figure about whom you would like to learn more—and write a biographical sketch of him or her in the space below. Briefly describe the life and accomplishments of your figure and explain why he or she is important in American history. You may wish to conduct additional research before you write your sketch.

Quiz and Review

ONLINE QUIZ
Take a practice quiz for each section in this chapter.

CHAPTER REVIEW
Use the online Chapter Review to help you prepare for the chapter test.

Activities

HISTORICAL DOCUMENTS
Read and explore key documents that shaped African American history.

VIRTUAL FIELD TRIP
Take a virtual field trip to experience key sites from African American history.

VOICES OF HISTORY
Experience African American history and culture through recordings of key people and documents.

Partner

CONNECTING TO OUR PAST
Examine artifacts from **Howard University's Moorland-Spingarn Research Center** that bring to life the study of African American history.

African Americans Help Create a New Nation

CHAPTER SUMMARY

SECTION 1 Blacks in Colonial America

- The southern colonies were home to the largest number of African slaves, due in large part to the plantation system.
- In the middle colonies, slavery was less common than in the South, though no less harsh.
- Slavery was relatively rare in the New England colonies.

SECTION 2 The Revolutionary War Era

- Disputes over taxation led to increased tension between the colonies and Great Britain.
- Even as colonists began to call for freedom from British rule, some called for an end to slavery.
- African Americans sided with both the colonists and the British during the Revolutionary War.

SECTION 3 Citizenship in the New Nation

- Many Americans began to call for an end to slavery after the American Revolution, leading to the end of slavery in the North.
- Free blacks had to work hard to overcome limited opportunities and discrimination.
- Debates over slavery helped shape the U.S. Constitution.

SECTION 4 African American Culture

- Slaves worked to keep elements of their traditional African culture alive in the Americas.
- Most Africans in the United States became Christian, but they often had to form their own churches in which to worship.
- Opportunities for schooling for black students were limited in the early United States.
- African Americans made significant contributions to the arts and sciences in the new nation.

African Americans in the NEW REPUBLIC

Southern slaves gather in front of their living quarters on a southern plantation in this early American painting.

Detail of *The Old Plantation*, c. 1790

EXPRESSING YOUR OPINION

In the 1800s a lively debate raged about whether slavery should continue in the United States and about how the government could put a stop to it. Write a letter to the editor of a local newspaper expressing your opinion about the best way to end American slavery.

The Slave System in the South

1. **TAKING NOTES** Use a graphic organizer like this one to take notes on the rise of "king cotton," the slave trade, and life under slavery. Use the **Reading Focus** questions on the next page to help guide your note taking.

2. As you read the section, underline or highlight definitions and descriptions of the **Key Terms** listed on the next page.

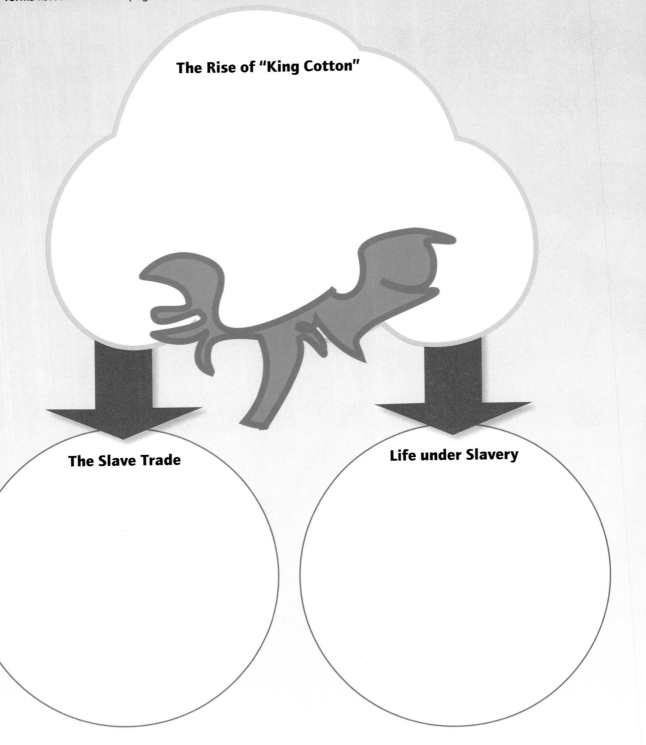

The Rise of "King Cotton"

The Slave Trade

Life under Slavery

BEFORE YOU READ

MAIN IDEA

As the economy of the southern states came to rely on the production of cotton, the need for slave labor grew.

READING FOCUS

- How did the increasing importance of cotton affect the South?
- What were the results of the ban on the foreign slave trade?
- What were some key elements of slave life and culture?

KEY TERMS

cotton gin
Industrial Revolution
cotton belt
antebellum period
domestic slave trade
spirituals

BUILDING BACKGROUND

By the early 1800s slavery had come to an end in all the northern states. In the South, however, the growing importance of cotton led to an increasing demand for slaves. As a result, the institution of slavery became more entrenched than ever in the South. ■

The Rise of "King Cotton"

By the early 1800s the United States was changing rapidly. Westward expansion and new technologies were transforming the nation. Advances in cotton production would lead to a transformation of the southern economy and the spread of slavery.

The Cotton Boom

Life in the South had long revolved around agriculture. Southern farmers had relied on cash crops such as tobacco, rice, and indigo before the American Revolution. By the late 1700s, however, prices for these crops had dropped dramatically. To make up for the lost income, southern farmers were forced to look for more <u>lucrative</u> crops.

Many southerners hoped that cotton would help their economy. Eventually, some southern farmers began planting short-staple cotton, which was easy to grow but difficult and time-consuming to process. Workers spent hours picking the seeds from cotton fibers, so short-staple cotton was expensive to produce. In 1793 northerner Eli Whitney revolutionized cotton production. Working as a tutor on a Georgia plantation, Whitney began experimenting with a machine that would remove seeds from short-staple cotton. Within six months, he had built the first **cotton gin**. His new device could clean seeds from cotton fibers 50 times faster than by hand. Thanks to the cotton gin, the large-scale production of cotton in the South was possible.

By the late 1790s cotton production was on the rise, as was the demand for U.S. cotton. A key reason for the growing demand was the booming textile, or cloth, industry. The **Industrial Revolution**, a period of rapid growth in using machines for manufacturing and production, had transformed how most textiles were produced.

ACADEMIC VOCABULARY

1. Use the context, or surrounding words in the sentence, to write a definition of **lucrative**.

_____

_____

_____

The Cotton Kingdom, 1820–1860

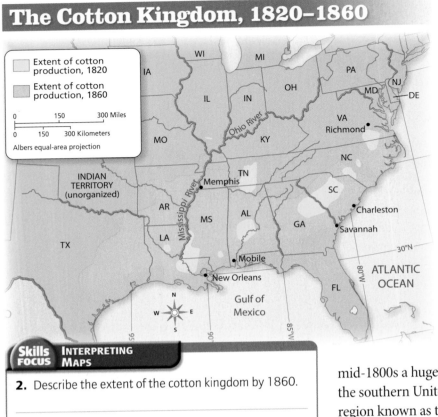

Extent of cotton production, 1820

Extent of cotton production, 1860

0   150   300 Miles
0   150   300 Kilometers
Albers equal-area projection

Skills FOCUS   INTERPRETING MAPS

2. Describe the extent of the cotton kingdom by 1860.

_____

_____

Rather than make cloth by hand, workers could now use machines to produce cloth much faster than ever before. As a result, the demand for cotton skyrocketed.

The combination of the new cotton gin and the growing demand for cotton encouraged many southern growers to plant cotton. Wealthy farmers established huge cotton plantations throughout the South. As a result, cotton production in the United States soared. By 1820 farmers in the United States were producing more than 300,000 bales of cotton per year. U.S. production jumped to more than 1 million bales per year by 1840. The amount of land devoted to growing cotton also rose dramatically. By the mid-1800s a huge band of cotton farms stretching across the southern United States as far west as Texas formed a region known as the **cotton belt**.

Cotton soon became America's most valuable crop. Farmers in the cotton belt cultivated, cleaned, and shipped vast quantities of cotton to mills in Great Britain to be made into cloth. Northerners profited from cotton as well. They helped transport and sell cotton and opened mills and factories where cotton cloth was produced. By the mid-1800s the economy of the South was firmly based on cotton. As South Carolina Senator James Henry Hammond declared in 1858, "Cotton is king!"

Slavery and the Cotton Boom

As cotton grew in importance in the South, so, too, did slavery. Growing, harvesting, and cleaning cotton demanded great amounts of labor. Rather than pay wages to free workers, wealthy planters increasingly relied on slave labor. They knew that the more slaves they used, the more cotton they could produce and the more profit they could make. Thus, slavery was a key contributor to the economic success of the South.

KEY FACTS

3. Use the graphic organizer below to identify the causes and effects of the cotton boom in the South.

With the expansion of cotton farming came an expansion in slavery. The slave population in the United States grew rapidly. In 1790 there were fewer than 700,000 slaves in the United States. By 1810 the slave population had increased to about 1 million, and by 1840, to nearly 2.5 million. The cotton boom also led to the spread of slavery to new regions in the United States. As farmers moved south and west in search of new lands on which to grow cotton, they often took slaves with them. As a result, slavery spread throughout the cotton belt into Alabama, Mississippi, Arkansas, and Texas.

Cotton Boom

Causes	Effects

Not all southerners, however, had slaves. Only about one-fourth of white families in the South owned slaves. The majority of slaveholders in the South owned fewer than 5 slaves and held small farms. Wealthy planters who owned more than 20 slaves made up only a small portion of slave owners. Due to their wealth, however, these planters dominated economic and political life in the South. In 1866 President Andrew Johnson recalled that "there were 27 non-slaveholders to one slaveholder [in Tennessee], and yet the slave power controlled the state." ✔

✔**Reading Check**
4. Analyze Why did slavery expand into new states and territories?

The Slave Trade

During the **antebellum period**—the period before the Civil War—slave traders met the growing demand for slave labor by importing new slaves from Africa and the Caribbean. In 1803, for example, some 20,000 enslaved Africans were imported into Georgia and South Carolina. However, this foreign slave trade soon faced opposition.

As you learned in the previous chapter, in 1787 delegates to the Constitutional Convention agreed to allow the foreign slave trade for only 20 years. In the early 1800s, as the 20-year deadline drew close, antislavery advocates began speaking out in favor of outlawing the foreign slave trade. Congress eventually agreed, and on January 1, 1808, a ban on the importation of slaves to the United States went into effect.

Despite the ban on the foreign slave trade, slaves continued to arrive on U.S. shores. Slave merchants turned to smuggling shipments of slaves into the United States, where southern planters eagerly purchased them. At the same time, the federal government often failed to enforce the ban on the foreign slave trade. Although the importation of slaves persisted, the supply of newly imported slaves was drastically reduced.

Congress's ban against the foreign slave trade did not put an end to the sale and purchase of slaves in the United States, however. The **domestic slave trade**, or the sale and transportation of slaves within the United States, remained legal. Slave owners and traders were free to buy and sell slaves within the country. As a result of the decline of the foreign slave trade, the domestic slave trade soon flourished.

The constant demand for slaves meant a boom in the domestic slave trade. Slave owners in the Upper South—where cotton was not widely grown—began selling their slaves to farmers in the cotton belt. By 1815 the domestic slave trade had become one of the country's major industries. Breeding slaves for sale became as profitable for some farmers as working them in the fields. Businesses were established that specialized in the sale of slaves. Slave traders sometimes kidnapped free African Americans and sold them into slavery in other parts of the country. Bustling slave markets existed in many cities, including Baltimore, Maryland; Charleston, South Carolina; and Washington, D.C. ✔

THE GRANGER COLLECTION, NEW YORK

Cotton Farming
The labor of slaves on cotton plantations was key to the economic success of the South.

✔**Reading Check**
5. Explain How did slave traders try to get around the ban on the importation of slaves?

Life under Slavery

With the dramatic rise of "king cotton," the southern economy came to depend on the work of slaves. Slave life was one of hard labor and strict rules. For many slaves, culture and family were their only escape from a life of grueling work.

Slaves and Work

The slave's life centered around work. For the vast majority of slaves, that work took place on rural farms or plantations. Slaves on small farms performed a variety of jobs, such as planting and harvesting crops or preparing food. They were managed—and often worked alongside—their owners.

On plantations, however, slaves often held specific jobs, such as field hands or household servants. Field hands had some of the most difficult jobs on plantations. They worked long hours planting, plowing, and harvesting crops. Most field hands worked six days a week, all year long, with only a few days off each year. Women and children older than about 10 were expected to perform the same tasks as men. One slave described the work performed by female slaves in Louisiana.

PRIMARY SOURCES

A Slave Spiritual

One characteristic of slave culture was music. Many slaves enjoyed singing spirituals while they worked. Generally religious in nature, spirituals told of the hardships and hopes of slaves.

"When Israel was in Egyptland
Let my people go
Oppressed so hard they could not stand
Let my people go.

Go down, Moses,
Way down in Egyptland
Tell old Pharaoh
'Let my people go . . .

'No more shall they in bondage toil [work],
Let my people go;
Let them come out with Egypt's spoil,
Let my people go.'"

Skills FOCUS ANALYZING PRIMARY SOURCES

6. Explain What hope does this spiritual express?

_____

_____

_____

HISTORY'S VOICES

[Women] perform their share of all the labor required on the plantation. They plough, drag, drive team, clear wild lands, work on the highway, and so forth. Some planters, owning large cotton and sugar plantations, have none other than the labor of slave women.

—Solomon Northup, *Twelve Years a Slave*, 1853

Most field hands endured poor living conditions. They often lived in rugged cabins and received simple clothes and small rations of food. After working long hours in the fields, they usually had to tend to their own needs, such as cooking and caring for children.

Other slaves worked in the planter's household as butlers, cooks, or nurses. These slaves often had better food, clothing, and shelter than did field hands. However, they typically worked longer hours and were expected to serve the planter's family 24 hours a day.

Slave Culture

Despite the difficult labor and harsh conditions, many enslaved Africans managed to find comfort in their culture and community. To relieve the hardship of their lives, slaves often turned to cultural activities and to the comfort of their families.

Religion was a key factor of slave culture. For many slaves, religion provided the hope of salvation in this life and in the next. On many plantations slaves were allowed to gather to worship, often under the leadership of a slave preacher. One common feature of slave religion in the South was the slave spiritual. **Spirituals** are emotional songs that often express religious beliefs. Slaves sometimes used spirituals to express their joys and their sorrows or sang spirituals to keep a steady rhythm while working in the fields.

Religious gatherings and other celebrations offered many slaves an opportunity to socialize. Many such gatherings featured singing, dancing, and storytelling, which were important aspects of slave culture on the plantation. These activities often provided comfort and entertainment for slaves. One slave musician remarked that "had it not been for my beloved violin, I scarcely can conceive how I could have endured the long years of bondage."

Because laws often prevented slaves from learning to read or write, most songs and stories were handed down by word of mouth. Over the years, slave work songs, spirituals, and folk tales have been preserved.

Families were another vital part of slave life. For many slaves, family was the most important aspect of their lives. Marriage among slaves was common throughout the South. In fact, slave owners often encouraged marriage among their slaves. Slaves with families, they believed, would be less likely to rebel or run away.

Slave families, however, faced many challenges. Marriages could be dissolved by slave owners. Parents often did not have enough time to care for their own children. Because slave owners were free to sell their slaves at any time, families were constantly threatened with being split apart. ✔

FACES OF HISTORY

George Moses HORTON
c. 1797–c. 1883

North Carolina slave George Moses Horton is best remembered as a talented poet. As a child, Horton became interested in books and taught himself to read. He soon developed a love of hymns and poems and eventually began composing his own poetry.

As a young man, Horton held a job selling produce at a market near the University of North Carolina. There, he attracted attention for his gift of poetry. University students often purchased love poems that Horton composed and dictated. With the help of community members, Horton learned to write and eventually published his first poem. In 1829 he released *The Hope of Liberty*, his first collection of poems. Horton, who later published two more poetry collections, is still widely admired for his literary achievements.

7. Draw Conclusions To what might the title of Horton's first poetry collection, *The Hope of Liberty*, refer?

_____

_____

✔ **Reading Check**
8. Identify What were some key elements of slave culture?

_____

_____

_____

---

go.hrw.com
Online Quiz
Keyword: SAAH HP4

Reviewing Ideas, Terms, and People

9. Identify Main Ideas How did the cotton gin affect life in the South?

_____

_____

10. Identify Cause and Effect What led to the rise of the domestic slave trade?

_____

_____

11. Evaluate What do you think was the most important aspect of slave culture? Why?

_____

_____

Interpreting Visuals

Understand the Skill

Visual images are important sources of historical information. By studying visuals, such as paintings, sketches, and photos, we can learn a great deal about the attitudes of a particular time period or group of people as well as important details from that period. For example, a sketch of factory workers can indicate what clothes people wore in that period, what tools and technology were available, and what working conditions were like. Visuals, like written documents, can also indicate the artist's or photographer's point of view. Interpreting visual images is a crucial skill for understanding history.

Learn the Skill

Use the strategies below to analyze visuals.

1. Identify the creator of the image and the type of artwork.
2. Identify the subject of the image and examine the details.
3. Determine how the creator of the visual depicts the subject and identify the point of view represented in the image.
4. Compare the image with what you know about the historical time period.

The First Cotton Gin
William L. Sheppard, 1800s

The Granger Collection, New York

Use the strategies you learned at left to analyze the illustration, *The First Cotton Gin*, and then answer the questions below.

1. Identify Who created the illustration, and when was it created?

_____

_____

2. Explain What is the subject of the image? What other details are depicted in it?

_____

_____

3. Identify Points of View What is the point of view of the illustration? What details in the image indicate that to you?

_____

_____

_____

4. Draw Conclusions What does this image tell you about the historical period in which it was created?

_____

_____

_____

5. Elaborate Write a paragraph in which you compare what you know of the period with what is depicted in the image. How do the two compare?

_____

_____

_____

_____

_____

_____

_____

_____

_____

_____

_____

_____

_____

_____

_____

Free African Americans

1. **TAKING NOTES** Use a graphic organizer like this one to take notes on free blacks in the antebellum period and westward expansion. Use the **Reading Focus** questions on the next page to help guide your note taking.

2. As you read the section, underline or highlight definitions and descriptions of the **Key Terms and People** listed on the next page.

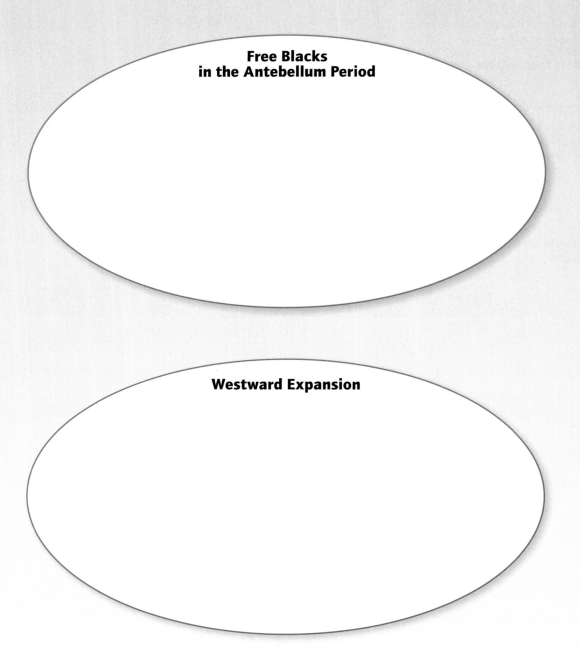

**Free Blacks
in the Antebellum Period**

Westward Expansion

BEFORE YOU READ

MAIN IDEA

Free African Americans lived in every region of the United States in the early 1800s, but in each region they faced different challenges.

READING FOCUS

- What opportunities and restrictions did free blacks in the North and the South face?
- What roles did free blacks play in westward expansion in the early 1800s?

KEY TERMS AND PEOPLE

Louisiana Purchase
York
James Beckwourth

BUILDING BACKGROUND

From the earliest days of the American colonies, some African Americans were free. In the years before the Civil War, the number of free blacks increased dramatically. The growing free black population faced many new challenges and opportunities. ■

Free Blacks in the Antebellum Period

Since colonial times, free blacks had lived and prospered in the United States. In the antebellum period, or the years before the Civil War, the free black population slowly began to increase. Free blacks in the South and the North faced many challenges.

Becoming Free

As you have just read, the slave system remained strong in the South through the early 1800s. How then did the free black population in that region grow so much? Several factors contributed to the increase. Some slaves continued to save money to buy their freedom, while others served owners who, perhaps overtaken by feelings of guilt, released their slaves from bondage—at least until states passed laws making the emancipation, or freeing, of slaves much harder. Just as slaves had been granted freedom for fighting in the Revolutionary War, thousands more were released for their service in the War of 1812. A few slaves were granted freedom for some extraordinary service they performed. For example, a slave in Georgia was made free in 1834 after he saved the state capitol from burning. The free black population also increased naturally, as free blacks got married and had children.

Free Black Society in the South

Though they did not have to work as slaves, southern free blacks did not lead easy, carefree lives. State laws denied them such basic rights as voting, testifying in court, and receiving an education. Furthermore, free blacks in some parts of the South had to be wary even just walking down the street, because unscrupulous slave traders sometimes kidnapped free blacks and sold them into bondage. Nevertheless, hundreds of free blacks in the South persevered and even prospered.

> **KEY FACTS**
>
> **1.** What are some ways in which African Americans gained their freedom?

U.S. SLAVE AND FREE BLACK POPULATIONS, 1820–1860

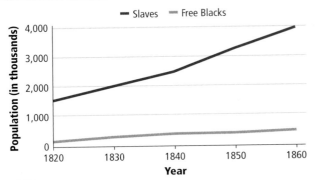

— Slaves — Free Blacks

Source: *Historical Statistics of the United States*

Skills FOCUS INTERPRETING GRAPHS

2. Approximately how many more slaves than free blacks lived in the United States in 1860?

_____

_____

ACADEMIC VOCABULARY

3. Use the context, or surrounding words in the sentence, to write a definition of the word **apprenticed**.

_____

_____

_____

VIRTUAL FIELD TRIP
Go online to experience a virtual field trip to key sites from the antebellum period.

go.hrw.com
Chapter Activity
Keyword: SAAH CH4

The jobs available to free blacks were, in most cases, limited by law. States passed laws that barred African Americans from working in certain jobs. For example, in South Carolina they could not be clerks, and in Georgia they could not be typesetters. Even jobs not forbidden to free African Americans often required a special license, such as the license black shop owners needed to sell wheat or corn in Maryland.

Despite the restrictions limiting their job opportunities, most free blacks managed to find employment. Many found positions as skilled artisans, working as cobblers, blacksmiths, and carpenters. Others hired themselves out as general laborers, often for low wages. Still others were farmers. Blacks had little choice but to work. Laws in every southern state required that free blacks work. States passed laws declaring that any black person who could not furnish proof of employment could be sentenced to forced labor. Children of those sentenced would be taken away and sent to live with white families.

Black Slave Owners

Through their efforts, some free blacks became quite wealthy. Some free African Americans used their wealth to purchase slaves and become slave owners themselves. For example, William Ellison was born a slave on a small plantation in South Carolina. Rather than work in the fields, Ellison was apprenticed to a cotton gin builder to learn how to make and repair the machines. At age 26 he was granted his freedom and went into business for himself. His business was quite successful, and by 1860 Ellison had saved enough to buy a plantation and as many as 60 slaves.

According to the U.S. census, about 3,400 blacks owned slaves in the United States by 1840. However, not all of them were plantation owners like William Ellison. The majority lived in southern towns and cities where they ran businesses or factories that used slaves as their primary source of labor. Many of the black slave owners were not typical slave owners. In many cases, when slaves were freed, their family members often remained enslaved. Former slaves sometimes purchased their wives and children. Southern laws during the antebellum period, however, made granting a slave his or her freedom very difficult. As a result, many free blacks officially owned members of their own families as slaves.

Free Blacks in Florida

In one area of the South, Florida, the free black community was very different from that in the rest of the South. Most of the black residents of Florida were escaped slaves who had fled to the area in the early 1800s. At that time, Florida had been a Spanish colony and had not permitted slavery. When the British took Florida from the Spanish in 1763, thousands of these escaped slaves fled to Havana, Cuba. Others, however, chose to stay in Florida, where they established hidden settlements in the Florida wilderness.

In the wilderness, free blacks met and settled with Native American peoples, the Seminoles. In general, each group had its own communities, but some blacks lived in Seminole settlements, either free or as slaves. Those blacks who were slaves were often better off than they had been under the British. For example, they were given land of their own to farm and weapons with which to hunt.

In 1816 when U.S. general Andrew Jackson led troops into Spanish Florida, runaway African Americans fired on Jackson's troops. He responded by capturing the men and selling them into slavery. Over the next several years, free blacks and their Seminole allies were involved in several disputes with the U.S. Army. The conflict died off for a time when Florida became part of the United States in 1821 and free blacks there were guaranteed their freedom. Before long, however, the Seminole Wars broke out, and black soldiers once more fought against the U.S. Army. By 1842 the wars were over, and the Seminoles were forced to leave Florida.

Blacks in the North

African Americans living in the South viewed the North as a land of freedom and opportunity. To an extent, they were right. Northern blacks did have more rights than those who lived in the South. Since the Revolutionary War, for example, most African Americans in the North had had the right to vote. They could serve on juries and had more careers open to them. Additionally, black citizens in the North had more freedom to move around from place to place than did free blacks in the South.

Northern free blacks still faced discrimination, though, and over time their rights were gradually stripped away. Even in the North, few white people considered black people their equals, and the prejudice showed. In Philadelphia, for example, African Americans were not admitted into concert halls, churches, and orphanages or on public transportation. Gradually, they were also banned from certain careers.

During the antebellum period, black voting rights in the North slowly eroded as well. New Jersey banned free blacks from voting in 1807, as did Pennsylvania in 1838. Connecticut and New York placed voting restrictions on black men. The only states in which voting rights were never limited for black men were Maine, New Hampshire, Vermont, and Massachusetts. ✔

INFO TO KNOW
Free blacks in the North also lived with the threat of being kidnapped and sold into slavery. In 1841 Solomon Northup, a free black from New York, was abducted and enslaved. He worked as a slave for 12 years before winning back his freedom.

✔ Reading Check
4. Compare What rights did free blacks in the North have that those in the South did not?

_____

_____

_____

_____

_____

Kidnapping Free Blacks
This 1840s wood engraving from an antislavery publication shows free blacks being kidnapped by slave traders.

Skills FOCUS ANALYZING VISUALS

5. Draw Conclusions What was the likely purpose of this illustration? What indicates that to you?

_____

_____

_____

James Beckwourth was one of many African Americans who helped settle the western frontier.

Westward Expansion

After 1800 the United States began rapidly acquiring new land to the west of what was then its borders. The largest acquisition of land was the **Louisiana Purchase** of 1803. The Louisiana Territory, purchased from France by U.S. President Thomas Jefferson, included all the land drained by the Mississippi River and its tributaries, a vast expanse that more than doubled the size of the United States.

Jefferson sent a 33-person expedition out to explore the newly purchased territory. Led by explorers Lewis and Clark, the expedition journeyed all the way across North America to the Pacific and mapped much of the Louisiana Territory. Among the people who made up the expedition was **York**, Clark's African American slave and personal servant. According to the expedition's journals, York was a first-rate hunter, swimmer, and fisher; York is also said to have worked with the famous Native American guide Sacagawea in interpreting for the rest of the party. When the party returned home after their exploration, York asked Clark for his freedom, but it was not immediately granted. York had to wait 10 years to be free.

Once Lewis, Clark, and the others had mapped out the new American territory, people began heading west to settle. When the United States gained most of what is now the western United States in the 1840s—including the Oregon Territory and Texas—the move west accelerated. African Americans played some key roles in the westward expansion. **James Beckwourth**, for example, established an important pass through the Sierra Nevadas to California. Later, he became a chief of the Crow people and was renamed Morning Star. George Washington Bush, a free black who had fought bravely for the United States during the War of 1812, was one of the founders of Oregon. Bush Prairie bears his name today. In California, 26 of the original 46 settlers of the settlement now known as Los Angeles were black, some of them free, some slaves. In the 1790s one black settler, Francisco Reyes, was elected mayor of Los Angeles. Free black people also helped settle other communities in California, including San Jose, Santa Barbara, San Francisco, and Monterey. ✔

✔ Reading Check

6. Draw Conclusions Why do you think many African Americans were eager to move west?

SECTION 2 ASSESSMENT

go.hrw.com
Online Quiz
Keyword: SAAH HP4

Reviewing Ideas, Terms, and People

7. Identify What difficulties did free blacks in the South face?

---

8. Explain How did the rights of African Americans in the North change over time?

---

9. Make Judgments If you were a free African American living in the early 1800s, in which region would you have wanted to live? Why?

Writing a Poem

During the antebellum period free blacks in the United States faced many challenges, from discrimination to fear of abduction to limited job opportunities. Despite these challenges, free blacks often prospered.

Write a poem that focuses on the challenges or the successes of free blacks in the antebellum period. Be sure to use descriptive language to enhance your poem. Use the space provided to write your poem.

Title:

As You Read

African Americans Resist Slavery

1. **TAKING NOTES** Use a graphic organizer like this one to take notes on slave revolts, the journey to freedom, and the colonization movement. Use the **Reading Focus** questions on the next page to help guide your note taking.

2. As you read the section, underline or highlight definitions and descriptions of the **Key Terms and People** listed on the next page.

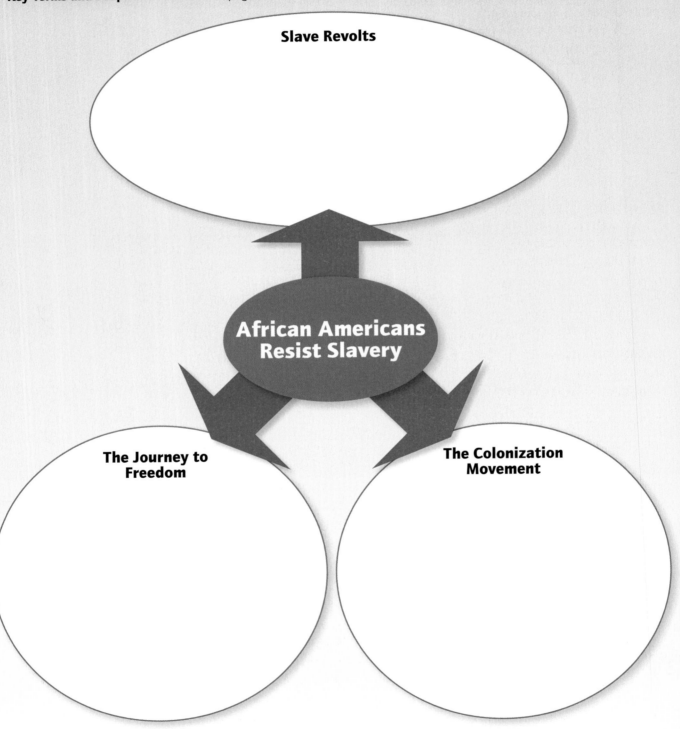

Slave Revolts

African Americans Resist Slavery

The Journey to Freedom

The Colonization Movement

African Americans Resist Slavery

BEFORE YOU READ

MAIN IDEA

African Americans used a variety of methods to escape and protest enslavement.

READING FOCUS

- Why did some African Americans resort to violent slave revolts?
- How did the Underground Railroad allow blacks to resist slavery?
- What were the arguments for and against the resettlement of blacks in Africa?

KEY TERMS AND PEOPLE

Gabriel Prosser
Denmark Vesey
Nat Turner
Amistad mutiny
Underground Railroad
Harriet Tubman
Levi Coffin
colonization

BUILDING BACKGROUND

Enslaved blacks did everything they could to resist slavery. Some made attempts to escape. Others chose to fight for their freedom. Still other slaves preferred death to captivity. The goal, however, was always the same—freedom. ◼

Slave Revolts

As you have learned, slavery took on new importance during the antebellum period as southern farmers came to depend on slave labor to earn a profit. As a result, the slave population grew, and restrictions on slaves became more oppressive than ever. Many slaves resisted their enslavement by rebelling.

Gabriel's Conspiracy

One of the first great slave revolts of the antebellum period never actually took place. In August 1800 the white inhabitants of Richmond, Virginia, uncovered a planned rebellion in the region. The plot was organized by slave **Gabriel Prosser**. A blacksmith, Gabriel was often hired out by his owner. As a result, he was relatively free to travel and communicate with other slaves, free blacks, and white laborers. He used this freedom to recruit more than 1,000 people to join his revolt. Gabriel's plot called for armed rebels to storm the arsenal in Richmond and use the weapons they found there to take over the city and, eventually, the entire state.

On the night of the planned attack, rains washed out roads and bridges, forcing Gabriel to postpone the uprising. During the delay, however, two slaves exposed the plot. Authorities rounded up slaves suspected of involvement, including Gabriel and more than 60 others. Some 35 slaves, including Gabriel, were put to death.

Although Gabriel's uprising never took place, it did have a significant impact in the South. Slave owners became increasingly suspicious of revolts. This fear led Virginia's state legislature to pass laws restricting the movement of slaves without permission. The hiring of slaves was also restricted in many places.

INFO TO KNOW

Evidence indicates that among the many people involved in Gabriel's plan were at least two white conspirators. Although evidence of their involvement was turned over to authorities, they were never charged.

Nat Turner, leader of the bloodiest slave revolt in U.S. history, evaded arrest for six weeks before his capture, trial, and execution.

Denmark Vesey

Like Gabriel, former slave **Denmark Vesey** encouraged his fellow African Americans to fight for freedom. Vesey, who lived in Charleston, South Carolina, had purchased his freedom in 1800. He believed that slavery was morally wrong and was determined to do what he could to stop it.

Inspired in part by the successful slave revolt in Haiti, Vesey spent years organizing a rebellion. He and an estimated 9,000 black rebels living in and near Charleston planned to attack guardhouses and arsenals, murder white citizens, and burn down the city in the summer of 1822. Shortly before the day of the attack, word of the plot got out. South Carolina authorities mounted a massive search for those responsible. At least 139 people were arrested, including Denmark Vesey and four white men who had encouraged the plot. The authorities hanged Vesey and some 34 other conspirators.

Nat Turner's Rebellion

In Southampton County, Virginia, rebels came closer to success than any slave revolt in the United States. They were led by **Nat Turner**, a Virginia slave. A deeply religious man, Turner believed that he had been chosen to lead his people out of slavery.

On August 21, 1831, Turner and seven other slaves launched an uprising. After killing Turner's owner and family, the rebels moved from farm to farm, killing as they went. Within two days, about 60 white people had been killed. Turner had expected hundreds of slaves to join his rebellion, but only about 75 slaves rallied to his cause. Soon, Turner and his fighters were outnumbered by a force of 3,000 white soldiers and armed citizens, and many of the rebels were killed or captured. As the uprising fell apart, Turner fled. For six weeks he eluded capture but was finally tracked down and brought to trial. Turner was executed on November 11, 1831.

Turner's rebellion was the bloodiest slave uprising in U.S. history. Frightened and fearful of more revolts, local white people killed more than 100 blacks, many of whom had nothing to do with the revolt. Slave owners feared more uprisings. Several southern states passed new laws to restrict slaves. Laws restricted slave gatherings and their freedom of movement. These strict laws failed, however, to prevent rebellions, and the fear of slave uprisings continued to haunt the South.

The *Amistad* Mutiny

In 1839 African captives began a revolt, known as the ***Amistad* mutiny**, that led to their freedom. Captives aboard the Spanish slave ship, *Amistad*, revolted against the crew. Led by Joseph Cinque, the Africans demanded that the navigator return them to Africa. Instead, the ship sailed north and was captured by the U.S. Navy.

Once in the United States, the captives were arrested and held in prison. In 1840 a trial was held to determine if they should be returned to Spain. Antislavery activists helped defend the captives. The *Amistad* case eventually made its way to the U.S. Supreme Court, which determined that the kidnapped Africans had a right to defend themselves. The following year, they were at last allowed to return to Africa. ✔

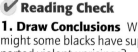

✔ Reading Check
1. Draw Conclusions Why might some blacks have supported violent uprisings?

The Journey to Freedom

Very few slaves took part in slave uprisings like that of Nat Turner. Most slaves chose other ways of resisting slavery. Thousands of African Americans challenged slavery by purchasing their freedom, escaping along the Underground Railroad, and undertaking daring journeys to freedom.

Earning Freedom

As you have learned, one route out of slavery was to purchase one's freedom. Some slaves worked long hours, scrimped and saved, and were able to buy their own freedom or that of a family member. One such example is the story of Lunsford Lane from Raleigh, North Carolina. In his spare time, Lane made pipes and raised chickens to earn money to pay his owner for his freedom. Benjamin Bradley also purchased his freedom. A talented inventor, Bradley used earnings from his <u>innovations</u> to buy his freedom. In Washington, D.C., Alethia Browning Tanner saved money she earned selling vegetables to pay more than $1,000 for her freedom. Over the years, Tanner saved enough money to purchase the freedom of 13 of her family members.

ACADEMIC VOCABULARY

2. Use the context , or surrounding words in the sentence, to write a definition of the word **innovations**.

_____

_____

_____

The Underground Railroad

African American slaves used every means they could to gain their freedom. The most common way—and the most dangerous—was to escape to the North or to Canada. Across the United States, from New York to San Francisco, a network of Americans who opposed slavery grew into a revolutionary organization. Known as the **Underground Railroad**, this organization helped slaves escape their owners and make their way to safety. The stations of the Underground Railroad were the homes and barns of sympathizers—both white and black—who hid escaped slaves, gave them food and shelter, and transported them to the next station. Individuals known as conductors helped smuggle fugitives to safety. Conductors often placed their own lives at risk to help lead others to safety.

Routes to Freedom

- Free state
- Slave state
- Territory where slavery is permitted by local decision
- → Route to freedom

The Underground Railroad

Thousands of slaves traveled along the routes of the Underground Railroad to freedom in foreign countries or in the North.

On to Liberty, Theodor Kaufman, 1867, Metropolitan Museum of Art New York

Skills FOCUS ANALYZING VISUALS

3. What difficulties might escaping slaves have faced?

_____

_____

_____

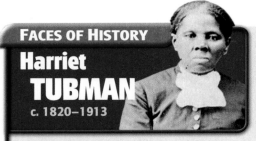

FACES OF HISTORY
Harriet TUBMAN
c. 1820–1913

Harriet Tubman, a celebrated conductor on the Underground Railroad, was a woman of uncommon courage. Born a slave on a Maryland plantation, Tubman escaped as a young woman. With the help of a sympathetic white neighbor, Tubman eventually made her way to Pennsylvania.

An extraordinary woman with nerves of steel, Tubman was determined to help others escape slavery. Within a year of her escape, she returned to Maryland to lead members of her family to freedom. As a conductor for the Underground Railroad, Tubman helped an estimated 300 slaves to freedom in the North, making some 19 trips to the South.

4. Explain In what ways did Tubman exhibit great courage?

_____

_____

_____

Escape along the Underground Railroad was perilous. Conductors often led their charges under the cover of night to escape detection, using the North Star as a guide. They often went to great lengths to see that their "passengers" reached freedom. **Harriet Tubman**, one of the best-known conductors, was said to have threatened fugitive slaves with a gun to keep them quiet. To avoid detection, conductors often hid slaves in boxes or at the bottom of wagons, and they would communicate through secret messages and signals. According to some accounts, slaves may have used quilts to leave secret codes for escaping slaves.

According to one estimate, by 1858 some 3,000 people were involved in the Underground Railroad in one way or another. They are said to have guided about 75,000 slaves to freedom between 1851 and 1861. One of the leading conductors was **Levi Coffin**, a fierce opponent of slavery. Originally from North Carolina, Coffin and his wife, Catharine, settled in Newport, Indiana, where they frequently hid fugitives. Through his work with the Underground Railroad, Coffin is believed to have helped more than 2,000 slaves escape to freedom.

Great Escapes

Not all slaves escaped along the Underground Railroad. Many accounts tell of slaves who planned and carried out their own daring escapes to freedom.

Henry Brown of Richmond, Virginia, found a unique way to escape. In 1848 Brown, with the aid of a friend, folded himself into a box and had himself mailed to Philadelphia and freedom. With only a few air holes and a pouch of water, Brown almost died on the journey. After this dangerous journey, Brown was delivered in his box to friends in Philadelphia. Brown told of his escape.

INFO TO KNOW
While some stories claim that African Americans used secret messages in quilts, that detail has been questioned by historians. Because of the secretive nature of the Underground Railroad, little evidence exists today that supports that claim.

✔ **Reading Check**
5. Make Inferences Why were the operations of the Underground Railroad kept secret?

_____

_____

_____

_____

_____

HISTORY'S VOICES

"I took my place in this narrow prison, with a mind full of uncertainty as to the result. It was a critical period of my life . . . but if you have never been deprived of your liberty, as I was, you cannot realize the power of that hope of freedom."

—George Stearns, *Narrative of Henry Box Brown by Himself*, 1849

Other African Americans used their ingenuity to escape. One slave on a Virginia plantation brought a young white man named Thomas Jackson pine knots to burn so he could stay warm as he studied for his military school exams. In exchange, Jackson taught the young slave to read and write. The slave was then able to write a pass saying that he was a free man. He successfully escaped to the North, and the young white man passed his exams. Jackson eventually became a famous southern leader during the Civil War—General Thomas "Stonewall" Jackson. ✔

The Colonization Movement

Beginning as early as 1714 some Americans proposed a new way to fight the discrimination that plagued many black Americans. This plan was **colonization**, the resettlement of black people in Africa. Americans were soon divided on the issue.

Support for Colonization

The first attempt at colonization took place in 1815, when business owner Paul Cuffe took 38 African Americans to Sierra Leone, a British colony in West Africa. Cuffe received moral support from fellow black business leaders James Forten and John Russworm. These men believed, as Forten put it, that African Americans "will never become a people until they come out from amongst the white people."

Supporters of colonization argued that blacks would never be fully accepted in U.S. society. Blacks, however, would be accepted in Africa. They also argued that Africa would offer more opportunities than life in the United States. Others believed that colonization was a first step toward ending slavery.

Colonization gained popularity, especially among white Americans. In December 1816 a group of white northerners formed the American Colonization Society. Their aim was to finance any African Americans who wanted to leave the United States for Africa. Members included author Francis Scott Key and politician Henry Clay. They lost no time in petitioning Congress to get land in Africa where blacks could be sent.

Backed by powerful legislators, the United States established a U.S. colony called Liberia on Africa's west coast. Almost immediately black people left for the colony. By 1830 more than 1,200 black Americans had arrived. Most were free, though some had been slaves who were freed and sent to Liberia. The American Colonization Society eventually sent more than 10,000 blacks to Africa.

HISTORICAL DOCUMENT
Go online to to read a historical document relating to the colonization movement.

go.hrw.com
Chapter Activity
Keyword: SAAH CH4

Resisting Slavery

KEY FACTS

6. Use the graphic organizer to identify the ways in which African Americans resisted slavery during the antebellum period.

Revolts	Escapes	Colonization

7. Use the graphic organizer to identify the arguments for and against the colonization movement.

For Colonization

Against Colonization

✔ **Reading Check**

8. Draw Conclusions Why do you think some African Americans supported colonization?

_____

_____

_____

_____

Opposition to Colonization

Almost from the start, many free African Americans rejected the idea of going back to Africa. In 1817 some 3,000 free blacks in Philadelphia held a huge convention to voice their opposition to colonization. The convention rejected the idea of colonization. Many believed that it only served the best interests of slave holders.

Opponents of colonization were vocal in their protests. One of their chief arguments was that black Americans had earned the right to live in the United States. Free blacks had contributed greatly to the development of the country without getting payment or recognition. African Americans would be better off to stay in the United States and purchase property and develop businesses.

Many African Americans also objected to the American Colonization Society's degrading view of black people. The society had publicly stated that African Americans were "notoriously ignorant, degraded and miserable, mentally diseased [and] broken-spirited." It said they would "wander unsettled and unbefriended" or "sit indolent, abject and sorrowful" if they were not sent back to Africa.

Some opponents of colonization argued that the policy would benefit slave owners. They argued that proponents of colonization did not wish to free the slaves, but merely to get rid of free blacks who might encourage slaves to rebel. Some members of the American Colonization Society opposed educating African Americans or giving them more rights in society. African Americans believed that they supported colonization because it was a way to avoid dealing with free blacks.

Still other African Americans opposed colonization because they did not approve of simply dumping black people in distant locations. They saw such a move as being filled with complications. For example, African Americans might have difficulty blending into African societies culturally, socially, and politically. Born and raised in the United States, they were likely to be viewed as outsiders. Another concern was economic. Without financial support, African Americans might find it difficult to support themselves once in Africa. The debate over colonization raged for some years. While some Americans saw it as a solution to racial problems in the United States, many agreed that it avoided the highly controversial issue of slavery. ✔

SECTION 3 ASSESSMENT

go.hrw.com
Online Quiz
Keyword: SAAH HP4

Reviewing Ideas, Terms, and People

9. Recall What did Gabriel Prosser, Denmark Vesey, and Nat Turner have in common?

_____

_____

10. Identify Cause and Effect What effect did the slave revolts in the early 1800s have on slaves in the South?

_____

_____

11. Make Judgments Would you have supported colonization? Why or why not?

_____

_____

Creating an Illustrated Time Line

Use the key events discussed in the section to create an illustrated time line. Start by selecting five key events. Then sketch a scene or symbol that represents each event on the time line. Be sure to include a caption and date for each event.

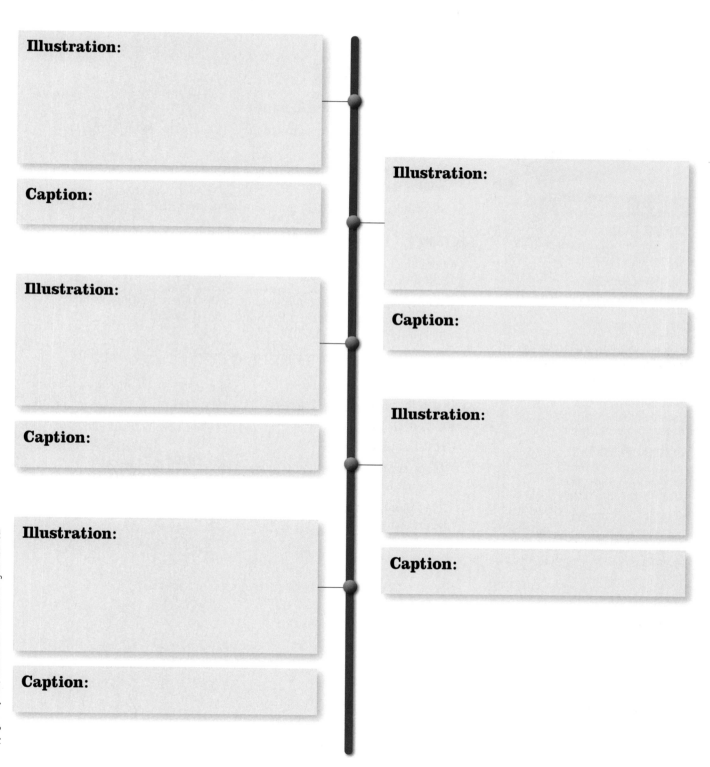

Illustration:

Caption:

Illustration:

Caption:

Illustration:

Caption:

Illustration:

Caption:

Illustration:

Caption:

Online Resources

Visit **go.hrw.com** for review and enrichment activities related to this chapter.

go.hrw.com
Chapter Home Page
Keyword: SAAH CH4

Quiz and Review

ONLINE QUIZ
Take a practice quiz for each section in this chapter.

CHAPTER REVIEW
Use the online Chapter Review to help you prepare for the chapter test.

Activities

HISTORICAL DOCUMENTS
Read and explore key documents that shaped African American history.

VIRTUAL FIELD TRIP
Take a virtual field trip to experience key sites from African American history.

VOICES OF HISTORY
Experience African American history and culture through recordings of key people and documents.

Partner

CONNECTING TO OUR PAST
Examine artifacts from **Howard University's Moorland-Spingarn Research Center** that bring to life the study of African American history.

African Americans in the New Republic

CHAPTER SUMMARY

SECTION 1 Slavery in the South

- A cotton boom lead to a growing reliance on slave labor in the southern states.
- Most southern slaves faced many difficulties, including poor living conditions and harsh punishments.
- Slave culture centered on family, religion, and African traditions.

SECTION 2 Free African Americans

- Free blacks in the South often experienced discrimination and limited rights.
- While blacks in the North often had better opportunities available to them than free blacks in the South did, they still faced discrimination.
- Free African Americans played many important roles in settling the West.

SECTION 3 Resisting Slavery

- Some slaves and free blacks carried out slave revolts in an effort to resist slavery.
- Many slaves escaped the bounds of slavery with the help of conductors on the Underground Railroad.
- The colonization movement sparked controversy among black and white Americans.

CHAPTER 5

1850–1865

Steps to FREEDOM

Black troops from the Union Army's 54th Massachusetts Infantry lead a heroic attack on Confederate-controlled Fort Wagner.

EXPRESSING YOUR OPINION

List some reasons that countries go to war. Then write a paragraph explaining some of the reasons why you might be willing to fight for your country.

Storming Fort Wagner, by Kurz and Allison, 1890/The Granger Collection, New York

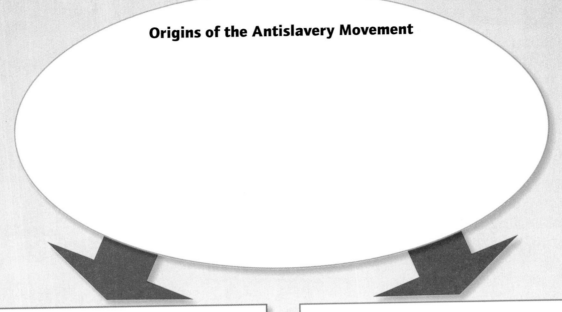

As You Read

The Antislavery Movement

1. **TAKING NOTES** Use a graphic organizer like this one to take notes on the origins of the antislavery movement, the role of black abolitionists, and the role of white abolitionists. Use the **Reading Focus** questions on the next page to help guide your note taking.

2. As you read the section, underline or highlight definitions and descriptions of the **Key Terms and People** listed on the next page.

Origins of the Antislavery Movement

Role of Black Abolitionists

Role of White Abolitionists

1 The Antislavery Movement

BEFORE YOU READ

MAIN IDEA

Both black and white Americans helped support the antislavery movement in the early to mid-1800s.

READING FOCUS

- What were the origins of the antislavery movement, and what led to its growth in the early 1800s?
- Who were some black abolitionists, and what methods did they use?
- Who were some white abolitionists, and what methods did they use?

KEY TERMS AND PEOPLE

abolition movement
David Walker
Frederick Douglass
Sojourner Truth
discrimination
William Lloyd Garrison
John Brown

BUILDING BACKGROUND

In the early 1800s reform movements swept the nation. Reformers sought to improve conditions for white Americans in factories, prisons, and crowded cities. In addition, a growing number of reformers turned their attention to the issue of slavery. Both black and white Americans grew increasingly vocal in their opposition to the South's "peculiar institution." These reformers demanded change—and they would be heard. ■

Origins of the Antislavery Movement

The antislavery movement in the United States dates back to before the American Revolution. Early colonists, such as the Quakers, had long protested against slavery on moral grounds. As the colonists' struggle for independence from Great Britain intensified, more people in the colonies joined the call to end slavery. In fact, the first antislavery society in North America was formed in Philadelphia in 1775.

The antislavery movement did not become a major force in American society until the early 1800s, however. At that time, a religious revival known as the Second Great Awakening spread across the United States. This rebirth of religious fervor encouraged some Americans to try to reform, or improve, society. The increased focus on religion and social reform contributed to the growth of the antislavery movement. A growing number of Americans viewed slavery as a moral wrong that went against their religious beliefs. Social reformers began to unite and form organizations to oppose slavery. The antislavery movement soon became one of the most prominent—and controversial—reform movements of the period. ✔

✔ Reading Check

1. Analyze What contributed to the growth of the antislavery movement in the early 1800s?

_____

_____

_____

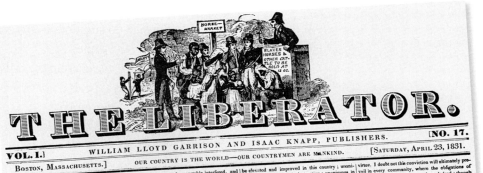

◀ *The Liberator,* a popular antislavery newspaper

Black Abolitionists

American antislavery groups differed in their goals. For example, some groups opposed the spread of slavery but wanted to keep the system in areas where it already existed. Other antislavery groups supported the **abolition movement**, a campaign to abolish, or end, slavery. The supporters of this movement were called abolitionists. Among the most vocal abolitionists were free blacks, who often risked their freedom and even their very lives to try to end slavery.

Black Militants

KEY FACTS

2. Underline or highlight the description of David Walker's significance to the black antislavery movement.

Some of the first outspoken black abolitionists were militants, people who aggressively support a cause. Many militant black abolitionists favored the use of force to end slavery. Their rousing writings and speeches called on African Americans to resist slavery by any means necessary. One such militant abolitionist was a free black merchant named **David Walker**. In 1829 Walker published a controversial pamphlet calling on African Americans to rise up against slavery.

> **HISTORY'S VOICES**
>
> "They want us for their slaves, and think nothing of murdering us in order to subject us to that wretched condition—therefore, if there is an *attempt* made by us, kill or be killed . . . Had you not rather be killed than to be a slave to a tyrant, who takes the life of your mother, wife, and dear little children?"
>
> —David Walker, *Appeal to the Colored Citizens of the World*

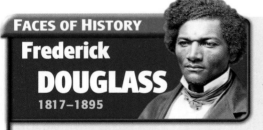

FACES OF HISTORY

Frederick DOUGLASS

1817–1895

Frederick Douglass was born into slavery in Maryland. He learned to read and write and in 1838 cleverly wrote his own pass to escape to the North. There, Douglass began giving speeches describing his terrible ordeals under slavery. A brilliant speaker with a sharp intellect, he mesmerized audiences and soon became a leading spokesperson for the abolitionist cause. Douglass proved to be a gifted writer as well. Today his autobiography, *Narrative of the Life of Frederick Douglass*, is considered a classic of American literature.

During the Civil War, Douglass advised President Abraham Lincoln, urging him to enlist black soldiers and to make ending slavery a goal of the war. After the war, Douglass focused on causes such as racial prejudice, land rights for former slaves, women's rights, and lynching. In 1889 he became the first African American to hold a high rank in the U.S. government when he was appointed U.S. minister to Haiti.

3. Analyze What skills made Douglass a persuasive abolitionist?

_____

_____

_____

Walker was not alone in his call for the use of force to end slavery. New York abolitionist Henry Highland Garnet urged slaves to resist their slaveholders. In an 1843 speech he declared, "Brethren, arise, arise! Strike for your lives and liberties . . . Let every slave throughout the land do this." Such calls for resistance shocked some black abolitionists, who looked for more peaceful methods to end slavery.

Frederick Douglass

One black abolitionist who opposed the use of force was **Frederick Douglass**. A former slave who had escaped, Douglass was a gifted writer and speaker for the abolition movement. He published an antislavery newspaper, *The North Star*, and described his life under slavery in *Narrative of the Life of Frederick Douglass*. In addition, Douglass traveled throughout the United States and the British Isles giving speeches on the evils of slavery. His eloquent appeals drew many people to the abolition movement.

The Black Abolition Movement

Douglass was just one of many free blacks who worked to try to abolish slavery during the early to mid-1800s. To promote their cause, black abolitionists gave public speeches and held antislavery conventions to push for freedom. In addition, black abolitionists wrote movingly about the evils of slavery. By 1860 African Americans were publishing more than a dozen antislavery newspapers in the United States. These papers included Douglass's *North Star* and the *Mystery,* a Pittsburgh paper published by Martin R. Delany. Some black abolitionists who had once been enslaved, such as Douglass, also wrote slave narratives. These personal accounts of slave life helped educate Americans about the horrors of slavery.

Black abolitionists included brave women as well as men. One of the best-known female black abolitionists was **Sojourner Truth**. A tall, charismatic woman, Truth had escaped from slavery. She went on to become a leading abolitionist and women's rights activist. Truth wrote a stirring slave narrative about her life and captivated audiences with her fiery speeches and songs. In 1851 she delivered her most famous speech, "Aint I a Woman," in which she spoke about the power of women.

In addition to working to end slavery, black abolitionists protested against racial **discrimination**, the unfair treatment of people of a certain race. Although African Americans in the North were free, they often faced unequal treatment because of their race. Some black abolitionists took direct action to fight racial discrimination. For example, Elizabeth Jennings of New York City fought a horse-drawn streetcar company that refused to let her ride in the car reserved for white passengers. She boldly sued the Third Avenue Railway Company—and won! Jennings received $225 in damages. More important, her case paved the way for a second legal case, after which the company decided to let black passengers ride its streetcars. ✔

White Abolitionists

African Americans were not the only people to speak out against slavery in the United States. Thousands of white activists also joined the antislavery movement during the mid-1800s. Many of these white activists were strong abolitionists who and became leaders in the movement and worked tirelessly to end slavery.

William Lloyd Garrison

White journalist **William Lloyd Garrison** became one of the foremost abolitionists in the nation. In 1831 Garrison founded a leading antislavery newspaper, *The Liberator.* In the first issue he made his commitment to abolition clear.

HISTORY'S VOICES

"I will be as harsh as truth, and as uncompromising as justice. On this subject, I do not wish to think, or to speak, or write, with moderation . . . I am in earnest—I will not equivocate—I will not excuse—I will not retreat a single inch—AND I WILL BE HEARD."

—William Lloyd Garrison, *The Liberator,* January 1831

As his statement shows, Garrison was a radical abolitionist. He challenged calls for gradual abolition and instead demanded an immediate end to slavery. In 1854 Garrison caused a sensation when he burned a copy of the U.S. Constitution, which he claimed supported the institution of slavery.

VIRTUAL FIELD TRIP
Go online to experience a virtual field trip to key sites from the antislavery movement and the Civil War.

go.hrw.com
Chapter Activity
Keyword: SAAH CH5

✔ **Reading Check**
4. Contrast How did militant abolitionists differ from other black abolitionists?

Skills Focus ANALYZING PRIMARY SOURCES

5. What is Garrison's attitude toward slavery? How can you determine his attitude?

John Brown supported using violence to oppose slavery.

The Granger Collection, New York

Over the years, Garrison worked hard to end slavery. He helped found the New England Anti-Slavery Society and the American Anti-Slavery Society. He and other white abolitionists contributed their own money to pay for lecture tours and to purchase the freedom of many slaves. Like black abolitionists, white abolitionists also often risked their lives in their attempts to end slavery. For example, in 1835 a mob in Boston physically attacked Garrison during a speech until he was rescued.

Other White Abolitionist Leaders

To abolish slavery, abolitionists needed to persuade people to join their cause. White abolitionists, like black abolitionists, used many methods to spread their message. Some white abolitionists, such as Garrison, published antislavery newspapers. Other white abolitionists, such as Theodore Weld, published antislavery pamphlets and books. Weld's 1839 pamphlet *Slavery As It Is* helped inspire one of the most famous abolitionist literary works—*Uncle Tom's Cabin* by Harriet Beecher Stowe. This novel, published in 1852, depicts the terrors and tragedies of slave life. The novel sold some 300,000 copies the first year and drew new supporters to the antislavery cause.

Some white abolitionists used political means to oppose slavery. The New York abolitionists Arthur and Lewis Tappan favored the use of legislation rather than protest to oppose slavery. More moderate than Garrison and his followers, the Tappan brothers thought that the U.S. government should end slavery. In 1839 they helped establish the Liberty Party, the first antislavery political party in the United States.

Some white abolitionists were willing to take more drastic steps to oppose slavery. One of these militant white abolitionists was **John Brown**. Like black militants, Brown thought that only force could end slavery. In 1849 he moved his family to a black community in North Elba, New York. There, he learned firsthand from former slaves of the evils of the slave system. Brown came to believe that nothing short of war could end slavery. In time, his belief would come true. ✔

✔ Reading Check

6. Find the Main Idea What methods did white abolitionists use to spread their message?

---

go.hrw.com
Online Quiz
Keyword: SAAH HP5

SECTION 1 ASSESSMENT

Reviewing Ideas, Terms, and People

7. Recall What was the abolition movement, and who were some important male and female leaders in the movement?

8. Infer Why did militant abolitionists inspire some people and shock others?

9. Evaluate Which method do you think was most successful in drawing new supporters to the abolition movement? Why?

Analyzing Primary Sources

Understand the Skill

Primary sources are documents or other historical sources created by people who were present at historical events either as witnesses or participants. Letters, diaries, newspaper stories, and speeches are all examples of primary sources. By analyzing primary sources, historians can learn valuable information about people's attitudes during a specific period in history.

Learn the Skill

Use the strategies shown at right to learn how to analyze primary sources.

Fellow-citizens; above your national, tumultuous joy, I hear the mournful wail of millions! whose chains, heavy and grievous yesterday, are, to-day, rendered more intolerable by the jubilee shouts that reach them . . . My subject, then fellow-citizens, is AMERICAN SLAVERY. I shall see, this day, and its popular characteristics, from the slave's point of view. Standing, there, identified with the American bondman, making his wrongs mine, I do not hesitate to declare, with all my soul, that the character and conduct of this nation never looked blacker to me than on this 4th of July! Whether we turn to the declarations of the past, or to the professions of the present, the conduct of the nation seems equally hideous and revolting. America is false to the past, false to the present, and solemnly binds herself to be false to the future. Standing with God and the crushed and bleeding slave on this occasion, I will, in the name of humanity which is outraged, in the name of liberty which is fettered [held back], in the name of the constitution and the Bible, which are disregarded and trampled upon, dare to call in question and to denounce, with all the emphasis I can command, everything that serves to perpetuate slavery—the great sin and shame of America!

—Frederick Douglass, "What to the Slave Is the Fourth of July?" speech, presented to the Rochester Ladies' Antislavery Society, July 5, 1852

Step 1 Identify the author or creator and the purpose of the primary source.
Who gave this speech, and what was his or her purpose?

_____
_____
_____
_____

Step 2 Determine the point of view of the author or creator.
What is the speaker's attitude toward his subject?

_____
_____
_____
_____
_____

APPLY THE SKILL

1. **Infer** Douglass was originally asked to give his speech on July 4, but he refused. Why might Douglass have refused to give this speech on that day?

_____

_____

2. **Evaluate** How would this source help a historian understand the speaker's views on slavery?

_____

_____

The Coming Conflict

1. **TAKING NOTES** Use a graphic organizer like this one to take notes on the key events and key disagreements that led up to the secession of the southern states. Use the **Reading Focus** questions on the next page to help guide your note taking.

2. As you read the section, underline or highlight definitions and descriptions of the **Key Terms and People** listed on the next page.

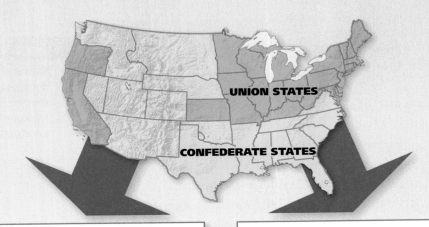

UNION STATES

CONFEDERATE STATES

Key Events	Key Disagreements
1820s–1840s	**1820s–1840s**
1850s	**1850s**
1860s	**1860s**

The Coming Conflict

BEFORE YOU READ

MAIN IDEA

Disagreement over the expansion of slavery led to conflict between the North and the South, and in time to the secession of southern states.

READING FOCUS

- How did the expansion of slavery create rising tensions between the North and the South?
- How did black and white northerners react to the Fugitive Slave Act?
- What conflicts intensified the debate over slavery into a crisis?
- What further events led the nation to split apart?

KEY TERMS AND PEOPLE

Missouri Compromise
Compromise of 1850
popular sovereignty
Fugitive Slave Act
Kansas-Nebraska Act
Dred Scott decision
Republican Party
Abraham Lincoln
Confederate States of America

BUILDING BACKGROUND

As tensions over slavery intensified, the North and the South edged closer to conflict. Disputes over the expansion of slavery began to escalate and erupt into violence. Could the country continue like this—half slave states and half free states? The rising tensions between these two opposing forces would soon tear the country apart at its seams. ◼

Rising Tensions

For years Americans had looked hopefully to the West. Some Americans hoped to find wealth by moving west. Others just hoped to be able to obtain land of their own. Whatever the reason, growing numbers of Americans had begun settling the West. As they did so, the issue of slavery's expansion soon arose. Would settlers be allowed to bring slaves into the new territories? By the early 1800s the expansion of slavery had become a tense issue that threatened the peace and unity of the nation.

The Missouri Compromise

The tensions between the slave states and the free states began to increase in the early 1800s. In 1819 the leaders of the Missouri Territory applied to enter the Union as a slave state. At the time, the nation was equally balanced with 11 slave states and 11 free states. This balance meant that the slave states and the free states had the same number of senators in the U.S. Congress. If Missouri joined the Union as a slave state, this balance in the Senate would be upset. The Missouri issue caused an uproar in Congress. Many northern members did not want to lose power in the Senate to the South, and still others opposed the expansion of slavery on moral grounds.

Eventually, Congress resolved the issue with the **Missouri Compromise** of 1820. Under this agreement, Missouri was admitted as a slave state and Maine as a free state. In addition, the compromise banned slavery north of the 36°30' N latitude in the unorganized territory of the Louisiana Purchase. The Missouri Compromise helped maintain the delicate balance in the U.S. Senate. Nonetheless, tensions remained high between the North and the South over the expansion of slavery.

> **KEY FACTS**
>
> **1.** Why was the westward expansion of slavery an explosive issue in the U.S. Congress?

Compromises over Slavery KEY FACTS

Examine the maps below. In the space provided, write a description of each of the compromises that addressed the issue of the expansion of slavery.

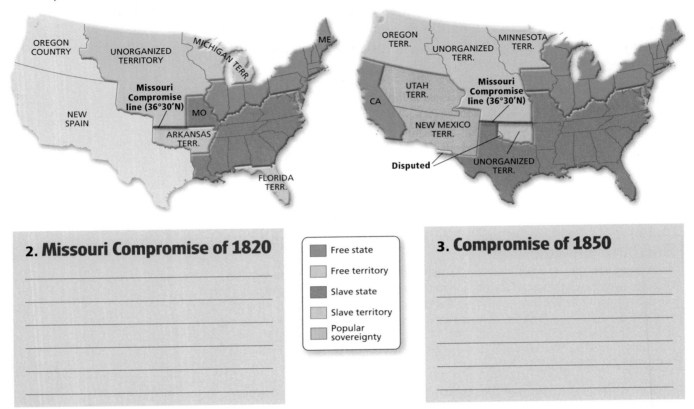

2. Missouri Compromise of 1820

_____
_____
_____
_____
_____
_____

Free state
Free territory
Slave state
Slave territory
Popular sovereignty

3. Compromise of 1850

_____
_____
_____
_____
_____

The Compromise of 1850

As time passed and new territories sought statehood, the leading question remained: Would each new territory become a slave state or a free state? While many politicians struggled and fought over this issue, a few worked furiously to maintain the balance. In 1848, however, the United States gained a vast amount of land in the West as a result of the Mexican-American War. Almost immediately, a debate began in Congress over whether new territories in the region should allow slavery.

The conflict over slavery in the newly <u>acquired</u> region went unresolved until California, a part of the region, applied for statehood in 1849. California's leaders wanted their territory to be a free state. However, this move would once again upset the balance in the U.S. Senate between the slave states and the free states.

To leaders in the South, an imbalance of power was unacceptable. Outraged southern leaders feared that the South would lose economic and political power. As a last resort, some southerners in Congress even threatened that their states would secede, or break away, from the United States if the balance of power was upset.

"Let them secede!" countered some northerners scornfully. Sentiment among a growing number of people in the North was that slavery had outlived its usefulness. The *Cleveland Plain Dealer* stated bluntly, "Rather than see slavery extended one inch beyond its present limits, we would see this Union rent asunder [split apart]!"

ACADEMIC VOCABULARY

4. Use the context, or surrounding words in the sentence, to write a definition of **acquired**.

_____
_____
_____

In Congress, veteran senator Henry Clay of Kentucky, who had helped develop the Missouri Compromise, came up with a plan to solve the California problem. After debating Clay's plan for months, Congress agreed to a series of laws called the **Compromise of 1850**. Under this compromise, California joined the Union as a free state. The rest of the land gained from Mexico was then organized into the New Mexico and Utah territories. In each territory, the issue of whether to allow slavery would be decided by **popular sovereignty**, or by the popular vote of the people. In addition, the Compromise of 1850 ended the slave trade in the District of Columbia and, to appease the slave states, created a tougher fugitive slave law. Although neither the North nor the South was completely satisfied with the compromise, it had prevented a larger conflict from occurring—for the time being. ✔

The Fugitive Slave Act

Although the Compromise of 1850 seemed to settle one dispute in the battle over slavery, it triggered another. One part of the compromise was the **Fugitive Slave Act**, which established strict new measures concerning runaway slaves. For years, southern slaveholders had complained that northerners ignored fugitive slave laws by aiding escaped slaves. In an effort to stop such actions, the Fugitive Slave Act made assisting runaway slaves a federal crime. Federal commissioners were appointed to enforce the law, and all citizens were expected to "aid and assist" in its execution. Under the new law, people who helped or hid fugitive slaves were subject to heavy fines and imprisonment. Federal marshals could enter northern states where slavery was illegal and arrest fugitive slaves, even those who had been free for decades. Furthermore, African Americans accused of being runaways had to prove that they were free, often a difficult or impossible task. The law put many black northerners—both those who were legally free and those who had escaped slavery—at risk.

Fighting the Fugitive Slave Act

The Fugitive Slave Act infuriated many northerners and encouraged more of them to support the fight against slavery. Across the North, people openly resisted the new law and organized to fight it. As slave catchers began capturing fugitive slaves, many abolitionists urged African Americans to prepare to defend themselves.

HISTORY'S VOICES

"What is life to me if I am to be a slave in Tennessee? . . . My home is here, and my children were born here . . . I will not live a slave, and if force is employed to reenslave me, I shall make preparations to meet the crisis."

—Reverend Jermain Wesley Loguen, "I Won't Obey the Fugitive Slave Law," 1850

Harriet Tubman, the famous black conductor for the Underground Railroad, was determined to help fight the Fugitive Slave Act. In 1860 in Troy, New York, Tubman learned that a man named Charles Nalle had been captured and was to be returned to slavery in Virginia. Determined to help Nalle, Tubman bravely rushed to the U.S. commissioner's office, where he was being held. There, she waited along with a large crowd that had gathered. As Nalle was being escorted out of the office, the crowd pushed forward and tore him away from his captors. Tubman stated that she tied her bonnet to the man's head so that he could escape undetected through the crowd.

✔ Reading Check
5. Find the Main Idea Why were the Missouri Compromise of 1820 and the Compromise of 1850 necessary?

_____

_____

_____

_____

CAUTION!!
COLORED PEOPLE
OF BOSTON, ONE & ALL,
You are hereby respectfully CAUTIONED and advised, to avoid conversing with the
Watchmen and Police Officers of Boston,
For since the recent ORDER OF THE MAYOR & ALDERMEN, they are empowered to act as
KIDNAPPERS
AND
Slave Catchers,
And they have already been actually employed in KIDNAPPING, CATCHING, AND KEEPING SLAVES. Therefore, if you value your LIBERTY, and the Welfare of the Fugitives among you, Shun them in every possible manner, as so many HOUNDS on the track of the most unfortunate of your race.
Keep a Sharp Look Out for KIDNAPPERS, and have TOP EYE open.
APRIL 24, 1851.

▲ **This 1851 poster warned African Americans in Boston to keep alert for slave catchers in the area.**

Black Self-Protection Groups

As the threat of capture for escaped slaves increased, many black communities in the North organized groups to protect themselves. On more than one occasion, one of these self-protection groups helped save African Americans from capture. One such incident involved a black self-protection group in Christiana, Pennsylvania. A former slave named William Parker had organized the group. As in similar groups in the North, the group's members had developed a plan in which they would alert one another if slave catchers were seen in the area.

In September 1851 a Maryland slaveholder accompanied by a U.S. marshal and an armed group pounded on Parker's door. The slaveholder had warrants for four black men staying in Parker's house and claimed that they had escaped from him. When the slaveholder demanded the men's return, Parker's wife blew a horn for help. Neighbors came to the Parkers' aid, and the battle was on. The intruders shot at Parker and his group, who fired back. In time, the group of slave catchers retreated. The Parkers and their friends had successfully defended the four men's freedom. During the shooting, however, the slaveholder was killed and a few other people were badly wounded. Many southerners demanded vengeance. Authorities eventually arrested two white abolitionists and several African Americans for treason. William Parker became a fugitive and had to flee, leaving his family behind. ✔

The Conflict Becomes a Crisis

Throughout the 1850s the dispute over slavery raged on. Three key events—the passage of the Kansas-Nebraska Act, the *Dred Scott* decision, and John Brown's raid—would bring the crisis between the North and the South to a head.

The Kansas-Nebraska Act

No sooner had the Compromise of 1850 cooled rising tensions, then another crisis heated them up again. In 1854 Congress passed the **Kansas-Nebraska Act**. This act organized Kansas and Nebraska into territories and, overriding the Missouri Compromise, allowed the issue of slavery in them to be decided by popular sovereignty. Thus, the people of each territory would vote whether or not to allow slavery there.

The Kansas-Nebraska Act bitterly divided the nation. Both proslavery and antislavery forces sent supporters to live in Kansas to help influence the vote there. Some abolitionists, such as John Brown, settled in Kansas to provide additional support. Heated exchanges between proslavery and antislavery forces soon led to violence. "Bleeding Kansas," as the situation was called, became yet another battleground in the dispute over the expansion of slavery.

Dred Scott, by Louis Schultze, 1881

Dred Scott "had no rights which the white man was bound to respect," ruled Chief Justice Roger Taney.

The *Dred Scott* Decision

As conflict raged in Kansas, a case came before the U.S. Supreme Court in 1857 that was to have landmark significance. The case dealt with Dred Scott, an enslaved Missouri man. Scott had traveled with his slaveholder to Illinois and the Wisconsin Territory, both areas where slavery was illegal. When Scott returned to Missouri, he sued for his freedom. He argued that living on free soil had made him free.

Scott's case made its way to the U.S. Supreme Court. In the *Dred Scott* **decision**, a deeply divided Court ruled against Scott's argument. Led by Chief Justice Roger Taney, the Court stated that Scott could not sue in federal court because he was not a citizen under the U.S. Constitution. The Court further stated that the Missouri Compromise, which had prohibited slavery in certain territories, was unconstitutional. The Court explained that the Fifth Amendment of the U.S. Constitution protected the property rights of slaveholders and that the Missouri Compromise deprived slaveholders of those rights without due process of law.

Even though many white southerners viewed the *Dred Scott* decision as a victory, abolitionists were outraged. Did the ruling mean the U.S. Supreme Court was on the side of slavery? Frederick Douglass declared that the decision should serve as a "link in the chain of events preparatory to the downfall and complete overthrow of the whole slave system."

John Brown's Raid

Radical abolitionist John Brown contributed another link in the growing chain of events in the dispute over slavery. By 1859 Brown had decided that force was the only way to end slavery. He came up with a plan to raid a federal arsenal at Harpers Ferry, Virginia. An arsenal is a place where weapons are stored. Brown's plan was to seize the weapons and use them to arm a slave revolt. Although some abolitionists, such as Harriet Tubman, supported Brown's plan, others warned him against it.

Despite such warnings, Brown struck on the night of October 16, 1859. Along with a band of 21 comrades, he successfully broke into the federal arsenal. Then a snag occurred. Few slaves in the area were willing to run away and join Brown. The next afternoon local militias trapped Brown's group inside the arsenal.

Brown's raid inflamed many white southerners. In contrast, many northerners viewed Brown and his comrades as heroes. After being convicted in a trial, John Brown was sentenced to hang on December 2, 1859. On that day, church bells tolled across the North in salute of Brown. ✔

PRIMARY SOURCES

John Brown's Raid: A Letter

Among the members of John Brown's unsuccessful raid at Harpers Ferry were five African Americans. One of them was John Copeland, who wrote this letter to his brother shortly before being executed.

"Not that I am terrified by the gallows which I see staring me in the face, and upon which I am so soon to stand and suffer death for doing what George Washington . . . was made a hero for doing . . . Washington entered the field to fight for the freedom of the American people—not for the white men alone, but for both black and white . . . It was a sense of the wrongs which we have suffered that prompted the noble but unfortunate Captain Brown and his associates to attempt to give freedom to a small number, at least of those who are now held by cruel and unusual laws, and by no less cruel and unjust men."

Skills FOCUS ANALYZING PRIMARY SOURCES

7. What is Copeland's opinion of John Brown?

✔ **Reading Check**

8. Sequence What series of events in the mid- to late 1800s led to increased conflict between the North and the South?

The Nation Splits Apart

During the 1850s unpopular compromises, laws, and court decisions had deepened the divisions in the United States. Many Americans feared that ideological, economic, and political divisions over slavery would permanently rip the nation apart.

The Election of 1860

Since the 1840s, groups had formed antislavery political parties, but they had limited political success. Spurred on by the Kansas-Nebraska Act, though, antislavery forces united to try once again. In 1854 they formed the antislavery **Republican Party**. The new party quickly gained support across the North. In 1856 Illinois lawyer and politician **Abraham Lincoln** joined the Republican Party and soon became one of its leaders. Addressing the Illinois Republican convention, he made a dire prediction.

> **HISTORY'S VOICES**
> "'A house divided against itself cannot stand.' I believe this government cannot endure, permanently half *slave* and half *free.* I do not expect the Union to be *dissolved*—I do not expect the house to *fall*—but I do expect it will cease to be divided. It will become *all* one thing or *all* the other."
> —Abraham Lincoln, address to the Illinois Republican Convention, June 16, 1858

✔ **Reading Check**
9. Draw Conclusions Why did many southerners oppose Lincoln's election to the presidency in 1860?

In 1860 the Republican Party chose Lincoln as its presidential candidate. Southerners vowed to defeat Lincoln and the antislavery Republicans. However, a division in the Democratic Party, which dominated the South, split the southern vote. As a result, Lincoln won the presidency despite receiving less than 40 percent of the popular vote and not winning a single southern state.

The First Southern States Secede

Many southerners were irate over Lincoln's election. "A party founded on the . . . hatred of African slavery is now the controlling power," wrote the *New Orleans Delta*. The election propelled seven southern states—South Carolina, Mississippi, Florida, Alabama, Georgia, Louisiana, and Texas—to secede. In December 1861, they formed the new nation of the **Confederate States of America**, or the Confederacy. ✔

go.hrw.com
Online Quiz
Keyword: SAAH HP5

Reviewing Ideas, Terms, and People
Choose the letter of the term at right that best matches each description.

_____ **10.** This agreement allowed one new slave state and one new free state to enter the Union and banned slavery in part of the Louisiana Purchase.

_____ **11.** This law established strict new laws for the capture of escaped slaves.

_____ **12.** His election led directly to the secession of seven southern states.

_____ **13.** This agreement allowed California to enter the Union as a free state.

_____ **14.** Violence erupted as a result of this controversial legislation.

a. Abraham Lincoln
b. Compromise of 1850
c. Fugitive Slave Act
d. Kansas-Nebraska Act
e. Missouri Compromise

Creating a Time Line

The years leading up to the secession of the southern states were some of the most turbulent in U.S. history. The conflict over slavery led to political disagreements, protests, and even violence. Use your notes from Section 2 to complete the time line of key events that led to increasing tensions between the North and the South.

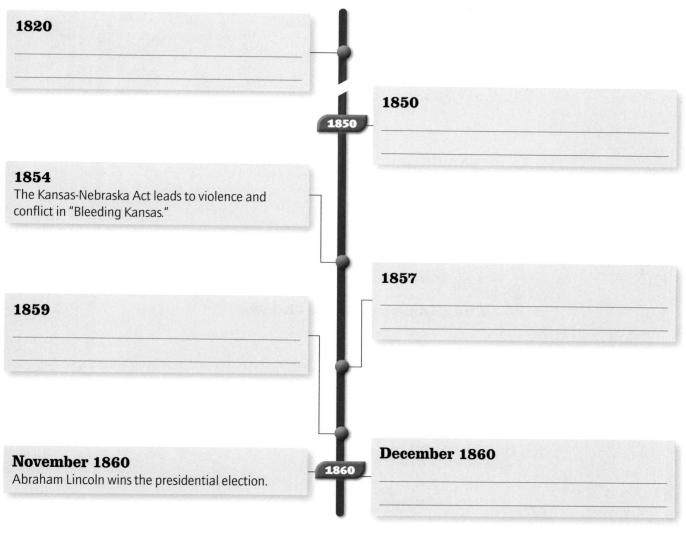

1820

_____

_____

1850

_____

_____

1850

1854
The Kansas-Nebraska Act leads to violence and conflict in "Bleeding Kansas."

1857

_____

_____

1859

_____

_____

November 1860
Abraham Lincoln wins the presidential election.

1860

December 1860

_____

_____

ASSESS YOUR KNOWLEDGE

1. Recall What event on the time line resulted from Lincoln's election as president?

_____

_____

2. Compare What two events on the time line were attempts to settle conflicts between the free states and the slave states?

_____

_____

The Civil War—Freedom Won

1. **TAKING NOTES** Use a graphic organizer like this one to take notes on the outbreak of the Civil War, African Americans in the Civil War, and the Emancipation Proclamation. Use the **Reading Focus** questions on the next page to help guide your note taking.

2. As you read the section, underline or highlight definitions and descriptions of the **Key Terms** listed on the next page.

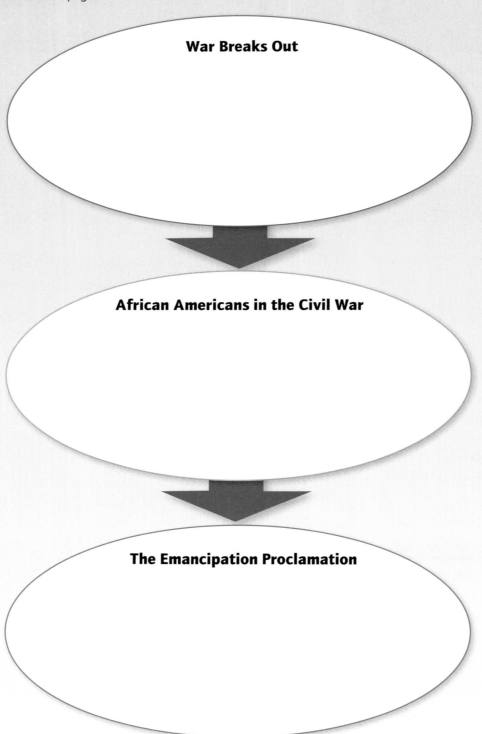

War Breaks Out

African Americans in the Civil War

The Emancipation Proclamation

3 The Civil War— Freedom Won

BEFORE YOU READ

MAIN IDEA

The Civil War led to new roles, rights, and freedoms for African Americans in the North and the South.

READING FOCUS

- What events led to the outbreak of war between the Union and the Confederacy?
- In what ways did African Americans contribute during the Civil War?
- What led Lincoln to issue the Emancipation Proclamation?

KEY TERMS

contrabands
First Louisiana Native Guards
54th Massachusetts Infantry
border states
Emancipation Proclamation
Juneteenth

BUILDING BACKGROUND

After years of painful dispute, the United States broke apart. Several southern states formed the Confederate States of America to protect their way of life, including the institution of slavery. Secession, however, did not end the dispute between the North and the South. The tense situation would require only a spark to unleash the heat of war. ◢

War Breaks Out

On March 4, 1861, Abraham Lincoln became president of the United States. He immediately set out to assure southerners that the U.S. government would not provoke war. Like most Americans, Lincoln hoped the southern states would return peacefully to the Union. In less than two months, however, civil war had broken out.

An Attack Leads to War

During the months before Lincoln took office as president, Confederate officials had begun seizing federal arsenals, forts, and other property in the South. Once in office, Lincoln declared that all federal property, even that in the Confederacy, belonged to the United States. He then ordered the U.S. military to protect all such property.

In South Carolina, Confederates were determined to take Fort Sumter, which guarded Charleston Harbor. U.S. forces were equally determined to keep the fort. To help defend Fort Sumter, President Lincoln sent in ships with <u>essential</u> supplies. When Confederate leaders learned of the ships, they worried that troops might follow. Before that could happen, the Confederates decided to take action. On April 12, 1861, Confederate forces began firing on Fort Sumter. After more than 30 hours of cannon fire, the U.S. forces at the fort surrendered. The Civil War had begun.

In response to the fall of Fort Sumter, Lincoln declared that the South was in a state of rebellion. He called on each state to send troops to put down the rebellion. Most states rallied to his call. However, several of the slave states that were still in the Union refused. Instead, shortly after Lincoln's call for troops, Virginia, Arkansas, Tennessee, and North Carolina seceded and joined the new Confederacy.

ACADEMIC VOCABULARY

1. Use the context, or surrounding words in the sentence, to write a definition of **essential**.

_____

_____

_____

Preparing for War

With the outbreak of war, armies on both sides prepared to fight. When U.S. leaders called for volunteers, many black men in the North were eager to join. Army officials hesitated to accept them, however. Many northerners did not consider African Americans to be equals and were afraid of arming them. As a result, the Union army turned away black volunteers, although the navy accepted them. Unable to serve in the army, African Americans in some northern cities created informal military units. The units then trained in preparation for the day they might be called to duty.

A few Union generals disagreed with the decision not to use black troops and took African Americans into their ranks. Many of these African Americans were escaped Confederate slaves, who became known as **contrabands**. Shortly after the war began, runaway slaves had begun showing up at Union army camps seeking protection and offering to help. Soon, Union leaders compromised and allowed some black men to join the army in noncombat positions such as cooks or hospital orderlies. Meanwhile, the U.S. Navy approved the active enlistment of black men in September 1861.

In the Confederacy, African Americans contributed to the war effort as well. Slaves on farms and plantations grew much of the food for the South. The labor of these slaves freed up white men to fight for the Confederacy. Slaves also performed many Confederate noncombat jobs, such as cooking and driving wagons. ✔

African Americans in the Civil War

African Americans eventually received the chance to fight in the Union army. Once able to participate, they played a crucial role in the war effort by going on dangerous missions as soldiers and spies as well as serving in other capacities.

The Enlistment of Black Troops

The Union did not experience the quick victory in the Civil War that leaders had expected at first. As the war continued and more soldiers died, northern attitudes about the use of black troops began to change. In July 1862 the U.S. Congress approved the limited enlistment of black men in areas of the South where the fighting was heaviest.

African American Union Soldiers
Black soldiers, such as those in the 4th U.S. Colored Infantry shown below, and in the 54th Regiment, fought bravely in the Civil War.

NOW IN CAMP AT READVILLE!
54th REGIMENT!
MASS. VOLUNTEERS. composed of men of
AFRICAN DESCENT
Col. ROBERT G. SHAW.
Colored Men, Rally 'Round the Flag of Freedom!
BOUNTY $100!
AT THE EXPIRATION OF THE TERM OF SERVICE.
Pay, $13 a Month!
Good Food & Clothing!
State Aid to Families!
RECRUITING OFFICE
COR. CAMBRIDGE & NORTH RUSSELL STS.
BOSTON.
Lieut. J. W. M. APPLETON, Recruiting Officer.

By the end of 1862 several black regiments had been formed in areas of the South under Union control. One such regiment was in New Orleans, Louisiana. This black regiment had been part of a Louisiana state militia. After Union forces gained control of New Orleans in 1862, General Benjamin F. Butler organized the regiment into the **First Louisiana Native Guards**, also known as the Corp d'Afrique. Within a few months, Butler had enough volunteers to field two additional black regiments.

In 1863 the U.S. Congress approved the general recruitment of black soldiers. Recruiting efforts began immediately, and black leaders such as Frederick Douglass called on African Americans to join the fight against the South. One of the first black regiments organized under the new law was the **54th Massachusetts Infantry**. At first, the regiment was allowed to perform only manual labor. Later, however, the members of the regiment fought in battle and distinguished themselves as some of the Union's most heroic soldiers.

In March 1865 the Confederacy also began to recruit black troops. Few black men enlisted, though. Less than a month later, Confederate general Robert E. Lee surrendered to Union general Ulysses S. Grant. The Civil War was over.

Hardships and Heroism

During the Civil War black troops faced hardships not shared by white troops. For example, black troops often received fewer supplies and less training than white troops, as well as less pay at first. Many African Americans took steps to counter such discrimination. Members of the 54th Massachusetts Infantry, for instance, protested unequal wages by refusing pay for more than a year. The U.S. government eventually agreed to pay black troops the same wage as white troops. In addition, black soldiers faced more severe treatment if captured. Confederate troops enslaved or executed captured black soldiers but held captured white soldiers as prisoners of war.

In spite of discrimination and hardship, more than 186,000 black men bravely served in the Union's armed services during the Civil War. African Americans were especially noted for their service in the U.S. Navy. Fully one-fourth of all Union sailors in the Civil War were black. These heroic black sailors, such as Robert Smalls, proved their bravery and loyalty to the Union.

In all, black troops fought with distinction in more than 250 skirmishes and battles. Black soldiers also won 23 Congressional Medals of Honor, the nation's highest military award. One of the black soldiers awared this medal was Sergeant William H. Carney of the 54th Massachusetts Infantry. During the regiment's famous assault on Fort Wagner in 1863, Carney risked his life to protect the Union flag.

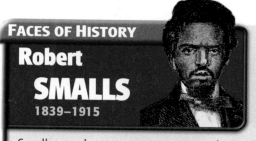

FACES OF HISTORY

Robert SMALLS
1839–1915

Born into slavery in South Carolina, Robert Smalls was hired out to work on steamboats as a youth. Intelligent and a quick learner, Smalls soon became an expert steamboat pilot. In 1861, after the Civil War began, he was forced to serve in the Confederate navy aboard the *Planter*, a medium-sized warship.

On May 12, 1862, the ship's white officers went ashore, leaving Smalls and seven other black men to guard the ship in Charleston Harbor. During the night, Smalls piloted the ship out of the harbor. After stopping briefly to pick up family and friends, he steered the ship into Union territory and then handed it over to officials.

Smalls's heroic exploit gained him fame and admiration. Lincoln made him a pilot in the U.S. Navy, and Smalls later became a captain, the highest rank of any black naval officer at that time.

3. Identify What event gained Smalls fame and admiration?

_____

_____

KEY FACTS

4. Identify the steps that led to the recruitment of black troops in the Civil War.

_____
_____
_____
_____
_____
_____
_____
_____
_____
_____
_____
_____
_____
_____
_____
_____

Sojourner Truth, a former slave and a leading abolitionist, helped support black troops in the war.

Heroic Black Women in the Civil War

Black women also displayed outstanding bravery during the Civil War. Many of these women served as nurses, while others traveled with the troops and helped cook, sew, and wash.

The most common job for women during the Civil War was that of nursing the sick. One well known black nurse was Susie King Taylor, whose husband was an officer in the First South Carolina Volunteers. Not only did Taylor nurse the sick and cook for the troops but she also taught many soldiers to read and write in her spare time.

Sojourner Truth, a leading black abolitionist, also worked to support the war effort. During the war, Truth helped raise money and supplies for southern black refugees. In addition, she met with President Lincoln, who convinced her to nurse wounded black soldiers in the Freedmen's Hospital.

Black Military Spies

Some African Americans contributed to the Union war effort by serving as military spies. Union officials soon learned that black spies could more easily pass on valuable Confederate information without being detected than white spies could.

One black spy was Harriet Tubman, the famous conductor for the Underground Railroad. Tubman spied for three years by gathering information from southern slaves. Union general Rufus Saxton praised her "remarkable courage, zeal and fidelity."

Mary Elizabeth Bowser was another well-known black spy. Bowser, who pretended she could not read, worked as a servant in the home of Confederate president Jefferson Davis. There, she listened to conversations and examined documents. Later, she passed on any valuable military information to Union officials. ✔

The Emancipation Proclamation

During the first part of the Civil War, one crucial question remained unanswered: What would President Lincoln do about the issue of slavery? Many abolitionists argued that the war was pointless if it was not being fought to end slavery. Yet many white northerners opposed emancipation, or the freeing of slaves.

Resolving the Issue of Slavery

Such differing opinions put Lincoln in a difficult position. Although he was opposed to slavery, he did not want to lose northern support for the war. He knew that many white northerners would not risk their lives for African Americans. Therefore, Lincoln did not initially make ending slavery a war aim. Rather, the war was being fought to restore the Union. In addition, Lincoln feared that ending slavery might lead to the secession of the slave states still in the Union. The slave states of Delaware, Kentucky, Maryland, and Missouri—known as the **border states**—had stayed in the Union. Because of their location between the North and the Confederacy, these border states had strategic military importance. The Union could not risk losing them.

✔ Reading Check

5. Summarize In what ways did African Americans contribute to the war effort for both the North and the South?

_____

_____

_____

_____

_____

_____

INFO TO KNOW
President Abraham Lincoln also worried that freeing millions of slaves would lead to unrest in American society. For this reason, he favored the voluntary colonization of African Americans in Africa, Central America, or the Caribbean. Support for the colonization movement faded over time, however.

Yet the issue of slavery continued to come up as the war progressed. As Union troops pushed into Confederate territory, thousands of contrabands sought refuge with them. At first, the Lincoln administration supported returning contrabands to slaveholders. Some Union commanders even did so. Such actions infuriated abolitionists, however. They pointed out that every enslaved African American who left the South meant one less person to help the Confederacy.

Lincoln and his advisors soon decided he had to take some action against slavery. The president faced a dilemma, though. He did not think the U.S. Constitution gave the president the power to end slavery. Lincoln therefore proposed a plan for compensated emancipation in the border states. Under this plan, the border states would receive federal funds in exchange for passing state laws to abolish slavery over time. Although loyal to the Union, the border states were not ready to end the slave system on which their economies were based. All four states rejected Lincoln's plan.

As Union forces struggled in the war, however, Union leaders convinced Lincoln that ending slavery in the South was of military importance. They explained that the Confederacy would be crippled without slave labor. Lincoln decided that he could use his constitutional power as commander in chief to end slavery in the areas that were rebelling. He began forming a new emancipation plan. In April 1862, Lincoln and Congress took the first step by ending slavery in the District of Columbia. Soon after, Congress outlawed slavery in all U.S. territories.

Lincoln wanted to wait for a major Union victory before announcing his full emancipation plan. In September 1862 the victory came at the bloody Battle of Antietam. With the win he wanted, Lincoln announced his new plan. Once again he offered compensated emancipation to slaveholders in the border states. More important, though, he declared that on January 1, 1863, he would free all enslaved African Americans in rebel areas of the South.

Response to Lincoln's Plan

The reaction to Lincoln's announcement was mixed. Some abolitionists were hopeful that his plan would deal a deathblow to the institution of slavery. Other abolitionists were angry, however, because Lincoln's plan did not end slavery everywhere in the United States. Slavery would continue in areas that were not in rebellion, such as in the border states and those parts of the Confederacy under Union control.

Some other northerners also opposed Lincoln's plan. As he had feared, some white Union soldiers resigned rather than fight to end slavery in the South. In addition, many unskilled workers in the North were upset. These workers feared that ending slavery would lead to a flood of black workers from the South who would increase job competition. When the U.S. government had hired former slaves to help harvest crops in Illinois in 1862, white workers had rioted in protest. Similar riots had occurred in other northern cities.

Yet many northerners rallied behind Lincoln and his plan. These Americans hoped that freeing the Confederacy's slaves would help shorten the war. One Cincinnati newspaper declared that Lincoln was destroying the "labor system *which feeds the enemy.*" Many Union soldiers supported the plan as well. A Union colonel noted that even though few of his soldiers were abolitionists, they were eager "to destroy everything that . . . gives the rebels strength."

KEY FACTS

6. Use the graphic organizer below to identify the arguments for and against emancipating enslaved African Americans.

For Emancipation

Against Emancipation

Lincoln Issues the Emancipation Proclamation

The night before Lincoln's plan was to go into effect, black and white abolitionists gathered anxiously at watch meetings across the North. On January 1, 1863, Lincoln issued the **Emancipation Proclamation**. This groundbreaking order proclaimed all enslaved African Americans in rebel areas to be emancipated, or free. As news of the Proclamation spread, many African Americans and abolitionists rejoiced. A major step toward the end of slavery in the United States had been achieved.

Although the Emancipation Proclamation had a large emotional impact in the North, it initially had little effect in the South. The Proclamation applied only to slaves in areas held by the Confederacy—the very areas in which the Union had no power to enforce the order. Gradually, though, the Proclamation did begin to have an impact in the South. As Union troops advanced into Confederate territory, they freed the slaves they encountered. Some historians estimate that Union troops liberated thousands of enslaved people each day. At the same time, many northern African Americans risked their lives to spread the word of freedom in Confederate-held parts of the South. Many slaves, on learning of their freedom, put down their rakes and hoes and escaped to Union lines.

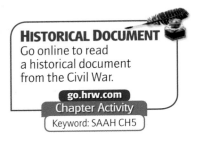

HISTORICAL DOCUMENT
Go online to read a historical document from the Civil War.

go.hrw.com
Chapter Activity
Keyword: SAAH CH5

As Union leaders had hoped, the Emancipation Proclamation began to weaken the Confederate war effort. The reduction in the slave labor force hurt the Confederacy's armies and plantations. In addition, the Proclamation ended any hope of foreign support for the South. Great Britain, a major importer of southern cotton, had considered aiding the Confederacy. However, abolitionism was strong in Britain. After the Union made ending slavery a war aim, Britain was no longer willing to help the South.

As Union leaders had hoped, the Emancipation Proclamation began to weaken the Confederate war effort. The reduction in the slave labor force hurt the Confederacy's armies and plantations. In addition, the Proclamation ended any hope of foreign support for the South. Great Britain, a major importer of southern cotton, had considered aiding the Confederacy. However, abolitionism was strong in Britain. After the Union made ending slavery a war aim, Britain was no longer willing to help the South.

While weakening Confederate forces, the Emancipation Proclamation strengthened Union forces. As mentioned earlier, the Union began the general recruitment of black soldiers in 1863, after the Proclamation. Most African Americans who served in the Union military enlisted during this period. These black soldiers and sailors played an important role in the Union victory. They knew that they were fighting not only for the preservation of the Union but also for the freedom of African Americans.

PRIMARY SOURCES

Emancipation Proclamation

President Abraham Lincoln issued the Emancipation Proclamation on January 1, 1863. The Proclamation freed all enslaved people in states under Confederate control and was a step toward the Thirteenth Amendment, which ended slavery in the United States.

"That on the 1st day of January, in the year of our Lord 1863, all persons held as slaves within any state or designated part of a state, the people whereof shall then be in rebellion against the United States, shall be then, thenceforward, and forever free . . .

And I further declare and make known that such persons of suitable condition will be received into the armed service of the United States to garrison [station troops in] forts, positions, stations, and other places, and to man vessels of all sorts in said service."

Skills FOCUS | **ANALYZING PRIMARY SOURCES**

7. In addition to freeing slaves in areas under Confederate control, what did the Emancipation Proclamation do?

_____

_____

_____

Most of all, the Emancipation Proclamation had a profound impact on enslaved African Americans. In the South, Union troops freed millions of African Americans from lives of cruel labor. In areas where the Proclamation did not apply, many slaves simply decided they were free as well and courageously escaped.

The Emancipation Proclamation is one of the key documents of American history. President Lincoln himself recognized the historical significance of his actions. In 1865 he called the Emancipation Proclamation "the central act of my administration and the great event of the nineteenth century." The Proclamation's main significance was that it set an important legal precedent for African Americans. It was the beginning of the end of slavery in the United States. Near the end of the Civil War, Congress passed an amendment to the U.S. Constitution that abolished slavery throughout the nation.

The Emancipation Proclamation's Legacy

Today a number of African Americans remember the legacy of the Emancipation Proclamation by celebrating **Juneteenth**. This event commemorates June 19, 1865, the date when the Emancipation Proclamation was announced in Galveston, Texas. Federal troops did not reach Texas and free the slaves there until after the Civil War was over. In Texas, June 19 came to be known as Juneteenth, on which African Americans celebrated their freedom.

In 1980 Juneteenth became a state holiday in Texas. Although not an official holiday elsewhere, Juneteenth has gradually gained popularity in other parts of the United States. In fact, some of the largest Juneteenth gatherings are now held in the northern cities of Minneapolis, Minnesota, and Milwaukee, Wisconsin. Juneteenth festivities take many forms, including public speeches, parades, rodeos, and picnics. Many people also gather with their families on the holiday to rejoice in the gains that African Americans have made and to reflect on their hopes for the future. ✔

Abraham Lincoln and his Emancipation Proclamation lithograph, by Strobridge & Co., c. 1888

▲ **The Emancipation Proclamation, issued on January 1, 1863, freed all enslaved African Americans in rebelling areas.**

✔ Reading Check
8. Summarize Whom did the Emancipation Proclamation free, and how did African Americans react to it?

_____

_____

_____

_____

SECTION 3 ASSESSMENT

go.hrw.com
Online Quiz
Keyword: SAAH HP5

Reviewing Ideas, Terms, and People

9. Recall What triggered fighting between the Union and the Confederacy in 1861?

_____

_____

10. Infer Why might Union black troops have faced more hardships than Union white troops during the Civil War?

_____

_____

11. Elaborate Do you think that President Lincoln should have freed all the slaves in the Union and Confederacy in 1863? Why or why not?

_____

_____

Designing a Storyboard

Imagine that you have been asked to create a short film focusing on the contributions and experiences of African Americans in the Civil War. Use your notes from this section to identify key ideas and events to depict in your film. Then use a storyboard like the one below to plan the main scenes for your film. Sketch the scenes and then write a brief description of the characters and action in each one.

Scene 1

Description

_____

_____

Scene 2

Description

_____

_____

Scene 3

Description

_____

_____

Scene 4

Description

_____

_____

ASSESS YOUR KNOWLEDGE

1. Summarize What message are you attempting to convey in your film?

_____

_____

2. Analyze How do the scenes you created convey that message?

_____

_____

Writing a Script

To complete preparations for your film, you need a script. Use the storyboard ideas you developed on the previous page to help you select a specific scene. Then write a two- to three-minute script for that scene. In your script, include details about the setting, the characters, and any important action that takes place in the scene. Most importantly, try to write interesting and informative dialogue.

Scene: _____
_____

Setting: _____
_____

Characters: _____   _____   _____
_____   _____   _____

Dialogue:

_____   _____
_____   _____
_____   _____
_____   _____
_____   _____
_____   _____
_____   _____
_____   _____
_____   _____
_____   _____
_____   _____
_____   _____
_____   _____
_____   _____

Quiz and Review

ONLINE QUIZ
Take a practice quiz for each section in this chapter.

CHAPTER REVIEW
Use the online Chapter Review to help you prepare for the chapter test.

Activities

HISTORICAL DOCUMENTS
Read and explore key documents that shaped African American history.

VIRTUAL FIELD TRIP
Take a virtual field trip to experience key sites from African American history.

VOICES OF HISTORY
Experience African American history and culture through recordings of key people and documents.

Partner

CONNECTING TO OUR PAST
Examine artifacts from **Howard University's Moorland-Spingarn Research Center** that bring to life the study of African American history.

Steps to Freedom

CHAPTER SUMMARY

SECTION 1 The Antislavery Movement

- In the late 1800s, the Second Great Awakening contributed to the growth of the abolition movement, a campaign to end slavery.
- Abolitionists included both black and white Americans.
- Some abolitionists called for militant efforts to end slavery, while others used more peaceful methods to spread their message.

SECTION 2 The Coming Conflict

- Disputes over the expansion of slavery as new states entered the Union led to rising tensions between northerners and southerners.
- The Missouri Compromise of 1820 and the Compromise of 1850 sought to resolve sectional disputes over the expansion of slavery.
- The Fugitive Slave Act, the Kansas-Nebraska Act, the *Dred Scott* decision, and John Brown's raid heightened tensions over slavery.
- The 1860 presidential election of Abraham Lincoln led several southern states to secede and form the Confederate States of America.

SECTION 3 The Civil War—Freedom Won

- The Civil War began on April 12, 1861, when Confederate forces attacked Fort Sumter in South Carolina.
- During the war, black men served as soldiers, spies, and laborers; black women served as spies, nurses, and support personnel.
- On January 1, 1863, President Lincoln issued the Emancipation Proclamation, freeing all slaves in rebel areas in the United States.
- On April 9, 1865, the Union won the Civil War.

6 BLACKS in the Reconstruction Era

After the Civil War, slavery ended. Many former slaves were thrilled to have the opportunity to attend school at last. This 1886 engraving shows a black primary school in Vicksburg, Mississippi.

Freedman's School, 1886/The Granger Collection, New York

EXPRESSING YOUR OPINION

List several important freedoms that you value having the most. Then write a paragraph explaining how you might feel if you had just gained those freedoms for the first time. Consider freedoms such as the right to receive an education or to travel.

As You Read

Life after Slavery

1. **TAKING NOTES** Use a graphic organizer like this one to take notes on life after the end of slavery, the Freedmen's Bureau, and landownership for freedpeople. Use the **Reading Focus** questions on the next page to help guide your note taking.

2. As you read the section, underline or highlight definitions and descriptions of the **Key Terms** listed on the next page.

The Thirteenth Amendment

Slavery Comes to an End

The Freedmen's Bureau

Landownership

Life after Slavery

BEFORE YOU READ

MAIN IDEA

Near the end of the Civil War, the U.S. government took action to end slavery and to help southerners, including newly freed African Americans.

READING FOCUS

- How did the end of slavery affect the lives of African Americans?
- In what ways did the Freedmen's Bureau help freedpeople and white southerners after the war?
- What steps did the U.S. government take to help freedpeople become landowners?

KEY TERMS

Reconstruction
Thirteenth
    Amendment
Freedman's Bureau
Southern Homestead
    Act

BUILDING BACKGROUND

On April 9, 1865, Confederate forces surrendered. The Union had won the Civil War. Although the war's end was a time of great rejoicing, it was also a time of great sadness. More than 500,000 military personnel had been killed—almost as many as in all other U.S. wars combined. In the South, the land lay in ruins. Countless homes and buildings were destroyed, and many farms and plantations had been abandoned. Confederate money had become worthless, and many southerners faced starvation and economic ruin. The U.S. government stepped in to help southerners—both black and white. ◼

Slavery Comes to an End

After the Civil War ended, the U.S. government faced the challenge of reuniting the nation and rebuilding the defeated South. This process was called **Reconstruction**. The period of Reconstruction lasted 12 years, from 1865 to 1877. One of the first actions that Congress took under Reconstruction was to abolish slavery.

Freedom at Last

The Emancipation Proclamation of 1863 had freed only enslaved African Americans in Confederate areas not under Union control. Slavery still existed in the rest of the South, including the border states. For this reason, Congress took action to ensure the freedom of all African Americans. On January 31, 1865—before the Civil War even ended—Congress proposed the **Thirteenth Amendment** to the U.S. Constitution. This amendment made slavery illegal throughout the entire United States.

The Thirteenth Amendment took effect on December 18, 1865. All of the more than 3.5 million African Americans who had endured bitter lives under slavery were free. When abolitionist William Lloyd Garrison heard the news, he declared that his work was finished. Not all abolitionists agreed, however. African Americans still did not have U.S. citizenship or the right to vote. Frederick Douglass, a black abolitionist leader, insisted "slavery is not abolished until the black man has the ballot [vote]."

Freedom—A New Way of Life

The end of slavery opened up a world of new opportunities for freed African Americans, or freedpeople. Black couples proudly held formal ceremonies to legalize their marriages. Former slaves eagerly sought to restore families ripped apart by slavery.

VIRTUAL FIELD TRIP
Go online to experience a virtual field trip to key sites from the Reconstruction era.

go.hrw.com
Chapter Activity
Keyword: SAAH CH6

KEY FACTS

1. Underline or highlight what the Thirteenth Amendment stated and the date when it was ratified, or took effect.

SAML. DOVE wishes to know of the whereabouts of his mother, Areno, his sisters Maria, Neziah, and Peggy, and his brother Edmond, who were owned by Geo. Dove, of Rockingham county, Shenandoah Valley, Va. Sold in Richmond, after which Saml. and Edmond were taken to Nashville, Tenn., by Joe Mick; Areno was left at the Eagle Tavern, Richmond

Respectfully yours,
SAML. DOVE.
Utica, New York, Aug. 5, 1865–3m

U. S. CHRISTIAN COMMISSION,
NASHVILLE, TENN., July 19, 1865.

New Freedoms

After slavery ended, many freedpeople traveled, as shown in the photo on the right of blacks leaving Richmond, Virginia. Other freedpeople searched for long-lost loved ones, as shown in the print advertisement above.

Free to travel without a pass, many former slaves journeyed thousands of miles to search for lost loved ones. Others traveled simply to test their new freedom. One woman explained, "I must go, if I stay here I'll never know I'm free."

Having been treated as inferior for so long, freedpeople also took steps to gain respect and equality. Under slavery, most black adults were given their slaveholders' last names and were addressed by their first names. After slavery ended, many black adults took new last names and insisted on being addressed as "Mister" or "Missus." Some freedpeople also worked to gain the same rights as white citizens. One freedman argued that "if I cannot do like a white man I am not free."

Seeking Economic Opportunity

With freedom, former slaves could look for better jobs. Some freedpeople left their former slaveholders to seek economic opportunities elsewhere. Many of these blacks no longer wanted to work on the same farms or plantations where they had been forced to endure backbreaking labor without pay. Some former slaveholders were shocked when freedpeople left. One planter tried to convince a freed family to return. The man of the family wrote that they would return only if the planter paid them back wages for all the years they had served him. The planter never replied.

A number of freedpeople moved to cities to seek work. Between 1865 and 1870 the black population of the South's 10 largest cities doubled. Other freedpeople left the South altogether. Some of them moved to cities in the North. Still others went west, where they started businesses or worked as miners, soldiers, or cowboys.

However, the majority of former slaves remained in the rural South, in part because of the many challenges they faced. Although often willing to work hard, freedpeople faced numerous obstacles to economic independence. Most freedpeople had little or no money and few belongings. In addition, few freedpeople had been educated, which severely limited the jobs they could obtain.

To add to these challenges, the South's economy had been badly crippled by the Civil War. At the same time, southerners had to create a new labor system to replace slavery. With such problems, job prospects were bleak for all southerners—both black and white. Across the South, many people were in desperate need of help. ✔

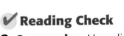

Reading Check

2. Summarize How did the Thirteenth Amendment affect the lives of African Americans?

_____

_____

_____

_____

_____

_____

_____

_____

The Freedmen's Bureau

To help the South, in March 1865 the U.S. government created the Bureau of Refugees, Freedmen, and Abandoned Lands, better known as the **Freedmen's Bureau**. This organization provided relief to needy southerners and assistance to help freedpeople move from slavery to freedom.

Relief for Southerners

The main goal of the Freedmen's Bureau was to provide relief to southerners—both black and white. As the nation's first large-scale relief organization, the Freedmen's Bureau provided food, clothing, fuel, and medical services to hundreds of thousands of southerners. For example, by 1867 the Bureau had set up 46 hospitals in the South and provided medical treatment to more than 450,000 people.

Education for Freedpeople

The Freedmen's Bureau also provided assistance to freedpeople, such as help finding work and locating loved ones.

FACES OF HISTORY

Charlotte FORTEN
c. 1817–1885

Charlotte Forten grew up in a free black family in Philadelphia, Pennsylvania. The family was well-off and were active abolitionists. In 1856 Forten began teaching in Salem, Massachusetts, the first African American to teach white students there. Driven to achieve, she was meanwhile active in the abolition movement and in expanding her knowledge. In time, this challenging schedule took its toll on her health, and she quit her job. She would continue to have similar bouts of poor health from overwork throughout her life.

In 1862, during the Civil War, Forten became a volunteer teacher in the Sea Islands off South Carolina. The Union had captured this area and begun schools for the former slaves there. In 1864 Forten described her experiences in an article, "Life on the Sea Islands," for *Atlantic Monthly* magazine. "I never before saw children so eager to learn," she wrote. In her journal, published later, she expressed sadness, though, that she had so little in common with her students.

3. Analyze What impressed you most about Forten's life? Why?

_____

_____

_____

Perhaps the most successful assistance provided was education. Denied schooling under slavery, few freedpeople could read or write. During the Civil War, northern groups such as the American Missionary Association had started black schools in Union-held areas of the South. Some former slaves had founded their own black schools as well. The Bureau built upon these early efforts.

During its existence, the Bureau founded more than 4,000 black schools. Thousands of black and white teachers, mainly from the North, volunteered at these schools. Charlotte Forten and Susie King Taylor were two black teachers who later wrote about their experiences. Taylor describes her students in the passage below.

HISTORY'S VOICES

"I had about forty children to teach, beside[s] a number of adults who came to me nights, all of them so eager to learn to read . . . I gave my services willingly for four years and three months without receiving a dollar."

—Susie King Taylor, *Reminiscences of My Life in Camp*, 1902

Although many freedpeople were eager to learn, many white southerners did not want former slaves to be educated. With an education, freedpeople could better compete for jobs and for economic and political power. Some white southerners even went so far as to burn down black schools and to attack teachers and students. Despite such opposition, by 1877 more than 600,000 African Americans had enrolled in schools in the South. ✔

✔ **Reading Check**
4. Find the Main Idea
What was the purpose of the Freedmen's Bureau?

_____

_____

_____

_____

_____

_____

During the Civil War, Union troops provided materials to help these former slaves transform an abandoned Sea Islands plantation into a village.

Landownership

Perhaps even more than wanting to gain an education, many freedpeople dreamed of owning land. They saw landownership as a means to economic independence and true freedom from white control. The U.S. government tried two main methods of helping freedpeople obtain land, with mixed results.

Abandoned Confederate Land

One method to help freedpeople obtain land was to offer them abandoned Confederate land. During the Civil War, some white southerners fled areas under Union control. In some cases, Union officials seized abandoned plantations and paid contrabands to work them. By saving their money, former slaves might then one day buy the land.

One such example took place in the Sea Islands off the Georgia and South Carolina coasts. Union forces captured these islands early in the war, and most of the white population fled. The U.S. government then seized the abandoned land and hired freedpeople to work some of it. In early 1865 Union general William T. Sherman divided the land and nearby mainland areas into 40-acre plots. He then offered freed families the plots along with army mules for plowing. By the end of the war, more than 40,000 freedpeople were farming land on the Sea Islands as their own.

After the war, "forty acres and a mule" became a slogan for freedpeople, who hoped U.S. leaders would continue to give them land. Many former slaves thought it was only fair that they receive free Confederate land. This land would make up for all the years that slaves had been forced to work without pay. In addition, the federal government had given free land to white settlers in the past.

Some more-radical Republicans in Congress agreed and proposed bills for giving Confederate land to freedpeople, but none of the bills passed. Nonetheless, freedpeople did obtain some abandoned Confederate land after the war. The Freedmen's Bureau distributed and leased some abandoned lands to former slaves. In addition, in some parts of the South, African Americans began working abandoned lands on their own. For example, in 1866 more than 800 freedpeople established a village called Slabtown on 600 acres of abandoned plantation land in Hampton, Virginia. J. T. Trowbridge, a northern writer, later marveled at the village's success.

HISTORY'S VOICES

"There was an air of neatness and comfort . . . The business of the place was carried on chiefly by freedmen, many of whom were becoming wealthy . . . I found no idleness anywhere. Happiness and industry were the universal rule."

—J. T. Trowbridge, *The South: A Tour of Its Battlefields and Ruined Cities*, 1866

Freedpeople did not get to keep much of this Confederate land, however. In time, U.S. leaders returned most of the land—including much of the land in the Sea Islands—to the original white owners. The thousands of former slaves who had settled and worked the land as their own had to leave or work for the white landowners.

INFO TO KNOW

The Sea Islands' black population was isolated and thus had retained many African customs. African Americans on the islands spoke Gullah, a mix of English and West African languages that few outsiders could understand. Today some Gullah words, such as *gumbo* and *voodoo*, have gained common use.

KEY FACTS

5. What two main methods did the U.S. government use to try to help freedpeople obtain their own land?

Public Land

Another method to help freedpeople obtain land was to give them public land. In 1866 Congress passed the **Southern Homestead Act**. This law set aside 45 million acres of public land in five southern states. Under the law, black and white southern families could obtain free 80-acre homesteads. Only about 4,000 black families took advantage of the offer, because few freedpeople could afford the supplies needed to work a farm. Of those who did take land, few were able to support themselves long enough to make their farms a success. The law was later repealed in 1872.

Challenges and Successes

Freedpeople faced discrimination in obtaining land as well. Those who could afford to buy land often found that white landowners would not sell to them. By refusing to sell to African Americans, white southerners hoped to maintain control over blacks and a supply of cheap labor. "Freedom and independence are different things," a Mississippi planter wrote in his diary. "A man may be free and yet not independent."

Despite such challenges, some freedpeople were able to buy land. In Mississippi, for example, 1 out of every 12 black families owned land by 1870. One of these families was that of Isaiah T. Montgomery, who turned a tragedy into success. In 1865 Montgomery and some of his relatives leased the Mississippi plantation where they had been slaves. The Montgomerys prospered and by 1868 had saved enough to buy the land. Within a few years, they were the state's third-largest cotton producers.

Then tragedy struck. The heirs of the plantation's original white owners demanded the land back. Fearing violence, Montgomery signed over his property—worth at least $14,000—for $3,500. The *Mississippi Register* proclaimed, "A White Man in a White Man's Place. A Black Man in a Black Man's Place. Each according to the Eternal Fitness of Things." But Montgomery did not give up. He and a cousin bought swampland in Bolivar County and labored with others for years to clear the land. There, they founded the village of Mound Bayou, which still exists today. ✔

ACADEMIC VOCABULARY

6. Use the context, or surrounding words in the sentence, to write a definition of **repealed**.

✔ Reading Check

7. Analyze How successful was the U.S. government at helping freedpeople own land?

SECTION 1 ASSESSMENT

go.hrw.com
Online Quiz
Keyword: SAAH HP6

Reviewing Ideas, Terms, and People

8. Recall What was Reconstruction?

9. Summarize What types of challenges did freedpeople face following the Civil War and the end of slavery?

10. Evaluate What do you think was the most important accomplishment of the Freedmen's Bureau?

Creating a Newspage

On December 6, 1865, the states ratified the Thirteenth Amendment, which abolished slavery in the United States. Create a newspage for freedpeople celebrating this event. Use your notes from this section to identify key topics related to the end of slavery. Then use a template like the one below to create your newspage. Provide a masthead. Then write an article, with headline, about how slavery's end has affected African Americans. Consider both the gains and challenges that freedom brought.

December 1865

Wedding Announcements

Rufus Turner, the son of Fred Williams and Lucy Johnson, was united in holy matrimony with Judy Cornwall, daughter of Bernice Cornwall, on December 10, 1865, in Charlotte, North Carolina. Rufus Turner proudly served in the 35th United States Colored Troops.

Information Wanted

Martha Roscoe of Richmond, Virginia, wishes to know the whereabouts of her sister, Jane Bass, who was owned by Nathan Early, owner of a hardware store in Richmond. Jane was taken away early in the morning in 1847 or so when she was quite young and sold to Robert Reynolds, a hotelkeeper in Savannah, Georgia. Ministers, please read this notice in your churches.

George Adams of Nashville, Tennessee wishes to know the whereabouts of his son, Charles, and daughter, Elmira, who were owned by Joseph Grant of Murfreesboro, Rutherford County, Tennessee. They were taken away and sold in Nashville. A man named David Bell took them to Natchez, Mississippi.

Creating an Information Guide

To complete your newspage for freedpeople, create a Freedmen's Bureau Information Guide to appear on the back of the newspage. The information guide should provide a short introduction that explains what the Freedmen's Bureau is. The guide should then provide drawings or pictures that illustrate the main services that the Bureau provided to freedpeople. Use a template like the one below to create your information guide.

Freedmen's Bureau Information Guide

_____

_____

_____

Relief	Education

Land	Other

ASSESS YOUR KNOWLEDGE

1. **Summarize** How did the Freedmen's Bureau address the challenges that freedpeople faced in building new lives after slavery?

   _____

2. **Make Judgments** Do you think the Freedmen's Bureau did enough to help freedpeople after the end of slavery? Why or why not?

   _____

As You Read

The Politics of Reconstruction

1. **TAKING NOTES** Use a graphic organizer like this one to take notes on Reconstruction under Lincoln, Reconstruction under Johnson, and Congressional Reconstruction. Use the **Reading Focus** questions on the next page to help guide your note taking.

2. As you read the section, underline or highlight definitions and descriptions of the **Key Terms and People** listed on the next page.

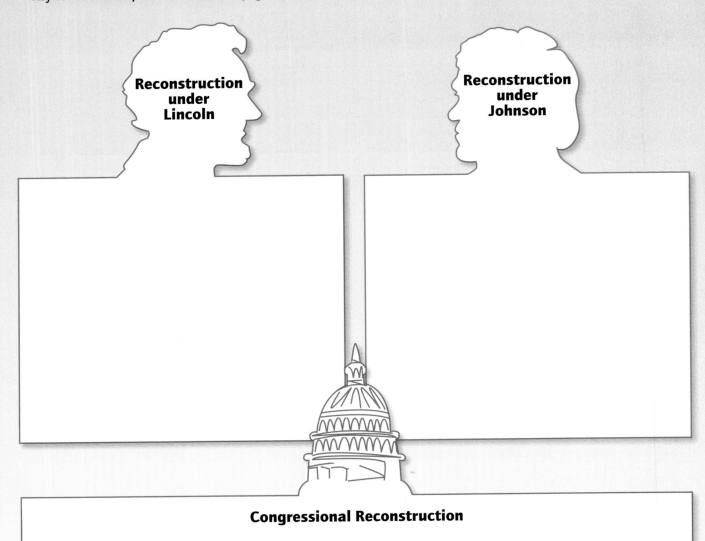

Reconstruction under Lincoln

Reconstruction under Johnson

Congressional Reconstruction

The Politics of Reconstruction

BEFORE YOU READ

MAIN IDEA

U.S. leaders had differing views about how to reconstruct the United States and about what rights to extend to African Americans.

READING FOCUS

- What were the main points of presidential Reconstruction under Lincoln?
- What were the main points of presidential Reconstruction under Johnson, and what conflicts arose between Johnson and Congress?
- What were the major policies and achievements of Congressional Reconstruction?

KEY TERMS AND PEOPLE

Ten Percent Plan
Wade-Davis Bill
John Wilkes Booth
Andrew Johnson
Black Codes
Radical Republicans
Charles Sumner
Thaddeus Stevens
Civil Rights Act of 1866
Fourteenth Amendment
Reconstruction Acts
Fifteenth Amendment

BUILDING BACKGROUND

After the Civil War, the U.S. government began Reconstruction, the process of rebuilding the South and reuniting the nation. While the government helped former slaves begin the difficult task of building new lives, northern leaders debated how to treat the defeated Confederate states. Deep-seated animosity remained between the North and the South, and many northerners supported stiff penalties for the rebel southern states. President Abraham Lincoln, however, stated in 1865 that he hoped northerners would treat the South "with malice toward none, with charity for all." ■

Reconstruction under Lincoln

During the Civil War, President Lincoln had hoped to reunite the United States as quickly as possible. In 1863, well before the war ended, he had developed a plan for restoring rebel states to the Union. A quick restoration was not to be, though. Opposition from Congress and a great tragedy would soon derail Lincoln's hopes.

Lincoln's Ten Percent Plan

Lincoln's Reconstruction plan included three main parts. First, southerners who took an oath of loyalty to the United States and agreed that slavery was illegal would receive amnesty and regain their citizenship. High-ranking Confederate officials were excluded, however. Second, at least 10 percent of a state's citizens who had voted in 1860 had to swear loyalty before they could form a new state government. Third, the state had to amend its constitution to ban slavery. Lincoln would then recognize the state and its new government as part of the Union. This plan became known as the **Ten Percent Plan**. By the war's end, Arkansas, Louisiana, and Tennessee had rejoined the Union under the plan and elected new members to Congress.

ACADEMIC VOCABULARY

1. Use the context, or surrounding words in the sentence, to write a definition of **amnesty**.

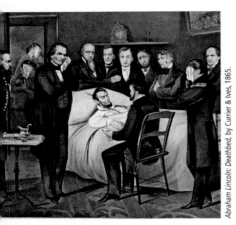

▲ **President Abraham Lincoln died on April 15, 1865, after John Wilkes Booth assassinated him.**

Opposition to Lincoln's Plan

Lincoln's Ten Percent Plan met with strong opposition from Congress. Many Republican members—particularly the more radical Republicans—thought the plan was too lenient. They wanted a more demanding Reconstruction plan that imposed stiffer penalties against the South. A Republican senator from Michigan expressed this view.

HISTORY'S VOICES

"The people of the North are not such fools as to . . . turn around and say to the traitors, 'all you have to do [to return] is . . . take an oath that henceforth you will be true to the Government.'"

—Senator Jacob Howard, 38th Congress, 1st Session, 1863–1864, quoted in *Reconstruction: America's Unfinished Revolution, 1863–1877,* by Eric Foner

Another reason that some members of Congress opposed Lincoln's plan had to do with a question of government power. Who had the power to allow the seceded states to rejoin the Union—the president or Congress? President Lincoln thought he did, but many members of Congress disagreed.

To show its opposition, Congress refused to seat the new members from the states admitted under Lincoln's Ten Percent Plan. Congress then proposed a stricter Reconstruction plan in the **Wade-Davis Bill**. Under this plan, a state had to meet two conditions to rejoin the Union. First, a majority of the state's adult white male citizens had to take a loyalty oath before the state could form a new government. Second, the state constitution had to be amended to abolish slavery and prohibit secession. In addition to these two conditions, the bill prohibited anyone who had voluntarily supported the Confederacy from voting or holding office.

This plan would make rejoining the Union much harder for southern states. At the time, the Civil War had not yet ended, and Lincoln thought the plan's tough conditions would make southerners more committed to fighting. He therefore refused to sign the Wade-Davis Bill into law. Many Republicans harshly criticized Lincoln for this action. Such criticism from Lincoln's own political party proved to be a sign of the bitter struggle that Reconstruction was to become.

The Assassination of Lincoln

What new Reconstruction plan Lincoln might have proposed remains unknown. On the evening of April 14, 1865—less than a week after the war's end—Lincoln and his wife attended a play at Ford's Theater in Washington. During the performance, a southerner named **John Wilkes Booth** sneaked into the president's theater box and shot him. The next morning, Lincoln died.

Lincoln's tragic death produced one of the greatest outpourings of grief in American history. As a train carried the president's body to Illinois for burial, huge crowds gathered along the way to show their respect. In a letter, black poet Frances Ellen Watkins Harper expressed her sadness. "Sorrow treads on the footsteps of the nation's joy . . . To-day a nation sits down beneath the shadow of its mournful grief. Oh, what a terrible lesson does this event read to us!" In the former Confederacy, some white southerners reacted to Lincoln's death with concern. Reconstruction was now in the hands of **Andrew Johnson**, Lincoln's vice president. A southerner who had supported the Union, Johnson was a traitor in the eyes of many people in the South. Meanwhile, many members of Congress hoped to find an ally in Johnson. ✔

INFO TO KNOW
To kill the Wade-Davis Bill, Lincoln used a pocket veto. This veto power is available only during the last 10 days that Congress is in session. During that time, the president can kill a bill simply by not signing it. Usually, if the president does not sign a bill while Congress is in session, the bill becomes law after 10 days. Congress cannot overturn a pocket veto.

✔ **Reading Check**
2. Find the Main Idea What was the Ten Percent Plan, and why did many Republicans in Congress oppose it?

Reconstruction under Johnson

Many Republicans in Congress hoped that Johnson, as the new president, would support more demanding Reconstruction policies. During the Civil War, Johnson had taken a tough stand against the Confederacy. "Treason is a crime," he had declared, "and crime must be punished." Conflict, however, would soon erupt between Johnson and Congress over Reconstruction.

Johnson's Reconstruction Plan

Johnson issued his Reconstruction plan in May 1865, less than a month after becoming president. In some ways, Johnson's plan was similar to Lincoln's. Almost all white southerners who took a loyalty oath to the United States would receive amnesty. They would then regain their U.S. citizenship and property, with the exception of their former slaves. However, high-ranking Confederate officials as well as southerners who owned property worth $20,000 or more had to obtain presidential pardons to receive amnesty. Unlike Lincoln's plan, Johnson's plan did not require a certain percentage of state voters to pledge loyalty. Instead, delegates at a state convention had to repeal secession, amend the state constitution to abolish slavery, and nullify all Confederate debts. Once these steps were taken, state voters could form a new state government and elect representatives to Congress.

Johnson's Reconstruction plan moved forward during the summer of 1865—with surprising results. Despite his strong words against treason, Johnson pardoned nearly every planter and former Confederate official who applied. He eventually pardoned several thousand southerners. These pardons enabled many prewar leaders and former Confederates to gain political office. In fact, southern voters elected to the U.S. Congress 10 former Confederate generals, two former Confederate cabinet members, and the former vice president of the Confederacy. Many Republicans in Congress, which was in recess during this period, were far from satisfied with this turn of events. When Congress met for its session in December 1865, the members refused to seat the newly elected southern representatives.

Black Codes

In the meantime, Johnson had approved most of the new southern state governments. The state's legislatures had then quickly begun passing discriminatory laws against African Americans. Called **Black Codes**, the laws resembled the slave codes that had controlled African Americans under slavery. Although slavery had ended, deep-rooted prejudice against African Americans remained in the South. Most white southerners hoped to restore the white power structure they had enjoyed before the war. The Black Codes were designed to control African Americans and to put them back into an inferior and slavelike condition. At the same time, the laws were meant to ensure white planters of a dependent black labor force.

The Black Codes, which varied by state, did ensure freedpeople of some rights. For example, in most states, blacks could marry and testify in court against other blacks. Most Black Codes, however, denied rights. Some states enforced segregation, or racial separation, in public areas. Some did not allow freedpeople to own guns. Many states banned interracial marriage and prohibited African Americans from testifying in court against white citizens.

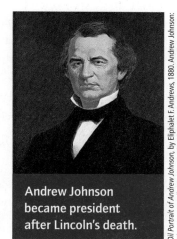

Andrew Johnson became president after Lincoln's death.

KEY FACTS

3. List the main requirements of President Johnson's Reconstruction plan.

Black Codes

Many white southerners were horrified and threatened by former slaves suddenly moving around freely. To control freedpeople, southern states passed laws known as Black Codes. The following is an excerpt from Mississippi's Black Code, passed in November 1865.

Section 7. Be it further enacted [passed], that every civil officer shall, and every person may, arrest and carry back to his or her legal employer any freedman, free Negro, or mulatto [person of mixed race] who shall have quit the service of his or her employer before the expiration [end] of his or her term of service without good cause, and said officer and person shall be entitled to receive for arresting and carrying back every deserting employee aforesaid [mentioned before], the sum of $5, and 10 cents per mile from the place of arrest to the place of delivery.

Skills FOCUS ANALYZING PRIMARY SOURCES

4. Draw Conclusions How does the excerpt above restrict the freedom of African Americans and resemble actions taken under slavery?

_____

_____

_____

✔ **Reading Check**

5. Identify Cause and Effect How did Johnson's Reconstruction plan affect African Americans in the South?

_____

_____

_____

_____

_____

_____

All the states' Black Codes limited former slaves' economic opportunities. For example, some states taxed freedpeople who did not work on plantations or as servants. Some states banned former slaves from buying land or renting property in certain areas. Most states required freedpeople to sign labor contracts, which bound workers to their employers for a certain period, such as a year. Workers who left before the period ended could be arrested or lose their wages. Even more, in many states, freedpeople without labor contracts or jobs could be arrested, fined, and then forced to work to pay off the fines.

The Freedmen's Bureau and the U.S. military were able to prevent some Black Codes from being enforced. In addition, the Bureau tried to help freedpeople obtain fair labor contracts. Even so, the Black Codes denied African Americans many rights and restored the South's white power structure. Southern blacks were subjected to curfews, arrest, and humiliating treatment. Local law officers invaded African Americans' homes and seized their property. Unable to obtain land or better jobs, many former slaves had to go back to the plantations to work under labor contracts.

The Black Codes angered and alarmed African Americans. One black Civil War veteran asked, "If you call this Freedom, what do you call Slavery?" To oppose the Black Codes, some black leaders in the South held conventions to call for change. In South Carolina, for example, a black convention sent a petition to state officials.

HISTORY'S VOICES

"We simply ask . . . that the same laws which govern _white men_ shall govern _black men_ . . . that, in short, we be dealt with as others are—in equity [equality] and justice."

—Convention of the Colored People of South Carolina, 1865

A few African Americans took more direct action to oppose the Black Codes. In Louisville, Kentucky, horse-drawn streetcars were restricted to white passengers. Some young black men began boarding the streetcars and refusing to leave until arrested. Their efforts helped convince the streetcar company to change its policy and allow black riders. Similar events occurred elsewhere. Such gutsy stands foreshadowed the struggles of the civil rights movement of the 1950s and 1960s. ✔

Congressional Reconstruction

Opposition to President Johnson's Reconstruction plan increased as the months passed. Many northerners were disturbed by the events taking place in the South. "Public sentiment [there] is still as bitter and unloyal as in 1861," the *New York Times* reported. These northerners thought that the nation's enormous wartime sacrifices would be wasted if the South returned to its prewar ways. A growing number of members in Congress agreed and soon moved to take control of Reconstruction.

HISTORICAL DOCUMENT

Go online to read a historical document from the Reconstruction era.

go.hrw.com

Chapter Activity

Keyword: SAAH CH6

Congress Opposes Johnson

In Congress, the members most fiercely opposed to Johnson's Reconstruction plan were the **Radical Republicans**. This small group was led by Senator **Charles Sumner** of Massachusetts and Representative **Thaddeus Stevens** of Pennsylvania. The Radicals wanted to impose harsh terms on the defeated southern states and to force them to make dramatic changes before rejoining the Union. "The whole fabric of southern society must be changed," proclaimed Stevens.

In addition, the Radicals criticized Johnson for not providing African Americans with the right to vote or with any role in the new state governments. In contrast, Johnson thought that each state should decide what black civil rights to provide, such as the right to vote. When some black leaders met with him to discuss black voting rights, Johnson declared, "It is the people of the states that must for themselves determine this thing." Black leader Frederick Douglass firmly responded, "You enfranchise [give the vote to] your enemies and disenfranchise your friends."

Most Republicans in Congress did not share the Radicals' views. These more moderate Republicans formed the largest group in Congress. Although they mainly disliked Johnson's Reconstruction plan, they hoped to work with him. At the same time, they opposed the Black Codes and saw the need to protect freedpeople's rights.

To do so, Congress passed two bills in early 1866. The first bill was the Freedmen's Bureau Bill. It extended the life of the Freedmen's Bureau and enabled it to try some legal cases involving African Americans, thereby removing such cases from possibly unfair southern courts. The second bill was the **Civil Rights Act of 1866**. This bill provided African Americans with the same legal rights as white Americans. Anyone who denied freedpeople their equal rights could be tried in a federal court.

Johnson vetoed both bills. He insisted they were unconstitutional and unnecessary. Freedpeople should not have equal rights, he declared, because they did not yet understand "our institutions." He further declared that Congress could not pass laws until all of the states were represented. Johnson's actions alienated many moderate Republicans in Congress. They joined forces with the Radicals and passed both bills over the president's vetoes. The battle for control of Reconstruction had begun.

The Veto, by Thomas Nast, 1866

The political cartoon above shows Johnson kicking a bureau labeled Freedmen, symbolizing the Freedmen's Bureau. The cartoon accuses Johnson of hurting freedpeople by vetoing the Freedmen's Bureau Bill.

6. What U.S. Supreme Court case did the Fourteenth Amendment overturn, and how did overturning that case help African Americans?

_____

_____

_____

_____

_____

_____

_____

The Fourteenth Amendment

Republicans in Congress worried that the U.S. Supreme Court might later overturn the Civil Rights Act of 1866. To ensure the rights it protected, Congress passed the **Fourteenth Amendment** to the U.S. Constitution. This amendment, which was ratified in 1868, granted U.S. citizenship to all people born or naturalized in the United States. This guarantee overturned the *Dred Scott* decision of 1857, in which the U.S. Supreme Court had ruled that African Americans were not U.S. citizens. In addition, the Fourteenth Amendment guaranteed all U.S. citizens equal protection under the law and prohibited any state from depriving a citizen's rights without due process of law. Last, the new amendment prohibited all prewar officials who had supported the Confederacy from holding state or national political office.

The Fourteenth Amendment infuriated many white southerners, and every seceded state but Tennessee refused to ratify it. President Johnson and many northern Democrats strongly opposed the amendment as well. Because of this opposition, civil rights for African Americans became a key issue in the 1866 congressional elections. In preparation, Johnson began a tour of the nation to promote his policies and the candidates who supported them. However, during the tour he often argued with his audiences and lost some people's support. About the same time, race riots broke out in Louisiana and Tennessee when white mobs attacked African Americans. Dozens of people—most of them black—were killed. These events helped increase support for the Republicans, and northern voters elected them in large numbers.

Radical Reconstruction

After the 1866 elections, the Radical Republicans in Congress had enough numbers and support to take control of Reconstruction. In 1867 and 1868 Congress passed several strong **Reconstruction Acts**. These laws invalidated the state governments

HISTORICAL DOCUMENT

Go online to read a historical document from the Reconstruction era.

go.hrw.com

Chapter Activity

Keyword: SAAH CH6

The Reconstruction Amendments

In the space provided, list what each amendment stated and when it was ratified.

7. Thirteenth Amendment	8. Fourteenth Amendment	9. Fifteenth Amendment

that Johnson had approved and divided the South into five military districts under U.S. Army control. Only Tennessee, readmitted to the Union in July 1866, was exempt. The other seceded states had to meet three conditions to rejoin the Union. First, they had to ratify the Fourteenth Amendment. Second, they had to give adult black male citizens the vote. Third, they had to let voters, including black men, elect new state government officials. Military commanders had the authority to register black voters and to remove southern officials who did not cooperate.

Johnson hotly denounced the Reconstruction Acts, which he claimed used "powers not granted to the federal government or any one of its branches." He vetoed each act in turn, but Congress overrode every veto. Tensions further heightened when Congress passed a law requiring Senate approval for the president to remove Cabinet members. Johnson refused to obey the law, and in 1868 the U.S. House of Representatives impeached him. The Senate, however, lacked one vote to convict Johnson and remove him from office. Nonetheless, Johnson's power as president was broken.

Later that year, Ulysses S. Grant was elected as the new president. The former general in chief of the Union forces, Grant was a popular war hero. He also supported Congressional Reconstruction. By the time he took office, Congress had admitted seven more southern states to the Union—Alabama, Arkansas, Florida, Georgia, Louisiana, North Carolina, and South Carolina.

The Fifteenth Amendment

The Reconstruction Acts gave the vote to black men—but only in the South. In much of the rest of the nation, black men still could not vote. To give all black men the vote, Congress passed the **Fifteenth Amendment** to the U.S. Constitution in 1869. This amendment, which was ratified in 1870, stated that no U.S. citizen could be denied the right to vote because of race, color, or previous condition of servitude. Abolitionist William Lloyd Garrison praised "this wonderful, quiet, sudden transformation of four millions of human beings from . . . the auction block to the ballot-box." ✔

Significant Election Scene at Washington, by A. W. McCallum, 1867

The Fifteenth Amendment gave all adult black men in the United States the right to vote.

✔**Reading Check**

10. Identify What did the Reconstruction Acts do?

_____

_____

_____

_____

_____

_____

go.hrw.com
Online Quiz
Keyword: SAAH HP6

SECTION 2 ASSESSMENT

Reviewing Ideas, Terms, and People

11. Recall What was Lincoln's plan for Reconstruction, and what was it called?

_____

_____

12. Compare How did the Black Codes resemble slavery?

_____

_____

13. Evaluate Which element of the Reconstruction Acts do you think was the most important?

_____

_____

Identifying Cause and Effect

President Andrew Johnson and the Republican leaders in Congress fought for control over Reconstruction. Use your notes from Section 2 to review Reconstruction under Johnson and Congress. Then use graphic organizers like the ones below to list some of the main points and effects of each Reconstruction plan. Some answers have been entered for you.

Reconstruction under Johnson

- White southerners, with some exceptions, who took a loyalty oath were provided amnesty. High-ranking Confederate officials and southerners who owned property worth $20,000 or more had to obtain presidential pardons to receive amnesty.

Effects

Congressional Reconstruction

- The Reconstruction Acts of 1867–1868 organized the former Confederacy, except Tennessee, into five military districts under the control of the U.S. Army.

Effects

Distinguishing Fact from Opinion

Understand the Skill

To analyze documents, historians must be able to tell facts from opinions. A statement is a claim of fact if evidence can prove or disprove the statement. For example, historical records can prove the following fact: "In December 1863, President Abraham Lincoln issued the Proclamation of Amnesty and Reconstruction." A statement is an opinion if evidence cannot prove or disprove the statement. For example, research cannot prove or disprove the following opinion: "Lincoln was the greatest president ever."

Learn the Skill

Use the strategy below to learn how to tell facts from opinions.

Step 1
Read a statement and ask yourself if the information can be either proved or disproved.

Step 2
If the answer is **yes**, the statement is a **claim of fact**.

If the answer is **no**, the statement is an **opinion**.

Step 3
If the claim is **true**, it is a **fact**.

Otherwise, the claim of fact is either false or untested.

APPLY THE SKILL

1. Find the Main Idea How does a fact differ from an opinion?

_____

2. Analyze Read the following passage, in which President Andrew Johnson explains why he is vetoing the Civil Rights Bill of 1866. Then identify whether each underlined statement is a fact or opinion.

a By the 1st Section of the bill, all persons born in the United States and not subject to any foreign power, excluding Indians not taxed, are declared to be citizens of the United States . . . [I]t is now proposed . . . to confer [grant] the rights of citizens upon all persons of African descent, born within the extended limits of the United States, while **b** persons of foreign birth who make our land their home must undergo a probation of five years and can only then become citizens upon proof that they are "of good moral character, attached to the principles of the constitution of **c** the United States" . . . To me the details of the bill seem fraught with evil.

Fact or Opinion?
a. _____

Fact or Opinion?
b. _____

Fact or Opinion?
c. _____

The Emergence of Black Political Leaders

1. **TAKING NOTES** Use a graphic organizer like this one to take notes on black state and local leaders, black congressional leaders, and Republican control in the South during Reconstruction. Use the **Reading Focus** questions on the next page to help guide your note taking.

2. As you read the section, underline or highlight definitions and descriptions of the **Key People** listed on the next page.

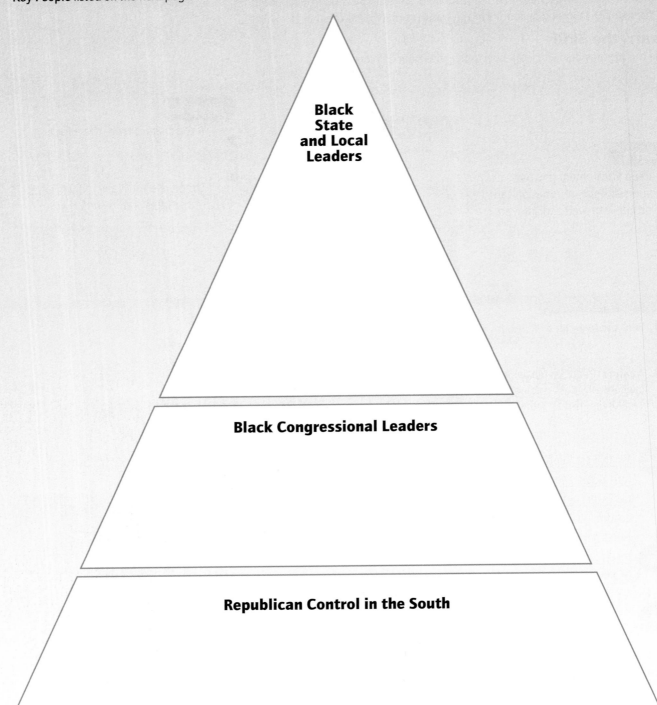

Black
State
and Local
Leaders

Black Congressional Leaders

Republican Control in the South

SECTION 3 The Emergence of Black Political Leaders

BEFORE YOU READ

MAIN IDEA

During Congressional Reconstruction, African Americans held political offices and worked to improve their lives.

READING FOCUS

- What key political offices did black state and local leaders hold?
- Who were some of the significant black congressional leaders?
- What changes did Republican control bring to the South?

KEY PEOPLE

P. B. S. Pinchback
Hiram Revels
Blanche K. Bruce
Joseph Rainey

BUILDING BACKGROUND

During 1867 and 1868 Congress and the U.S. Army took charge of Reconstruction. The southern state governments created under President Johnson were dismantled, and many white southerners lost political power. These changes enabled the Republicans to gain control in many southern states. Republican officials included loyal white southerners as well as northerners who had come south. However, by far the largest group of Republicans in the South was a newly empowered political group—black men. With the vote, African Americans would emerge as political leaders for the first time. ■

Black State and Local Leaders

Under Congressional Reconstruction, political power in the South shifted. Many pre-war southern officials and former Confederates lost the right to vote and hold office. At the same time, hundreds of thousands of southern black men gained these rights. In fact, black voters came to outnumber white voters in five southern states. This black political power would open new doors for African Americans in the South.

African Americans Participate in Government

Across the South, determined African Americans began actively participating in government, despite white resistance. This participation began with the state constitutional conventions of 1867 and 1868. The Reconstruction Acts required that the seceded states hold these conventions to write new state constitutions. Moreover, the states had to let African Americans take part. Large numbers of black men turned out to vote for delegates to the state conventions, and black delegates were elected to every one. In fact, in Louisiana the number of black delegates equaled that of white delegates, and in South Carolina black delegates formed the majority. The *Charleston Daily News* praised the black delegates at the South Carolina convention.

HISTORY'S VOICES

"Beyond all question, the best men in the convention are the colored members . . . They have assembled neither to pull wires like some, nor to make money like others; but to legislate for the welfare of the race to which they belong."

—*Charleston Daily News*, 1868

P. B. S. Pinchback was a black delegate to the Louisiana constitutional convention. He was later lieutenant governor and briefly served as governor.

1. List the significant state political offices that African Americans held during Congressional Reconstruction.

_____

_____

_____

_____

_____

_____

_____

_____

_____

_____

The new state constitutions that black delegates helped create expanded democracy and improved life for African Americans in several ways. As the Reconstruction Acts required, all of the constitutions abolished slavery and gave the right to vote to black men. Many of the state constitutions also did away with property qualifications for voting and holding political office. Furthermore, several of the constitutions made more state offices elected rather than appointed, thus increasing voters' power.

African Americans Gain Political Office

After creating new state constitutions, the seceded states held elections. The large number of black male voters in the South overwhelmingly supported the Republican Party. With their help, the Republicans easily gained control of almost all of the new southern state governments. Moreover, for the first time, black men won a number of government offices. More than 600 African Americans were elected to southern state legislatures. Other black leaders won important state offices, such as lieutenant governor, secretary of state, and state treasurer. Even more African Americans were elected to local political offices. In all, during Reconstruction more than 1,500 African Americans admirably served in state and local offices in the South.

These black officeholders came from a variety of backgrounds. They included both southerners and northerners, both African Americans who had been enslaved and those who had been free from birth. In general, though, the black leaders who won political office tended to be better educated and wealthier than most African Americans in the South. These black officials were often community or church leaders, and many had gained political experience by participating in black conventions. In addition, at the state level, black officeholders were more likely to have been free before the war than enslaved. However, many freedpeople held local offices.

The political influence of African Americans during Reconstruction varied from state to state. Black political influence was strongest in South Carolina, which had a large black population. There, black members controlled the lower house of the state legislature until 1874. In addition, two black legislators—Samuel J. Lee and Robert B. Elliott—served as Speaker of the House. Other prominent black leaders in the state included Alonzo J. Ransier and Richard H. Gleaves, who both served as lieutenant governor; Jonathan Jasper Wright, who served on the state Supreme Court; and Francis L. Cardozo, who served as both secretary of state and state treasurer.

Black political influence was also strong in Louisiana and Mississippi. In both states, blacks were well represented in the state legislatures, although they never held control. In Louisiana, three African Americans served as lieutenant governor—Oscar J. Dunn, **P. B. S. Pinchback**, and C. C. Antoine. In 1872 Pinchback became the first black governor when he held the office for more than a month when the elected governor was impeached.

▼ **This 1872 print by Currier & Ives honored the first black members of the U.S. Congress. In front from left to right are Hiram Revels (MS), Benjamin Turner (AL), Josiah Walls, (FL), Joseph Rainey, (SC), and Robert B. Elliott (SC). In back from left to right are Robert De Large (SC) and Jefferson Long (GA).**

The First Colored Senator and Representatives, by Currier & Ives, 1872

In Mississippi, four African Americans held significant state offices. A. K. Davis served as lieutenant governor, and James Hill served as secretary of state. T. W. Cardozo was the state superintendent of education, and John R. Lynch was Speaker of the House.

In the other southern states, black leaders held several offices but had less influence on state politics. For example, African Americans were underrepresented in the state governments in Alabama, Arkansas, Florida, North Carolina, and Tennessee. In Virginia, Democrats kept control of the state government, and few African Americans gained political office.

In some states, black officeholders faced fierce resistance from white southerners. For example, in Georgia, the state legislature initially refused to let the elected black members take their seats. Not until a year later, after the Georgia Supreme Court approved the black legislators, were they able to take office. ✔

FACES OF HISTORY

Blanche K. BRUCE

c. 1841–1898

Blanche K. Bruce was born into slavery in Virginia. Despite being enslaved, he received some schooling and later furthered his education. Early in the Civil War, Bruce escaped and made his way to Kansas. There, he founded the state's first black elementary school.

After the war, Bruce moved to Mississippi and bought land to farm. He soon became involved in Republican state politics and in 1874 was elected to the U.S. Senate. Bruce's start in the Senate was a rocky one, however. During the swearing-in ceremony, the senior senator from Bruce's state refused to escort him to his seat per tradition. Ignoring the insult, Bruce began walking to his seat alone. Seeing this, Roscoe Conklin, a Republican senator from New York, joined Bruce. Conklin befriended Bruce and went on to be his mentor in the Senate.

2. Draw Conclusions Explain the role that education played in Bruce's life.

_____

_____

_____

Black Congressional Leaders

In addition to holding offices at the state and local levels, several African Americans won election to the U.S. Congress during Reconstruction. James G. Blaine, a prominent white congressman, praised the conduct of these first black leaders in Congress. "The colored men who took seats in both [the] Senate and [the] House did not appear ignorant or helpless," Blaine wrote. "They were as a rule studious, earnest, ambitious men, whose public conduct . . . would be honorable to any race."

Black Senators

Two African Americans from Mississippi—Hiram Revels and Blanche K. Bruce—served in the U.S. Senate. **Hiram Revels** was a free-born minister and educator, originally from North Carolina. In 1870 he became the nation's first black senator when he took over the seat of Jefferson Davis, the former president of the Confederacy. Revels served in the U.S. Senate until 1871. While in office, he fought against racial segregation and earned respect for his skill as a speaker.

Blanche K. Bruce served in the U.S. Senate from 1875 to 1881, the first African American to serve a full six-year Senate term. While in office, Bruce became known for taking strong stands. He attacked election fraud and corruption and championed increased civil rights for African Americans as well as for Chinese immigrants and Native Americans. In addition, Bruce worked to increase education funding and to improve commerce along the Mississippi River. In 1879 he again made history when he briefly presided over the U.S. Senate, the first African American to do so. After his term ended, Bruce held several other federal positions in Washington.

✔**Reading Check**
3. Identify Cause and Effect How did black men gaining the right to vote affect southern state governments?

_____

_____

_____

INFO TO KNOW
Only five African Americans had served in the U.S. Senate as of 2007. Following Reconstruction, another black U.S. senator was not elected until 1967, when Edward Brooke of Massachusetts took office. In 1992 Carol Moseley Braun of Illinois became the first black woman in the Senate. The most recent black senator, Barack Obama of Illinois, took office in 2005.

Black Representatives

A total of 20 African Americans served in the U.S. House of Representatives from 1870 to 1901. The first black congressman in the House was **Joseph Rainey** of South Carolina. Born into slavery, Rainey had escaped during the Civil War. After the war, he became involved in state politics and briefly served in the South Carolina Senate. He later won election to the U.S. House of Representatives, where he served three terms from 1871 until 1879. While in office, Rainey focused on improving civil rights for African Americans.

Another prominent black congressman was Robert B. Elliott. Highly educated, Elliott graduated from Eton College in England before going to South Carolina to practice law. After holding several state offices, he served in the U.S. House from 1871 to 1874. Outspoken in his views, Elliott fought, without success, to have the vote taken away from all southern white men. ✔

Republican Control in the South

The Republican-dominated state governments in the South made many progressive reforms under Congressional Reconstruction. These reforms included improvements in civil rights, education, state facilities, and transportation. At the same time, African Americans formed their own institutions to improve their lives in the South.

Southern State Governments

The South's Republican state governments worked to expand and protect citizens' rights, including those of African Americans. The new state constitutions had already expanded voting rights and made government more democratic. Building on this foundation, all southern states repealed the Black Codes. Furthermore, some states in the Lower South made discrimination against African Americans illegal in hotels, on trains, and in other public facilities. Several states also expanded rights for married women.

Republican governments improved state services and facilities as well. One of the most significant improvements was the creation of public school systems, which were virtually nonexistent in the South before Reconstruction. With the spread of public education, the number of black children enrolled in school skyrocketed between 1870 and 1880, as the graph on the left shows. In addition, Republican governments built badly needed state facilities, such as hospitals, orphanages, and mental institutions. However, in most of the South white and black citizens were not allowed to use the same schools or state facilities.

To help rebuild the South and its economy, Republicans funded an extensive building program. Workers built new bridges and thousands of miles of new roads and railroads. Black leaders sought land reform as well to help freedpeople achieve economic independence, but with little success. A few states passed laws to try to help freedpeople buy land, but none approved seizing Confederate lands.

PERCENTAGE OF BLACKS ENROLLED IN SCHOOL, 1850–1880

Source: *Historical Statistics of the United States*

Skills FOCUS **INTERPRETING GRAPHS**

5. How much did the percentage of African Americans enrolled in schools increase from 1870 to 1880?

_____

_____

The needs in the South were great, and the Reconstruction state governments spent millions of dollars on improvements and building programs. To raise this money, the governments issued bonds and raised taxes, particularly taxes for large landowners. Meanwhile, Republicans decreased taxes for poor southern farmers. These government changes angered many of the white southern leaders and planters who had previously controlled the South. This anger further inflamed the hatred that many white southerners had for African Americans and white Republicans.

Black Institutions

While Republican state leaders worked to reform the South, industrious African Americans established institutions to help themselves. Black groups raised money to form institutions such as soup kitchens, orphanages, schools, and employment agencies. Some of the most important black institutions were churches. Under slavery, African Americans had often been forced to worship in white churches. With freedom, however, black men and women began to found and build their own churches. In addition, many black southerners joined northern black religious groups, such as the American Methodist Episcopal (AME) Church, founded in Pennsylvania in the 1790s. In the South, black churches quickly began to serve as important community centers; and black ministers, as community leaders—roles that continue today.

Some black churches founded southern black colleges to provide African Americans with greater access to a higher education. Springfield Baptist Church founded Morehouse College in Georgia in 1867 to educate ministers and teachers. Today the college is best known for its most famous graduate—Martin Luther King Jr., who did his early studies there. The Freedmen's Bureau and other groups founded black colleges as well. Howard University, named after the head of the Freedmen's Bureau, was founded in Washington, in 1867. A Union general who had led black troops during the Civil War founded Hampton Institute in Virginia in 1868. Hampton's focus on job training became the model for most black colleges in the South. The American Missionary Association founded seven black colleges during this period, including Fisk University in Nashville, Tennessee. Unlike many other black colleges, Fisk stressed obtaining a higher education rather than job training. ✔

Skills FOCUS — DISTINGUISHING FACT FROM OPINION

6. Is the underlined sentence in the paragraph to the left a fact or an opinion? How can you tell?

_____

_____

_____

✔ Reading Check

7. Summarize What did the Republican-dominated state governments accomplish under Congressional Reconstruction?

_____

_____

_____

_____

_____

_____

SECTION 3 ASSESSMENT

go.hrw.com
Online Quiz
Keyword: SAAH HP6

Reviewing Ideas, Terms, and People

Choose the letter of the name at right that best matches each description.

_____ **8.** The first African American to serve in the U.S. House of Representatives

_____ **9.** The black congressman who unsuccessfully tried to have the right to vote taken away from all southern white men

_____ **10.** The first African American to serve a full six-year term in the U.S. Senate

_____ **11.** The first African American to serve in the U.S. Senate

_____ **12.** The black lieutenant governor who briefly served as governor of Louisiana

a. Hiram Revels

b. Blanche K. Bruce

c. Joseph Rainey

d. P. B. S. Pinchback

e. Robert B. Elliott

Creating a Hall of Fame Display

A number of African Americans were elected to political office during Reconstruction. Imagine that you have been chosen to create a display of leading black politicians for a Reconstruction Hall of Fame. Use your notes from Section 3 to identify key black leaders. Then use a template like the one below to create your display.

Reconstruction Hall of Fame: Black Officeholders

U.S. Congress: Senators

Name: _____

Term of Office: _____

Achievements: _____

_____

Name: _____

Term of Office: _____

Achievements: _____

_____

U.S. Congress: Representatives

Name: _____

Term of Office: _____

Achievements: _____

_____

Name: _____

Term of Office: _____

Achievements: _____

_____

State Political Leaders

Name: _____

State Office: _____

Achievements: _____

_____

Name: _____

State Office: _____

Achievements: _____

_____

ASSESS YOUR KNOWLEDGE

1. **Draw Conclusions** Why were the rights to vote and hold political office important for African Americans during Reconstruction?

_____

2. **Make Generalizations** How can being active in politics help minority groups in the United States today?

_____

Creating an Award Certificate

Under Congressional Reconstruction, the southern state governments made many improvements and changes to the South. Imagine that you have been chosen to create an award certificate honoring the achievements of the Reconstruction state governments. Use your notes from Section 3 to identify the main accomplishments of the state governments. Then use a template like the one below to create your award certificate.

Award of Excellence

is given to

Reconstruction State Governments

in recognition of

_____

_____

_____

_____

_____

_____1867–1877_____

Date

_____

Signature

ASSESS YOUR KNOWLEDGE

1. **Identify Cause and Effect** How did the actions of the Reconstruction state governments help southern African Americans in particular?

_____

_____

2. **Evaluate** What do you think was the most important reform or accomplishment of the Reconstruction state governments?

_____

_____

Reconstruction Comes to an End

1. **TAKING NOTES** Use a graphic organizer like this one to take notes on white resistance and violence, new labor systems and economic hardship, and the end of Reconstruction. Use the **Reading Focus** questions on the next page to help guide your note taking.

2. As you read the section, underline or highlight definitions and descriptions of the **Key Terms and People** listed on the next page.

White Resistance and Violence	New Labor Systems and Economic Hardship

The End of Reconstruction

4 Reconstruction Comes to an End

BEFORE YOU READ

MAIN IDEA

In time, various forces led to the end of Reconstruction, and African Americans lost many of the rights and freedoms they had gained.

READING FOCUS

- What problems did Reconstruction lead to, and how did they affect black and white southerners?
- Why and when did Reconstruction come to an end?

KEY TERMS AND PEOPLE

Ku Klux Klan
Enforcement Acts
sharecropping
tenant farming
Samuel J. Tilden
Rutherford B. Hayes
Compromise of 1877

BUILDING BACKGROUND

By 1870 five years of Reconstruction had produced some major achievements. Congress had readmitted all of the former Confederate states to the Union. The United States was whole once again. At the same time, Reconstruction amendments and laws had greatly expanded democracy. After some 200 years of slavery, African Americans had gained not only freedom but also citizenship and political power. But in 1870 the Democrats began to regain power in the South, and blacks soon lost many of the gains they had made. ◼

Problems with Reconstruction

Despite the progress that Republicans made in the South, the majority of white southerners strongly opposed Congressional Reconstruction. They disliked having federal soldiers stationed in their states and disapproved of black men holding political office. In addition, white southern Democrats accused the Republican governments of spending too much and claimed that they were corrupt. This white opposition led to recurring violence across the South during Reconstruction.

White Resistance and Violence

White southerners' rage and fear over the changes occurring under Reconstruction frequently erupted into violence. White mobs attacked African Americans and burned black churches and schools—sometimes with the help of local police. Race riots broke out in cities and towns. Many African Americans and the white Americans who supported them were injured or killed.

To try to restore white supremacy, some white southerners organized terrorist groups. The best-known group was the **Ku Klux Klan**. Founded in Tennessee in 1866, the Klan began as a social club but quickly developed into a secret terrorist society. Members wore hoods and robes to hide their identities and often carried out attacks at night. The Klan used threats, burnings, beatings, whippings, and even murder to scare and punish blacks, especially those who were successful or leaders. White Republicans and other southerners who supported blacks were also targets.

> **Skills FOCUS** DISTINGUISHING FACT FROM OPINION
>
> **1.** Is the underlined sentence in the paragraph to the left a fact or an opinion? How can you tell?

▲ This 1874 political cartoon refers to the violence of white terrorist groups such as the Ku Klux Klan as "worse than slavery."

Worse than Slavery, by Thomas Nast, 1874

The Ku Klux Klan spread rapidly throughout the South. All types of white southerners joined the Klan's hooded night riders, from poor farmers to influential and respectable citizens. Many similar terrorist groups existed in the South as well, among them the White League and the Knights of the White Camelia. Although only a small minority of white southerners actually joined terrorist groups, many people supported their goals. Moreover, local officials in the South rarely prosecuted white citizens who committed terror or violence against blacks.

In 1870 and 1871 Congress passed three **Enforcement Acts** to try to stop the violence in the South. These laws banned the use of disguises to deprive any person of his or her rights and set heavy penalties for anyone attempting to prevent a citizen from voting. The new laws also empowered the U.S. Army and the federal courts to arrest and punish members of the Ku Klux Klan. Federal marshals arrested thousands of Klansmen, and within a few years the Klan's power was broken. Other white terrorist groups continued to operate actively throughout the South, however.

New Labor Systems and Economic Hardship

The violence of the Ku Klux Klan and other white terrorist groups was just one of the many problems with Reconstruction. Another problem was the government's failure to provide adequate support to enable freedpeople to gain economic independence. Although some former slaves became successful and even grew wealthy, the majority remained trapped in poverty.

Because few African Americans in the South could afford to buy or even rent land, many former slaves returned to working on plantations. However, most African Americans were not content with the low wages that planters were willing to pay. In addition, black farm laborers no longer wanted to work in supervised groups as they had under slavery.

As a result, a new agricultural labor system gradually developed in the South. Under this system, called **sharecropping**, a landowner provided a worker with land, seed, tools, a mule, and a cabin. The worker then farmed the land in exchange for a share, or a part, of the crop. For this reason, farmworkers became known as sharecroppers. The system benefited landowners because they no longer had to pay their workers—and money at the time was scarce. The sharecropper benefited by having a specific plot of land to farm. By the end of the 1870s most freedpeople and many poor white southerners had become sharecroppers.

Sharecroppers who saved up enough money could move up to **tenant farming**. Tenant farmers rented their land, which enabled them to grow whatever crops they wanted. Sharecroppers were often forced to grow cotton. Many tenant farmers preferred growing food crops because they provided food as well as an income.

KEY FACTS

2. Use the graphic organizer to compare and contrast sharecropping and tenant farming.

Similarities

Differences

Most sharecroppers and tenant farmers hoped to save enough money that they could one day buy their own farms. Only a few ever achieved this dream, however. Instead, most sharecroppers and tenant farmers became trapped in a cycle of debt that kept them in poverty. Because most farmers had little if any cash, they had to buy their food and other goods on credit. Later, when the farmers sold their crops, they hoped to pay off these debts. However, bad weather, poor harvests, or low crop prices often made paying off debts nearly impossible. Thus, with each passing year, many sharecroppers and tenant farmers found themselves deeper in debt.

The sharecropping system also helped keep the South's economy tied to one-crop agriculture. Sharecroppers often grew cotton, one of the South's major cash crops. When too many farmers planted cotton, though, the supply became too great. As a result, the price per bale of cotton dropped. In 1873 a nationwide depression caused cotton prices to fall for several years. In response, southerners grew even more cotton to try to increase their profits. But crop surpluses only drove prices lower, plunging many sharecroppers and tenant farmers even deeper into debt. ✔

✔ **Reading Check**
3. Find the Main Idea How did terrorist groups and the rise of sharecropping affect African Americans in Reconstruction?

The End of Reconstruction

By the early 1870s, support for Reconstruction was declining in both the North and the South. A number of factors contributed to this loss of support, among them the ongoing violence in the South. Eventually, Reconstruction came to an end in 1877. With its end, African Americans saw many of their gains and hopes fade away.

Declining Support for Reconstruction

As the violence in the South continued, northern support for Reconstruction declined. The continuing need for federal military forces to keep peace in the South dismayed many northerners. They wondered how effective the southern Republican governments could be if they were not able to stop the violence themselves. This reaction was exactly what the white terrorist groups in the South wanted.

In Congress, support for Reconstruction was declining as well. The two strongest supporters of Reconstruction—Representative Thaddeus Stevens and Senator Charles Sumner—had both died. Several other Radical Republicans had retired or left office. Many of the new leaders in Congress were more concerned with other issues than with Reconstruction and the problems of freedpeople.

In the South, Republicans began losing faith in Reconstruction. Southern blacks remained unhappy about their widespread poverty and the lack of land reform. Southerners of both races were discouraged by the region's poor economic condition, despite the Republicans' costly programs. Moreover, the high cost of these programs had plunged the southern states into debt. Just as bad, southern Democrats accused some Republican officials, especially those tied to railroad building, of corruption.

In 1870 white Democrats began to regain control of state governments in the South. The General Amnesty Act of 1872 contributed to this change. This act pardoned many former Confederates and let them once again vote and hold political office. Many prewar southern leaders began to be elected, replacing black officeholders. Most of the new white leaders belonged to the Democratic Party, which became known in the South as the party of white supremacy.

KEY FACTS

4. List the gains and hopes that African Americans lost as Reconstruction came to an end.

KEY FACTS

5. Identify the U.S. presidents that held office during the Reconstruction era.

Reconstruction Presidents

1861–
1865: _____
        (Republican)

1865–
1869: _____
        (Republican)

1869–
1877: _____
        (Republican)

1877–
1881: _____
        (Republican)

✔ **Reading Check**

6. Summarize What factors and events contributed to the end of Reconstruction?

_____

_____

_____

_____

_____

_____

While losing support in the South, Republicans also began to lose support at the national level. Several scandals plagued the Republican administration of President Grant. Although voters re-elected Grant in 1872, the scandals in his administration cost him and the Republican Party the support of many voters. This loss of support helped the Democrats regain control of the U.S. House of Representatives in 1874.

Economic problems then further weakened support for Reconstruction. The Panic of 1873 marked the start of a severe five-year economic downturn. Soon, an estimated 2 million Americans were out of work. Both Republican and Democratic leaders began to focus less on Reconstruction and more on economic issues.

As support for Reconstruction declined, violence in the South increased. Some white southern Democrats began using intimidation, violence, and other methods to regain political control. On election days, armed Democrats stole or destroyed ballot boxes and drove black voters from the polls. Republican candidates and their supporters were threatened, beaten, and even murdered in broad daylight. When Mississippi's governor asked for federal help in 1875, President Grant refused, saying that the public was "tired out" by the South's problems. The U.S. Supreme Court then began to limit the Fourteenth and Fifteenth amendments' protection of blacks' civil rights, including blacks' right to vote. By 1876 white Democrats had regained control of all but three southern states—South Carolina, Louisiana, and Florida.

The final blow to Reconstruction came with the presidential election of 1876. In that election, the Democratic candidate, **Samuel J. Tilden**, beat the Republican candidate, **Rutherford B. Hayes**, by an extremely narrow margin of victory. However, Republicans challenged the election results in four states, three of them in the South. In the **Compromise of 1877**, the Democrats agreed to let Hayes become president if Republican leaders agreed to remove all remaining federal troops from the South. The Republicans agreed, and with the removal of the troops Reconstruction ended. White control once again reigned over black destiny in the South. Even as times grew worse for blacks in the South, though, some African Americans were determined to one day regain the rights they had briefly held. ✔

SECTION 4 ASSESSMENT

Reviewing Ideas, Terms, and People

7. Recall What was the Ku Klux Klan, and how did it and similar groups disrupt life in the South during Reconstruction?

_____

_____

8. Explain Why did African Americans lose some of the gains they had made?

_____

_____

9. Evaluate What were the effects of Reconstruction on the economic life of African Americans?

_____

_____

Creating a Before-and-After Chart

In 1877 Reconstruction came to an end with the withdrawal of federal troops from the South. The end of Reconstruction deeply changed life in the South, particularly for African Americans. Use your notes from the entire chapter to review how life in the South changed during and after Reconstruction. Then use a graphic organizer like the one below to create a chart that describes life in the South for African Americans before and after the end of Reconstruction. You might use a bulleted list, drawings, slogans, and pictures to provide information in your chart.

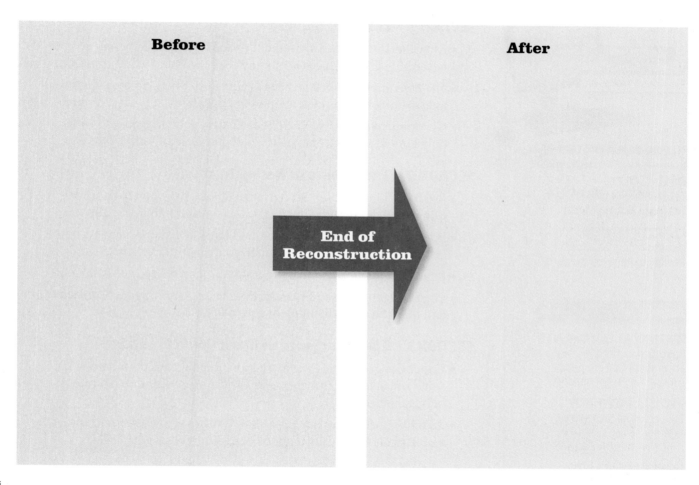

Before

End of Reconstruction

After

ASSESS YOUR KNOWLEDGE

1. **Infer** How might African Americans have felt about the loss of the freedoms and rights they had gained during Reconstruction?

   _____

   _____

2. **Make Judgments** Do you think that the Republicans should have tried to keep federal troops in the South longer than they did? Why or why not?

   _____

   _____

Online Resources

Visit **go.hrw.com** for review and enrichment activities related to this chapter.

go.hrw.com
Chapter Home Page
Keyword: SAAH CH6

Quiz and Review

ONLINE QUIZ
Take a practice quiz for each section in this chapter.

CHAPTER REVIEW
Use the online Chapter Review to help you prepare for the chapter test.

Activities

HISTORICAL DOCUMENTS
Read and explore key documents that shaped African American history.

VIRTUAL FIELD TRIP
Take a virtual field trip to experience key sites from African American history.

VOICES OF HISTORY
Experience African American history and culture through recordings of key people and documents.

Partner

CONNECTING TO OUR PAST
Examine artifacts from **Howard University's Moorland-Spingarn Research Center** that bring to life the study of African American history.

Blacks in the Reconstruction Era

CHAPTER SUMMARY

SECTION 1   Life after Slavery

- After the Thirteenth Amendment ended slavery, freedpeople sought new rights but also faced economic challenges and white opposition.
- The Freedmen's Bureau provided relief to southerners in need as well as assistance such as education to freedpeople.
- Government attempts to help former slaves obtain land met with only limited success, and few freedpeople became landowners.

SECTION 2   The Politics of Reconstruction

- President Lincoln's Ten Percent Plan faced strong opposition from Congress, who thought the plan was too lenient on the South.
- President Johnson's Reconstruction Plan enabled prewar southern leaders to regain control and led to conflict with Congress.
- Radical Republicans in Congress gained control of Reconstruction.
- The Fourteenth Amendment made African Americans U.S. citizens, and the Fifteenth Amendment gave adult black men the vote.

SECTION 3   The Emergence of Black Political Leaders

- Under Congressional Reconstruction, Republicans dominated most southern state governments, and African Americans held numerous political offices.
- Republican governments in the South made progressive reforms, and African Americans founded black churches and colleges.

SECTION 4   Reconstruction Comes to an End

- Many white southerners resisted Reconstruction, and violence against blacks and white Republicans was widespread in the region.
- The sharecropping system kept many blacks in debt and poverty.
- Political, economic, and social issues combined to decrease support for Reconstruction, which ended with the Compromise of 1877.

THE SEPARATION of the RACES

In response to racial tension and violence in the late 1800s and early 1900s, groups like the NAACP were founded. This flag was often flown outside the New York headquarters of the NAACP to increase the public's awareness of the dangers faced by African Americans on a daily basis.

A MAN WAS LYNCHED YESTERDAY

EXPRESSING YOUR OPINION

Make a list of ways in which people of various heritages have contributed to American society. Then choose one item from your list and write a paragraph about how your life might be different without this contribution.

163

The Jim Crow Era

1. **TAKING NOTES** Use a graphic organizer like this one to take notes on African Americans losing ground, the legalization of segregation, barriers to voting, and the rise of racial violence. Use the **Reading Focus** questions on the next page to help guide your note taking.

2. As you read the section, underline or highlight definitions and descriptions of each of the **Key Terms and People** listed on the next page.

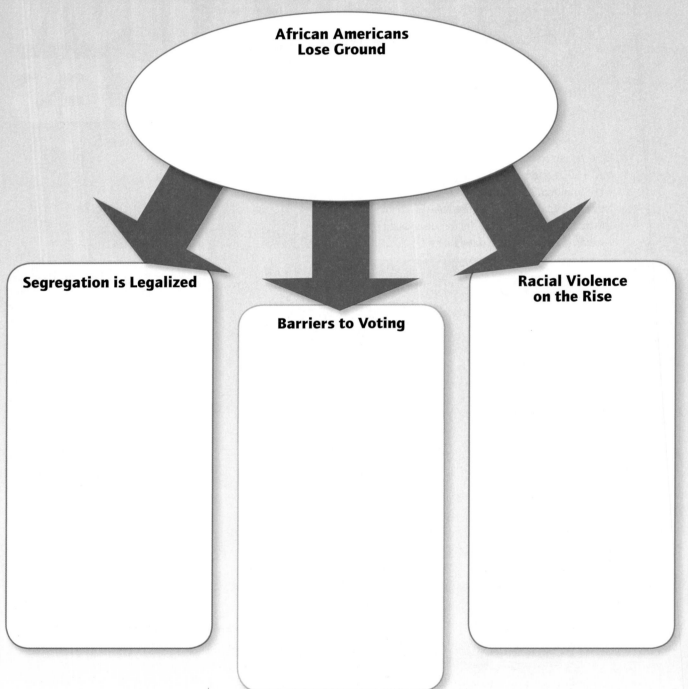

African Americans Lose Ground

Segregation is Legalized

Barriers to Voting

Racial Violence on the Rise

The Jim Crow Era

BEFORE YOU READ

MAIN IDEA

By 1900 many of the gains made by African Americans during Reconstruction had been taken away, and relations between blacks and whites had grown strained.

READING FOCUS

- What rights did black citizens lose after the end of Reconstruction?
- What court cases helped legalize segregation in the United States?
- What barriers were raised to keep African Americans from voting?
- What caused a rise in racial violence in the 1900s?

KEY TERMS AND PEOPLE

integration
segregation
Jim Crow era
Slaughterhouse Cases
Plessy v. *Ferguson*
poll tax
grandfather clause
lynchings
Ida Wells-Barnett

BUILDING BACKGROUND

Reconstruction had been an effort to heal the United States after years of conflict and war. As part of the healing, many Americans wanted to improve the lives of African Americans and protect their rights. These efforts were somewhat successful during Reconstruction, but after the period ended discrimination actually increased. ◼

African Americans Lose Ground

During Reconstruction, the central issue for African Americans had been how to legitimize their place in American society. With the support of the federal government, black people had helped rewrite state constitutions and worked to gain civil rights. These efforts were designed to put African Americans on par with their white counterparts—formally and legally.

Different Approaches

Faced with opposition from many whites, African Americans had to decide how best to work for equality. What would be the best approach toward reaching equal status? Debates raged in the black community. Most Africans Americans favored social integration. To integrate means to bring all the parts of something together to make it whole. **Integration** sought to place blacks on an equal basis with whites within American society by leveling social, economic, and political barriers and by creating equal opportunity among people of all races.

On the other hand, many blacks—and some whites—called for a racial separation, a mutually agreed upon and respectful division of the races into their own communities. Many people believed that blacks had to develop their own social, educational, and economic institutions independent of white society. Only then would they be able to gain self-respect and live free of white control.

Still, many whites looked for ways to keep the races separate and unequal. They sought to do this through voluntary **segregation**, or a separation of the races in daily life. Before long, the segregation laws, rules, and customs that arose after Reconstruction led to a new era of discrimination. It was called the **Jim Crow era** and it lasted nearly 100 years.

KEY FACTS

1. Underline the descriptions of the different approaches towards African Americans that existed at the turn of the century.

VIRTUAL FIELD TRIP
Go online to experience a virtual field trip to key sites from the Jim Crow era.

go.hrw.com
Chapter Activity
Keyword: SAAH CH7

The Rise of Jim Crow

The name *Jim Crow* came from a song originally sung by black children at play. The song took on a different meaning during the 1820s when a white performer named Thomas Dartmouth "Daddy" Rice appeared on stage as "Jim Crow," a highly stereotyped black character. In his performances, Rice wore dark makeup called blackface as he danced around and sang in an exaggerated accent.

> **HISTORY'S VOICES**
>
> "Come listen all you galls and boys I's jist from Tuckyhoe,
> I'm going to sing a little song, My name's Jim Crow,
> Weel about and turn about and do jis so,
> Eb'ry time I weel about and jump Jim Crow."
>
> —Thomas Dartmouth "Daddy" Rice, "Jump Jim Crow," 1828

Rice's Jim Crow song-and-dance routine was a big hit with white audiences across the United States. Soon, the term *Jim Crow* became a racial slur used by others to demean African Americans. By the late 1800s, the meaning of Jim Crow changed again to refer to the laws and customs used to oppress and to discriminate against blacks, especially in the South.

Redeemer Governments and Jim Crow Laws

As you have read, in the 1870s white Democrats who favored segregation began to gain power in the South. They were elected to state governments, replacing African American politicians who had been elected during Reconstruction. Southerners began to refer to these new governments as Redeemer governments, because they thought the new leaders would "redeem" the South by reversing Reconstruction policies. Firm believers in white supremacy, these leaders wanted to limit the power of black citizens.

In the late nineteenth century, Redeemer lawmakers began passing laws to establish separate facilities for black people. These laws became known as Jim Crow laws. From 1890 to 1910, Jim Crow laws spread across the South. For example, in 1890 Louisiana formally instituted Jim Crow seats on streetcars. These were certain cars, or sections of cars, reserved only for black people. Other southern states later followed Louisiana's example. Throughout the South, African Americans were forced to ride in separate railway cars, eat in separate restaurants, attend separate schools, and live in separate neighborhoods.

In the North, Jim Crow laws were less widespread than in the South. Still, blacks had to deal with all kinds of prejudice. For example, in many northern cities African Americans were denied admittance to certain places, such as hotels, restaurants, and theaters.

Blacks also faced prejudice at the United States Military Academy at West Point. In 1870 J. W. Smith became the academy's first black cadet. Smith had to deal with almost daily abuse, both verbal and physical. For a time, he accepted the abuse from his fellow cadets stoically. But finally the malicious cadets provoked Smith. Frustrated by the constant harassment, he struck a white cadet and was expelled. It was not until a few years later, on June 14, 1877, that Henry O. Flipper became the first black cadet to graduate from West Point.

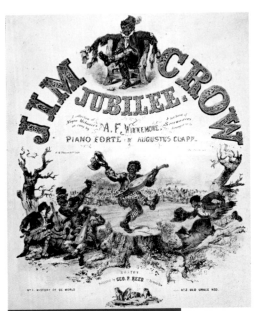

The character Jim Crow became a derogatory symbol for African Americans after Reconstruction.

Reading Check

2. Sequence What events led to the passing of Jim Crow laws in the South?

_____

_____

_____

_____

_____

_____

Segregation is Legalized

As Reconstruction ended, states in the South began writing new constitutions. Many incorporated Jim Crow principles. In addition, federal court rulings set precedents that states used to support segregation policies. Among these were two Supreme Court rulings that became the legal basis for segregation in the United States.

The Slaughterhouse Cases

The first decision to help set a precedent for segregation appeared, on first glance, to have nothing to do with race relations at all. In 1873 three separate cases regarding the meatpacking industry in New Orleans were brought before the Supreme Court. Together, these cases are called the **Slaughterhouse Cases**. A few years before the cases were filed, the state of Louisiana decided to create a new corporation to run all slaughterhouses in the city of New Orleans, largely for health and sanitation reasons. The owners of slaughterhouses objected to the new corporation, stating that it would be an unlawful monopoly that threatened their livelihood.

When their case reached the Supreme Court, the slaughterhouse owners argued that the Louisiana law violated their rights under the Fourteenth Amendment. One clause of that amendment had declared that no state could impede the rights and privileges of its citizens. Unfortunately for the plaintiffs, the Supreme Court did not agree. It said that the Fourteenth Amendment only protected the rights of national citizenship, the rights granted to Americans by the Constitution. It did not protect rights, such as business ownership, that had been granted by states.

Though they did not deal outright with segregation, the Slaughterhouse Cases were later used to justify Jim Crow laws and the creation of separate facilities for blacks and whites. After all, schooling, housing, transportation, and the like were rights granted to citizens by states, not the federal government, and therefore states had the right to determine how those rights were interpreted.

Plessy v. Ferguson

In 1892 another case about discrimination came up. Liberal white and black attorneys protested a Louisiana law that prohibited blacks and whites from riding in the same railroad car. One man, Homer Plessy, challenged that law. By blood, Plessy was one-eighth black, as his great-grandmother had been black. Under Louisiana law, this made Plessy black as well—though he looked white—which meant that he could only ride on streetcars set aside for black travelers.

Supported by a group of political activists, Plessy refused to <u>comply</u> with the law. In 1892 he took a seat in a white streetcar compartment. Plessy declared that, as he was seven-eighths white, he deserved to sit there. When challenged, Plessy refused to move and was arrested. In court, Plessy's attorneys argued that forcing black people into separate cars branded them as inferior. Louisiana courts disagreed, claiming that separate facilities did not demean blacks, as long as those facilities were equal.

Plessy appealed the state's decision, and the case landed before the U.S. Supreme Court. In the landmark case ***Plessy v. Ferguson***, the Court sided with the lower court. It agreed that segregation was lawful as long as blacks and whites had access to equal facilities. This became known as the "separate but equal" doctrine.

KEY FACTS

3. How did the Supreme Court interpret the Fourteenth Amendment in the Slaughterhouse cases?

_____

_____

_____

_____

ACADEMIC VOCABULARY

4. Use the context, or surrounding words in the sentence, to write a definition of **comply**.

_____

_____

_____

The only justice who disagreed with the *Plessy* v. *Ferguson* decision was John Marshall Harlan. Harlan argued that the decision would only worsen racial tension.

HISTORY'S VOICES

"What can more certainly arouse hate, what more certainly create and perpetuate a feeling of distrust between these races, than state enactments, which, in fact, proceed on the grounds that colored citizens are so inferior and degraded that they cannot be allowed to sit in public coaches occupied by white citizens?"

—John Marshall Harlan, *Plessy* v. *Ferguson* dissent, 1896

✔ **Reading Check**

5. Describe What were the results of the Supreme Court decision in *Plessy* v. *Ferguson*?

_____

_____

_____

_____

As Harlan feared, most whites saw Jim Crow separatism as a way to keep blacks in the position of second-class citizens. The facilities available to African Americans were seldom equal to those used by whites. In the South, for instance, 80 percent of the money spent on education went to white schools, and little to black schools. ✔

Barriers to Voting

The voting rights of African Americans became a major issue of concern for white politicians. Some whites wanted to ensure that blacks had the right to vote—as long, that is, as they voted to support certain policies. Other conservative white politicians did not want black voters to have any say in the government at all.

Black Disenfranchisement

With the end of Reconstruction, white legislators across the South enacted new black codes, including unfair voting laws, to keep black people from voting. For example, they added literacy tests to their voting restrictions. Because many blacks had received no education, they could not pass the tests. In addition, to keep poor blacks from voting, states charged a fee to vote called a **poll tax**.

Because literacy tests and poll taxes also prevented poor and illiterate whites from voting, some states included a **grandfather clause** in their laws. Such clauses stated that if a person's grandfather had been eligible to vote, then that person could vote as well. These clauses prevented most blacks from voting because very few had grandfathers who had been able to vote. Other states used a so-called clause of understanding, which waived literacy requirements if a voter could explain the meaning of a phrase taken from the Constitution. Since the explanations were judged by white officials, such clauses were easily exploited to only allow whites to vote. Some southern states also banned blacks from taking part in primary elections. They argued that because the primaries were sponsored by political parties, not by the government, they were not covered under the Fourteenth and Fifteenth Amendments.

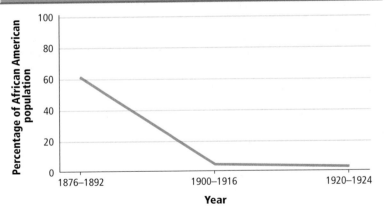

ESTIMATED AFRICAN AMERICAN VOTER TURNOUT IN THE SOUTH, 1876–1924

Source: *Who Voted? The Dynamics of Electoral Turnout, 1870–1980*

Skills FOCUS **INTERPRETING GRAPHS**

6. Between 1876 and 1924, what was the greatest percentage of black voter turnout, and when did it occur?

_____

As a result of these restrictions on voting, black voters had little say in who was elected to office in the South. This meant that within a few decades after the Civil War, many African American men were right back where they started—unable to vote and with little say in the government.

The Populist Movement

Among those who supported blacks' voting rights were members of the Populist movement. This movement had begun in the 1880s largely to support and protect farmers. In 1892 the Populists officially banded together as a new political party.

To gain support for their programs and candidates, some Populist leaders turned to black voters. In places where blacks had been blocked from voting, the Populists often worked on behalf of black citizens, trying to win back voting rights they had lost. Many black voters did indeed cast their ballots for Populist candidates. This, in turn, angered conservative white Democrats. Fearing the increasing political power of black voters, many conservative white leaders sought new ways to keep African American citizens from voting.

With support from the Populists, black voters elected a few black politicians to office in the South. Once such black office holder was George Henry White, who was elected to the U.S. House of Representatives from North Carolina. When elected, he was the only black representative in Congress. White took his position as a representative of his whole race very seriously. For example, in response to a proposed new tariff bill White spoke eloquently.

FACES OF HISTORY

Ida WELLS-BARNETT
c. 1862–1931

Ida Wells-Barnett, a Populist and fierce crusader against lynching in the United States, was born in Mississippi, the daughter of slaves.

After the Civil War, she was educated at a school for free blacks and later at Fisk University in Tennessee. While in Tennessee, she sued a railroad company that had physically removed her from a seat on a train after she refused to give up the seat to a white passenger. Although she lost the suit, Wells-Barnett was inspired to fight for civil rights.

After three of her friends were lynched in 1892, Wells-Barnett began writing editorials attacking the concept of lynching. Her writing angered many people, some of whom attacked and destroyed her newspaper office. She did not quit, however, and in fact became more prominent than ever. For the rest of her life, Wells-Barnett traveled the country, speaking on behalf of the rights of blacks and women.

7. Make Generalizations How did Ida Wells-Barnett embody the ideals of the Populist movement?

_____

_____

_____

HISTORY'S VOICES

"I am here to speak, and I do speak, as the sole representative on this floor of 9,000,000 of the population of these United States, 90 per cent of whom are laborers. Under this bill they are protected; they are given an opportunity to earn their living. Bread and butter are what we want, not fine-spun Democratic campaign theory. We have had enough of that."

—George Henry White, Speech to the House of Representatives, March 31, 1897 ✔

✔ Reading Check
8. Identify What were two common practices used to keep African Americans from voting?

_____

_____

_____

_____

Racial Violence on the Rise

Life under Jim Crow was often dangerous for African Americans. Jim Crow laws and customs were backed with threats of violence. Blacks who violated Jim Crow laws and customs, for example, by acting "too proud" or by trying to vote, risked their homes, their jobs, their own lives, and even the lives of their family members.

Lynching

Among the most common—and most horrible—forms of racial violence in the late 1800s were **lynchings**, or murders of individuals—usually by hanging—without a trial. In the mid-1800s, lynch mobs and the majority of their victims were white men. Most of the victims were accused of some sort kind of crime, like horse or cattle theft. After Reconstruction, lynchings of blacks became more common. By the late 1890s, it was estimated that one African American was lynched every other day.

In total, nearly 900 blacks were lynched between 1882 and 1892. Many had committed no crime, but had offended a white person. Despite extreme danger, black journalists, such as **Ida Wells-Barnett**, fought to expose the scale of white violence, end lynchings, and defend the memories of black victims.

Race Riots

Race riots also provoked fear among blacks. During the Jim Crow era the number of race riots increased dramatically. Most race riots occurred in cities when large numbers of white people took to the streets to punish blacks accused of crimes or misbehavior. Often, the rioting mob would target an entire black community.

The first major race riot of the Jim Crow era took place in 1898 in Wilmington, North Carolina. Wilmington was home to a number of black professionals. In fact, the majority of the city's population was black, which led to the election of a Republican government. In 1898 a group of white supremacists grabbed weapons and stormed through the streets. The mob killed at least 10 black citizens and forced the city's mayor to step down. Another major riot took place in Atlanta, Georgia. In 1906 rumors began to spread that black men in that city had been attacking white women. In response, thousands of angry whites formed a mob. During the violence that followed, about 27 black citizens were killed and 70 more were injured.

Though lynchings and race riots were more common in the South, both forms of violence were known in the North. Still, neither state nor federal agencies made any sort of concerted effort to stop the violence or punish those who committed it. ✔

✔ Reading Check

9. Analyze What was the cause of most lynchings and race riots?

---

go.hrw.com
Online Quiz
Keyword: SAAH HP7

Reviewing Ideas, Terms, and People

10. Define What were Jim Crow laws, and why were they passed?

11. Identify Cause and Effect What were the underlying causes of segregation and racial violence in the South after Reconstruction?

12. Elaborate How did the Supreme Court decision in *Plessy* v. *Ferguson* support racial inequality?

Analyzing Effects

The late 1800s and early 1900s saw a rise in discrimination toward African Americans, discrimination characterized in the figure of Jim Crow, a stereotypical and offensive portrayal of black people. Use the graphic organizer below to list the effects of Jim Crow attitudes on society of the time.

Attitudes

_____
_____
_____
_____
_____
_____
_____

Segregation

_____
_____
_____
_____
_____
_____
_____
_____

Voting

_____
_____
_____
_____
_____
_____
_____
_____

Violence

_____
_____
_____
_____
_____
_____
_____
_____
_____
_____

ASSESS YOUR KNOWLEDGE

1. Explain Why were southern leaders determined to keep blacks from voting?

_____

2. Predict What effects do you think the *Plessy* v. *Ferguson* case had on the fight for African American equality?

_____

Analyzing Visuals

The Jim Crow era was a time of terrible violence, with brutal crimes inflicted on people across the country. Driven by intolerance and fear, these crimes led hundreds of Americans, especially African Americans, to live in fear that they would soon be victims. The image below is a French artist's conception of the race riot in Atlanta, Georgia, in 1906. Examine the image carefully and then answer the questions on the next page.

1. **Analyze** Examine the image on the previous page. What is happening? Who appears to be committing a crime, and against whom is it committed?

_____

_____

2. **Interpret** Based on this image, what do you think the French opinion of racial violence in the South was? Why?

_____

_____

3. **Elaborate** Look at the image on the previous page again. Use this image and information from the section you have just read to write a paragraph describing relations between white and black Americans in the South in the early 1900s.

_____

_____

_____

_____

_____

_____

_____

_____

_____

_____

_____

_____

_____

_____

_____

_____

_____

_____

_____

_____

_____

_____

_____

The Progressive Movement

1. **TAKING NOTES** Use a graphic organizer like this one to take notes on the black self-reliance and protest movements and on black Progressive organizations. Use the **Reading Focus** questions on the next page to help guide your note taking.

2. As you read the section, underline or highlight definitions and descriptions of each of the **Key Terms and People** listed on the next page.

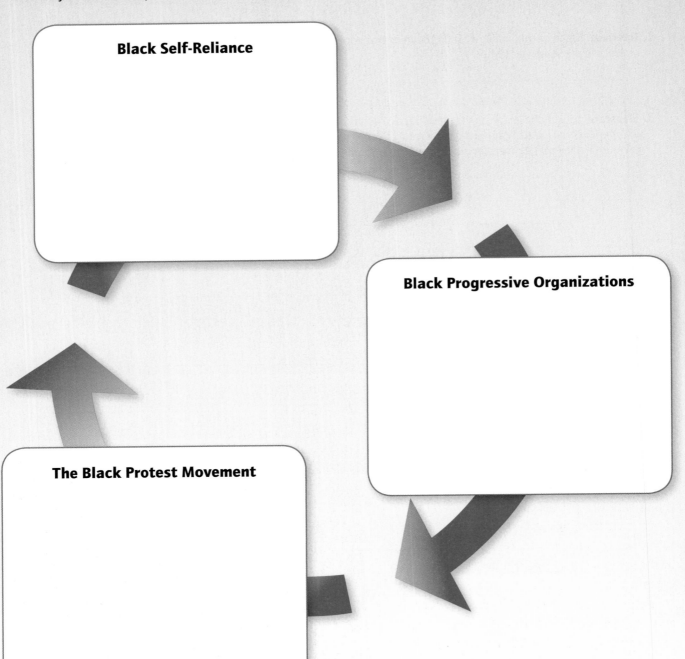

Black Self-Reliance

Black Progressive Organizations

The Black Protest Movement

The Progressive Movement

BEFORE YOU READ

MAIN IDEA

Countless individuals and groups worked tirelessly to improve the lives and situations of African Americans during the late 1800s and early 1900s.

READING FOCUS

- What was the Progressive movement, and what did Progressives want to achieve?
- Why did some black activists protest the Progressives?
- What goals were black Progressive organizations founded to achieve?

KEY TERMS AND PEOPLE

Progressive movement
Booker T. Washington
Atlanta Compromise
W. E. B. Du Bois
Niagara Movement
National Urban League
National Association
  for the Advancement
  of Colored People
  (NAACP)

BUILDING BACKGROUND

By 1900 African Americans had seen the denial of their political rights. Even worse, they had witnessed the destruction of basic human rights. But African Americans were not alone in noticing the hardships they faced. At the beginning of the century, reformers from all over the country—mostly white members of the middle class—banded together to fight injustice in society. ■

Black Self-Reliance

The reform movement of the late 1800s and early 1900s was called the **Progressive movement**. Among the key issues that Progressives challenged with their actions were terrible poverty, unfair business practices, the lack of rights for women, and racial discrimination.

The Progressives tried to change society by publishing articles and photographs that exposed evils in society. For example, Progressive journalists published photos of the horrible living conditions faced by the urban poor and wrote moving pieces about the unfair treatment of black Americans.

Among the Progressives who called for reform and improved conditions for African Americans were many black activists. The heart of their message was the idea of self-reliance, that blacks should not have to depend on anyone else to succeed. To attain self-reliance, they argued, black people needed the same educational and economic opportunities that whites enjoyed.

Education

Most people saw education as key to black self-reliance. These students attended the Tuskegee Institute.

Booker T. Washington thought that poor blacks needed to work together with whites in order to win equality and tolerance.

Black Progressives included both men and women. Among the most prominent supporters of African American rights were two black women, Ida Wells-Barnett and Mary Church Terrell. As you have already read, Wells-Barnett was an outspoken critic of lynching, but she also wrote passionately for increased rights for blacks and women. Likewise, Terrell traveled around the country calling for the same rights.

Booker T. Washington

The most vocal of all the black Progressives was an energetic young man named **Booker T. Washington**. Washington was a prominent educator and speaker.

Washington had been born a slave in 1856 in Virginia to a black mother and a white father. After the slaves were freed, he moved with his mother and stepfather to Malden, West Virginia, where he was put to work in a salt factory.

Young Washington's greatest dream was to learn to read and write. Eventually his mother saved enough to buy him a secondhand spelling book. Then a black school finally opened in the next town. Washington, still working a full day in the salt factory, walked to school at night. At the age of 16, he made his way to the Hampton Institute in Virginia. After graduation, Washington got a job as a teacher.

On September 18, 1895, Washington made a speech to the Cotton States and International Exposition in Atlanta. During his speech, Washington mesmerized his audience, black and white alike, with his vision of the future. He saw African Americans working diligently and humbly alongside whites to make money for the good of the South, and ultimately the country as a whole.

"Learn a trade" was Washington's enthusiastic advice to black citizens. He was convinced that once black people had taught themselves to be efficient workers, they would later be granted their rights as citizens. His philosophy came to be known as vocational education. In a statement known as the **Atlanta Compromise**, Washington declared that blacks and whites would have to work together to achieve racial equality. Tolerance was not something that could be forced on people.

HISTORY'S VOICES

"The wisest among my race understand that the agitation of questions of social equality is the extremist folly, and that progress in the enjoyment of all the privileges that will come to us must be the result of severe and constant struggle rather than of artificial forcing. No race that has anything to contribute to the markets of the world is long in any degree <u>ostracized</u>. It is important and right that all privileges of the law be ours, but it is vastly more important that we be prepared for the exercise of these privileges."

—Booker T. Washington, speech to the Cotton States and International Exposition, September 18, 1895

Many whites in the audience approved of Washington's message. At the close of Washington's speech, Georgia's former Governor Rufus Bullock publicly shook Washington's hand. Later, President Grover Cleveland wrote him a congratulatory letter.

But many people, primarily African Americans, were outraged. They thought he had done terrible harm to their fight for equal rights. According to his own writings years later, Washington acknowledged that he knew only too well the tightrope he walked that day. But he felt he had no choice. He was determined to help black people in the South keep from starving any way he could.

ACADEMIC VOCABULARY

1. Use the context, or surrounding words in the sentence, to write a definition of **ostracized**.

_____

_____

_____

Tuskegee Institute

Throughout his life, Washington felt that one way he could help black people succeed was by teaching them. That was why he accepted the chance to open the Tuskegee Institute in 1881.

When Washington arrived at Tuskegee, Alabama, he found that the new school was nothing more than a rundown old plantation and a barn. He had to borrow money from a friend to open the place on July 4, 1881. Undaunted, he and his 30 students cleared land, cut timber, and, over the next fifteen years, built all the school facilities themselves. By his death in 1915, the institute had an annual endowment in excess of $2 million, 1,400 students (including undergraduates from Africa and the Caribbean), 2,300 acres of land under student cultivation, and 66 school buildings.

The Tuskegee Institute had been founded to train teachers and to teach poor blacks trades so they could succeed. In this, the school was successful. Eventually, its focus changed from vocational training to a more traditional college curriculum and began offering college degrees. Now called Tuskegee University, the school today has an enrollment of more than 3,000.

Black Education Movement

Inspired by Washington and wanting to help black students receive a quality education, many benefactors from around the country began to give money to support black schools. Rich business owners from the North, including George Peabody, who had established museums at Harvard and Yale, gave more than $2 million to open public schools in the South. Likewise John D. Rockefeller, the oil tycoon, established schools in the South that were open to all students, black or white.

Other philanthropists paid to open schools that were only open to black students. One such donor was Anna Jeanes, the daughter of a Philadelphia merchant. In the early 1900s she donated $1 million to black schools in the South. Julius Rosenwald likewise established a fund dedicated to building and improving rural black schools. Jeanes and Rosenwald were not alone in their generosity; many wealthy individuals worked to help black students gain new opportunities and improve their lives. ✔

The Black Protest Movement

As you have read, not all African Americans agreed with Washington about the best way to gain equality and opportunity. Many were not happy with Washington's acceptance of discrimination in exchange for economic opportunity. They felt that it was necessary for black Americans to fight bitterly against discrimination and segregation, to protest the status quo and work for a positive change in society.

W. E. B. Du Bois

One of the leaders of the Black Protest movement was **W. E. B. Du Bois**, a brilliant young professor of economics at Atlanta University. Du Bois feared that if African Americans gave up their struggle and just waited to gain full equality, as Washington suggested, they would be headed back to slavery. After all, what good were a house and farm if they could be looted by whites at any time? What use was a loving family if one's mother or father could be lynched any day?

W. E. B. Du Bois believed that the core of educated and talented African Americans could bring about changes for all.

✔ **Reading Check**
2. Explain What role did education play in Booker T. Washington's vision of African American success?

_____

_____

_____

_____

AFRICAN AMERICANS AT THE TURN OF THE CENTURY **177**

3. Use the graphic organizer below to compare and contrast the views of Booker T. Washington and W. E. B. Du Bois.

KEY FACTS

Similarities

Differences

✔ **Reading Check**

4. Identify What was the goal of the Niagara Movement?

_____

_____

_____

_____

Du Bois's point of view, like Washington's, was shaped in no small part by his upbringing. Du Bois was born to free parents in 1868 in Great Barrington, Massachusetts. At an early age, Du Bois showed such signs of brilliance that he won a scholarship to Fisk University. Eventually, he went on to receive a master's degree and a Ph.D. from Harvard University, the first black student ever to do so.

Early in his career, Du Bois gained fame as a scholar. His first major work, *The Suppression of the African Slave Trade to the United States of America, 1638–1870*, established his reputation in the field of history. In 1899 he published *The Philadelphia Negro*, the first in-depth sociological examination of African Americans. And in 1903, greatly disappointed by Booker T. Washington, Du Bois penned *The Souls of Black Folk*. In it, he pointed out how wasteful it was for whites to keep blacks down, instead of allowing them to be productive members of society.

HISTORY'S VOICES

"Actively we have woven ourselves [into] this nation—we have fought their battles, shared their sorrow, mingled our blood with theirs, and generation after generation have pleaded with a headstrong, careless people to despise not Justice, Mercy, and Truth, lest the nation be smitten with a curse. Our song, our toil, our cheer and warning have been given to this nation in blood brotherhood. Are not these gifts worth the giving? Is not this work and striving? Would America have been America without her Negro People?"

—W. E. B. Du Bois, *The Souls of Black Folk*, 1903

Like Booker T. Washington, Du Bois wanted better lives for African Americans. But the two men differed on how to bring those lives about. Washington focused on getting the black working class what it needed to survive. Du Bois, on the other hand, believed that the black middle class was the only group with the resources, both material and mental, to pull the working class out of poverty. He dubbed those young black people with the most potential for leadership the Talented Tenth. He thought that the skills and talents of the Tenth could pull all black citizens up from hardship.

The Niagara Movement

Du Bois, unlike some intellectuals, did not simply sit around and talk about the problems in society. He set out to change them. He was determined that black Americans have three things: the right to vote, civic equality, and the education of youth according to their ability.

On July 11, 1905, Du Bois and 29 other determined young black intellectuals met at Fort Erie, Ontario, in Canada, just across the Niagara River from Buffalo, New York. Du Bois's original plan had been to hold the meeting in Buffalo, but the hotel at which he wanted to stay refused to rent rooms to African Americans.

Du Bois and his young intellectuals were determined to create an organization which would aggressively push for full civil rights for all African Americans. The group incorporated itself as the **Niagara Movement** and, to underscore their determination, met the following year at the site of John Brown's failed slave revolt, Harpers Ferry.

The next year, in 1907, the Niagara Movement met in the old abolitionist stronghold of Faneuil Hall in Boston. In 1908, after a shocked nation heard the news of a major race riot in the city of Springfield, Illinois, many young liberal whites decided to join with their black counterparts to take up the civil rights banner. ✔

Niagara Movement's Declaration of Principles

After the first meeting of the Niagara Movement in 1905, its members published a list of the basic principles for which they stood. The list addressed topics as diverse as education, military service, religion, and work. Three articles from the declaration are printed below.

"Protest: We refuse to allow the impression to remain that the Negro-American assents to inferiority, is submissive under oppression and apologetic before insults. Through helplessness we may submit, but the voice of protest of ten million Americans must never cease to assail the ears of their fellows, so long as America is unjust.

Color-Line: Any discrimination based simply on race or color is barbarous, we care not how hallowed it be by custom, expediency or prejudice.

Differences made on account of ignorance, immorality, or disease are legitimate methods of fighting evil, and against them we have no word of protest; but discriminations based simply and solely on physical peculiarities, place of birth, color of skin, are relics of that unreasoning human savagery of which the world is and ought to be thoroughly ashamed.

"Jim Crow" Cars: We protest against the "Jim Crow" car, since its effect is and must be to make us pay first-class fare for third-class accommodations, render us open to insults and discomfort and to crucify wantonly our manhood, womanhood and self-respect."

Skills FOCUS **ANALYZING PRIMARY SOURCES**

5. Draw Conclusions Why do you think the members of the Niagara Movement wanted a clear statement of their principles?

_____

_____

_____

Progressive Organizations

Booker T. Washington and W. E. B. Du Bois recognized the importance of African Americans banding together. Both men helped found large organizations in efforts to improve African American lives. But Washington and Du Bois were not alone. In the late 1800s and early 1900s, dozens of national organizations dedicated to bettering the African American experience were created.

Economic Organizations

Booker T. Washington organized the first successful national black business association of the early twentieth century. At the group's 1900 meeting, he urged the more than 400 delegates who came from 34 states to start as many businesses as possible. Indeed, by 1907 the National Negro Business League had 320 branches.

Between 1906 and 1910, three different organizations were formed in New York City to press for economic advancement for African Americans. By 1911 the three organizations decided to centralize their efforts. The new organization was called the National League on Urban Conditions Among Negroes. It still exists today as, simply, the **National Urban League**.

Since its creation, the National Urban League has devoted itself to helping African Americans in cities make progress in all walks of life. Over the years, it has assisted in everything from helping newly arrived southern blacks adjust to the North, to working to develop training programs to help people progress beyond unskilled jobs.

HISTORICAL DOCUMENT
Go online to read a historical document from the Niagara Movement.

go.hrw.com
Chapter Activity
Keyword: SAAH CH7

NAACP's Campaign Against Lynching

On July 28, 1917, an estimated 10,000 men, women, and children marched in New York City as part of a "silent parade" organized by the NAACP to protest racial violence.

The NAACP

On February 12, 1909, the one hundredth anniversary of Abraham Lincoln's birth, the **National Association for the Advancement of Colored People (NAACP)** was born and dedicated to advancing the position of black Americans. W. E. B. Du Bois and the Niagara Movement joined with white reformers to found the NAACP. Among the white founders were Mary White Ovington, a New York social worker, and Oswald Garrison Villard, grandson of abolitionist William Lloyd Garrison.

In May 1910 Du Bois created a magazine in which the leaders of the new organization could share their views. The magazine was aptly entitled *The Crisis*. By 1920 *The Crisis* was selling as many as 100,000 copies a month. Du Bois explained the purpose of the magazine in its first editorial.

HISTORY'S VOICES

"The object of this publication is to set forth those facts and arguments which show the danger of race prejudice, particularly as manifested today toward colored people. It takes its name from the fact that the editors believe that this is a critical time in the history of the advancement of men . . . Finally, its editorial page will stand for the rights of men, irrespective of color or race, for the highest ideals of American democracy, and for reasonable but earnest and persistent attempts to gain these rights and realize these ideals."

—W. E. B. Du Bois, Editorial in *The Crisis*, 1910

White and black attorneys soon joined the NAACP and began waging the battle against injustice—a battle that continues today. They won three landmark cases in the NAACP's first 15 years of existence:

• *Guinn* v. *United States* (1915), in which the Supreme Court declared the "grandfather clauses" in Oklahoma to be illegal.

• *Buchanan* v. *Warley* (1917), in which a Louisville, Kentucky, law that had forced black people to live only in certain sections of town was declared unconstitutional.

• *Moore* v. *Dempsey* (1923), in which 5 black men convicted of murder in Arkansas who protested that their rights had been violated due to public pressure on the judge and jury were given a new trial.

These cases became precedents for attorneys in other parts of the country to argue the rights of African Americans.

Labor and Political Organizations

The National Urban League and the NAACP attracted black professionals and activists as members. Most black Americans, however, were farmers and workers who lived quiet lives, relying on their own enterprise to get ahead. To help get what they needed to thrive, they formed unions, business organizations, and banks.

In spite of efforts to integrate unions, racial separation remained the order of the day. In 1866 the National Labor Union was formed. The NLU made some overtures toward black workers about joining, but old attitudes were hard to change. The union ended up accepting black members only in separate local chapters. A black labor leader named Isaac Myers then organized the Colored National Labor Union in 1869. But by 1872 the CNLU had virtually disappeared.

Two major unions were formed in the 1880s. The first, the Knights of Labor, actually agreed to welcome black workers into their ranks. Some 95,000 black people paid their money and joined the union—one-seventh of the union's total membership. But after a series of unpopular strikes, membership dropped sharply, and by the 1890s the union had declined. The other new union, the American Federation of Labor (AFL), claimed to welcome black members as well. However, few African Americans were actually allowed to join, though many did join unions affiliated with the AFL. It was not until years later, after the emergence of another large union, the Congress of Industrial Organizations (CIO), that black people were able to join a major integrated union.

As part of their desire to have more say in their lives, black Americans also began to rethink their political affiliations. Most black voters still sided with the Republican Party, the party of Lincoln that had put an end to slavery. Some black citizens, however, believed that the Republicans had begun to take their support for granted. After all, the Democrats made no effort to gain black support, so Republican candidates could generally assume they would win the black vote.

By the early 1900s changing political attitudes led some black voters to abandon the Republicans for the Democrats. Blacks in many northern cities learned that they could get concessions from local Democratic organizations in exchange for their support. As a result, black Democrats formed a group called the National Independent Political League to encourage their fellow African Americans to consider voting for Democratic candidates. ✔

INFO TO KNOW
In addition to African American workers, the Knights of Labor also welcomed women and unskilled workers. It excluded, among others, bankers, gamblers, and liquor sellers.

✔ **Reading Check**
6. Identify Cause What was the purpose of the creation of organizations such as the NAACP and the National Urban League?

_____

_____

_____

_____

SECTION 2 ASSESSMENT

Reviewing Ideas, Terms, and People

7. Identify What organizations were founded to help improve the lives of black Americans in the late 1800s and early 1900s?

_____

_____

8. Compare and Contrast How were the goals of Booker T. Washington and W. E. B. Du Bois similar? How were their opinions different?

_____

_____

9. Evaluate Do you think the Progressive movement helped improve the lives of African Americans? Why or why not?

_____

_____

Writing a Letter to the Editor

The Progressive Era was a time of strong opinions and vocal complaints. Both Progressives and their opponents spoke out proudly against what they saw as the wrongs of society. In today's society, one common method to voice these types of complaints is to write a letter to the editor of a newspaper. Such a letter allows you to express your views and share them with a potentially large readership, who may be swayed by your words. Imagine you were a member of society during the Progressive Era. Write a letter than could have been published in a local newspaper, expressing your opinions about a wrong you see in American society. Be sure to include specific examples in your letter so your readers know what your complaint is.

Designing a Flyer

During the Progressive Era, dozens of organizations were created to promote the equality and rights of African Americans. Some of these organizations were huge, like the NAACP. Others were much smaller neighborhood groups. Whatever their size, these organizations campaigned tirelessly to get their messages across. In the space below, design a flyer that such an organization might have used to spread its ideas through a community. Make sure that your flyer uses vivid words and/or images and makes clear what the organization's position is.

ASSESS YOUR KNOWLEDGE

1. Identify What was the goal of Progressive organizations?

_____

_____

2. Describe From what parts of society did the Progressives draw support?

_____

_____

As You Read

African Americans Move West

1. **TAKING NOTES** Use a graphic organizer like this one to take notes on the move west, blacks in the Old West, and the buffalo soldiers. Use the **Reading Focus** questions on the next page to help guide your note taking.

2. As you read the section, underline or highlight definitions and descriptions of each of the **Key Terms and People** listed on the next page.

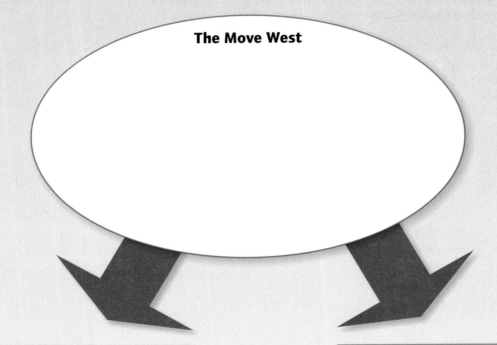

The Move West

Blacks in the Old West

Buffalo Soldiers

BEFORE YOU READ

MAIN IDEA

Beginning in the 1870s thousands of African Americans moved west to escape discrimination and to find new opportunities.

READING FOCUS

- Why did many black southerners move west in the 1870s and 1880s?
- What were some achievements of black cowhands in the Old West?
- Who were the Buffalo soldiers, and for what were they known?

KEY TERMS AND PEOPLE

Benjamin "Pap" Singleton
Exodus of 1879
Exodusters
buffalo soldiers
Spanish-American War

BUILDING BACKGROUND

In the mid-1800s Congress passed two bills that created new opportunities for African Americans. Called the Homestead Act and the Morrill Act, these bills opened up the American West for settlement. As a result of these two bills, people from all over the country began to move westward in search of new lives. Among those who moved were thousands of African Americans, mostly from the South, who saw the West as a land of new possibilities. ■

The Move West

"The whole South—every single state in the South—had got into the hands of the very men that held us as slaves . . . We said there was no hope for us and we better go." So reported one black southerner to a committee of Congress investigating why so many African Americans were leaving the South in the late 1870s. To escape the widespread discrimination they faced in the South, many headed north. Others went west.

The Exodusters

In 1879 more than 15,000 black southerners packed up their belongings and headed west to Kansas, the home of John Brown and thus a symbol of black freedom. Led by a former slave named **Benjamin "Pap" Singleton**, this mass migration was known as the **Exodus of 1879**. Those who took part in the exodus were called **Exodusters**.

Singleton's plan was to create independent black communities in the West. While he believed that blacks in the South would eventually gain freedom and equality, he didn't think it would occur during his lifetime. As a result, he was determined to find a place where he could enjoy his life.

HISTORY'S VOICES

"Well, my people, for the want of land—we needed land for our children—and their disadvantages—that caused my heart to grieve and sorrow; pity for my race, sir, that was coming down, instead of going up—that caused me to go to work for them."

—Benjamin "Pap" Singleton, Testimony before Congress, April 17, 1880

HISTORICAL DOCUMENT
Go online to read a historical document from the **Exodus of 1879**.

go.hrw.com
Chapter Activity
Keyword: SAAH CH7

Skills FOCUS ANALYZING PRIMARY SOURCES

1. Why does Singleton say he wanted to try to improve the live of black Americans?

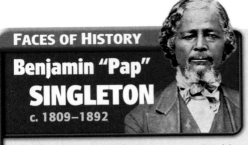

Benjamin "Pap" SINGLETON
c. 1809–1892

After escaping from slavery before the Civil War, Benjamin Singleton, affectionately known as "Old Pap," settled in Detroit, Michigan. After the war, he returned to his native Tennessee as a free man. There he worked to obtain affordable housing for poor black citizens, but local white residents refused to sell Singleton productive land. Unable to get land in Tennessee, he set out for Kansas, where he bought land that he later used to establish his first colony.

Although his second colony was a success, Singleton eventually became discouraged by the prejudice he faced from white settlers in Kansas. Finally concluding that African Americans would never be allowed to succeed in the United States, he joined a movement to help blacks relocate to Africa. His plan never got off the ground, and Singleton retired from his life of political activism.

2. Make Generalizations What was Pap Singleton's major goal in life?

_____

_____

_____

✔ **Reading Check**
3. Explain Why did many African Americans move west in the late 1800s?

_____

_____

_____

_____

Black Communities in the West

Once they arrived in Kansas, African Americans created their own communities. Singleton himself had founded two settlements even before the exodus, both called Singleton. Many of the people who moved to the Singleton colonies had little money and few possessions when they arrived. The first colony soon failed, after rich deposits of lead were discovered in the area and real estate prices skyrocketed. In the second colony, however, most people were able to find work and, within a few years, the community was thriving.

With the arrival of the Exodusters, several more African American communities were established. All in all, about 20 black towns were founded in the 1870s and 1880s. The largest of these towns—and the most successful—was Nicodemus, Kansas. Founded in 1877 by six black settlers and two white settlers, the town was home to about 500 people by 1880. However, crop failures and hostility from nearby towns took their toll on Nicodemus, and the town was down to only 200 people by 1910. By that time, it was the only all-black town in all of Kansas. ✔

Blacks in the Old West

When most people today think of the Old West, they picture cowhands on horseback driving huge herds of cattle over long distances. This image has its basis in truth. But did you know that large numbers of the cowhands on those cattle drives were black? Historians estimate that black cowboys represented one out of every four of this country's cowhands around the turn of the century. Because they lived solitary lives that, for the most part, went undocumented, most of the Old West's black cowboys remain nameless, but information about a few has survived.

Nat Love was one of the best-known black cowboys of the 1880s. Born a slave in Tennessee in 1854, he ventured west in 1869. Through sheer perseverance, Love taught himself to ride wild horses and shoot a Colt .45 pistol with deadly accuracy. In Deadwood, Dakota Territory, Love entered a horse roping competition which earned him a reputation as the champion rider in the West.

The inventor of the modern rodeo sport of steer wrestling was another African American cowboy, Bill Pickett. Born in southern Texas around 1870, Pickett was skilled in roping and in handling cattle for wagon trains. He was most famous, however, for subduing bulls using a trick he learned by watching herd dogs. To stop an angry bull, Pickett would actually sink his teeth into the animal's tender upper lip! In later years, he travelled internationally to demonstrate this amazing trick.

Black women also made names for themselves in the Old West. For example, Mary Fields single-handedly ran a stagecoach line through the often treacherous Montana Territory. Six feet tall and strong as many a man, for more than eight years Fields was responsible for getting the mail through the Montana wilderness, sometimes having to tote the mail herself when her wagon broke down in winter weather. Artist Leonora Russell was another noted black westerner. ✔

Buffalo Soldiers

Not all of the African Americans who moved to the West had done so looking for economic opportunities. Some were there as part of the U.S. Army. The region was home to four regiments of African American troops known as the **buffalo soldiers**.

The buffalo soldiers had their origin in the years after the Civil War. An 1866 law allowed the army for the first time to form regiments of black soldiers in peacetime, though these regiments had to be led by white men. Under the new law, the army formed two cavalry and four infantry regiments, later consolidated into two.

Fighting in the West

Based in Kansas, Montana, and Utah, the buffalo soldiers served mostly in the West. They spent their days escorting stagecoaches and trains and hunting down cattle rustlers, but their main job was protecting settlers in the area from hostile Native Americans and bandits. In fact, the name buffalo soldiers was given to the troops by the Native Americans they fought, though no one is quite sure what the name meant.

The buffalo soldiers were widely respected for their courage in battle and their strict discipline. Between 1870 and 1890, no fewer than 19 members of the group were honored with the Medal of Honor, the highest award the army gives for bravery. The soldiers were well behaved; drunken behavior, which was a major problem for most army units, was seldom seen in their ranks. In addition, few members of the buffalo soldiers ever deserted or committed crimes. ✔

Reading Check
4. Draw Conclusions Why do you think the life of a cowboy appealed to many young black men?

_____

_____

_____

_____

_____

_____

INFO TO KNOW
Some people think the name *buffalo soldiers* was given in response to buffalo-hide cloaks worn by the soldiers. Others think it referred to the soldiers' dark hair. Still others think it was because of their fierceness as opponents.

Buffalo soldiers
Four regiments of African American soldiers stationed in the West bore the name buffalo soldiers. The regiments were distinguished for their successful record in battle.

Skills FOCUS INTERPRETING INFORMATION

5. For what qualities were the buffalo soldiers known?

_____

_____

_____

_____

THE GRANGER COLLECTION, NEW YORK

The Spanish-American War

In the **Spanish-American War** of 1898, the buffalo soldiers further distinguished themselves. The war between the United States and Spain started in Cuba, a Spanish colony in which American businesses had invested. For years, Spain's rulers had put down Cuban revolutionaries who had sought independence for the island. In 1898, the sinking of the U.S. battleship *Maine* in Havana Harbor, in which 22 black sailors were among the 260 men who lost their lives, brought a harsh response from the United States. Assuming that Spain was responsible for the explosion aboard the *Maine*, Congress quickly passed a declaration of war. Among the first army regiments sent to Cuba to fight in the war were the buffalo soldiers. In addition, thousands more African Americans volunteered to fight for the liberation of the Cuban people.

The Spanish-American War lasted just over twelve weeks. Nevertheless, the 10th Cavalry, one regiment of the buffalo soldiers, was honored for its efforts at the Battle of Las Guásimas. In addition, the 9th and 10th Cavalry regiments provided crucial backup for Teddy Roosevelt and his troops called the Rough Riders at the decisive Battle of San Juan Hill.

All in all, five brave black soldiers, ranking from private to sergeant major, received Medals of Honor during the Spanish-American War. One of them was Private George H. Wanton. On June 30, 1898, along with several other fighting units, the 10th Cavalry attacked rebel strongholds in Tayabacoa, Cuba. Private Wanton watched many of his fellow fighting men fall. Finally, after several attempts failed to save the wounded men, Private Wanton volunteered for the job. Under heavy enemy fire, he brought many wounded soldiers to safety.

Despite continuing prejudice and discrimination, black soldiers of the late 1800s worked hard and fought well, so much so that they won the admiration of many of their white counterparts. Said one white southerner, "I've changed my opinion of the colored folks, for of all the men I saw fighting, there were none to beat the Tenth Cavalry, and the colored infantry at Santiago, and I don't mind saying so." ✔

✔ Reading Check

6. Summarize What were the major achievements of the buffalo soldiers?

_____

_____

_____

_____

_____

SECTION 3 ASSESSMENT

go.hrw.com
Online Quiz
Keyword: SAAH HP7

Reviewing Ideas, Terms, and People

7. Describe What roles did black settlers and soldiers play in the West?

_____

_____

8. Explain Why did many Exodusters want to establish black communities in Kansas?

_____

_____

9. Develop How do you think the buffalo soldiers helped change some people's views of African Americans?

_____

_____

Interpreting Graphs

Understand the Skill

Graphs are an excellent tool for analyzing statistical or numerical data. By presenting the data visually, graphs allow us to easily interpret patterns and spot changes over time. Historians use many different types of graphs in their work—bar graphs, line graphs, pie graphs, and so on. Each type is best suited to presenting a different type of information.

Learn the Skill

Use the notes and strategies to the right to learn how to best read and interpret the data found in graphs and to choose the right type of graph for data.

Step 1 Line graphs and bar graphs are used to show how data changes over time. *According to the line graph on this page, did the black population of the Northeast increase or decrease between 1860 and 1920?*

_____

_____

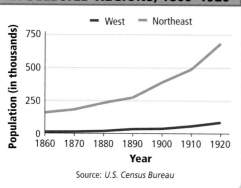

GROWTH OF BLACK POPULATION IN SELECTED REGIONS, 1860–1920

West — Northeast

Population (in thousands): 750, 500, 250, 0

Year: 1860 1870 1880 1890 1900 1910 1920

Source: *U.S. Census Bureau*

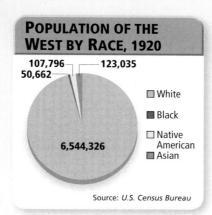

POPULATION OF THE WEST BY RACE, 1920

107,796 — 123,035
50,662
6,544,326

White
Black
Native American
Asian

Source: *U.S. Census Bureau*

Step 2 Pie graphs are best at showing percentages, the relative size of elements within a single unit. *According to the pie graph, what percentage of the West's population was black in 1920?*

_____

_____

APPLY THE SKILL

1. **Interpret** Look at the graphs above. Did the black population of the west increase more between 1860 and 1870 or between 1910 and 1920? Which graph did you use to find this information?

   _____

   _____

2. **Analyze** Which group made up the largest part of the West's population in 1910? Which graph did you use to find this information?

   _____

   _____

3. **Make Judgments** If you wanted to create a graph that showed how many black farmers moved west each year from 1870 to 1885, what kind of graph would you use? Why?

   _____

   _____

Black Achievements After Reconstruction

1. **TAKING NOTES** Use a graphic organizer like this one to take notes on black colleges and universities, writers and poets, businesses, and scientists and explorers. Use the **Reading Focus** questions on the next page to help guide your note taking.

2. As you read the section, underline or highlight definitions and descriptions of each of the **Key Terms and People** listed on the next page.

Colleges and Universities

Writers and Poets

Black-owned Businesses

Scientists and Explorers

Black Achievements After Reconstruction

BEFORE YOU READ

MAIN IDEA

In the early twentieth century, black Americans made great advances in education, literature, business, and science, among other fields.

READING FOCUS

- Where were black colleges and universities founded?
- In what types of writing did black writers and poets excel?
- What were some prominent black-owned businesses of the early twentieth century?
- What achievements could black scientists and explorers claim?

KEY TERMS AND PEOPLE

historically black colleges and universities (HBCUs)
Paul Laurence Dunbar
Madame C. J. Walker
Elijah McCoy
George Washington Carver
Matthew Henson

BUILDING BACKGROUND

Despite the hardships of segregation and discrimination, black Americans of the early twentieth century made great achievements. Some of the things they accomplished helped shape life in the United States for at least a century. ◼

Colleges and Universities

One of the greatest advances for African Americans after Reconstruction was the founding of new colleges and universities for them to attend. In 1850, just a few years before the Civil War, there had only been one college available to black students, the Institute of Colored Youth, later renamed Cheyney University. Over the course of the next century, the number of colleges that enrolled mostly black students had grown to more than 100.

During Reconstruction, a number of colleges for black students had been established in the South. Howard University in Washington, D.C., and Morehouse College in Atlanta, for example, were both begun through private grants in 1867. By 1877 other black colleges had popped up throughout the country, but mostly in the South.

Unlike many Reconstruction programs, the establishment of black colleges did not stop in 1877. You have already read about the creation of the Tuskegee Institute by Booker T. Washington in 1881. The establishment of private universities like Tuskegee, Howard, and Morehouse continued, but so did the creation of public schools like Florida A&M University. In addition, some colleges, like Spelman in Atlanta, were created specifically to educate black women.

Historically Black Colleges and Universities (HBCUs)

Many of the colleges founded to teach black students in the years that followed Reconstruction have been designated by Congress as **historically black colleges and universities (HBCUs)**. By definition, an HBCU is an accredited school founded before 1964 "whose principal mission was, and is, the education of black Americans."

LARGEST HBCUs BY ENROLLMENT

1	Florida A&M University Tallahassee, Florida
2	Howard University Washington, D.C.
3	Southern University Baton Rouge, Louisiana
4	Tennessee State University Nashville, Tennessee
5	St. Philip's College San Antonio, Texas

Source: U.S. Department of Education, *Historically Black Colleges and Universities, 1976 to 2001*

AFRICAN AMERICANS AT THE TURN OF THE CENTURY **191**

Since their founding, HBCUs have played a vital role in educating African Americans and shaping black culture. In 1999, for example, 24 percent—nearly a quarter—of all bachelor's degrees obtained by African Americans were issued by HBCUs, which make up only 3 percent of all colleges and universities in the United States. In addition, a significant percentage of prominent African American political, economic, and cultural leaders received their educations at HBCUs.

Black Fraternities and Sororities

College life was not always easy for black students. Attempting to obtain degrees in the Jim Crow era, many faced discrimination at every turn. Even on campuses home to mostly black students, it was not possible to escape discrimination completely. In order to succeed in college, many students felt that they needed some sort of support system.

To provide this support for themselves and each other, black students at colleges across the country banded together in fraternities and sororities. The first fraternity for African American men, Alpha Phi Alpha, was founded in 1906 by seven students at Cornell University in Ithaca, New York. The only black men enrolled at mostly white Cornell, they wanted the fraternity to be an organization that could provide moral support, housing, and study aid for themselves and black students who followed. The fraternity was a success. Chapters soon opened at other colleges across the country, and similar organizations were founded for black men and women. ✔

✔ Reading Check

1. Infer Why was the creation of black fraternities and sororities significant to African Americans?

_____

_____

_____

_____

_____

PRIMARY SOURCES

The Poetry of Paul Laurence Dunbar

Many of Paul Laurence Dunbar's most famous poems deal with sorrow, both his own sorrow and the collective sorrow of African Americans who had endured hardship. This collective sorrow is the theme of one of Dunbar's most popular poems, "Sympathy," first published in 1899.

"I know why the caged bird sings, ah me,
When his wing is bruised and his bosom sore,—
When he beats his bars and would be free;
It is not a carol of joy or glee,
But a prayer that he sends from his heart's deep core,
But a plea, that upward to Heaven he flings—
I know why the caged bird sings!"

Skills FOCUS ANALYZING PRIMARY SOURCES

2. Interpret What does Dunbar mean by "I know why the caged bird sings"?

_____

_____

_____

Writers and Poets

Education was not the only field in which African Americans made great strides after the turn of the century. Black authors penned memoirs, stories, novels, and poems that both entertained and challenged their readers.

Memoirs

A popular writer of the period was Elizabeth Keckley. Keckley was not a professional writer. Nevertheless, her account of her years as dressmaker and confidante to Abraham Lincoln's wife, Mary Todd Lincoln, aroused a great stir when it appeared in 1868. The book was called *Behind the Scenes, or, Thirty Years a Slave, and Four Years in the White House*. In addition to describing Mrs. Lincoln's struggles after her husband's assassination, Keckley's memoirs outlined the challenges she herself faced as a young black woman trying to get ahead. She also included details about private life in the White House, as in this passage about President Lincoln.

"He reached forth one of his long arms, and took a small Bible from a stand near the head of the sofa, opened the pages of the holy book, and soon was absorbed in reading them. A quarter of an hour passed, and on glancing at the sofa the face of the president seemed more cheerful. The dejected look was gone, and the <u>countenance</u> was lighted up with new resolution and hope."

—Elizabeth Keckley, *Behind the Scenes,* 1868

Stories and Novels

One of the most prolific black short story writers and novelists of the day was Charles Waddell Chesnutt. He used his own experiences to write a series of short stories for the *Atlantic Monthly* magazine. He later published three novels: *The House Behind the Cedars* (1900), *The Marrow of Tradition* (1901), and *The Colonel's Dream* (1905).

Another prolific African American novelist of the early twentieth century was Sutton E. Griggs. A Baptist minister, Griggs wrote novels like *The Hindered Hand* that he hoped would inspire cooperation between races. However, his works were never widely read, largely because Griggs published and distributed them himself.

Poetry

Paul Laurence Dunbar was the first widely recognized African American poet. While working as an elevator operator, he published his first collection of poems at his own expense. After an address he gave at his high school reunion drew the attention of several white editors, Dunbar found his early poems widely published in America and England. His first book of poetry, *Oak and Ivy*, appeared in 1893. His next big break came when his book *Majors and Minors* got a full-page review in *Harper's Weekly* in 1895. He spent the next years writing furiously and lecturing as the darling of the liberal literary set.

Dunbar's wife, Alice Moore Dunbar Nelson, was also a talented poet. Like her husband, Dunbar Nelson wrote many poems that dealt with the challenges faced by African Americans and women. One of her most famous poems, for example, expresses a woman's frustration with what was seen as a typical woman's role.

"I sit and sew—a useless task it seems,
My hands grown tired, my head weighed down with dreams—
The panoply of war, the martial tred of men,
Grim-faced, stern-eyed, gazing beyond the ken
Of lesser souls, whose eyes have not seen Death,
Nor learned to hold their lives but as a breath—
But—I must sit and sew."

—Alice Moore Dunbar Nelson, "I Sit and Sew," 1920

Frances Ellen Watkins Harper was another well-known black female poet. Along with her fierce dedication to antislavery and human rights activities, she devoted herself to the temperance movement, an effort to ban the consumption of alcohol in the United States. Her *Poems on Miscellaneous Subjects* was published in 1854. ✔

ACADEMIC VOCABULARY

3. Use the context, or surrounding words in the sentence, to write a definition of the word **countenance**.

_____

_____

_____

_____

✔ **Reading Check**

4. Make Generalizations
What were some common themes in African American literature in the early 1900s?

_____

_____

_____

_____

Cosmetics tycoon Madame C. J. Walker was the first female millionaire in the United States.

Black-Owned Businesses

By the turn of the century, in the North as well as in the South, a small percentage of African Americans had managed to build sizeable businesses. Among the fields in which black business owners achieved great success were the press, manufacturing, banking, and insurance.

The Black Press

Though black-owned newspapers had been rare in the 1800s, by 1900 three daily black newspapers and 150 black weekly newspapers were published in 26 states. However, none of them was as influential as the *Guardian*, first published in Boston in 1901 by activists Monroe Trotter and George Forbes. The *Guardian's* pages were open to young militants who argued for full and immediate civil and political rights for all African Americans, and the paper soon became the star of the black press.

In 1905 another very influential paper, the *Chicago Defender,* made its debut as a four-page weekly. Its publisher, Robert S. Abbott, wanted to print news for the average black person, rather than just for intellectuals. Still published today, the paper worked to defend the rights of African American people by publishing accounts of discrimination and calling for social equality.

Manufacturing

African Americans also made great advances in manufacturing that affected the lives of millions. For example, Jan Ernst Matzeliger, a black Massachusetts shoemaker, was a pioneer in shoemaking technology. In the late 1800s Matzeliger invented a machine to automate the shoemaking process. Thanks to his invention, high-quality footwear became more affordable and thus available to the general public.

Sarah Breedlove Walker, better known as **Madame C. J. Walker**, was the first black woman to become a millionaire. Walker invented a special hair softener, a straightening comb, and a variety of cosmetics marketed to both black and white women. Before she was 40, Walker's business had grown into a million-dollar cosmetic manufacturing company.

Banking and Insurance

Maggie Lena Walker, an African American, was the first American woman to become president of a bank. A native of Virginia, Walker was a member of the Independent Order of St. Luke, a group dedicated to caring for the sick and the elderly and to promoting self-reliance among African Americans. As secretary-treasurer of the order in 1899, she helped it grow strong enough to establish its own bank, the Consolidated Bank and Trust Company. Walker was named chairman of the board and had a long and successful tenure. As a successful businesswoman mindful of the needs of less fortunate women, Walker also helped establish The Council of Colored Women, as well as serving on the board of the National Urban League. By the time she died in 1934, she had established a legacy for young black women to follow.

In 1898 Dr. Aaron McDuffie Moore and John Merrick formed the first successful black insurance company, North Carolina Mutual and Provident Association. In 1905 Alonzo F. Herndon started the Atlanta Life Insurance company. ✔

INFO TO KNOW
In addition to being a successful business owner, Madame C. J. Walker was a generous humanitarian. She donated large sums of money to churches and the poor, and even founded a school for girls in West Africa.

✔**Reading Check**
5. Identify In what fields did African American business owners make significant contributions to society?

_____
_____
_____
_____

Scientists and Explorers

Hungry for knowledge, black Americans made great contributions to science. Clever black scientists created hundreds of new devices to make life easier for themselves and others. Skillful black doctors pioneered new procedures to save lives, while intrepid explorers set out in search of places never before visited by any human.

Black Inventors

In the years after the Civil War blacks patented hundreds of inventions. In fact, according to the United States Patent Office, by 1913 several hundred African Americans had taken out patents for inventions of their own, and hundreds more had contributed to the work of others. For example, a black engineer and drafter named Lewis Latimer worked with both Alexander Graham Bell on the development of the telephone and Thomas Edison on the development of the light bulb. Clearly, African Americans were prominent in the drive for invention that had taken hold of America in the late nineteenth century.

In 1872 **Elijah McCoy** devised a machine that automatically lubricated trains and factory equipment. McCoy's invention, a special cup that carefully dripped oil into machines while they were still moving, meant that train engines and steam boilers could be oiled without interruption, thus saving valuable time. This proved to be a tremendous boon to industry. Historians cite McCoy's invention as the inspiration for the phrase "the real McCoy." All in all, McCoy took out at least 72 patents with the U.S. Patent Office on the various devices he designed during his lifetime.

The work of another black inventor greatly improved the safety of the nation's railroads. Granville T. Woods invented an automatic air brake and a method of sending telegraph signals between trains, both of which significantly reduced collisions. He was also part of the team which invented the third rail, still in use today, which carries the electrical current used to power many modern trains.

Science and Medicine

One of the most brilliant scientists of the early 1900s was **George Washington Carver**, a researcher at the Tuskegee Institute. Carver was interested in agriculture, particularly in the potential uses of three crops—peanuts, soybeans, and sweet potatoes. He encouraged southern farmers to grow these crops on their land for two reasons. First, growing and selling these crops would help end the South's dependence on cotton. Second, growing peanuts and beans, both from the family of plants known as legumes, would restore nutrients to soil drained by years of cotton growing. As part of his plan to prove the usefulness of these crops, Carver developed more than 400 products that could be made from them. Some 300 of these products—including forms of cheese, milk, coffee, flour, ink, plastic, soap, and cosmetics—were made from peanuts. More than 100 more came from sweet potatoes, including vinegar, molasses, rubber, ink, and postage stamp glue.

KEY FACTS

6. Underline the new products created by George Washington Carver.

George Washington Carver, a researcher at the Tuskegee Institute, discovered hundreds of new uses for peanuts, soybeans, and sweet potatoes.

Explorer Matthew Henson was one of the first people to reach the North Pole.

Carver's diligence and determination brought him to the attention of people around the world. Presidents Calvin Coolidge and Franklin Roosevelt visited Carver's lab, and he was offered jobs by inventor Thomas Edison and Josef Stalin, both of whom he refused. Before he died, George Washington Carver donated his fortune to establish the Carver Research Center at Tuskegee to continue his research.

Black scientists were also making history in medicine during the period. In 1893 a black doctor, Daniel Hale Williams, performed the first successful heart operation. President Grover Cleveland later appointed Williams head of Freedmen's Hospital in Washington, D.C. Earlier, Williams had started the nation's first unsegregated hospital, Provident Hospital in Chicago, as well as a school for black nurses.

Exploration

Did you know that one of the first men to reach the North Pole was black? His name was **Matthew Henson**, and he reached the pole on April 6, 1909 with Robert E. Peary. Henson had spent years as chief guide to Peary, having learned to speak the language of the Inuits of northern Canada and Greenland.

After several attempts, Henson and Peary finally reached the North Pole in 1909. As Henson later wrote, their journey had been very long and difficult.

✔ **Reading Check**

7. Draw Conclusions How did advances by black scientists and explorers improve society?

_____

_____

_____

_____

_____

HISTORY'S VOICES

"We had been travelling eighteen to twenty hours out of every twenty-four. Man, that was killing work! . . . We used to travel by night and sleep in the warmest part of the day. I was ahead most of the time with two of the Eskimos."

—Matthew Henson, Interview with Lowell Thomas, 1939

In all, Henson devoted 22 years of his life to working with Peary in exploration. In 1944 Congress awarded him a medal for his service in the field of science. ✔

---

go.hrw.com
Online Quiz
Keyword: SAAH HP7

SECTION 4 ASSESSMENT

Reviewing Ideas, Terms, and People

Choose the letter of the term at right that best matches each description.

_____ **8.** Researcher who discovered new uses for peanuts and other crops

_____ **9.** Cosmetics tycoon and first black female millionaire

_____ **10.** Poet whose works deal largely with sorrow

_____ **11.** Memoir writer who worked for the Lincolns

_____ **12.** Polar explorer

_____ **13.** Inventor whose name became a popular saying

_____ **14.** First female bank president in the United States

_____ **15.** Poet who protested against traditional women's duties

_____ **16.** Doctor who performed the first successful heart operation

_____ **17.** Famous black novelist of the early 1920s

_____ **18.** Publisher of the *Defender* newspaper

a. Robert S. Abbott

b. George Washington Carver

c. Charles Waddell Chesnutt

d. Paul Laurence Dunbar

e. Matthew Henson

f. Elizabeth Keckley

g. Elijah McCoy

h. Alice Moore Dunbar Nelson

i. Madame C. J. Walker

j. Maggie Lena Walker

k. Daniel Hale Williams

Creating a Time Capsule

Time capsules are collections of items carefully chosen to represent particular eras or cultures. Suppose you have been asked to create a time capsule to represent African American culture and achievements during the early twentieth century. What items would you include? Choose five items. In each of the boxes below, draw the item. Then on the lines below the boxes, identify your choice and explain why it should be included in the time capsule.

African American Time Capsule: The Early Twentieth Century

Item: _____

Why Included: _____

_____

_____

Item: _____

Why Included: _____

_____

_____

Item: _____

Why Included: _____

_____

_____

Item: _____

Why Included: _____

_____

_____

Item: _____

Why Included: _____

_____

_____

ASSESS YOUR KNOWLEDGE

1. **Elaborate** If you could meet any African American from the early twentieth century for a conversation, who would it be? Why? What would you discuss?

_____

_____

Online Resources

Visit **go.hrw.com** for review and enrichment activities related to this chapter.

go.hrw.com
Chapter Home Page
Keyword: SAAH CH7

Quiz and Review

ONLINE QUIZ
Take a practice quiz for each section in this chapter.

CHAPTER REVIEW
Use the online Chapter Review to help you prepare for the chapter test.

Activities

HISTORICAL DOCUMENTS
Read and explore key documents that shaped African American history.

VIRTUAL FIELD TRIP
Take a virtual field trip to experience key sites from African American history.

VOICES OF HISTORY
Experience African American history and culture through recordings of key people and documents.

Partner

CONNECTING TO OUR PAST
Examine artifacts from **Howard University's Moorland-Spingarn Research Center** that bring to life the study of African American history.

The Separation of the Races

CHAPTER SUMMARY

SECTION 1   The Jim Crow Era

- In the late 1800s and early 1900s, African Americans lost many rights that they had once enjoyed.
- Supreme Court cases in the late 1800s established a legal precedent for segregation.
- State and local officials sought ways to keep African American citizens from voting, especially in the South.
- Lynchings and race riots increased during the Jim Crow era.

SECTION 2   The Progressive Movement

- Booker T. Washington encouraged black workers to seek education and try to win acceptance from whites through hard work.
- W. E. B. DuBois and the Niagara Movement argued that talented African Americans could improve their own lots in life.
- African Americans founded groups like the National Urban League, the NAACP, and labor unions to increase and protect their rights.

SECTION 3   African Americans Move West

- Thousands of Exodusters moved to Kansas to escape discrimination and make new lives.
- African Americans played many roles in the settling of the West.
- The buffalo soldiers were all-black regiments of the U.S. Army that won recognition for their service, bravery, and discipline.

SECTION 4   Black Achievements After Reconstruction

- Many universities were founded to fill the educational needs of black students after Reconstruction.
- Black writers and poets expressed their views of discrimination.
- Black business owners achieved success and fame in many fields.
- Black scientists and inventors improved the lives of people of all races.

A NEW CENTURY
and New
Opportunities

In the early 1900s Harlem became the center of black politics and culture. Venues such as the Cotton Club served as gathering places for African American leaders, artists, and thinkers.

EXPRESSING YOUR OPINION

In the 1920s the Harlem district of New York City was a center of African American artistic expression and innovation. Write a short paragraph describing something you wrote or created that served as a form of self-expression.

The World War I Years

1. **TAKING NOTES** Use a graphic organizer like this one to take notes on imperialism in Africa, World War I, and African American participation in World War I. Use the **Reading Focus** questions on the next page to help guide your note taking.

2. As you read the section, underline or highlight definitions and descriptions of each of the **Key Terms and People** listed on the next page.

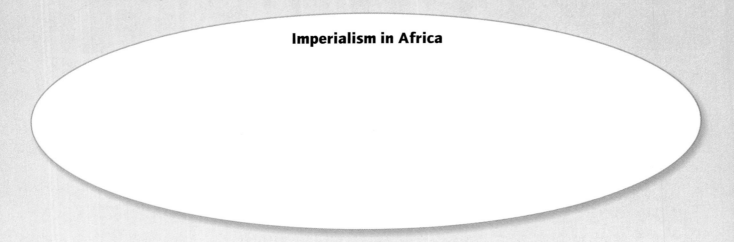

Imperialism in Africa

World War I

African Americans in World War I

The World War I Years

BEFORE YOU READ

MAIN IDEA

In the early 1900s imperialism in Africa and World War I affected people of African descent worldwide.

READING FOCUS

• How did people of African descent react to European imperialism in Africa in the late 1800s?

• How did World War I begin?

• What roles did African Americans play in World War I?

KEY TERMS AND PEOPLE

imperialism
Pan-Africanism
neutral
Eugene Jacques Bullard
369th Infantry

BUILDING BACKGROUND

As Americans were busy settling new territories in the West in the late 1800s, powerful European countries were expanding as well. Many countries rushed to establish colonies around the globe. This race for colonies would eventually play a part in the outbreak of one of the most devastating wars in history—World War I. ■

Imperialism in Africa

For hundreds of years Western nations such as Spain, Great Britain, and France had controlled colonies around the world. This practice, known as **imperialism**, gave powerful nations control of the governments and people of weaker nations. Ruling countries benefited tremendously from imperialism, as colonies supplied valuable raw materials—such as metals, cotton, and timber—for European factories. Because people in the colonies also purchased manufactured goods made in Europe, colonies also served as a market for European goods.

In the late 1800s and early 1900s, a new wave of imperialism led Western nations to seek out even more colonies. Africa became one of their chief targets. Eager to gain access to rich natural resources, European nations raced to acquire colonies throughout Africa. For example, Belgium's King Leopold II established the Congo Free State in Central Africa. Under his rule, companies exploited the people of the region, who were forced to collect resources, such as rubber and palm oil, for export.

Other nations colonized Africa as well. France and Great Britain controlled much of the continent, including French West Africa and British colonies in Egypt, Nigeria, and southern Africa. Germany, Italy, Portugal, and Spain also held African colonies. By 1914 only two African nations—Liberia and Ethiopia—remained independent.

Angry at the takeover of Africa, opponents of imperialism joined in protest. In 1900 black leaders held the first Pan-African Conference in London. At the conference, people of African descent from the United States, the Caribbean, Europe, and Africa gathered to address issues facing blacks, including racism and imperialism. W. E. B. Du Bois, one of the organizers of the conference, soon took up the idea of Pan-Africanism. **Pan-Africanism** is the idea that people of African heritage from around the world should work together to achieve freedom and equality. Pan-Africanism would serve as a powerful influence for future black activists. ✔

ACADEMIC VOCABULARY

1. Use the context, or surrounding words of the sentence, to write a definition of **exploited**.

_____

_____

✔ Reading Check

2. Identify Cause and Effect What conditions led to the creation of the Pan-African movement?

_____

_____

_____

World War I Begins

Imperialism eventually led to conflict. As European nations challenged each other for dominance around the world, a tangled system of political alliances and rivalries resulted in increasing tensions. In 1914 those tensions exploded into a war that came to involve all of the world's Western powers.

The United States Enters the War

World War I began in 1914 when the empire of Austria-Hungary declared war on Serbia, a small nation in southeastern Europe. Within weeks, the war in Europe grew more intense as a network of treaties and alliances pulled almost every country in Europe into the fighting. On one side were the Allied Powers of France, Great Britain, Italy, and Russia. Opposing them were the Central Powers of Austria-Hungary, Bulgaria, Germany, and the Ottoman Empire.

For three years the United States remained **neutral**, or chose not to take sides. Despite sympathies for the Allies, most Americans did not want to get involved in a bloody war overseas. Eventually, however, German attacks on U.S. merchant ships and the deaths of American civilians led to increasing outrage. Finally, on April 6, 1917, the United States joined the war on the side of the Allied Powers.

The Call for Troops

The U.S. declaration of war had a dramatic effect. Across the country, thousands of men poured into recruiting stations to volunteer for military service. Among those eager to serve their country were African American men. However, as at the beginning of the Civil War, most black volunteers were turned away.

African Americans themselves were divided over the issue of serving in World War I. Some black leaders wondered why African Americans, who were denied full rights at home, should be expected to die overseas to defend freedom for others.

INFO TO KNOW
During World War I Emmett J. Scott, former secretary to Booker T. Washington, served as special assistant to the U.S. secretary of war. His role was to consult on matters concerning African American military personnel such as morale, discrimination, and other issues.

African American Troops Prepare for War

Members of the New York National Guard's all-black 15th Regiment parade through the streets of New York City in 1916. The regiment soon became part of the United States Army.

Other black leaders, such as Robert S. Abbott, publisher of the *Chicago Defender*, and W. E. B. Du Bois, supported the war effort. Du Bois urged African Americans to volunteer for military service in spite of the discrimination they faced at home.

HISTORY'S VOICES

"Let us not hesitate. Let us, while the war lasts, forget our special grievances and close our ranks shoulder to shoulder with our own white fellow citizens and the allied nations that are fighting for democracy. We make no ordinary sacrifice, but we make it gladly and willingly with our eyes lifted to the hills."

—W. E. B. Du Bois, *The Crisis*, July 1918

In May 1917 Congress passed the Selective Service Act, which required men of all races between the ages of 21 and 30 to register to be drafted into the armed forces. African American men were now allowed to serve their country in what was being called "the war to end all wars." Black troops, however, would face discrimination in the armed forces much like the discrimination they faced in civilian life. ✔

African Americans in World War I

Many African Americans lent their support to the war effort with the hope that, in time, their sacrifices would improve their political and social status at home. They believed that, as Du Bois argued, "Out of the war will rise . . . an American Negro, with the right to vote, and the right to work and the right to live without insult."

Blacks Serve in the War

As soon as the United States entered the war, the African American troops already in the armed forces were called to duty. Some 10,000 black troops were already serving in the U.S. Army. Another 10,000 black troops served in state National Guard units.

By the end of the war, some 370,000 African Americans had served in the military. They were segregated into all-black divisions commanded by white officers and trained in separate camps away from white troops. Some white army officers and southern politicians objected to black troops receiving training with weapons, worrying that African Americans who could use guns might pose a threat after the war ended. As a result, few African Americans were trained for combat. Only 40,000 saw action on the battlefield. Most black troops were limited to non-combat roles, performing behind the front lines in support roles such as drivers and laborers.

One African American who saw combat was **Eugene Jacques Bullard**, the world's first black fighter pilot. Born in Georgia, Bullard lived in Europe as a young man and joined the French Foreign Legion at the outbreak of war in 1914. Bullard eventually served as a pilot in the French air force, where he flew on some 20 missions. Despite his distinguished service record, the U.S. Army Air Service rejected him when he sought to fly for his native country—black pilots were not welcome.

Black Army Officers

At the time the United States entered World War I in 1917, there were only three African American commissioned officers in the entire U.S. military. As hundreds of thousands of black troops joined the military, black leaders protested the military's discrimination against black officers.

✔**Reading Check**
3. Analyze How did African American attitudes toward serving in World War I differ?

▲ **African Americans served bravely in World War I despite discrimination.**

Harlem Hell Fighters
Nicknamed the "Harlem Hell Fighters" by the Germans, the 369th spent more time in continuous combat than any other American unit in World War I.

Black leaders argued that the government should not deny "the right of our best [Negro] men to lead troops of their race into battle." In May 1917 the U.S. Army finally relented and established a training camp in Iowa for black officers. By the end of the war, this camp commissioned more than 600 black officers, although most were assigned to command black labor battalions serving behind the front lines.

Black Troops in Combat

Only two African American units saw combat overseas during the war—the 92nd and the 93rd infantry divisions. The 92nd arrived on the front lines in France in August 1918. Many of the unit's soldiers were assigned to build roads, but some members of the 92nd saw heavy fighting against German troops. Many received the Croix de Guerre, the French government's award for military bravery.

The 93rd Division saw even more action on the battlefield. The 93rd's most famous unit, the **369th Infantry**, also known as the Harlem Hell Fighters, was the first all-black U.S. combat unit to be sent overseas during the war. This unit had an impressive war record.

The 369th was originally formed as the 15th Regiment of the New York National Guard. After becoming part of the U.S. Army, the 369th shipped out for Europe in December 1917. When the unit arrived in France, U.S. and British army leaders refused to allow black men to fight alongside their troops. Members of the 369th were given manual labor duties rather than serving on the front lines. In the spring of 1918, the unit was assigned to serve with the French army. Already accustomed to fighting with black soldiers from France's African colonies, French troops did not object to integrating their forces.

When the members of the 369th were finally given the opportunity to fight, they did so bravely. The unit spent a total of 191 days fighting on the front lines. Near the war's end, the 369th became the first Allied unit to fight through enemy lines to reach the Rhine River in Germany. But their service came at a high cost—almost 1,500 Harlem Hell Fighters died in combat. By the end of the war, 171 members of the 369th had received the Legion of Honor, France's highest award.

KEY FACTS

4. Use the graphic organizer below to identify the achievements of African Americans during World War I.

Black Officers

369th Infantry

Black Nurses

The two most highly honored African American soldiers in World War I were both members of the 369th—Henry Johnson and Needham Roberts. In May 1918 the two men, both privates, were guarding an isolated obsevation post when a German patrol of some 24 soldiers attacked their post. Johnson and Roberts fought off the attack despite severe wounds and a lack of ammunition. Both were later honored by the French government with the Croix de Guerre for their bravery.

Black Nurses

Several years before the outbreak of World War I, a group of black women organized the National Association of Colored Nurses. They were determined that African American nurses gain proper recognition for their work and be accepted as professionals.

The U.S. Army did not call upon the services of black nurses until just before the end of the war. In September 1918, a devastating worldwide flu epidemic broke out. In desperate need of nurses, the army sent 18 black nurses to hospitals in Ohio and Illinois. Because of the shortage of medical personnel, these nurses tended both black and white patients and earned high praise from the hospital administrators with whom they worked.

After the War

World War I ended in November 1918. When African American veterans returned home, they received little recognition for their sacrifices during the war. The 369th Infantry was honored in a parade for war veterans in New York City, but other areas largely ignored blacks' contributions to the war. Many African American veterans refused to accept these insults quietly. In St. Joseph, Missouri, for example, black veterans would not agree to march at the back of a victory parade, believing that this discrimination went against the democratic ideals for which they had fought. After helping to fight for freedom overseas, many believed that they had earned the right for greater freedoms at home.

▲ **A wounded veteran of the 369th Infantry marches in a 1919 victory parade in New York City.**

✔ **Reading Check**

5. Summarize What roles did African Americans play in the course of World War I?

_____

_____

_____

_____

SECTION **1** **ASSESSMENT**

go.hrw.com
Online Quiz
Keyword: SAAH HP8

Reviewing Ideas, Terms, and People

6. Describe What did leaders at the 1900 Pan-African Conference hope to achieve?

_____

_____

7. Summarize What were the achievements of the 369th Infantry?

_____

_____

8. Support a Position Do you think that African Americans should have supported the war effort even though they were denied full citizenship at home? Why?

_____

_____

Developing Arguments For and Against

After the United States entered World War I, controversy swept through the African American community. Black Americans were divided over the issue of whether or not they should support the war effort. In the space provided, develop two lists of arguments—one in favor of the U.S. war effort and one against it. Be sure to provide specific reasons for each of your arguments.

For	Against
_____	_____
_____	_____
_____	_____
_____	_____
_____	_____
_____	_____
_____	_____
_____	_____
_____	_____
_____	_____
_____	_____
_____	_____
_____	_____
_____	_____

ASSESS YOUR KNOWLEDGE

1. **Make Generalizations** What techniques might supporters of each side have used to effectively make their arguments to the public?

   _____

   _____

2. **Evaluate** Which argument would you have found most convincing? Why?

   _____

   _____

Writing a Persuasive Speech

Imagine that the year is 1917 and your community is divided over whether or not African Americans should serve in World War I. Leaders have called for a meeting to debate the issue, and they have asked you to deliver a speech expressing your point of view on the war effort. First, determine what point you will argue, then use the note cards below to plan your speech. Your speech should include an introduction, key points in support of your stance, and a conclusion. Be sure to address opposing points of view, use persuasive language, and call for support for your stance.

1

2

3

4

5

6

Changes in Black Society

1. **TAKING NOTES** Use a graphic organizer like this one to take notes on the Great Migration, the Red Summer of 1919, and the rise of black nationalism. Use the **Reading Focus** questions on the next page to help guide your note taking.

2. As you read the section, underline or highlight definitions and descriptions of each of the **Key Terms and People** listed on the next page.

The Great Migration

Red Summer of 1919

The Rise of Black Nationalism

Changes in Black Society

BEFORE YOU READ

MAIN IDEA

The migration of African Americans to the North and the birth of black nationalism resulted in changes for black society.

READING FOCUS

- What led thousands of southern blacks to migrate to the North?
- What events led up to the Red Summer of 1919?
- How did black nationalism and social gains lead to changes in the United States?

KEY TERMS AND PEOPLE

Great Migration
blues
Red Summer
Marcus Garvey
black nationalism

BUILDING BACKGROUND

As the United States entered World War I in Europe, changes were taking place at home. Tired of years of discrimination and poverty in the South, thousands of African Americans began moving to the North in record numbers. This migration of people led to many changes in the United States. ◾

The Great Migration

In the years following World War I, thousands of African Americans left the South in search of better opportunities. As black Americans moved North in record numbers, they had a powerful effect on the economy and culture of the North.

African Americans Move North

With the beginning of U.S. involvement in World War I, the demand for war equipment and supplies surged. Northern factories were booming. However, hundreds of thousands of white men were leaving their jobs to fight in the war, and the flow of new immigrants was sharply limited. As a result, many northern businesses looked to the South for workers to fill the new jobs. African Americans from the South moved north in search of better lives.

Southern blacks were eager to move north for a variety of reasons. Chief among those reasons was their desire for better economic opportunities. For many black Americans, the promise of good jobs pulled them to the North. Northern cities like Chicago, Pittsburgh, and Detroit held the promise of steady jobs and good pay. African American newspapers such as the *Chicago Defender* also played a key role in encouraging black southerners to move north. They frequently published articles and letters from readers describing the advantages of life in the North.

At the same time, life in the South was pushing many African Americans to leave. Years of discrimination, violence, and disenfranchisement pushed southern blacks to move to the North. Black southerners hoped to escape the segregation, poverty, and racial violence they often faced in the South, where many had little choice but to work as sharecroppers or in other low-paying jobs. Economic troubles also pushed many African Americans to leave the South. During the war, farmers and laborers suffered from damaged crops, poor harvests, and a sharp drop in wages.

KEY FACTS

1. Identify the push and pull factors that led to the Great Migration.

Push and Pull Factors
Push
Pull

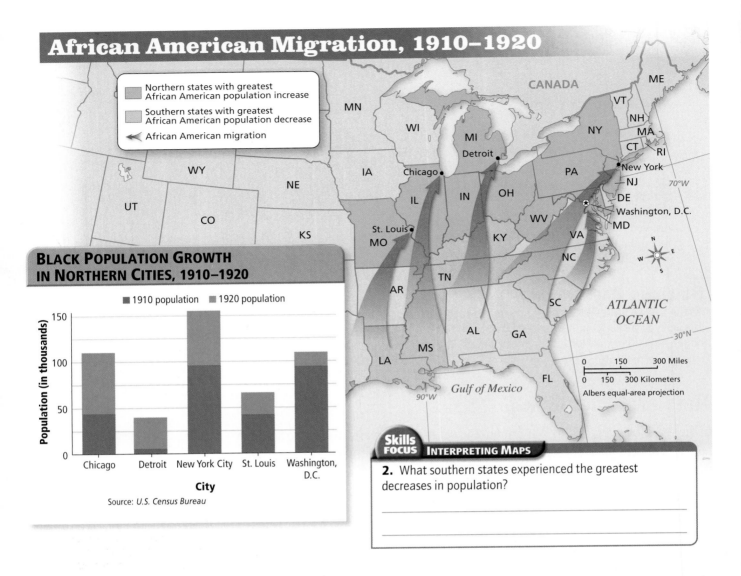

African American Migration, 1910–1920

Legend:
- Northern states with greatest African American population increase
- Southern states with greatest African American population decrease
- African American migration

BLACK POPULATION GROWTH IN NORTHERN CITIES, 1910–1920

- 1910 population
- 1920 population

Population (in thousands) vs. City (Chicago, Detroit, New York City, St. Louis, Washington, D.C.)

Source: *U.S. Census Bureau*

SKILLS FOCUS INTERPRETING MAPS

2. What southern states experienced the greatest decreases in population?

_____

_____

Reading Check

3. Summarize How did the Great Migration lead to changes in the North?

_____

_____

_____

_____

_____

INFO TO KNOW
Originally an African American musical style, the blues later influenced the growth of jazz, soul, rock, and other types of music.

Effects of the Great Migration

This combination of factors resulted in an unprecedented movement of African Americans to the North. From 1910 to 1920 an estimated 330,000 black southerners moved north. This enormous movement of people became known as the **Great Migration**.

The Great Migration brought many changes to the United States. A key result was the rapid growth of many northern cities. Black Americans moved in record numbers to industrial cities in the North. Cities such as St. Louis, Chicago, and Detroit experienced tremendous growth. In Detroit, for example, the black population grew from less than 6,000 in 1910 to more than 40,000 in 1920.

This massive movement of people also influenced northern culture. As African Americans settled in northern cities, they brought southern customs with them. For example, black musicians from the South introduced the blues to many northern cities. Born in the Mississippi Delta and nurtured in the city of New Orleans, the **blues** is a form of music that combines instrumental rhythms and expressive vocals to convey deep emotions, especially sadness or love. Southern blues musicians such as W. C. Handy introduced the blues to northern cities, where it became an important part of the cultural scene in places such as Chicago and St. Louis. ✔

Red Summer of 1919

While many African Americans did find the new opportunities they sought in the North during World War I, they could not escape the racism and discrimination they were fleeing. In fact, racial tension in the United States grew even more severe after the end of World War I, reaching a peak in the summer and fall of 1919 when race riots broke out across the country. Black writer and civil rights activist James Weldon Johnson later named these months of bloody racial violence the **Red Summer**.

Racial Tensions Rise

Racial tensions rose after World War I for several reasons. Many of the factory jobs created in the North during the war were in war-related industries. When the war ended, demand for these products fell suddenly and many workers lost their jobs. As American soldiers returned home and tried to find work, they found themselves competing with African Americans for factory jobs that had grown scarce. The resulting competition between black and white workers for suddenly limited jobs led to a sharp increase in tensions in many cities.

At the same time, African American expectations had begun to change. Many blacks believed that they had earned greater freedom at home after helping fight for freedom overseas during the war. Some whites were determined to resist any changes brought about by this new attitude, and as a result many African Americans grew increasingly frustrated and angry.

Violence Breaks Out

In the South, some whites began to punish anyone who encouraged black people to move north or otherwise assert their independence. The cities of Birmingham, Alabama, and Jacksonville, Florida, levied heavy fees—as much as $1,000—against agents sent to recruit black workers. In some other places, laws made it illegal to sell or distribute black publications such as the *Chicago Defender* or the NAACP's magazine *The Crisis*, both of which encouraged black southerners to seek better lives in the North. In this tense atmosphere, whites attacked blacks in a number of race riots that broke out in the summer of 1919. All together 25 such riots were recorded in cities such as Charleston, South Carolina; Washington, D.C.; Knoxville, Tennessee; Longview, Texas; Elaine, Arkansas; Omaha, Nebraska; and Chicago, Illinois.

The direct offshoot of simmering racial tension, most of these race riots were triggered by what could have been harmless events. For example, the Chicago riot began when a black man out for a swim in Lake Michigan drifted into a section of the water reserved for white swimmers. A white crowd gathered on the beach yelled and threw stones at the black swimmer, who drowned. Though his body—recovered a few days later—showed no signs of being hit by stones, the discovery came too late to stop the 13-day race riot that began when angry African Americans—who believed the man had been murdered—took to the streets.

Some other riots had more intentional beginnings. The riots in Knoxville and Omaha both began when mobs tried to protect African Americans accused of attacking white citizens. The Longview riot was begun by a group of white men who went to the black section of town to punish a schoolteacher who had written a condemnation of recent lynchings for the *Chicago Defender*. ✔

ACADEMIC VOCABULARY

5. Use the context, or surrounding words in the sentence, to write a definition of **levied**.

✔ **Reading Check**

6. Identify What led to the outbreak of race riots in 1919?

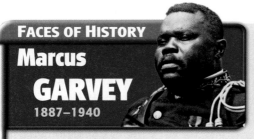

Marcus GARVEY
1887–1940

In the 1920s Marcus Garvey was arguably one of the most famous black men in the world. He was born the youngest of 11 children in St. Ann's Bay, Jamaica. At the age of 14, Garvey left school to work as printer's apprentice. He traveled throughout Central and South America, not returning to Jamaica until 1914. Determined to end the terrible exploitation of black workers that he witnessed in Jamaica and throughout his travels, he founded the Universal Negro Improvement Association (UNIA).

In 1916, at Booker T. Washington's invitation, Garvey moved to the United States. Garvey, a gifted orator, toured the nation lecturing on racial pride, unity, and self-reliance. He attracted supporters by the thousands. In time, he settled in Harlem and organized a chapter of the UNIA there. By 1919, the UNIA claimed more than a million members and over 30 chapters worldwide. It was the largest organized mass movement of African Americans in U.S. history.

7. Make Generalizations How did Garvey's travels as a young man shape his later beliefs?

_____

_____

_____

_____

HISTORICAL DOCUMENT
Go online to read a historical document from Marcus Garvey.

go.hrw.com
Chapter Activity
Keyword: SAAH CH8

Black Nationalism and Social Gains

The outbreak of violence during the Red Summer did little to deter black Americans from their efforts to work for change. In fact, African Americans, both individually and collectively, increased their efforts to end discrimination and win equal rights.

Marcus Garvey

One of the leaders of the fight against discrimination was **Marcus Garvey**, founder of the black nationalism movement. **Black nationalism** was the belief that black people around the world should create their own societies, separate and distinct from white societies. This was in direct contrast to the beliefs of Booker T. Washington, W. E. B. Du Bois, and the NAACP, who shared the goal of breaking down barriers between blacks and whites. Garvey feared that this goal threatened the racial purity of African Americans and that it discouraged the feelings of unity and strength he tried to foster in black communities worldwide.

In 1914, while still living in his native Jamaica, Garvey founded an organization known as the Universal Negro Improvement Association, or UNIA. The UNIA's ultimate goal was to encourage Africans from around the world to return to Africa and build a new nation there. Its slogan was "Back to Africa."

Believing that blacks would be respected and self-reliant only when they were strong economically, Garvey sought to build an independent black economy in the United States by founding businesses, including a shipping line, grocery stores, a restaurant, and a publishing house. Garvey also believed that blacks should take pride in their African heritage. His newspaper, *The Negro World*, boasted of the accomplishments of people of African descent and of the glories of African culture. Garvey spoke of a "new Negro" who would be proud of being black.

> **HISTORY'S VOICES**
>
> "The new Negro, through the Universal Negro Improvement Association, is speaking for himself. The new Negro is saying to the world: 'There can be no abiding peace until we are fully emancipated.'"
>
> —Marcus Garvey, Speech in Washington D.C., 1921

Garvey's message of self-reliance and black pride proved enormously popular, and the UNIA soon claimed some 2 million members. At the same time, however, Garvey made many enemies.

In 1922 Garvey and other members of the UNIA were indicted for mail fraud. Supporters of the UNIA felt that the charges were politically motivated; nevertheless, Garvey was convicted and imprisoned in 1925. He was released from jail in 1927, but was forced to leave the country. Without his leadership the UNIA soon declined.

New Labor Unions

Though African Americans had first begun to join labor unions in the late 1800s, the 1910s and 1920s saw a renewed effort by blacks to form organizations that would fight for better jobs and wages. In the 1910s, for example, Benjamin Fletcher organized several unions along the Eastern Seaboard under the auspices of the Industrial Workers of the World (IWW). Fletcher's unions included most of Philadelphia's black dockworkers. In 1925 the formation of the Brotherhood of Sleeping Car Porters under the leadership of A. Philip Randolph marked the creation of the country's first truly successful black labor union. But it remained dangerous for African Americans to try to unionize. Fletcher was arrested and sentenced to 10 years in jail for his unionizing efforts. The 1919 race riot in Elaine, Arkansas, had begun when whites attacked black farmers who were discussing their plans to join a union.

Victories Against Lynching

The NAACP's fight against lynching that began in the first decade of the 1900s continued through this period as well. Leaders of the NAACP had helped persuade President Woodrow Wilson to condemn lynching in 1918, but they believed that a federal anti-lynching law was the only way to bring an end to the horrible practice.

From 1901 to 1920, 16 anti-lynching bills had been introduced in Congress, but opponents had blocked their passage. Finally, in 1922 the House passed the Dyer Anti-Lynching Bill, which would make lynching a felony and require punishment both for those involved in a lynch mob and for those who failed to punish mob members. Despite support from the NAACP and President Warren G. Harding, the bill was again blocked in the Senate. In 1923 it was reintroduced, but no action was taken. Still, debate over the Dyer Bill had raised public outrage over lynchings. ✔

✔ **Reading Check**
8. Analyze What were three ways in which African Americans worked to improve their lives in the 1910s and 1920s?

_____

_____

_____

_____

_____

SECTION 2 ASSESSMENT

go.hrw.com
Online Quiz
Keyword: SAAH HP8

Reviewing Ideas, Terms, and People

9. Describe What was the goal of black nationalism?

_____

10. Explain How did the Great Migration lead to increased racial tension after the end of World War I?

_____

_____

11. Make Judgments Do you think Marcus Garvey's desire to create a new nation in Africa for black Americans was a good idea? Why or why not?

_____

_____

Writing a Newspaper Editorial

As you have read, shortly after World War I, African Americans moved to the North by the thousands. One black newspaper, the *Chicago Defender*, played a large role in encouraging black southerners to move north. In the space provided, write an editorial in which you discuss the benefits of moving to a northern city. Be sure to use persuasive language to convince readers in the South to leave.

Make Plans to Head North

_____

_____

_____

_____

_____

_____

_____

_____

_____

_____

_____

_____

_____

_____

_____

_____

_____

_____

_____

_____

_____

_____

_____

Analyzing Secondary Sources

Understanding the Skill

Secondary sources are accounts produced after a historical event by people who rely on primary sources to understand what happened at the event. Secondary sources often contain summaries and analyses of events and time periods. When a historian produces a secondary source, it often contains an interpretation of a historical event, or what the historian thinks actually happened and why. Historians build their interpretations on the basis of available facts and their own analysis. These secondary sources can be analyzed to determine whether they present a complete and accurate account of events.

Learn the Skill

Use the strategies at right to learn how to analyze secondary sources.

> The Thomas family arrived in Chicago in the spring of 1917. Like thousands of other black Southerners moving north at the time, their first task was to find a home. For a week they pounded the pavements of the South Side ghetto. To look elsewhere would have been futile. In Chicago the "black belt," along with a few other scattered neighborhoods, provided the only housing available to African Americans. The parents, their nineteen-year-old daughter, and a son two years younger crowded into a five-room apartment—cramped, but probably larger than the farmhouse they had left behind in Alabama.
>
> The second task was to find work. The men went off to the stockyards; the women turned to the familiar trade of wringing the dirt out of other people's clothing. Optimistic about the future, the teenagers spent their evenings in night school, hoping to improve on the grade-school education they had brought with them from a rural Southern schoolhouse. In their free time the family explored the leisure activities available on Chicago's South Side, carrying picnics into the park and venturing into theaters and ice-cream parlors.
>
> —James R. Grossman, "A Chance to Make Good: 1900–1929," 2000

Step 1 Identify the subject and author of the secondary source, and when the source was created. *Who wrote this passage? When did he or she write it?*

_____

_____

_____

Step 2 Determine which statements can be verified as facts and which statements appear to be the interpretations of the author. *Circle statements that are facts. Then underline or highlight statements that are the interpretations of the author.*

Step 3 Compare the author's interpretation of the facts with your own interpretation. *Do you think the author is biased or using faulty logic in his or her interpretation?*

_____

_____

_____

APPLY THE SKILL

1. Explain How does the author of this source use facts to support his analysis of the lives of African Americans moving north in the Great Migration?

_____

_____

2. Draw Conclusions How would this source be useful for understanding the experiences of African Americans who moved to Chicago during the Great Migration?

_____

_____

The Harlem Renaissance

1. **TAKING NOTES** Use a graphic organizer like this one to take notes on the roots of the Harlem Renaissance and key contributors to the movement. Use the **Reading Focus** questions on the next page to help guide your note taking.

2. As you read the section, underline or highlight definitions and descriptions of each of the **Key Terms and People** listed on the next page.

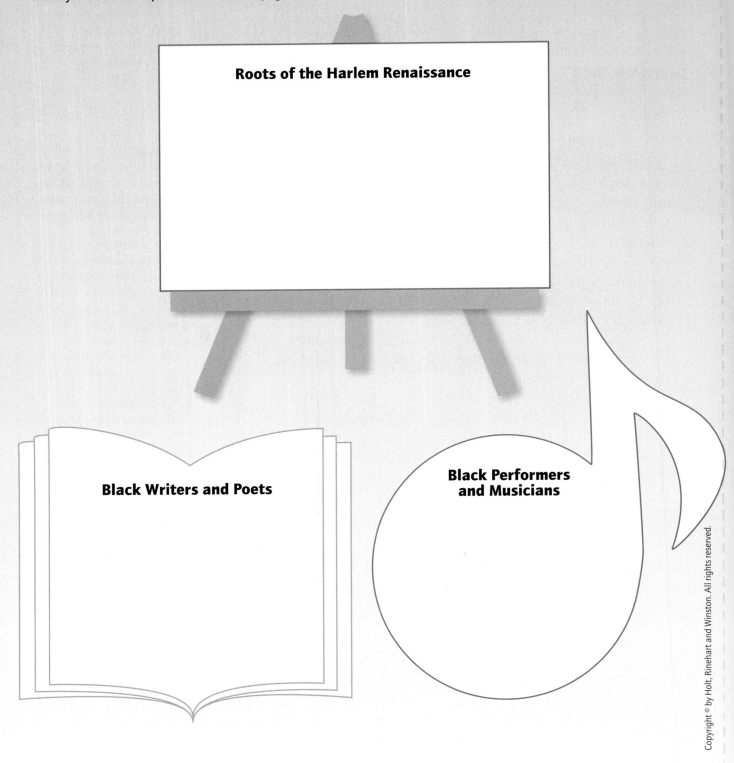

Roots of the Harlem Renaissance

Black Writers and Poets

Black Performers and Musicians

The Harlem Renaissance

BEFORE YOU READ

MAIN IDEA

Expressions of black culture, including literature, music, and art, reached new heights during the Harlem Renaissance of the 1920s and 1930s.

READING FOCUS

- Why was Harlem home to an outpouring of African American cultural expression?
- Who were some key writers and poets of the Harlem Renaissance?
- What roles did black performers and musicians play in the Harlem Renaissance?

KEY TERMS AND PEOPLE

Harlem
Harlem Renaissance
Langston Hughes
James Weldon Johnson
Zora Neale Hurston
folklore
jazz
vaudeville

BUILDING BACKGROUND

During the Great Migration, New York City was a prime destination for many black migrants to the North. There, thousands of African Americans hoped to build better lives for themselves. In one New York neighborhood, black artists and intellectuals would begin a vibrant artistic and literary movement that would shape American culture. ◼

Roots of the Harlem Renaissance

During the Great Migration thousands of African Americans flocked to New York City. Many migrants to New York settled in the neighborhood known as **Harlem**. Located in the northern portion of Manhattan Island, Harlem had first become a popular neighborhood for African Americans at the end of the 1800s. After World War I, Harlem became a center of black social and cultural life and activism.

Many of the African Americans living in Harlem felt a strong sense of racial pride and identity. This spirit attracted a great many talented African American artists, writers, thinkers, and musicians, who shared their experiences and encouraged one another to greater creative heights. A common theme was resistance to white prejudice and a pride in African American culture and heritage. For example, Harlem was home to the first branch of the NAACP, which opened in 1910. Marcus Garvey's Universal Negro Improvement Association was also headquartered in Harlem.

A number of African Americans played an important role in encouraging and promoting the growth of black culture in Harlem. For example W. E. B. Du Bois served as the editor of the NAACP's magazine, *The Crisis*. Published in Harlem, the magazine addressed issues of importance to African Americans across the nation. It also featured African American writing and poetry and helped promote racial pride and identity. The National Urban League also helped promote racial pride. Like the NAACP, the Urban League published a magazine, *Opportunity*, that highlighted black culture. Another notable figure in the development of African American culture in the early 1900s was Alain Locke. A philosophy professor at Howard University, Locke encouraged black artists to connect to their African heritage. He also pushed black authors to write about African American life. By 1917, emphasis on black culture had led to the artistic and literary movement known as the **Harlem Renaissance**. ✔

✔ Reading Check

1. Draw Conclusions Why do you think that Harlem was home to an African American cultural movement?

_____

_____

_____

_____

Black Writers and Poets

Throughout the 1920s and 1930s the Harlem Renaissance dominated African American cultural life. During this period, artists expressed new ideas about black culture and black life in the United States. Among the most vocal artists of the new cultural movement were writers and poets.

PRIMARY SOURCES

The Poetry of Langston Hughes

One of the most celebrated poets of the Harlem Renaissance was Langston Hughes, who often wrote about the black experience. In one of his most famous poems, "I, Too," Hughes expresses his pride in being African American.

I, too, sing America.

I am the darker brother.
They send me to eat in the kitchen
When company comes,
But I laugh,
And eat well,
And grow strong.

Tomorrow,
I'll be at the table
When company comes.
Nobody'll dare
Say to me,
"Eat in the kitchen,"
Then.

Besides,
They'll see how beautiful I am
And be ashamed—

I, too, am America.

Skills FOCUS ANALYZING PRIMARY SOURCES

2. Draw Conclusions What point is Hughes trying to convey in the poem?

_____

_____

_____

A Burst of Creativity

The emphasis on African American life and culture was initiated by white writers who focused on the black experience in the United States. Their works served to inspire African American writers and poets who burst onto the U.S. cultural scene during the Harlem Renaissance. Leading African American magazines, such as *The Crisis* and *Opportunity*, promoted the works of talented black writers. The National Urban League also encouraged African American writers by hosting an annual literary contest. The contest helped propel black writers into the mainstream of American literature. Some common themes among these writers were racial pride and resistance to prejudice.

Langston Hughes

One of the best-known writers of the Harlem Renaissance was poet, essayist, and playwright **Langston Hughes**. Hughes first drew national attention in 1921 at the age of 19 when his poem "The Negro Speaks of Rivers" appeared in *The Crisis*. In 1925 he won a poetry prize from *Opportunity* magazine, and he soon became one of the leading figures of the Harlem Renaissance.

Hughes produced poems, plays, and novels that focused on black life and culture in the United States. He believed that black writers should express their "individual dark-skinned selves without fear or shame." Many of his works used African American slang and musical rhythms and expressed the joy, suffering, and pride of being a black American. Hughes, who continued writing until his death in 1967, is still celebrated as one of the leading writers in American literature.

Other Writers and Poets

In addition to Langston Hughes, dozens of other gifted writers took part in the cultural explosion in Harlem. Among them was **James Weldon Johnson**. In 1900 he co-wrote the song "Lift Every Voice and Sing," which later became the official anthem of the NAACP. A political activist, Johnson helped organize anti-lynching activities for the NAACP and pushed for the passage of the Dyer Bill. As a writer, Johnson is perhaps best known for his 1927 book of poetry, *God's Trombones*, a collection of African American sermons written in verse. Some consider the collection to be among the finest works produced during the Harlem Renaissance.

Another writer of the period was Claude McKay. McKay was considered the spokesperson for the more militant group of young black writers. One of his most famous poems, "If We Must Die," deals with the violence of the Red Summer of 1919. McKay was one of the first writers of the Harlem Renaissance to gain widespread success. His 1928 best-selling novel, *Home to Harlem*, was the most successful novel by an African American writer up to that time.

Zora Neale Hurston was also a major contributor to the new literary movement in Harlem. Hurston's writing was deeply influenced by **folklore**, or traditional stories, sayings, and other art forms. Her interest in folklore led to the publication in 1935 of *Mules and Men*, a collection of African American oral folktales gathered during a study in Florida. Hurston also wrote plays, novels, and short stories. Her most famous novel, *Their Eyes Were Watching God*, explores the world of a young black woman in the early 1900s still feeling the legacy of slavery and discrimination.

Hurston was not the only female writer to emerge during the Harlem Renaissance. As literary editor for *The Crisis*, Jessie Redmon Fauset not only helped promote the careers of writers such as Hughes and McKay, but was also a successful novelist herself. Nella Larsen was another celebrated Harlem writer. Like Hurston and Fauset, Larsen often focused on the lives of African American women.

The popularity of the writers of the Harlem Renaissance soon led to the spread of the literary movement beyond New York. Black writers across the nation were inspired to publish their own works. From Washington, D.C. to Nashville to Los Angeles, writers emerged to contribute to the revitalization of black culture that was taking place. As writers like Claude McKay and Langston Hughes traveled the world, they influenced writers outside the United States as well. ✔

FACES OF HISTORY

Zora Neale Hurston
1891–1960

A talented novelist and anthropologist, Zora Neale Hurston, was a key figure in the Harlem Renaissance. After spending much of her childhood in the all-black town of Eatonville, Florida, Hurston moved north in the Great Migration and began her literary career.

In 1925 Hurston moved to New York City, joining artists and intellectuals such as Langston Hughes and Alain Locke in Harlem. While in New York, Hurston studied anthropology—the study of human cultures—at Barnard College and Columbia University. Her interest in anthropology led to a series of studies of African American folklore in the South and the Caribbean.

Despite her many successes, Hurston died poor and largely forgotten. Since the 1970s, however, her writings have experienced a remarkable resurgence in popularity.

3. Elaborate Why do you think that Hurston's writings became popular in the 1970s?

_____

_____

_____

✔ **Reading Check**
4. Summarize What topics did writers of the Harlem Renaissance address?

_____

_____

_____

_____

Harlem's Jazz Age

Harlem was home to widely popular clubs such as the Savoy and the Cotton Club, where people crowded in to see jazz musicians such as Duke Ellington and his band.

VIRTUAL FIELD TRIP
Go online to experience a virtual field trip to key sites from the Harlem Renaissance.

go.hrw.com
Chapter Activity
Keyword: SAAH CH8

Musicians, Artists, and Performers

Literature was not the only focus of the Harlem Renaissance. African American musicians, artists, and performers also took center stage in Harlem in the early 1900s.

The Jazz Age

By the late 1920s, Harlem was the hotspot for a new form of music called **jazz**. The birth of jazz can be traced back to turn-of-the-century New Orleans, where African American musicians blended several musical styles, including spirituals, blues, ragtime, marching band music, hillbilly music, and various European traditions. The result was a wholly original American form of music that was new, different, and very exciting. As African Americans moved to northern cities like Chicago and New York, jazz traveled with them.

Part of what made jazz so exciting was that, while a jazz song might start with a known melody or theme, much of the music was improvised, or composed on the spot. Jazz could be fast or slow, and it was easy to dance to. In short, jazz was not defined by a clear set of rules but rather by its spirit and creativity. "Man, if you have to ask what it is," legendary jazz musician Louis Armstrong once stated, "you'll never know."

Louis Armstrong was a leading performer on the Harlem jazz scene, which was centered at clubs such as the Savoy Ballroom and the Cotton Club. Fans flocked to Harlem to hear Armstrong and other leading performers of the day, including Cab Calloway and composers Duke Ellington and Fats Waller. Club-goers also came to Harlem ready to dance. Jazz fans invented new dance steps as the music inspired them, including the jitterbug and the Lindy Hop (named after Charles Lindbergh).

Jazz fans also came to Harlem to see Bessie Smith, "the Empress of the Blues." Smith began her career as a teenager, singing her own "down-home" version of the blues in small cafes throughout the South. By 1923, she had moved to New York City and signed with Columbia Records. Smith's first release, "Down-Hearted Blues," sold over 2 million copies. Over the next few years, Smith would record with all of the top Jazz Age musicians and earn an incredible $2,000 a week for her performances. Together with Louis Armstrong, she is credited with developing the tradition of jazz singing.

Black Artists

Alongside writers such as Langston Hughes and Zora Neale Hurston, black painters, sculptors, photographers, and filmmakers contributed to the creative energy in Harlem during the 1920s and 1930s. These artists were united by a desire to create art that expressed the history and experiences of African Americans.

Painter Aaron Douglas was among the leading artists of the Harlem Renaissance. Often called the "father of African American art," Douglas was the first black artist to experiment with modernism and to use symbols from African art in his paintings, murals, and illustrations. By contrast, sculptor and art educator Augusta Savage crafted stunningly realistic symbols of black pride and aspirations, including sculptures of W. E. B. Du Bois and Marcus Garvey. Together with other Harlem Renaissance artists—Loïs Mailou Jones, James VanDerZee, and William H. Johnson to name a few—they captured the black experience in clay, on canvas, and on film.

Black Performers

Before the Harlem Renaissance, African Americans had few opportunities in the theater world. At the turn of the century, most theatrical productions were the creation of white playwrights and performers. Black actors were generally limited to minor roles that encouraged racial stereotypes.

Over time, however, African American performers began taking part in theatrical productions in Harlem. In 1917 an all-black group of actors gained praise for their performances in a series of one-act plays performed at the Garden Theater in New York's Madison Square Garden. African American performers scored another success with the 1921 production of *Shuffle Along*. A musical written, performed, and produced by blacks, the show brought African American theater to popularity.

Many talented African American performers got their start in New York theater during this period. Some starred in **vaudeville**—a sort of early variety show that combined acting, music, and comedy—such as Bill "Bojangles" Robinson, whose tap dance performances amazed audiences in New York and around the world. He went on to become one of the first black American stars on Broadway and in Hollywood. Actor Paul Robeson also drew critical acclaim for his dramatic performances.

The Harlem Renaissance — KEY FACTS

5. Describe some of the key contributions of African American artists of the Harlem Renaissance.

▲ Claude McKay's book *Home to Harlem* focused on life and culture in Harlem.

The Harlem Renaissance Draws to a Close

The Harlem Renaissance, a time of great cultural achievement, was not confined only to New York. Black writers, musicians, and artists had great appeal around the nation and the world. Jazz styles gained popularity in Chicago, Paris, and other cities. Writers and poets across the nation imitated the styles of Harlem writers. Black and white Americans alike were captivated by the new styles that originated in Harlem. In later years, historians noted the spread of the ideas of the Harlem Renaissance to other parts of the United States.

6. What is the authors' interpretation of the influence of the Harlem Renaissance?

_____

_____

_____

_____

HISTORY'S VOICES

"Gradually the scope of the Harlem Renaissance came to be the whole of the United States. African Americans everywhere became more articulate. There were poetry circles in Houston and Detroit, little theaters in Chicago and Los Angeles, and interested students of painting in Cleveland and Nashville. Long before the beginning of the Depression the groups in Harlem could claim no monopoly, but they could claim some credit for the widespread interest in the new efforts at self-expression in various parts of the country."

—John Hope Franklin and Alfred A. Moss Jr., *From Slavery to Freedom*, 1998

✔ **Reading Check**

7. Draw Conclusions Why might the styles of the Harlem Renaissance have been so widely popular?

_____

_____

_____

_____

The Harlem Renaissance had roared through the 1920s. By the 1930s, however, the period was drawing to a close. As several leaders of the movement, such as W. E. B. Du Bois and James Weldon Johnson, moved away from Harlem, the movement lost some of its steam. Another key factor in the decline of the Harlem Renaissance was the economic depression that struck the United States in 1929. As Americans struggled to find work and earn a living, the artistic movement that had flourished in the 1920s slowly declined.

While the movement eventually came to a close, its influence did not. Writers such as Langston Hughes and artists such as Aaron Douglas continued their popularity through the 1930s and beyond. In fact, many participants from Harlem still influence the arts today. The Harlem Renaissance had created a unique cultural movement of which all Americans could be proud. ✔

SECTION 3 ASSESSMENT

go.hrw.com
Online Quiz
Keyword: SAAH HP8

Reviewing Ideas, Terms, and People

8. Describe How did the literature of the Harlem Renaissance reflect black history?

_____

_____

9. Make Generalizations How did changes in American society lead to the end of the Harlem Renaissance?

_____

_____

10. Elaborate How might jazz be seen as a symbol of the entire Harlem Renaissance?

_____

_____

Creating an Advertisement

During the Harlem Renaissance a new generation of black writers began to be noticed for their depictions of African American life. In the space below, design an advertisement for a key book from the Harlem Renaissance. Be sure to include the title and author of the book, and a specific reason that the book is important.

ADVERTISEMENT

ASSESS YOUR KNOWLEDGE

1. **Analyze** How does your advertisement relay the importance of the book you have chosen from the Harlem Renaissance?

2. **Evaluate** Do you think the book you chose is still important to read today? Explain.

Online Resources

Visit **go.hrw.com** for review and enrichment activities related to this chapter.

go.hrw.com
Chapter Home Page
Keyword: SAAH CH8

Quiz and Review

ONLINE QUIZ
Take a practice quiz for each section in this chapter.

CHAPTER REVIEW
Use the online Chapter Review to help you prepare for the chapter test.

Activities

HISTORICAL DOCUMENTS
Read and explore key documents that shaped African American history.

VIRTUAL FIELD TRIP
Take a virtual field trip to experience key sites from African American history.

VOICES OF HISTORY
Experience African American history and culture through recordings of key people and documents.

Partner

CONNECTING TO OUR PAST
Examine artifacts from **Howard University's Moorland-Spingarn Research Center** that bring to life the study of African American history.

A New Century and New Opportunities

CHAPTER SUMMARY

SECTION 1   The World War I Years

- In response to European imperialism in Africa, black leaders from around the world joined the Pan-African movement.
- Though the United States remained neutral in the early years of World War I, many Americans—including African Americans—pushed for the country to join the war effort.
- Brave African Americans served as both soldiers and nurses in World War I.

SECTION 2   Changes in Black Society

- The Great Migration was a mass movement of African Americans out of the South to escape discrimination and segregation.
- During the Red Summer of 1919, African Americans across the country faced terrible violence and increased discrimination.
- The black nationalism movement sought to promote feelings of unity and strength in the black community

SECTION 3   The Harlem Renaissance

- An emphasis on black culture during the 1910s led to a new arts movement called the Harlem Renaissance.
- Writers like Langston Hughes and Zora Neale Hurston expressed new ideas about black culture in their writings.
- During the Harlem Renaissance, black performers gained national reputations in such styles as vaudeville and jazz.

The GREAT DEPRESSION and World War II

This 1943 poster shows factory workers at an integrated aircraft plant during World War II. Propaganda posters, pamphlets, and films were produced by the government to elicit support for the war.

EXPRESSING YOUR OPINION

Would you be willing to fight for a country that denied you rights and opportunities? Write a short paragraph explaining why or why not.

UNITED WE WIN

WAR MANPOWER COMMISSION · WASHINGTON, D. C.

OWI PHOTO BY LIBERMAN

Depression and Recovery

1. **TAKING NOTES** Use a graphic organizer like this one to take notes on the change from times of economic prosperity to economic depression, the effects of the Depression, and ways that New Deal programs brought relief. Use the **Reading Focus** questions on the next page to help guide your note taking.

2. As you read the section, underline or highlight definitions and descriptions of each of the **Key Terms and People** listed on the next page.

From Prosperity to Depression

The Effects of the Depression

New Deal Brings Relief

Depression and Recovery

BEFORE YOU READ

MAIN IDEA

The economic hardship of the Great Depression led to widespread unemployment and poverty, with increased challenges for black Americans.

READING FOCUS

- What caused the shift from prosperity to depression in the United States in the 1920s?
- What were the economic and social effects of the Great Depression?
- How did the New Deal bring relief to the American people?

KEY TERMS AND PEOPLE

assembly line
Great Depression
Franklin D. Roosevelt
Mary McLeod Bethune
Black Cabinet
New Deal
A. Philip Randolph

BUILDING BACKGROUND

Following World War I, the United States enjoyed prosperity and growth during the 1920s. The Roaring Twenties, however, ended in a dismal time when jobs were scarce and poverty was widespread. African Americans were especially hard hit. ■

From Prosperity to Depression

The early 1920s witnessed a dramatic upsurge in the American economy. New industrial practices led to great wealth for some business owners and more options for consumers. Unfortunately, this time of prosperity would not last.

Prosperity in the 1920s

The automobile industry offers a good example of the prosperity of the 1920s. Most early cars were too expensive for the average consumer. In 1908 Henry Ford changed that. He built a line of affordable cars called the Model T using the mass-production methods of modern factories. The Model T was made on an **assembly line**. In an assembly line, a product moves from worker to worker, each one performing one step. As more Americans were able to buy cars, Ford quickly became prosperous. Realizing that his employees were potential car buyers, Ford raised workers' wages.

Ford's employees were not the only ones to prosper from the new economy. Along with other American workers, some African Americans benefited from the boom times of the 1920s. Thousands of African Americans moved to cities, especially in the North, to work. Even with little schooling, they could find better jobs in northern factories. Unfortunately, agricultural laborers in the South saw little benefit from the growing economy.

Although employment increased, most black workers labored for low pay, often under difficult conditions. For example, the black porters and maids who worked on board the nation's trains were on duty for long hours, traveling some 10,000 miles per month but earning only about $60 a month.

KEY FACTS

1. Why did some African Americans move to Northern cities?

Stock Market Crash

The good feelings of the 1920s hid a growing economic problem, and despite the boom, only a small percentage of the population truly prospered. A number of ordinary Americans had begun to invest in the stock market. The stock market is a place where stocks are bought and sold. *Stock*, or ownership in a company, is sold in units called *shares*. Buying shares allows a person to own a piece of a corporation. If a corporation's value increases, the value of its stock rises and investors make money. If a corporation's value declines, stock owners can lose the money they have invested. Some American investors used credit to purchase stocks. Though risky, this practice became increasingly common during the 1920s as the stock market rose sharply.

During the fall of 1929 signs of trouble appeared. Some manufactured products did not sell as well as predicted, and some businesses began to fail. Rumors began to circulate that some big investors were taking their money out of the stock market. On October 24 nervous investors started selling their stock. Soon the market was flooded with stock for sale, but no one was buying. Within a few days, many Americans who had invested heavily went broke as their stock became worthless. This series of events was called the stock market crash of 1929. Investors who had bought stock on credit were in especially bad shape; they were obligated to repay their loans even though they had suffered great losses.

The stock market crash was one factor that led to the most severe economic depression in the nation's history, called the **Great Depression**. Many banks ran out of money, and countless people were out of work. ✔

✔ Reading Check

2. Identify What was the Great Depression?

_____

_____

_____

_____

_____

The Effects of the Depression

Although many bankers and business owners did suffer during the Depression, some were fortunate enough to have other resources to get them through the hard times. People on the fringes of American society, however—including most African Americans—faced disaster.

Hard Times

Unemployed men wait in line outside a depression era soup kitchen.

Skills FOCUS   INTERPRETING GRAPHS

3. According to the graph, how much higher was the unemployment rate for black men than for white men?

_____

_____

UNEMPLOYMENT RATES FOR MALE WORKERS, 1931

☐ Unemployed   ■ Employed

White Workers

31.7%

African American Workers

52%

Source: *Negroes and the Great Depression: The Problem of Economic Recovery*

Conditions around the Country

In the North, where the economy was based mainly on manufacturing, many black workers lost their jobs. Sometimes, factory owners who wanted to reduce their workforces kept white employees and let the black employees go. The practice was legal. Domestic workers such as maids and cooks, many of whom were black, also lost their jobs when their employers could no longer pay them. African American communities had some of the highest unemployment rates in the country during the Depression. In Harlem, a primarily black neighborhood in New York City, for example, the unemployment rate reached 50 percent in 1932.

During the Depression the southern economy was primarily agricultural. Farmers—especially black farmers—were not protected from the Depression's ravages. As sellers dropped prices on various products to make a sale, the prices on farm products also dropped. In fact, they dropped so low that farmers could not make enough money to fulfill their basic needs. Many lost their land and had to work for other farmers, planting or picking crops. With so many workers competing for those jobs, they had to settle for wages so low that starvation was a threat.

Religious and charity organizations brought relief to many Americans. Some of these groups, however, barred African Americans from receiving the free food offered to others. In some places where government jobs were available, often only white applicants were given consideration. When the government gave money to families in need, in some communities black families received much less than white families. ✔

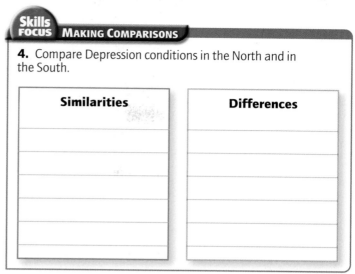

✔ Reading Check

5. Describe What forms of discrimination did many African Americans face during the Depression?

_____

_____

_____

_____

The New Deal Brings Relief

Economic opportunities had brought large numbers of African Americans to the North, where they formed new communities, like Harlem. With the onset of hard times and the search for ways to improve the lives of poor black Americans, these communities became centers of black political power. The citizens of these communities banded together and worked for change in the political system. In 1928, for example, black voters in Chicago were influential in electing Oscar DePriest, a black politician, to Congress—the first black representative elected since 1900.

Political Shifts

One significant change in politics at this time was a shift in party affiliations. Many African Americans were becoming frustrated with the Republican Party, which they thought was neglecting blacks to ally with white candidates and voters. This alignment with white voters gave the Republicans new popularity in the South. For example, southern voters had helped Republican Herbert Hoover win the presidency in 1928. To carry the South, the Republicans had to limit the power of previously influential black party leaders.

6. Use the context, or surrounding words in the sentence, to write a definition of the word **resurgence**.

_____

_____

_____

By 1932 many black voters had decided to vote for non-Republican candidates in response to the abandonment they felt from the party. However, few seemed willing to support the Democratic candidate for president, **Franklin Delano Roosevelt**. African Americans feared that a Democratic victory would lead to a resurgence of the discrimination they had suffered around the turn of the century. This fear was heightened when Roosevelt chose John Nance Garner of Texas—a southerner—as his vice presidential running mate. As a result, Roosevelt never received the full support of the African American community some had predicted.

Roosevelt and Black Americans

The Roosevelt administration, however, turned out to be the one most sympathetic to African Americans since Reconstruction. Many black voters rewarded Roosevelt with their support, shifting their allegiance to the Democratic Party.

Among Roosevelt's chief supporters was a remarkable woman, **Mary McLeod Bethune**. When he began the unprecedented practice of meeting with black leaders to hear their views on civil rights, he included Bethune. In fact, Roosevelt named her as an official presidential advisor. From 1936 to 1944 Bethune's official title was Director of the Division of Negro Affairs of the National Youth Administration. Her fearless championing of the rights of black students, especially in the South, helped lead to such changes as recognition of Negro History Week. Roosevelt named more African Americans to federal positions than any president had before him. He appointed the first black federal judge in U.S. history, William Hastie. By 1939 some of Roosevelt's influential appointees were being called the **Black Cabinet**.

HISTORICAL DOCUMENT
Go online to read a historical document from the **New Deal**.

go.hrw.com
Chapter Activity
Keyword: SAAH CH9

FACES OF HISTORY

Mary McLeod BETHUNE

1875–1955

The fifteenth child of former slaves, Mary McLeod Bethune overcame great hardships to win a position of influence in the government. In 1904, without much funding, Bethune founded the Daytona Normal and Industrial Institute for Negro Girls. This institution later merged with the Cookman Institute to become Bethune-Cookman College.

Bethune was a powerful speaker and a tireless activist. Her activities were noticed by people around the country. Among them was Eleanor Roosevelt, the wife of the president. Eventually, the two became friends. Roosevelt saw to it that Bethune had access to important educational circles—access that eventually helped her become the first African American woman to head a federal agency.

7. Describe What were some of Bethune's major accomplishments?

_____

_____

_____

_____

The New Deal

Roosevelt's primary goal as president was to rescue the country from the ravages of the Great Depression. To do so, he created a far-reaching program of reforms that he called the **New Deal**. The New Deal had three goals: to provide relief for those suffering the effects of the Great Depression, to bring about the recovery of the depressed American economy, and to enact reforms in order to prevent another terrible depression from happening in the future.

As part of the New Deal, the federal government took a much more active role in people's business and personal lives than it ever had before. For example, some New Deal programs forced businesses to work together to set fair prices. Other programs provided money for people in need. Still others created massive work programs designed to help people find employment and get back on their feet.

While African Americans benefited from some New Deal programs, they still faced discrimination. Many never saw real benefits from any New Deal program. Claiming that all his efforts to do so had been blocked by southern Democrats in Congress, Roosevelt did nothing for many years to end this discrimination. In 1941, however, the actions of **A. Philip Randolph** led to a new law banning discrimination in hiring practices.

Randolph was a union organizer who had come to national prominence in 1925 for challenging the Pullman Company. As head of a union of railway porters and maids, Randolph secured pay raises and increased rights for those he represented. But even with the threat of another war looming, blacks were being turned away from military and defense organizations. In protest, Randolph organized a march in Washington, D.C. Randolph was adamant in his position.

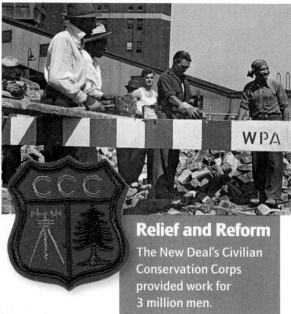

Relief and Reform

The New Deal's Civilian Conservation Corps provided work for 3 million men.

HISTORY'S VOICES

"[I]f American democracy will not give jobs to its toilers because of race or color; if American democracy will not insure equality of opportunity, freedom and justice to its citizens, black and white, it is a hollow mockery and belies the principles for which it is supposed to stand."

—A. Philip Randolph, *The Black Worker*, 1941

✔ **Reading Check**

8. Explain How did Randolph help fight discrimination?

_____

_____

_____

_____

_____

_____

In response to Randolph's demand, Roosevelt issued Executive Order 8802, also known as the Fair Employment Act, just one week before the scheduled march. The order decreed: "There shall be no discrimination in the employment of workers in defense industries and in Government because of race, creed, color, or national origin." The decree also set up the nation's first Committee on Fair Employment Practices. This group was charged with investigating violations of the executive order. Triumphantly, Randolph called off the march. ✔

SECTION 1 ASSESSMENT

go.hrw.com
Online Quiz
Keyword: SAAH HP9

Reviewing Ideas, Terms, and People

9. Describe How did Mary McLeod Bethune and A. Philip Randolph help improve the lives of African Americans?

_____

_____

10. Explain What was the purpose of the New Deal, and how did it affect African Americans in particular?

_____

_____

11. Elaborate What increased hardships did black Americans in particular face as a result of the Great Depression?

_____

_____

Preparing a Lesson

Imagine that you have been asked to teach a lesson on the New Deal to a middle school class. Prepare an outline to help you organize your lesson. Conduct research using online or print resources to learn more about the New Deal. Be sure to include information you find that you think would be of interest to younger students. Use the notebook paper below to help you organize your work and prepare your outline.

I. Introduction
   A.
   B.

II.
   A.
   B.
   C.

III.
   A.
   B.
   C.

IV. Conclusion
   A.
   B.

ASSESS YOUR KNOWLEDGE

1. **Identify** Describe at least three New Deal programs that you found through your research.

_____

_____

2. **Describe** If you were going to teach the lesson, how could you present the material in order to keep the attention of younger students?

_____

_____

Writing a Speech

Imagine that it is graduation day for the first class of the Daytona Normal and Industrial Institute for Negro Girls. Write a commencement speech for the students as if you were Mary McLeod Bethune, the school's founder. Think about what she might say to inspire, motivate, and encourage her students to succeed.

African Americans in World War II

1. **TAKING NOTES** Use a graphic organizer like this one to take notes on war in Europe and the Pacific, African American contributions at home and on the front, and discrimination. Use the **Reading Focus** questions on the next page to help guide your note taking.

2. As you read the section, underline or highlight definitions and descriptions of each of the **Key Terms and People** listed on the next page.

War in Europe and the Pacific

African Americans Do Their Part

African Americans in World War II

African Americans on the Home Front

Blacks Face Discrimination

African Americans in World War II

BEFORE YOU READ

MAIN IDEA

During World War II, African Americans made heroic contributions both in battle and on the home front, though many still faced discrimination.

READING FOCUS

- What events led to the outbreak of war in Europe and the Pacific?
- What parts did African Americans play in World War II?
- How did African Americans contribute to the war effort on the home front?
- What forms of discrimination did blacks face during World War II?

KEY TERMS AND PEOPLE

World War II
D-Day Invasion
Battle of the Bulge
island hopping
Benjamin O. Davis
Tuskegee Airmen

BUILDING BACKGROUND

Imagine going to bed one night and waking up the next day to find out that your country is at war. That situation happened on December 7, 1941. Japanese fighter planes had dropped their deadly payloads on the U.S. fleet anchored in Hawaii's Pearl Harbor. The United States was at war. ■

War in Europe and the Pacific

At first, many Americans opposed entering World War II. Two years after the war had begun in Europe, however, events in the Pacific sparked American involvement.

War Begins in Europe

Even before the war began, Hitler infuriated people worldwide with his expressions of racism. He believed that Germans belonged to a "master race" and promoted a belief in the racial superiority of the German people. Hitler blamed Jews for the world's problems and claimed that other groups were subhuman. Poles, Slavs, the Romany, people of color, homosexuals, and people with disabilities were also targets for Nazi prejudice.

In an effort to realize his dream of uniting all ethnic Germans, Hitler tried to force the Austrian government to agree to union with Germany in 1938. When Austria refused, Hitler sent troops into the country. Later that year he seized land from neighboring Czechoslovakia. When Hitler invaded Poland on September 1, 1939, **World War II** began. Finally, Great Britain and France had enough of his actions, and both countries declared war on Germany and Italy, its ally.

At first, the United States stayed out of the conflict. After victory in World War I, many Americans thought that the United States should remain uninvolved in this new war. They favored a policy of isolationism, or noninvolvement in world affairs. Isolationists thought that World War II was a European problem that need not concern the United States. President Franklin Roosevelt disagreed. However, public attitudes against the war prevented him from getting the country involved.

ACADEMIC VOCABULARY

1. Use the context, or surrounding words in the sentence, to write a definition of the word **seized**.

Among those who fought bravely against the Japanese at Pearl Harbor was a young kitchen attendant named Dorie Miller. When Miller's ship, the USS *West Virginia*, was hit in the initial Japanese attack, he carried wounded soldiers to safety. Witnessing Miller's actions, an officer sent him to help the ship's captain, who had been mortally wounded in the attack. Before long, Miller began firing at the enemy with an anti-aircraft gun he had never before used. As Miller later said, "It wasn't hard. I just pulled the trigger and she worked fine. I had watched the others with these guns. I guess I fired her for about fifteen minutes. I think I got one of those [Japanese] planes. They were diving pretty close to us." For his extraordinary courage in the battle, he was awarded the Navy Cross—the first African American to receive such an honor.

2. Summarize How did Miller demonstrate courage during the Pearl Harbor attack?

_____

_____

_____

The Attack on Pearl Harbor

Those attitudes changed when Germany's other ally, Japan, attacked the Pearl Harbor Naval Base in the Hawaiian Islands, a U.S. territory, in 1941. Early on the morning of December 7 of that year, Japanese fighter planes appeared in the sky above Pearl Harbor. The planes rained down bombs on the unprepared American fleet. American troops valiantly tried to repel the attack, but they had been so surprised by the arrival of the Japanese that they were not even able to launch planes into the air before they were destroyed. In less than two hours, the Japanese hit eight battleships, sinking four, and destroyed nearly 200 aircraft. Even worse, more than 2,000 American soldiers died in the attack.

Within a day of the attack, Roosevelt asked Congress for and received a declaration of war against Japan. In response, Germany and Italy declared war on the United States. As a result, the United States sent troops to Europe as well. The nation had entered World War II.

The Course of the War

With heavy fighting taking place in both Europe and the Pacific, World War II was truly a global conflict. It was the largest and bloodiest war in all of world history, taking the lives of more than 40 million people and causing billions of dollars worth of damages. That World War II changed the world forever is no exaggeration.

In Europe, the war had been going badly for the Allied powers before 1941. The arrival of American forces, however, helped turn the tide. Still, fierce fighting continued in western, eastern, and southern Europe.

The major turning point in the war in Europe came in June 1944 with the **D-Day Invasion**. On June 6, 1944, more than 150,000 Allied troops stormed the beaches of Normandy, France, where a German army was camped. By July, nearly 1 million soldiers had come ashore. Though costly, the D-Day Invasion was successful. From Normandy the Allies marched steadily east, coming closer and closer to Germany. Despite a heavy German counterattack known as the **Battle of the Bulge**, which slowed the Allied advance for several months, the Germans could not stop them. Finally, on May 8, 1945, Germany surrendered. The war in Europe was over.

Fighting in the Pacific was just as deadly. After Pearl Harbor, the Japanese won a string of victories in the Pacific, invading and claiming numerous islands. In late 1941 the Japanese invaded the Philippines, an American-controlled territory, which Japan conquered after a few months of fighting. The war looked bleak for the Allies.

VIRTUAL FIELD TRIP
Go online to experience a virtual field trip to key sites from **World War II**.

go.hrw.com
Chapter Activity
Keyword: SAAH CH9

Shortly after the loss of the Philippines, however, the Allies' fortunes changed. Led by the Americans, the Allies won significant victories in the Battles of the Coral Sea, Midway, and Guadalcanal. Following these victories, the Allies began a strategy called **island hopping**. They used air, sea, and ground forces to capture key islands, from which they launched offensives against other strategic points. Through this strategy, Allied forces slowly advanced on Japan.

Despite many losses, Japan refused to surrender. Finally, U.S. president Harry S Truman decided to take drastic measures. He ordered the army to use America's newest weapon, the atomic bomb, to bring the Japanese to surrender. After two incredibly deadly bombs destroyed the cities of Hiroshima and Nagasaki—and killed more than 100,000—Japan finally surrendered on August 14, 1945. ✔

✔ **Reading Check**
3. Identify Cause and Effect What was the turning point for the Allies in the Pacific?

African Americans Do Their Part

At home and on the war front, African Americans contributed to the eventual victory over Germany and Japan. About a million black men and women served in the armed forces. The military remained segregated until 1948, however, and most blacks were assigned to service and support positions. One black recruit complained, "We can take no pride in our armed forces. We can become no more than flunkies in the army and kitchen boys in the navy."

African American Soldiers

As the war went on, African Americans made slow gains. In all, 22 black combat units fought in Europe. Among them, the 969th Field Artillery won a Distinguished Unit Citation for outstanding courage. Near the end of the war in Europe, during the decisive Battle of the Bulge, black and white soldiers fought side by side to drive back a fierce German attack. General George S. Patton told his troops, "I don't care what color you are, so long as you go up there and kill [Germans]." But segregation returned to all units after the German surrender in 1945.

Despite the racism that existed in the armed forces, some black soldiers managed to rise through the ranks. For example, in 1940 **Benjamin O. Davis** became the first African American general in the army. Subsequent tours of duty took Davis to the Philippines, Africa, Europe, and various places within the United States. Davis also taught at Tuskegee Institute and Wilberforce University. In 1942 he became Adviser on Negro Problems in Europe and in 1944 was named Special Assistant to the Commanding General in France.

During his years in the military, General Davis rendered invaluable service, earning the Distinguished Service Medal and the Bronze Star. He also won several foreign awards and honors, including the Croix de Guerre with Palm from France. After 50 years of service, he retired in 1948.

General Benjamin O. Davis oversees a Signal Corps crew erecting poles in France.

Propaganda Poster

This World War II poster features an image of a Tuskegee fighter pilot. The Tuskegee Airmen were the first African American flying unit in the U.S. military. Hundreds of airmen were trained, and many saw combat action.

Skills FOCUS ANALYZING PRIMARY SOURCES

4. Interpreting Visuals What is the message of this poster? How effective do you think it was?

The Tuskegee Airmen

Among the African American groups who fought valiantly in World War II were the **Tuskegee Airmen**, a division of the Army Air Corps. The division was formed in 1941 after black soldiers protested that they were not being allowed to take an active role in the war. With support from the NAACP and black newspapers, the soldiers finally convinced the army to allow them to fight in combat.

The Tuskegee Airmen got their name from Tuskegee Institute in Alabama, where they trained. They were fighter pilots, about 1,000 of them in total. Their first commander was Lieutenant Colonel Benjamin O. Davis Jr., the son of the famous general. Davis later became the first black general in the U.S. Air Force. The group escorted bombing missions and attacked enemy airfields, supply centers, and communication lines.

During the war the Tuskegee Airmen won great acclaim for their bravery and their successful record. They flew nearly 16,000 missions and destroyed hundreds of enemy aircraft. For their efforts, members of the group won more than 900 medals and honors, and in 2006—more than 60 years after the end of World War II—Congress voted to award them the Congressional Gold Medal, the highest honor that Congress can give.

African American Women in the War

African American women also made great contributions to the war effort. In July 1943, the U.S. Congress created the Women's Army Corps. At first, the African American women who joined were only allowed such duties as hospital service for black soldiers. As the war continued, however, their tasks were expanded to such positions as lab technicians and librarians.

In 1944 the army opened its hospital doors to black nurses. By the end of the year, African American nurses were treating white soldiers. On March 8, 1945, Phyllis Mae Daley became the first black woman in the Navy Nurse Corps. In later wars, black women served successfully in the Nurse Corps as well.

INFO TO KNOW
The Tuskegee Airmen have long been credited as the only U.S. escort group to have never lost a bomber to enemy fire. Recent scholarship suggests, however, that the group did in fact lose some bombers. Though the number of planes lost is undetermined, the figure is believed to be quite low.

✔**Reading Check**
5. Describe What roles did African Americans play in WWII?

In 1945 some 800 black women formed the 688th Central Postal Battalion in Europe. This battalion was given the important mission of establishing a central postal directory in Europe. The unit received praise for its performance, which included arranging for the delivery of 3 million pieces of backlogged mail. ✔

African Americans on the Home Front

Not all of the contributions that African Americans made to winning World War II happened in Europe and the Pacific. Thousands of blacks in the United States worked to ensure victory by fighting the war on the home front.

Working on the Home Front

With so many young men away at war, factories were faced with a labor shortage. African Americans were now welcomed into the workforce along with other people of color. Thousands of black men found factory jobs, such as airplane builders, shipbuilders, welders, auto mechanics, and radio operators. Many black women also found themselves part of the workforce for the first time.

As African Americans entered the workforce, they joined labor unions to which no black members had previously belonged. African American union members took on prominent roles in unions such as the United Auto Workers and the Congress of Industrial Organizations.

Army Nurses

Though opportunities for minorities were limited, many women, like these nurses stationed in Australia, volunteered to serve in World War II.

Contributing to the War Effort

Black Americans also worked alongside their white neighbors to raise financial and moral support for the war effort. They bought war bonds, a type of savings bond that raised money to support the armed forces. They also held rallies in schools and churches to encourage others to support the war and to buy bonds.

In 1941 the government created the Office of Civilian Defense (OCD), whose goal was to maintain American morale and ensure that civilians remained safe in case of an attack against the United States. African Americans occupied many prominent positions within this organization. One of its high-level officers was Crystal Bird Fauset of Philadelphia, who served as the race relations advisor to the OCD. Previously, Fauset served as a state legislator, the first African American woman ever to hold that post.

African Americans also joined in efforts to conserve food and other goods during the war. Some planted "victory gardens" to help overcome food shortages and preserve valuable resources for the military. Others volunteered to work on ration boards that regulated the distribution of food products with limited availability, such as butter, coffee, sugar, and meat. Goods like gasoline, metal, glass, and rubber were also rationed. Americans, black and white alike, considered these sacrifices worthwhile if they helped even a little in winning the war. ✔

✔ **Reading Check**
6. Describe How did African Americans contribute to the war effort at home?

_____

_____

_____

_____

_____

Blacks Face Discrimination

Unfortunately, despite the great contributions many black citizens made to the war effort, widespread discrimination against them continued. As you have read, the armed forces did not want to accept black volunteers at the beginning of the war. Many civilian organizations felt the same way. African Americans who volunteered to help their country win the war often found their offers of help met with suspicion and distrust. As one journalist later noted, African Americans were fighting Adolf Hitler abroad even as they were still having to fight Jim Crow at home.

During the war thousands of African Americans left their homes in the South and moved to cities in the North and West in search of better jobs. The black populations of many cities skyrocketed. In Los Angeles, for example, the black population more than doubled in a decade, jumping from less than 65,000 in 1940 to more than 170,000 in 1950. City and state leaders worried that racial tension and violence would soon increase because of the rapidly changing demographics. The limited availability of housing and jobs contributed to the mounting racial tension.

Unfortunately, in some places, these fears proved correct. During the summer of 1943, for example, major race riots broke out in Harlem, Detroit, Los Angeles, and Beaumont, Texas. Perhaps the bloodiest began in Detroit on June 20, 1943. Several minor conflicts soon escalated into mob violence. Rumors about crimes that black and white citizens had committed against each other spread quickly. The fighting intensified, with the riot continuing over the course of three days. In total, 25 black residents and 9 white residents were killed. Hundreds more were arrested for looting and other crimes. Finally, the federal government had to intervene to end it. President Roosevelt declared a state of emergency and sent 6,000 troops into Detroit to stop the fighting. Troops occupied Detroit for six months.

Hoping to prevent a similar situation, some cities made efforts to prevent interracial problems. Although riots did occur around the country in 1943, some cities were able to diffuse tense situations by planning ahead to prevent violent outbursts.

Reading Check

7. Explain Why did the African American population of many cities in the North and the West increase after the war?

_____

_____

_____

_____

_____

SECTION 2 ASSESSMENT

go.hrw.com
Online Quiz
Keyword: SAAH HP9

Reviewing Ideas, Terms, and People

8. Identify How did African Americans contribute to the Allied victory in World War II?

_____

_____

9. Explain How did the shift in population during World War II contribute to discrimination against African Americans?

_____

_____

10. Elaborate How do you think some black troops may have felt upon their homecoming in 1945 after having helped defeat Hitler's forces?

_____

_____

Making Comparisons

Understanding the Skill

An important skill for analyzing history is the ability to make comparisons. Historians often examine certain time periods, people, places, and events for clues about how they are similar and different. Making comparisons is an essential part of identifying historical connections.

Learn the Skill

Use the strategies below to make comparisons.

1. Identify who or what you are going to compare.
2. Look for similarities and differences between the items you are comparing. Create a graphic organizer to identify the ways in which the items are alike and different. Use specific examples whenever possible.
3. Analyze your findings. Identify relationships between the similarities and differences and consider possible explanations for them.

Apply the Skill

Use the strategies you learned above to complete the chart and answer the questions that follow.

African Americans in World War I	African Americans in World War II
• Initially, African American volunteers were refused.	
• African American troops served in segregated units, such as the 369th Infantry.	
• African American women served overseas as nurses and worked in factories at home.	
• Following the war, thousands of African Americans moved north in the Great Migration.	

ASSESS YOUR KNOWLEDGE

1. **Identify** What time periods are you comparing in the chart above?

_____

_____

2. **Elaborate** Sum up the similarities and differences between African American participation in World War I and World War II.

_____

_____

_____

Social and Cultural Changes

1. **TAKING NOTES** Use a graphic organizer like this one to take notes on American soldiers returning from war, the push for equality, and African Americans in the arts. Use the **Reading Focus** questions on the next page to help guide your note taking.

2. As you read the section, underline or highlight definitions and descriptions of each of the **Key Terms and People** listed on the next page.

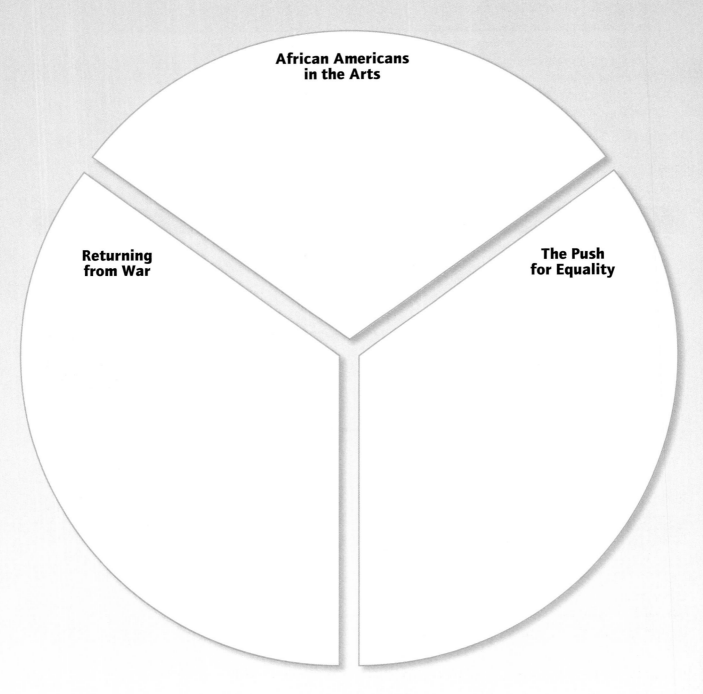

African Americans in the Arts

Returning from War

The Push for Equality

3 Social and Cultural Changes

BEFORE YOU READ

MAIN IDEA

After World War II, African Americans fought to win equality and create social and cultural changes in the United States.

READING FOCUS

- What opportunities were available to black soldiers returning from World War II?

- How did prominent African Americans contribute to the fight for equality?

- What contributions did African Americans make to the arts?

KEY TERMS AND PEOPLE

GI Bill
United Negro
  College Fund
Jesse Owens
Marian Anderson
swing
Lena Horne
Jacob Lawrence

BUILDING BACKGROUND

After World War II, African Americans began to play a larger role in the nation's cultural activities. The success of black artists, actors, writers, and athletes brought to the nation's attention the achievements of African Americans throughout the country. ■

Returning from War

American soldiers returning home from World War II found many new opportunities available to them. Even before the war had ended, President Roosevelt had signed what became known as the **GI Bill**, an act designed to help soldiers attend college or receive advanced training in a career. The bill also provided loans to returning soldiers who wished to buy farms or homes.

The GI Bill and Higher Education

Though the GI Bill was intended to apply equally to all returning soldiers, some African American soldiers found it difficult to take full advantage of the bill, for various reasons. Some could not afford to do so, as the grants often were not large enough to provide for families. Many ex-soldiers had no choice but to stay home and look for work rather than attend college. In addition, some prospective students faced discrimination from college admissions boards and the Department of Veterans' Affairs, an organization created to help meet the needs of returning soldiers.

Even with these obstacles, black college enrollment did increase greatly after the war. Not only were more black students enrolling in college but more institutions of higher learning were opening their doors to black students. Still, about half of these students were enrolled in historically black colleges and universities.

In the depressed economy that followed World War II, donations to private African American colleges decreased. Concerned, Dr. Frederick Patterson, then president of Tuskegee Institute, wrote to his peers to inquire if they were faced with the same difficulties. When he learned that they were, Patterson proposed a solution.

> **INFO TO KNOW**
> In the years following World War II a Second Great Migration took place as large numbers of African Americans once again moved north.

> **KEY FACTS**
> **1.** Underline the reasons why some African Americans were unable to take full advantage of the GI Bill.

He suggested that the schools collectively appeal to the nation for donations. A year later, in April 1944, the **United Negro College Fund** (UNCF) was created to give financial support to African American students pursuing a higher education. With support from President Roosevelt and John D. Rockefeller Jr., among others, the first campaign was a resounding success; together the 27 founding institutions raised three times as much money as they had raised independently the previous year.

Confronting Racism

Although racism and discrimination continued after World War II, the federal government did make an effort to end it. In 1948 President Harry S Truman issued an executive order that was intended to end segregation in the military.

> **HISTORY'S VOICES**
>
> "It is hereby declared to be the policy of the President that there shall be equality of treatment and opportunity for all persons in the armed services without regard to race, color, religion, or national origin."
>
> —Harry S Truman, Executive Order 9981, July 26, 1948

✔ Reading Check
2. Explain What was the purpose of the GI Bill?

Despite some resistance, the armed forces began the slow process of integration. At first, blacks were admitted into the armed forces on the basis of a quota system, and many continued to serve in segregated units. Military segregation officially ended in 1954 when the secretary of defense declared that the last remaining all-black unit had been disbanded. ✔

The Push for Equality

As the government was taking the first steps toward ending discrimination in this country, many African Americans were striving on their own to win recognition for their abilities and talents. They hoped to use their newfound recognition to gain acceptance for African Americans throughout the country.

African American Athletes

In one week, **Jesse Owens**, the son of a sharecropper and grandson to a slave, accomplished what no Olympian had ever achieved before. He won four gold medals in track and field in the 1936 Olympic Games in Berlin, Germany, then under Nazi rule. Owens had not only proved himself the fastest man in the world, he had, before Adolf Hitler's own eyes, crushed the myth of white supremacy.

Another popular athlete was Joe Louis. Known as the "Brown Bomber," Louis became the world heavyweight boxing champion in 1937, a title that he would hold on to until 1949. His first professional loss was to a German boxer named Max Schmeling in 1936. Louis faced off against Schmeling in a rematch in 1938 and won. At the time, many Americans viewed this fight as a symbol of the struggle between U.S. democracy and German Nazism. To this day, Louis is regarded by many as the greatest heavyweight boxer of all time.

What Joe Louis had done for African Americans just before World War II, famed boxer Jack Johnson did in the years before World War I. Johnson was the first black man to win international recognition as a sports figure when he became boxing's world heavyweight champion in 1908.

In the 1936 Olympic Games, Jesse Owens captured the world's attention by winning four gold medals.

Marian Anderson and Eleanor Roosevelt

Meanwhile, African Americans continued to demonstrate their persistence and commitment to excellence in arenas such as education and entertainment. One of the most public supporters of equality for African Americans was first lady Eleanor Roosevelt. A personal friend of Mary McLeod Bethune, Roosevelt helped Bethune gain influence with the government. When Eleanor Roosevelt was photographed walking with two black Howard University ROTC cadets, African Americans around the country circulated the image as an example of Roosevelt's commitment to her belief in promoting equal rights.

Renowned concert singer **Marian Anderson** is another talented African American who won the admiration of public figures such as Roosevelt. In 1939 Anderson attempted to schedule a booking at the famous Constitution Hall. However, the conservative group that owned the building—the Daughters of the American Revolution (DAR)—refused her permission to do so. Roosevelt was so upset by the racial snub that she resigned from the DAR in protest. Anderson ended up performing on the steps of the Lincoln Memorial in Washington, D.C., instead. The performance became the most famous of her career. A host of notables, including the first lady, attended the concert, which drew a crowd of 75,000 people. ✔

✔ **Reading Check**
3. Elaborate What steps were some blacks taking to gain mainstream acceptance?

African Americans in the Arts

As influential as African Americans were in sports and other fields, nowhere was their influence felt more than in the arts. From music to film to literature, black artists made major contributions to American culture in the 1930s and 1940s.

The Swing Era

In the 1930s a new type of music had captured the attention of the nation. Called **swing**, this music was a type of jazz that featured complicated, carefully planned orchestrations. Among the pioneers of swing music were many prominent African Americans.

Edward "Duke" Ellington was one of the top creative geniuses of the Jazz Age, as the period was often called. In the early 1920s Ellington made his way to New York and began working with a band called The Washingtonians. By 1927 Ellington and his band had a permanent gig at the famous Cotton Club in Harlem.

For more than fifty years, Ellington would perform elegantly in top hat and tails, leading his band in numbers that he had written. His compositions won fame for displaying one musical innovation after another. In 1943, for example, he interwove jazz into the traditional concert format in his smash hit "Black, Brown, and Beige."

Performing Arts

Actor Paul Robeson, blues singer Bessie Smith, and jazz musician Duke Ellington (from left to right) were among the most popular artists of the 1930s and 1940s.

4. Use a graphic organizer to identify African American contributors to the arts.

Contributions to the Arts	
Person	Contribution

A popular trend in swing music was the introduction of scat, a form of singing that uses random syllables rather than distinct words. Among the masters of this form of singing was black bandleader Cab Calloway. Scat features prominently in his biggest hit, "Minnie the Moocher," released in 1931.

Another popular black bandleader was William "Count" Basie. A brilliant piano player, Basie formed a band that became well known for its lively playing and the excellent recordings they made. In addition to their own music, Count Basie and his band won fame for inviting great vocalists to perform with them. Among the famous African Americans who performed with Count Basie and his band was Billie Holiday, considered by many to be one of the greatest female jazz singers ever.

Louis Armstrong of New Orleans was another famous musician and bandleader. Known as a phenomenal trumpet player, Armstrong—nicknamed Satchmo—toured the country with his band, selling out performances everywhere. He continued to play trumpet and sing into the 1960s, even knocking the Beatles out of the number-one spot on the charts with his release of "Hello, Dolly" in 1964.

African Americans on Stage

African Americans also made great contributions to theater and film. For example, Paul Robeson, a Columbia law school graduate, won great fame for his dramatic roles on stage. In New York, Robeson spent much of his spare time with the black literary crowd, which also included such liberal white writers and artists as Carl Van Vechten and Eugene O'Neill. Before long, O'Neill asked him to take the lead role in his new play *All God's Chillun Got Wings*. The daring play immediately became the center of furious controversy, because its theme was interracial marriage. Robeson was an activist who openly criticized racism. He was later blacklisted in the 1940s for his refusal to deny his suspected Communist leanings.

Black female playwrights of the period examined such issues as lynching, superstition, poverty, and ignorance. May Miller's 1933 play *Nails and Thorns* deals with the mob killing of a black man who is mentally handicapped. African American culture and black historical figures were also topics of examination. Shirley Graham was a composer, playwright, and biographer, among other things. Her 1932 opera *Tom-Tom* is credited by some as the first opera written by an African American woman.

Cabin in the Sky, the first big budget Hollywood movie with an all black cast, premiered in 1943.

African Americans in Film

By the 1930s African Americans were coming to more prominence in the movie industry. Though criticized by some for playing stereotypical roles, Hattie McDaniel won an Academy Award for Best Supporting Actress for her role as Mammy in *Gone with the Wind*. She was the first African American to win an Oscar, as well as the first African American to be nominated. Positive leading roles for African Americans in films, however, remained the exception.

Lena Horne, a talented singer and actor, was one of the most popular African American entertainers of the 1940s and 1950s. She was the first African American actor to sign a long-term contract with a major movie studio, MGM. A pioneer in the entertainment industry, she broke down racial barriers by refusing to play the subservient roles usually reserved for black actresses at that time. The studio, unwilling to risk losing the mostly segregated southern market, cast her in scenes that could be cut easily when shown in southern theaters. Still, Horne appealed to both black and white audiences and was the country's highest paid black actor in the mid-1940s.

African American Contributions to Art and Literature

Black artists, writers, and poets also made a great impression during this period. One such artist was **Jacob Lawrence**. He was encouraged from an early age to pursue his interests in art and African American history, subjects that are evident in his many paintings, prints, and murals. In 1941 Lawrence completed his best-known series of paintings, *The Migration of the Negro*.

> **INFO TO KNOW**
> Lawrence served in the Coast Guard's first racially integrated crew during World War II.

Black writers and poets also made a great impression during this period. One talented writer of the 1930s and 1940s was Richard Wright. In 1940 he wrote *Native Son*, a telling commentary on racism in American society. The story of a young black man indicted for murder in Chicago, *Native Son* became a bestseller. So did his equally passionate *Black Boy*, published in 1945, which told of Wright's own experiences with prejudice as a young African American man growing up in the South under Jim Crow laws.

The stirring, lyrical poetry of Gwendolyn Brooks so moved readers that she became the first African American poet to win a Pulitzer Prize. She won the prestigious award in 1950 for her book *Annie Allen*, whose poems loosely chronicle the life of an African American woman growing up in Chicago.

Another prominent black author of the day was Ralph Ellison. His novel *Invisible Man* won the National Book Award in 1953. A fictionalized autobiography, it tells the story of a young black man who feels overlooked by society because of his race. Ellison continued to win acclaim for his work. He was also a skilled musician, photographer, and professor. ✔

> ✔ **Reading Check**
> **5. Identify** What were some ways in which African Americans influenced the arts?
> _____
> _____
> _____
> _____

SECTION 3 ASSESSMENT

go.hrw.com
Online Quiz
Keyword: SAAH HP9

Reviewing Ideas, Terms, and People

6. Describe How did black athletes and artists work for equality in the 1930s and 1940s?
_____
_____

7. Explain How did the GI Bill help lead to changes in African American society?
_____
_____

8. Elaborate How could the presence of African American stars in films have helped change white attitudes toward black Americans?
_____
_____

Creating a Scrapbook Page

African Americans made great strides toward equality during the 1930s and 1940s. Use the space provided to create a scrapbook page that highlights some of the accomplishments of black Americans during this period. Be sure to include images, text, and other artifacts to tell the story of their many contributions.

Contributions to Culture and Society

ASSESS YOUR KNOWLEDGE

1. **Identify** What other sorts of artifacts might make a scrapbook on African Americans during this time period complete?

   _____

   _____

2. **Evaluate** Which contribution of African Americans during this period do you think was most important? Why?

   _____

   _____

Writing a Biopic

A biographical picture (often shortened to biopic) is a film that dramatizes the life of an actual person. A biopic attempts to tell a person's life story, though some films cover only a certain period of the person's life.

Research a jazz legend from the Swing Era. Choose someone mentioned in the text, or you may choose another person to research. Select an event or turning point to focus on and write a scene for a biopic. Remember to include detailed, vivid descriptions.

Scene 1

Description

_____

_____

_____

_____

_____

_____

_____

_____

_____

_____

The Great Depression and World War II

CHAPTER SUMMARY

SECTION 1   Depression and Recovery

- In the 1920s there was a shift from economic prosperity to economic depression.
- The Great Depression affected the lives of Americans from all economic and social backgrounds.
- Roosevelt's New Deal brought some relief to the American people.

SECTION 2   African Americans in World War II

- World War II began in Europe after Hitler invaded Poland in 1939.
- About 1 million African Americans served in the armed forces during World War II.
- African Americans made great contributions to the war effort on the home front.
- Though steps toward equality were made during World War II, discrimination against African Americans continued.

SECTION 3   Social and Cultural Changes

- New educational and employment opportunities were available to black soldiers returning from World War II.
- Prominent African Americans contributed to the fight for racial equality by using their recognition to gain acceptance for African Americans throughout the nation.
- African Americans made many contributions to music, art, and literature during the 1930s and 1940s.

First Steps Toward EQUALITY

Protesters arrive for the March on Washington, a massive civil rights rally in 1963. The rally was part of a modern civil rights movement that swept the nation in the 1950s and 1960s.

EXPRESSING YOUR OPINION

Would you be willing to take a stand to protest laws you thought were discriminatory? Write a paragraph explaining your response.

As You Read

Battling Segregation

1. **TAKING NOTES** Use a graphic organizer like this one to take notes on civil rights in the postwar period, school desegregation, and other calls for change. Use the **Reading Focus** questions on the next page to help guide your note taking.

2. As you read the section, underline or highlight definitions and descriptions of the **Key Terms and People** listed on the next page.

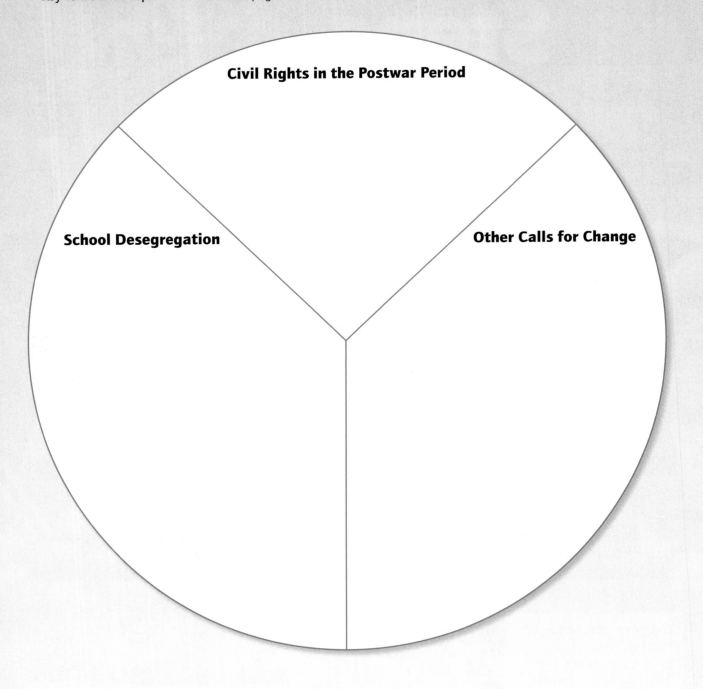

Civil Rights in the Postwar Period

School Desegregation

Other Calls for Change

Battling Segregation

BEFORE YOU READ

MAIN IDEA

In the late 1940s and early 1950s African Americans successfully broke down "separate but equal" barriers in education and professional baseball.

READING FOCUS

- What civil rights progress was made during the postwar period?
- What methods did civil rights activists use to desegregate public schools?
- What other events during this period led civil rights activists to call for change?

KEY TERMS AND PEOPLE

Thurgood Marshall
Sweatt v. *Painter*
Brown v. *Board of Education*
Little Rock Nine
Jackie Robinson
Emmett Till

BUILDING BACKGROUND

After World War II, black soldiers who had risked their lives to serve their country came home to face racial discrimination. Such treatment angered many blacks. "I paid my dues over there," said veteran James Hicks, "and I'm not going to take this anymore over here." Many black veterans joined with other African Americans to push harder for equality. Their efforts helped launch a civil rights movement that soon swept the nation. ▪

Civil Rights in the Postwar Period

The push for black civil rights in the United States gained new momentum after World War II. As black veterans came home, many of them were no longer willing to put up with discrimination. They and other African Americans began to call for an end to racial inequality. The result was a number of key gains for African Americans. As you have read, in 1948 President Harry S Truman desegregated the armed forces. That same year, Truman also banned discrimination in the hiring of federal employees. President Dwight D. Eisenhower, elected in 1952, took further steps to reduce racial discrimination in hiring practices. Meanwhile, at the state level, several northern and western states passed laws banning racial discrimination in public housing.

Despite these gains, many opportunities remained closed to African Americans in the 1950s. Although this period was a time of economic prosperity for many white Americans, few black Americans shared in this new wealth. Furthermore, white resistance to black equality remained strong. Such opposition was particularly evident in the South, where white citizens continued to use unfair laws, fear, and violence to try to keep black citizens from voting or from standing up for their rights.

One major barrier to equality for blacks was segregation. Custom and laws continued to separate black and white Americans in schools, housing, and jobs. Segregation was most rigid in the South, where Jim Crow laws forced blacks to use "colored only" waiting rooms, restaurants, and other facilities. The 1896 Supreme Court case *Plessy* v. *Ferguson* had established the "separate but equal" doctrine legalizing segregation. Separate black and white facilities were rarely equal, however. One glaring example of this inequality was the nation's black schools. A new generation of black leaders thus turned their attention to fighting segregation in education. ✔

VIRTUAL FIELD TRIP
Go online to experience a virtual field trip to key sites from the early civil rights movements.

go.hrw.com
Chapter Activity
Keyword: SAAH CH10

✔ **Reading Check**
1. **Summarize** What gains did African Americans make in the late 1940s?

School Desegregation

In most cases, the separate schools for black students were far inferior to the schools for white students. One reason was that states often spent far less on students in black schools than those in white schools. For example, in 1940 southern states spent less than $17 per black student and more than $40 per white student. Because of this limited funding, black schools often had out-of-date textbooks, old and inadequate buildings, and fewer extracurricular programs. Such inequalities had far-reaching effects on black children's later opportunities and success in life.

Fighting Segregation

Civil rights activists had long been fighting school segregation. In the 1840s Robert Morris, one of the nation's first black attorneys, and Charles Sumner, a white lawyer, sued the city of Boston. The lawsuit claimed that Boston's segregated schools violated the state constitution. The men lost the case, but it established an important principle that later activists would use—that segregated schools are inherently unequal.

In the 1930s Charles Hamilton Houston, head of the National Association for the Advancement of Colored People (NAACP), launched a campaign against segregation. Houston developed a strategy to chip away at the "separate but equal" doctrine, particularly in education. He hired **Thurgood Marshall**, a brilliant young black lawyer, to lead the team as the NAACP's chief legal counsel.

Under Houston and Marshall, NAACP lawyers won a series of court cases challenging the "separate but equal" doctrine. One victory was against the University of Missouri. The university had refused to admit Lloyd Gaines, a black student, to its law school because of his race. The university instead offered to help pay for Gaines to go to an out-of-state law school.

In the 1938 case *Gaines* v. *Canada*, the U.S. Supreme Court ruled that states had to provide equal educational facilities within their borders. Thus, each state had to provide separate black schools—including law schools—or admit black students to its white schools. The victory was a major step forward toward ending segregation in higher education.

Instead of integrating its law school, the University of Missouri created a black law school in St. Louis. Gaines never had the chance to attend the school, however. On March 19, 1939, he disappeared in Chicago, Illinois. He was presumed murdered, and the case remains unsolved.

ACADEMIC VOCABULARY
2. Use the context, or surrounding words in the sentence, to write a definition of **inherently**.

FACES OF HISTORY

Thurgood MARSHALL
1908–1993

The grandson of slaves, Thurgood Marshall spent much of his life fighting inequality and discrimination. Marshall himself faced discrimination when, as a young man, he was denied admission to the University of Maryland Law School because of his race. After attending law school at Howard University, Marshall joined a small law practice in Baltimore. There, his first major case was a lawsuit against the University of Maryland Law School on the part of another black student who had been denied admission. Marshall won that case and went on to win many other legal challenges to segregation. One of Marshall's greatest legal victories was his challenge to public school segregation in the landmark case *Brown* v. *Board of Education of Topeka, Kansas*. In 1967 Thurgood Marshall made history again when he became the first African American appointed to the U.S. Supreme Court.

3. Summarize What role did Thurgood Marshall play in ending racial segregation?

In 1946 Marshall and the NAACP represented Heman Sweatt, another black student denied access to a law school. The school in this case was the University of Texas. A lower court had ruled that unless the state of Texas established a "separate but equal" law school for black students, the university would have to admit Sweatt. To meet the requirement, the University of Texas created a black law school in the basement of a house. This makeshift law school did not even come close to being equal to the university's prestigious all-white law school.

The NAACP appealed, and in 1950 Marshall argued the case before the U.S. Supreme Court. In **Sweatt v. Painter** the Court ruled that the University of Texas black law school was inferior to its white law school. Furthermore, the Court ruled that separate law schools hurt the education of black law students. This major victory forced the nation's graduate and professional schools to integrate.

That same year, the NAACP took on another school segregation case. George McLaurin, a black student, had been admitted to the University of Oklahoma graduate program. However, the university had forced McLaurin to sit apart from white students in classrooms, the library, and the cafeteria. The U.S. Supreme Court ruled in *McLaurin* v. *Oklahoma State Regents* that these restrictions were unconstitutional.

These legal victories helped break down segregation in higher education. Yet the nation's public elementary and secondary schools remained segregated—and very unequal. The NAACP decided to push for the integration of all public schools.

Brown v. Board of Education

In 1954 Thurgood Marshall argued a case before the U.S. Supreme Court that forever changed education in the United States. The case was actually a combination of court cases challenging the constitutionality of segregated public schools. The Supreme Court combined the cases under the name of one of them, *Brown* v. *Board of Education of Topeka, Kansas*. In that case, NAACP members in Topeka tried to enroll their children, including Linda Brown, in white neighborhood schools. The schools refused to admit the black students, who had to attend black schools farther away.

The Supreme Court heard arguments in the case over a two-year period. In his arguments, Thurgood Marshall provided research suggesting that segregation harmed the self-image of young black students. The research helped influence the Court's final decision. In 1954 in **Brown v. Board of Education**, the U.S. Supreme Court unanimously ruled that the "separate but equal" doctrine in the nation's public schools was unconstitutional and therefore that racial segregation in public schools was illegal. Chief Justice Earl Warren wrote the landmark decision in the *Brown* case.

HISTORY'S VOICES

"It is doubtful that any child may reasonably be expected to succeed in life if he is denied the opportunity of an education. Such an opportunity, where the state has undertaken to provide it, is a right which must be made available to all on equal terms . . . Does segregation of children in public schools solely on the basis of race . . . deprive the children of the minority group of equal educational opportunities? We believe that it does . . . We conclude that, in the field of public education, the doctrine of 'separate but equal' has no place. Separate educational facilities are inherently unequal."

—Chief Justice Earl Warren, *Brown v. Board of Education of Topeka, Kansas,* May 17, 1954

KEY FACTS

4. Identify the four U.S. Supreme Court cases from 1938 to 1954 that challenged the doctrine of "separate but equal" in public education.

Case: _____
_____
Date: _____
Ruling: _____
_____
_____
_____

Case: _____
_____
Date: _____
Ruling: _____
_____
_____
_____

Case: _____
_____
Date: _____
Ruling: _____
_____
_____
_____

Case: _____
_____
Date: _____
Ruling: _____
_____
_____
_____

Integrating Central High School

The famous photograph above shows Elizabeth Eckford, one of the Little Rock Nine, walking to Central High School on September 4, 1957. The white girl shouting at Eckford's back is Hazel Massery. Later, Massery regretted her actions and in 1963 apologized to Eckford. The two women, at right, became friends and have spoken publicly about their experiences.

KEY FACTS

5. List the main events in the Little Rock crisis in the order in which they occurred.

Crisis in Little Rock

At the time of the *Brown* decision, 21 states had laws segregating public schools. Reaction to school integration in these states was mixed. Many black leaders praised the *Brown* decision, and a few white leaders agreed to start desegregating, or integrating, public schools. However, other white leaders strongly opposed school integration, and some even vowed to defy it. For example, in Virginia several white officials pledged to join forces to block school integration at all levels. The Virginia legislature did its part by passing laws forcing the closure of any school that integrated and by helping white students attend all-white private schools.

School segregation in the South moved slowly, and only three southern school districts had desegregated by the end of 1954. In 1955 the U.S. Supreme Court strengthened the *Brown* ruling by ordering public schools to desegregate "with all deliberate speed." Enforcing the order proved difficult, however. Demonstrations against integration took place in many parts of the South, and some white citizens even burned crosses in protest. In the end, a crisis in Little Rock, Arkansas, compelled President Eisenhower and the federal government to take action.

As in many other parts of the South, in Little Rock the school board adopted a plan to desegregate its public schools gradually, one at a time. In the fall of 1957 the board allowed nine outstanding black students to attend the city's white Central High School. These students became known as the **Little Rock Nine**. Arkansas governor Orval Faubus, in violation of a federal court order, called out the Arkansas National Guard to keep the nine students from entering the white high school. Faubus claimed that this action was necessary to protect the school from white extremists who had threatened violence.

On September 4, 1957, the first day of school, some local ministers brought eight of the nine black students to Central High School. An angry white crowd confronted the students. At the school door, the National Guard barred the way and refused to let the students enter. The ninth black student, 15-year-old Elizabeth Eckford, had not received a message about where to meet the other students. Arriving at the school alone, Eckford was surrounded by a hostile white crowd as she made her way toward the building. When the National Guard turned her away, someone in the crowd began yelling, "Lynch her! Lynch her!" As Eckford struggled to escape, a white woman came forward and helped her safely leave.

For nearly three weeks, members of the Arkansas National Guard prevented the Little Rock Nine from entering Central High School. The tense situation continued until President Eisenhower sent more than a thousand federal troops to Little Rock to end the standoff. On September 25, 1957, U.S. soldiers with fixed bayonets escorted the nine black students into Central High School.

Once in school, the black students endured frequent abuse. White students called them names and kicked and shoved them in the halls. The students even received death threats and had to be assigned guards for protection. Despite such difficulties, eight of the nine students remained at Central High, and in May 1958 Ernest Green became the school's first black graduate. Green recalled that none of his classmates clapped when his name was called. "But I figured they didn't have to," he said, "I had accomplished what I came there for." The Little Rock crisis revealed just how strong racism was in some areas, and school desegregation continued for decades. ✔

Other Calls for Change

In addition to fighting segregation in schools, African Americans battled segregation in other areas of society. One of these areas was Major League Baseball. In the late 1940s the NAACP took on this challenge with the help of a highly talented athlete.

Breaking the Color Line in Professional Baseball

In the early years of professional baseball, African Americans had played on major-league teams. In the 1880s, however, major-league teams began refusing to sign black players. Talented black ballplayers had few opportunities to play professionally until the 1920s, when the Negro League formed.

In the early 1940s black civil rights activists began working to end segregation in Major League Baseball. The breakthrough came when Branch Rickey, owner of the Brooklyn Dodgers, agreed to sign a black ballplayer. Rickey knew he needed not only a star black player but also one who could withstand the insults he would surely face. He chose **Jackie Robinson**, a gifted athlete who had lettered in four sports in college. On April 15, 1947, Robinson broke the color line in Major League Baseball when he played his first game with the Brooklyn Dodgers.

The decision to sign Jackie Robinson was a phenomenal success for the Brooklyn Dodgers. In his first year on the team, Robinson won the National League's "Rookie of the Year" award.

✔ **Reading Check**
6. Find the Main Idea What was the significance of the case *Brown v. Board of Education*?

_____
_____
_____
_____
_____
_____
_____

▼ **Jackie Robinson became a hero to millions by breaking the color line in Major League Baseball. He went on to become an award-winning player.**

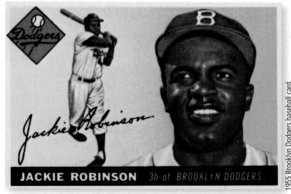

1955 Brooklyn Dodgers baseball card.
The Granger Collection, New York.

An amazing ballplayer, he went on to become the National League's Most Valuable Player in 1949. Rickey had asked Robinson not to talk or fight back when people shouted insults at him. Robinson's agreed, and his dignity combined with his immense talent earned him the admiration of millions of fans. He retired in 1956, and in 1962 became the first African American named to the Baseball Hall of Fame.

The Murder of Emmett Till

Despite early victories against segregation, blacks remained second-class citizens to many white Americans, particularly in the South. This truth gained nationwide attention in 1955 with the murder of **Emmett Till**, a 14-year-old boy from Chicago, Illinois. Till had gone to Mississippi to visit his great uncle. Having grown up in the North, the black teenager did not understand the South's strict racial etiquette.

Soon after arriving in Mississippi, Till and some other black teenagers went to a small grocery owned by a young couple, Roy and Carolyn Bryant. Roy was not in the store at the time. Egged on by his comrades, Till made a comment to Carolyn Bryant. She later claimed he asked her for a date and whistled at her, but historians do not know for certain. Whatever Till said, she took offense. Although she did not tell her husband, he soon found out about the incident.

Four days later, Roy Bryant and his half brother J. W. Milam kidnapped Till in the middle of the night. They brutally beat and shot him and then tossed his body in the Tallahatchie River. National reports of Till's murder deeply moved many Americans.

HISTORY'S VOICES

"His mother had done a bold thing. She refused to let him be buried until . . . thousands marched past his open casket in Chicago and looked down at his mutilated body. I felt a deep kinship to him . . . I couldn't get Emmett out of my mind."

—Muhammad Ali, boxer

Bryant and Milam stood trial for the crime, but a jury of 12 white men found them not guilty. Months later, the two men confessed to the killing to a reporter for *Look* magazine. Till's senseless murder—and his killers' acquittal—awakened more Americans to the racism that southern blacks faced and to the need for action. ✔

▲ This photograph shows Emmett Till with his mother, Mamie Till. She insisted on an open casket at Till's funeral in Chicago so that people could see what had been done to her son. Some 50,000 people attended Till's funeral.

✔ **Reading Check**

7. Analyze How did other events during this period affect the fight for civil rights?

_____

_____

_____

_____

_____

_____

_____

SECTION 1 ASSESSMENT

go.hrw.com
Online Quiz
Keyword: SAAH HP10

Reviewing Ideas, Terms, and People

8. Recall How did segregation and discrimination affect southern blacks in the 1950s?

_____

_____

9. Summarize How did NAACP cases open up education to black students?

_____

_____

10. Elaborate How did the murder of Emmett Till expose the racial hatred in the South?

_____

_____

Interpreting Political Cartoons

Understand the Skill

Political cartoons are drawings that express views on issues to influence public opinion. Often, political cartoons use both words and images to convey a specific message or viewpoint. In addition, political cartoons often include symbolism or caricatures. A caricature is a drawing that exaggerates the characteristics of a person or object.

Learn the Skill

Use the following strategies to learn how to interpret political cartoons.

Step 1 Identify the topic of the cartoon. *What issue, person, or event do you think this 1960 political cartoon addresses?*

_____

_____

_____

Step 2 Read all titles, labels, captions, and any other text in the cartoon. *What clues does the text provide about this cartoon's message?*

_____

_____

_____

"Inch by Inch." Copyright © 1960 by Bill Mauldin. Displayed courtesy of the William Mauldin estate.

Step 3 Study all the images in the cartoon. Determine if any of them are exaggerated and, if so, why. Identify the meaning of any symbols in the cartoon. *What exaggerated images does this cartoon contain?*

_____

_____

_____

Step 4 Analyze all the information you gathered to determine the cartoon's message. *What do you think is the message of this political cartoon?*

_____

_____

_____

APPLY THE SKILL

Draw Conclusions What does the political cartoon imply about school desegregation?

_____

_____

As You Read

The Civil Rights Movement Takes Shape

1. **TAKING NOTES** Use a graphic organizer like this one to take notes on protesting segregated transportation, Martin Luther King Jr., and nonviolent protest. Use the **Reading Focus** questions on the next page to help guide your note taking.

2. As you read the section, underline or highlight definitions and descriptions of each of the **Key Terms and People** listed on the next page.

Protesting Segregated Transportation

Martin Luther King Jr.

Nonviolent Protest

2 The Civil Rights Movement Takes Shape

BEFORE YOU READ

MAIN IDEA

With the victory over segregation in schools, civil rights activists fought to end segregation in transportation and other areas of American society.

READING FOCUS

- In what ways did civil rights activists protest segregation in public transportation?
- What was the significance of Martin Luther King Jr. in the civil rights movement?
- How did the strategy of nonviolent protest help civil rights activists in their cause?

KEY TERMS AND PEOPLE

Rosa Parks
Montgomery bus boycott
Martin Luther King Jr.
Southern Christian Leadership Conference (SCLC)
Mohandas Gandhi
James Lawson
sit-in
Student Nonviolent Coordinating Committee (SNCC)

BUILDING BACKGROUND

During the late 1940s and early 1950s civil rights activists successfully ended legalized segregation in the military and public schools. These victories were just a start, however. As the drive for equality gained momentum, activists fought segregation in other areas of society, and a civil rights movement began to take shape. ◼

Protesting Segregated Transportation

The Supreme Court's *Brown* decision striking down the "separate but equal" doctrine in public schools had a major impact on American society. However, segregation continued to be enforced in many other public places and facilities in the South. One major area that remained segregated was public transportation.

Baton Rouge Bus Boycott

African Americans had been fighting segregation in public transportation since the 1860s. For example, early activists had protested segregation on streetcar lines and trains. Despite some victories by activists, public transportation remained segregated in much of the South. In the early 1950s some civil rights leaders decided to fight this type of segregation by organizing boycotts of city buses.

One boycott took place in Baton Rouge, Louisiana, in 1953. The bus system in Baton Rouge reserved the first 10 seats for white passengers and the rest of the seats for black passengers. If all the "black" seats were taken, black passengers had to stand, even if a "white" seat was available. If a white passenger could not find a seat, a black passenger had to stand to let the white passenger sit.

T. J. Jemison, a black minister, decided to oppose the bus system's practice of reserved seating. He began speaking out against the practice and pressuring the Baton Rouge council to end it. The council eventually agreed to a compromise. Black passengers could sit in any empty seat as long as no white passengers were standing.

KEY FACTS

1. Underline or highlight the description of the way in which the Baton Rouge city buses were segregated.

FACES OF HISTORY

Rosa PARKS
1913–2005

Civil rights activist Rosa Parks is considered by many people to be the "mother of the civil rights movement." For much of her life, Parks was dedicated to improving the lives of black Americans. As a member of the NAACP, she worked with the black youth of Montgomery, Alabama. In 1955 her refusal to give up her seat on a public bus triggered the Montgomery bus boycott and a national civil rights movement that transformed the nation. In 1957 Parks and her family relocated to Detroit, Michigan. There, she helped create an organization that promotes education and activism among young people. During her lifetime, Parks was honored with many awards, among them the Presidential Medal of Freedom and the Congressional Gold Medal of Honor.

2. Infer Why might many people consider Parks the "mother of the civil rights movement"?

_____

_____

_____

_____

KEY FACTS

3. Use the graphic organizers below to list the key facts for each of the bus boycotts.

Baton Rouge Bus Boycott

Montgomery Bus Boycott

The Baton Rouge bus drivers refused to enforce the new law, however. When the bus company pressured them, the drivers went on strike. The Louisiana attorney general then struck down the Baton Rouge law, stating that it violated state laws enforcing segregation.

The bus drivers went back to work, but African Americans in Baton Rouge were outraged. In protest, Jemison and Raymond Scott, a black tailor, organized a boycott of the Baton Rouge bus system. By the next day, African Americans across the city had stopped riding the buses. Instead, boycott participants organized carpools or walked. Many of the protesters pooled their money to pay for gasoline, and a local gas station helped by selling them gasoline at cost.

After nearly a week, the boycott leaders reached a new compromise with city officials. The first two seats on city buses would be reserved for white passengers, and the back row would be reserved for black passengers. People of any race could sit in between. Jemison announced the decision at a meeting of protesters. Although some wanted to continue the boycott to end reserved seating entirely, most agreed to the compromise. The Baton Rouge bus boycott had succeeded after only five days.

Montgomery Bus Boycott

In 1955 a similar boycott began in Montgomery, Alabama. As in Baton Rouge, the Montgomery bus system required black passengers to sit in a "colored section" in the back of buses. Furthermore, black passengers were not allowed to share rows with white passengers. When a bus's "white section" was full, the driver expected an entire row of black passengers to stand so that one white passenger could sit.

The NAACP wanted to fight segregation on Montgomery's city buses. The organization found its test case with **Rosa Parks**, a 42-year-old seamstress and the secretary of the Montgomery chapter of the NAACP. On December 1, 1955, Parks boarded a city bus after a day at work and sat in the first row of the "colored section." When the "white section" filled up, the driver told Parks and three other black passengers to give their seats to white passengers. Parks refused and was arrested and taken to jail.

The NAACP recognized the opportunity that the arrest of Parks presented. With her cooperation, the organization called for a one-day boycott, which became known as the **Montgomery bus boycott**, of the city's bus system. Some two-thirds of bus passengers in Montgomery were black, and about 90 percent of them participated in the boycott. This level of success led black community leaders to extend the boycott. To coordinate efforts, they formed the Montgomery Improvement Association (MIA).

The individual chosen to lead the MIA was **Martin Luther King Jr.**, a 26-year-old black Baptist minister. King was an experienced activist and an executive committee member of the NAACP. He had also gained a reputation as a powerful speaker whose words could motivate and inspire others. In time, these talents would help King become one of the most significant voices of the civil rights movement.

The organizers of the Montgomery bus boycott hoped they would achieve a quick victory, but city officials refused to negotiate with them. Boycott participants did not give up, however, despite the many hardships they faced. Many of the black residents who participated in the boycott did not own cars and had depended on the buses to get to work or to do errands. To help these people, boycott leaders organized a carpool system. For more than a year, boycotters carpooled, took taxis, rode bicycles, or simply walked. King later recalled, "We came to see that, in the long run, it is more honorable to walk in dignity than ride in humiliation."

Many of Montgomery's white residents reacted to the bus boycott with anger. The local police harassed and arrested carpool drivers, and local insurance agents canceled some boycotters' auto insurance policies. A few white opponents even resorted to violence. King received hate mail and threatening phone calls; his house and the houses of other boycott leaders were bombed. Such events helped the boycott gain national attention, and African Americans began staging similar boycotts elsewhere.

Meanwhile, the NAACP filed a lawsuit in federal court challenging segregation on city buses. The case eventually went before the U.S. Supreme Court, which ruled in 1956 that segregation on city buses was unconstitutional. The ruling overturned Montgomery's bus segregation laws. A month after the ruling, King and other boycott leaders rode Montgomery's first integrated city bus. ✔

✔ **Reading Check**
4. Identify Who were two key African American activists in the Montgomery bus boycott?

Martin Luther King Jr.

The Montgomery bus boycott launched the modern civil rights movement and propelled Martin Luther King Jr. to its forefront. As one of the nation's most prominent civil rights leaders, he inspired millions. But what had brought King to this point?

The Road to Montgomery

Martin Luther King Jr. was born into a middle-class family in Atlanta, Georgia, in 1929. His father was a college-educated Baptist preacher, and young King received a solid education. He attended public school until age 15 and then went to Morehouse College, a historically black college in Atlanta. After graduating in 1948, King attended Crozer Theological Seminary in Pennsylvania. He earned a degree in theology in 1951 and then obtained a doctorate from Boston University in 1955.

While in Boston, King met a young woman named Coretta Scott. The two married in 1953 and in time had two sons and two daughters. In 1954 King became pastor of Dexter Avenue Baptist Church in Montgomery. By this time, he had joined the NAACP and become active in working for civil rights.

Montgomery Bus Boycott
On March 20, 1956, Martin Luther King Jr. and his wife, Coretta Scott King, speak to reporters before a trial in which King faced boycott charges.

Creation of the SCLC

The success of the Montgomery bus boycott inspired African Americans across the South. As groups began staging protests to fight segregation, King and other civil rights leaders realized they could achieve more by working together. In 1957 representatives of MIA and several other groups met in Atlanta, Georgia. They formed an organization called the **Southern Christian Leadership Conference (SCLC)** to coordinate civil rights campaigns. The group's members elected King as their first president. The SCLC was strongly influenced by the Christian faith, and many of its members were church leaders. However, the group came to include people of many faiths and races.

The SCLC highlights the important role that churches played in the civil rights movement. Black churches prepared members for activism by giving them leadership opportunities denied to African Americans elsewhere. Churches also helped provide the support and self-respect activists needed to stand up to racial hatred and violence. Most of all, churches promoted faith in a better life, a vision that inspired countless African Americans and their allies in the struggle for equality. ✔

Nonviolent Protest

The SCLC became one of several civil rights groups that shared a commitment to protest through nonviolent means. In the late 1950s and 1960s this strategy of nonviolence became a hallmark of the civil rights movement.

The Strategy of Nonviolence

The model for nonviolent protest was **Mohandas Gandhi**, who helped lead India's struggle for independence from Great Britain. Gandhi, who was inspired by nonviolent Hindu traditions as well as by writer Henry David Thoreau, rejected all violence. He instead led protesters in peacefully disobeying the law in an effort to change it. By exposing themselves to harm, the protesters hoped to expose injustice. Gandhi thought this approach was the best way to achieve change in a society in which other people held most of the power. King and several other civil rights leaders agreed.

KEY FACTS

> **HISTORY'S VOICES**
>
> "Violence as a way of achieving racial justice is both impractical and immoral. It is impractical because it is a descending spiral ending in destruction for all. The old law of an eye for an eye leaves everybody blind. It is immoral because it seeks to humiliate the opponent rather than win his understanding . . . Violence ends by defeating itself."
>
> —Martin Luther King Jr., *Strides toward Freedom*, 1958

A key civil rights leader committed to nonviolent protest was **James Lawson**, a black minister. In the early 1950s Lawson visited India to study Gandhi's teachings. With King's encouragement, he then began conducting SCLC workshops on nonviolent protest methods. Lawson held these workshops in Nashville, Tennessee, and on the campuses of black colleges across the South. Nonviolent protests often provoked violent responses from white opponents. For this reason, the workshops trained activists how to protect themselves and to remain peaceful in the face of violence. The activists whom Lawson trained included a number of future leaders in the civil rights movement, among them Diane Nash. She later described Lawson's workshops.

"Jim Lawson . . . conducted weekly workshops . . . We would practice things such as how to protect your head from a beating and how to protect each other. If one person was taking a severe beating, we would practice other people putting their bodies in between that person and the violence, so that the violence could be more distributed . . . We would practice not striking back if someone struck us."

—Diane Nash, quoted in *Voices of Freedom*, by Henry Hampton and Steve Fayer

The Sit-in Movement

One method of nonviolent protest that became popular in the civil rights movement was the **sit-in**, a demonstration in which protesters sit down in a location and refuse to leave. Civil rights activists had been using sit-ins since the 1940s to challenge segregation in both public places and private businesses. Like public facilities, many private businesses in the South were segregated and some did not serve black customers at all.

In 1960 four black college students decided to challenge segregation at Woolworth lunch counters in Greensboro, North Carolina. Woolworth was a popular department store that often had lunch counters inside. In Greensboro, Woolworth let white customers sit down at one end of the lunch counter but required that black customers eat standing up at the other end. On February 1, the four black male students went into Woolworth and sat at the "whites only" section of the lunch counter. Although denied service, the young men remained sitting until the store closed.

The next day, the four men returned with some more students and resumed the sit-in. By the third day, protesters almost filled the lunch counter. As the sit-in continued, it attracted hundreds of supporters—both black and white—and became national news. The students who began the sit-in had read about nonviolent protest and adopted the strategy. No matter how rude or hostile white onlookers were, the sit-in participants refused to respond. The strategy won the protesters the support of many white Americans.

As the daily sit-ins gained national exposure, a sit-in movement spread across the South. Soon, activists were staging similar protests in about 50 southern cities. For example, James Lawson and Diane Nash launched a series of sit-ins in Nashville. To help the many sit-ins, supporters of all races boycotted and picketed the targeted businesses. At the same time, white opponents tried to end the sit-ins by dumping food on the protesters and in some cases beating them.

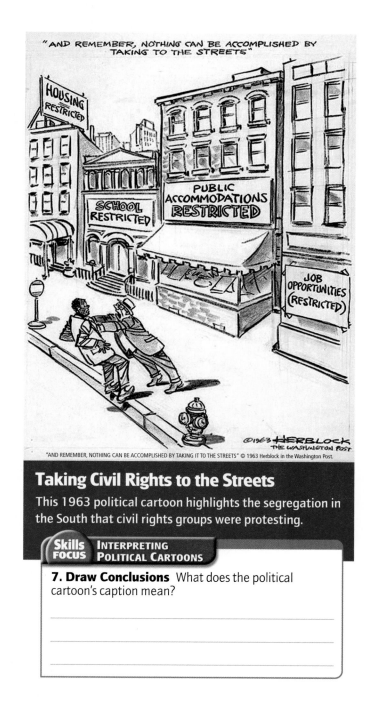

"AND REMEMBER, NOTHING CAN BE ACCOMPLISHED BY TAKING IT TO THE STREETS" © 1963 Herblock in the Washington Post.

Taking Civil Rights to the Streets

This 1963 political cartoon highlights the segregation in the South that civil rights groups were protesting.

Skills FOCUS INTERPRETING POLITICAL CARTOONS

7. Draw Conclusions What does the political cartoon's caption mean?

A Lunch Counter Sit-In

In this 1960 photograph, black and white protesters refuse to leave a segregated Woolworth lunch counter in Raleigh, North Carolina. In the background, two white waitresses watch them.

✔ Reading Check

8. Recall What event launched the sit-in movement, and when and where did this event occur?

_____

_____

_____

_____

_____

_____

By April 1960, police had arrested sit-in protesters across the South. Despite the arrests, several of the sit-ins were successful in getting business owners to change their policies. In May, many businesses in Nashville desegregated their lunch counters, and in July lunch counters in Greensboro did the same. By October, Woolworth and three other national chains had desegregated their lunch counters nationwide.

The sit-ins marked a shift in the civil rights movement. They demonstrated the success that black and white youth could achieve in the fight for civil rights. To organize future nonviolent protests, sit-in leaders formed the **Student Nonviolent Coordinating Committee (SNCC)**. The SNCC trained students in the strategy of nonviolence and organized civil rights demonstrations. The efforts of these and other young activists soon helped take the civil rights movement on the road. ✔

SECTION 2 ASSESSMENT

go.hrw.com
Online Quiz
Keyword: SAAH HP10

Reviewing Ideas, Terms, and People

9. Describe What were the results of the Montgomery bus boycott?

_____

_____

10. Draw Conclusions How did King's background prepare him for his role in the civil rights movement?

_____

_____

11. Elaborate Why do you think the sit-ins were so successful?

_____

_____

Creating a Problem-Solution Chart

Civil rights activists used various means to fight segregation during the 1950s and early 1960s. Using your notes from Section 2, create a chart describing the problems activists addressed during this period, the actions activists took to try to solve them, and the results of those actions. Use the template below to create your chart.

Problem	Solution/Actions	Results
1. segregation on city buses in the South		
2. numerous civil rights groups holding protests in the South during and after the Montgomery bus boycott		
3. segregated lunch counters in Woolworth and other private businesses in the South		

Copyright © by Holt, Rinehart and Winston. All rights reserved.

ASSESS YOUR KNOWLEDGE

1. **Summarize** What did civil rights activists achieve through the use of boycotts and sit-ins during this period?

_____

_____

2. **Analyze** Why were many civil rights activists committed to using nonviolent methods of protest?

_____

_____

The Movement Grows

1. **TAKING NOTES** Use a graphic organizer like this one to take notes on fighting discrimination on the road, the drive for voting rights, integrating higher education, and events in Albany, Birmingham, and Washington. Use the **Reading Focus** questions on the next page to help guide your note taking.

2. As you read the section, underline or highlight definitions and descriptions of each of the **Key Terms and People** listed on the next page.

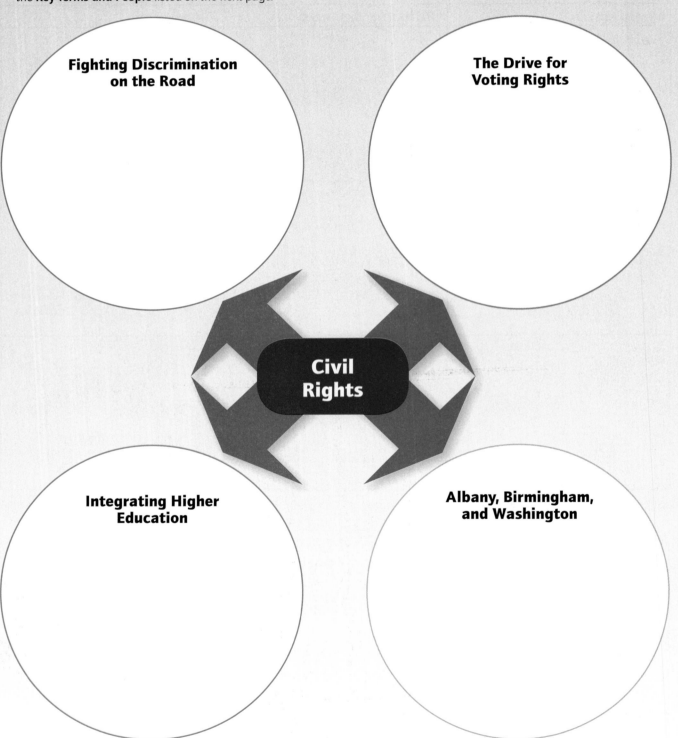

Fighting Discrimination on the Road

The Drive for Voting Rights

Civil Rights

Integrating Higher Education

Albany, Birmingham, and Washington

BEFORE YOU READ

MAIN IDEA

Through nonviolent protests and laws, civil rights activists made progress in the integration of interstate travel and higher education and in securing black voting rights.

READING FOCUS

- What further protests occurred to fight discrimination on the road?
- What key events occurred in the early drive for voting rights?
- In what ways did activists fight to integrate higher education?
- What protests occurred in Albany, Birmingham, and Washington, D.C.?

KEY TERMS AND PEOPLE

Congress of Racial Equality (CORE)
James Farmer
Freedom Rides
Civil Rights Act of 1957
James Meredith
Medgar Evers
March on Washington for Jobs and Freedom

BUILDING BACKGROUND

Nonviolent boycotts and sit-ins gained the civil rights movement national attention. Although not all of the protests were successful, many Americans were impressed with the courage and dignity of the black and white activists who took part in them. As public support for the civil rights movement grew, activists addressed new challenges in the struggle to gain full equality for African Americans.

Fighting Discrimination on the Road

The success of boycotts and sit-ins inspired civil rights activists to launch more nonviolent protests against segregation. Among the many areas of society that remained segregated was interstate bus and train travel. Although African Americans could ride buses and trains, blacks endured discrimination on cross-country journeys.

Riding for Freedom

In 1946 the U.S. Supreme Court had prohibited segregation in interstate bus travel. Yet, unofficial segregation continued in the South. Similar to the practice on city buses, black passengers on interstate buses were expected to sit in reserved areas and give up their seats to white passengers. In addition, black passengers had to use separate facilities, such as restrooms and water fountains, at interstate bus stations.

Some civil rights activists decided to protest the continuing segregation in interstate travel. These activists belonged to the **Congress of Racial Equality (CORE)**, a northern group founded in 1942 by **James Farmer** and others. In 1947 CORE sponsored the Journey of Reconciliation. In this protest, eight black men and eight white men boarded a bus in Washington, D.C., and rode it through the Upper South. Along the way, the activists were arrested and jailed several times. In North Carolina, a judge sentenced some of the black riders to 30 days on a chain gang. He then gave some of the white riders, whom he said had "upset the customs of the South," an even harsher sentence—90 days. The protest paved the way for later similar campaigns.

In 1960 the U.S. Supreme Court ordered the integration of interstate bus stations and facilities. Once again, many white southerners refused to follow the order. Members of CORE decided to stage another protest to draw attention to the situation.

ACADEMIC VOCABULARY

1. Use the context, or surrounding words in the sentence, to write a definition of the term **reconciliation**.

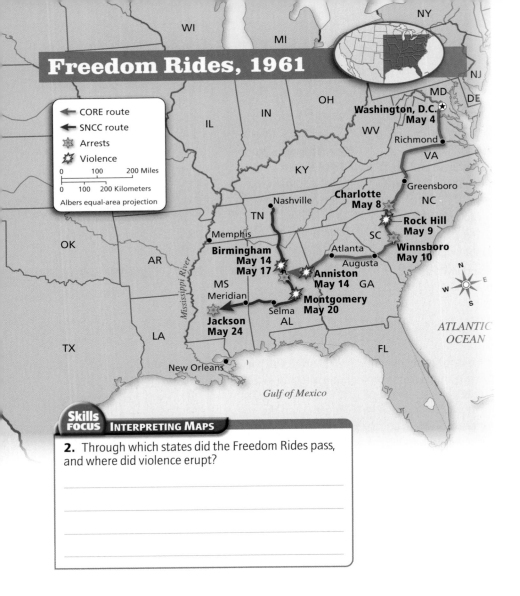

Freedom Rides, 1961

Legend:
← CORE route
← SNCC route
🏵 Arrests
✦ Violence

0   100   200 Miles
0   100   200 Kilometers
Albers equal-area projection

Washington, D.C.
May 4

Richmond

Greensboro

Charlotte
May 8

Rock Hill
May 9

Winnsboro
May 10

Nashville

Memphis

Birmingham
May 14
May 17

Atlanta
Augusta

Anniston
May 14

Montgomery
May 20

Meridian

Selma

Jackson
May 24

New Orleans

Gulf of Mexico

ATLANTIC
OCEAN

Skills FOCUS INTERPRETING MAPS

2. Through which states did the Freedom Rides pass, and where did violence erupt?

In 1961 CORE sent a group on **Freedom Rides**—bus trips through the South during which black and white activists tried to use segregated facilities. On May 4, a group that included James Farmer left Washington, D.C., on two buses bound for Louisiana.

Violence met the Freedom Riders as soon as they entered Alabama. On May 14, a white mob firebombed one of the buses and beat the riders as they tried to escape. The incident appeared on the front pages of newspapers nationwide. Then in Birmingham, Freedom Riders on the other bus were attacked by a group with baseball bats and metal pipes. The assaults severely injured one rider.

When the CORE riders were unable to continue the protest, the Student Nonviolent Coordinating Committee (SNCC) sent a second group to complete the Freedom Rides. Knowing they risked death, some riders made out their wills or wrote farewell letters.

Federal Intervention

President John F. Kennedy, elected in 1960, did not want the Freedom Rides to gain international attention and hurt America's image abroad. Although supporting civil rights, Kennedy asked the riders to end the protest. SNCC leader Diane Nash refused.

✔ **Reading Check**

3. Draw Conclusions Why were the Freedom Rides so successful?

HISTORY'S VOICES

"I strongly felt that the future of the movement was going to be cut short if the Freedom Ride had been stopped as a result of violence. The impression would have been given that whenever a movement starts, all you have to do is attack it with massive violence and the blacks will stop."

—Diane Nash, quoted in *Voices of Freedom*, by Henry Hampton and Steve Fayer

U.S. Attorney General Robert Kennedy had Alabama's governor, John Patterson, agree to provide the Freedom Riders with police protection. But when an angry mob attacked the riders in Montgomery, Alabama, the promised protection did not occur. Furious at Patterson's betrayal, Robert Kennedy sent federal marshals to protect the riders. The Freedom Rides ended in September 1961, when the Interstate Commerce Commission issued tougher laws against segregation in interstate travel. ✔

The Drive for Voting Rights

The civil rights movement was making steady progress in breaking down the racial barriers of segregation. However, blacks' political power remained severely limited. African Americans knew that true equality required that they have power in the voting booth. Although African Americans legally had the right to vote, unjust laws and threats often kept southern blacks from exercising this right or registering to vote.

Limited progress in black voting rights came with the **Civil Rights Act of 1957**. This act created a division within the U.S. Justice Department to investigate and enforce voting rights. Federal district judges were authorized to appoint officials to register voters in areas where voting rights were being denied. In addition, the act required that voting records be kept for up to 22 months so that federal investigators could determine if the law had been violated. The federal government then had the authority to prosecute anyone caught interfering with a person's right to vote.

Despite this new law, voting rights violations continued in the South. For example, in Mississippi almost half of the state's population was black. Yet only 5 percent of the eligible black adults in the state were registered to vote. In 1961 members of SNCC decided to target Mississippi for a voter registration drive in hopes of improving this situation. Robert Moses, a black SNCC leader, went to the town of McComb in July to start the drive. After a month, Moses had convinced only six blacks to register to vote. Even that modest success angered local white residents, though. Moses was beaten by the sheriff's cousin, chased by an angry mob, and jailed.

The violence increased in September when Henry Lee, a farmer who had been helping Moses, was killed. Despite strong evidence to the contrary, a jury ruled that the killing was in self-defense. SNCC workers and local high school students held a march in protest. More mob violence erupted, and police arrested many of the marchers. Moses finally left McComb after registering fewer than 24 new voters. Greater progress in black voting rights would have to wait several more years. ✔

Integrating Higher Education

While activists held nonviolent protests and sought voting rights, the NAACP continued its legal campaign to integrate schools. In the 1960s NAACP lawyers began to focus on enforcing integration in higher education. Two confrontations at universities in Mississippi and Alabama soon helped break down more school barriers.

In September 1962 the University of Mississippi refused to admit a black man named **James Meredith** because of his race. The NAACP then obtained a federal court order requiring the university to enroll Meredith. On September 30 the young black man arrived at the campus accompanied by federal marshals for protection. In protest of his arrival, a riot broke out on the campus. As the riot grew worse, President John F. Kennedy decided to send in army troops to restore order. "The eyes of the nation and the world are upon you," the president told Mississippians. "The honor of your university and the state [is] in the balance." After the troops arrived, the riot quickly ended. Two people, one of them a French reporter, had been killed, though, and hundreds more injured. Meanwhile, Meredith enrolled and, with the protection of marshals, began attending university classes. He graduated in 1963.

KEY FACTS

4. Underline or highlight the description of what the Civil Rights Act of 1957 did.

✔ **Reading Check**
5. Summarize What was the result of the voter registration drive in McComb, Mississippi?

_____

_____

_____

_____

_____

_____

INFO TO KNOW
James Meredith set out in June 1966 on a solitary "March Against Fear" from Memphis, Tennessee, to Jackson, Mississippi. During the protest march, he was shot and hospitalized. Other civil rights leaders continued the march to show support.

Reading Check

6. Compare How were the events that took place at the two universities similar?

_____

_____

_____

_____

_____

Another confrontation occurred on the campus of the University of Alabama. A federal judge had ordered the university to admit Vivian Malone and James Hood, two black students. On June 11, 1963, Alabama governor George C. Wallace stood in front of the enrollment building to try to keep Malone and Hood from going inside. National Guard troops walked alongside the two students as they approached Governor Wallace. Aware of the resistance they might meet, the soldiers had practiced how to physically lift and remove the governor if necessary. The action was not needed. After making a short speech about states' rights, Wallace let the black students pass. Civil rights leaders considered the events at the two universities to be major progress. ✔

Albany, Birmingham, and Washington

The protests of the civil rights movement varied in their rates of success. During this same period, a nonviolent protest in Albany, Georgia, fizzled and had only limited success. In contrast, protests in Birmingham, Alabama, and Washington, D.C.—and some tragic killings—focused nationwide attention on the civil rights movement.

The Albany Movement

In November 1961 SNCC members and local civil rights leaders in Albany, Georgia, began a series of nonviolent protests in that city. The campaign was known as the Albany Movement. After more than 500 protesters were arrested, Albany civil rights leaders invited Martin Luther King Jr. and the Southern Christian Leadership Conference (SCLC) to lead more nonviolent protests in the city. King and other SCLC members arrived, and not long after King was arrested for leading a protest march on the city hall. He refused to pay the fine, however, and vowed to remain in jail.

HISTORICAL DOCUMENT
Go online to read a historical document from the early civil rights movement.

go.hrw.com
Chapter Activity
Keyword: SAAH CH10

Albany, Birmingham, and Washington KEY FACTS

Briefly describe the civil rights protests that took place in Albany, Birmingham, and Washington, D.C., during the early 1960s.

Nov. 1961: Albany Movement

7. _____

April 1963: Birmingham Campaign

8. _____

Aug. 28, 1963: March on Washington

9. _____

▶ Birmingham firefighters blast young civil rights protesters with fire hoses. The immense force of the water knocked many of the young protesters off their feet, tore their clothes, and left some people bloody on the ground.

Albany's police chief worked to keep the movement from gaining national attention by meeting "nonviolence with nonviolence." He quietly arrested and jailed all the protesters. To make certain he had room for them, he arranged for surrounding towns to let him use their jails as well. Meanwhile, he had King released from jail. The news media had little to report, and King left Albany in August 1962. The movement received little national exposure, although it later had some success.

The Birmingham Campaign

King learned from the Albany Movement that nonviolent protest was more effective in gaining media publicity when met with violence. He also decided that the SCLC had more success staging its own demonstrations.

King and the SCLC next focused their efforts on Birmingham, Alabama, a hotbed of racism. In April 1963 the SCLC began a series of boycotts, marches, and sit-ins to challenge the city's segregation laws. Hundreds of protesters joined the campaign. After many were arrested, though, fewer adults were willing to participate.

To revive the campaign, another SCLC leader convinced King to recruit schoolchildren because they did not have jobs to lose if arrested. On May 2, more than 1,000 young people sang and chanted as they marched in protest through Birmingham. Hundreds of the children were arrested, but the next day, about 2,500 children continued the protest. This time, the nonviolence was met by open violence. Police Chief T. Eugene "Bull" Connor had his men use fire hoses, nightsticks, and dogs on the young protesters. Shocking scenes of the brutality flashed across television screens coast to coast. As a result, public support for the civil rights movement rose dramatically; and soon after, city officials agreed to many of the SCLC's demands.

The March on Washington

In response to the events in Birmingham, President Kennedy addressed the nation on July 11, 1963. "The fires of frustration and discord are burning, . . . North and South," he said. Kennedy then announced that he would ask for sweeping civil rights legislation. Just hours later, a black NAACP officer named **Medgar Evers** was murdered in front of his home in Jackson, Mississippi. The slaying horrified many Americans. Byron De La Beckwith, a Ku Klux Klan member, was tried for the murder but went free.

PRIMARY SOURCES

Letter from Birmingham Jail

Martin Luther King Jr. participated in the Birmingham protests and was jailed along with many others. When local white pastors ran a full-page newspaper ad condemning the protests, King replied in an eloquent statement. In this passage from his "Letter from Birmingham Jail," he presents the basis for his philosophy on nonviolence.

You express a great deal of anxiety over our willingness to break laws. This is certainly a legitimate concern. Since we so diligently urge people to obey the Supreme Court's decision of 1954 outlawing segregation in the public schools, at first glance it may seem rather paradoxical [inconsistent] for us consciously to break laws. One may well ask: "How can you advocate [support] breaking some laws and obeying others?" The answer lies in the fact that there are two types of laws: just and unjust. I would be the first to advocate obeying just laws . . . Conversely, one has a moral responsibility to disobey unjust laws. I would agree with St. Augustine that "an unjust law is no law at all."

Skills Focus ANALYZING PRIMARY SOURCES

10. Analyze Under what circumstances does King think disobeying the law is morally acceptable?

_____

_____

INFO TO KNOW

Byron De La Beckwith was set free after all-white juries in two separate trials failed to reach a verdict. In 1994 De La Beckwith was tried again for the murder of Medgar Evers based on some comments he had made. He was convicted, and died in prison in 2001.

March on Washington

Martin Luther King Jr. waves to the crowd after speaking.

✔ **Reading Check**

11. Recall Why was the March on Washington held?

_____

_____

_____

King and other civil rights leaders decided to hold a massive, peaceful rally in Washington, D.C. They hoped that a large rally in the nation's capital would put pressure on Congress to pass the civil rights bill Kennedy had proposed. The civil rights rally, called the **March on Washington for Jobs and Freedom**, took place on the National Mall on August 28, 1963, and included some 200,000 people of all races, backgrounds, and ages. From the steps of the Lincoln Memorial, several civil rights leaders addressed the crowd, with King being the last to speak. He began by reviewing the long history of the civil rights struggle. Then, at the urging of some friends nearby, he began to speak simply from his heart about his personal dream.

HISTORY'S VOICES

"I have a dream that one day this nation will rise up and live out the true meaning of its creed: 'We hold these truths to be self-evident; that all men are created equal.' . . . I have a dream that my four little children will one day live in a nation where they will not be judged by the color of their skin, but the content of their character. I have a dream today!"

—Martin Luther King Jr., "I Have a Dream" speech, August 28, 1963

King's stirring and eloquent "I Have a Dream" speech is considered one of the most famous in American history and helped King and the civil rights movement gain international acclaim. The next year, he was awarded the Nobel Peace Prize. In his acceptance speech in Oslo, Norway, King said, "I accept this award today with an abiding faith in America and an audacious faith in the future of mankind."

After the March on Washington, however, a wave of violence challenged the hopeful mood of civil rights activists. On September 15, 1963, a Birmingham church that was a meeting place for civil rights activities was bombed. The church was celebrating its Youth Day, and dozens of children were going into the building at the time. The blast killed four black girls and injured several other children. In response, violence erupted across the city, and two more black youths were killed by the day's end. The events led to public outrage and spurred on civil rights activists. ✔

SECTION 3 ASSESSMENT

go.hrw.com
Online Quiz
Keyword: SAAH HP10

Reviewing Ideas, Terms, and People

12. Identify What were the Freedom Rides, and what did they accomplish?

_____

_____

13. Contrast How did efforts to register black voters differ from those to integrate higher education?

_____

_____

14. Evaluate Why were the events of 1963 so important to the history of integration?

_____

_____

Creating a Flyer

Use your notes from Section 3 to identify the main events and accomplishments of the civil rights movement during the early 1960s. Then use a template like the one below to create a flyer for the March on Washington. The flyer should mention previous key civil rights events covered in Section 3, such as the Freedom Rides. The flyer should then explain the purpose and goals of the March on Washington and urge people to attend it.

March on Washington for Jobs and Freedom
August 28, 1963 • Washington, D.C.

ASSESS YOUR KNOWLEDGE

1. **Summarize** What gains did African Americans achieve as a result of the civil rights events covered in Section 3?

   _____

   _____

2. **Make Judgments** In your opinion, in what way did the March on Washington contribute to the civil rights movement? Explain your answer.

   _____

   _____

MOORLAND SPINGARN RESEARCH CENTER

First Steps Toward Equality

CHAPTER SUMMARY

SECTION 1 Battling Segregation

- In the 1950s few African Americans shared in the nation's prosperity, and blacks continued to face segregation in many areas of society.
- In 1954 the U.S. Supreme Court ruled that segregation in public schools was illegal, but some white leaders fought school integration.
- Jackie Robinson broke the Major League Baseball color line in 1947.
- The 1955 murder of black teenager Emmett Till heightened Americans' awareness of the extreme racism that existed in the South.

SECTION 2 The Civil Rights Movement Takes Shape

- During the 1950s civil rights activists used boycotts and the courts to end segregation on public city buses.
- Martin Luther King Jr. emerged as a significant leader of the civil rights movement.
- Many civil rights activists in the 1950s and 1960s used nonviolent methods of protest such as sit-ins to fight segregation.

SECTION 3 The Movement Grows

- The 1961 Freedom Rides challenged segregation in interstate travel.
- The Civil Rights Act of 1957 strengthened the enforcement of voting rights, but white southerners still kept many blacks from voting.
- Federal action forced southern universities to admit black students.
- Nonviolent protests and several tragic killings of African Americans focused national attention on the civil rights movement in 1963.

11 The MOVEMENT Continues

As the civil rights movement continued, African Americans across the country sought ways to show pride in their heritage. At the 1968 Olympic Games in Mexico City, sprinters Tommie Smith (center) and John Carlos (right) drew worldwide attention by raising their fists in a salute to black power.

EXPRESSING YOUR OPINION

How do people today display pride in their cultural heritage? Write a paragraph describing one or more ways in which you have expressed pride in your own heritage.

As You Read

Victories and Violence

1. **TAKING NOTES** As you read this section, use a graphic organizer like the one below to take notes on civil rights laws, the expansion of the movement north, and violence faced by protestors. Use the **Reading Focus** questions on the next page to help guide your note taking.

2. As you read the section, underline or highlight definitions and descriptions of each of the **Key Terms and People** listed on the next page.

The 1960s

Civil Rights Laws	Expanding the Movement North	Protestors Face Violence

BEFORE YOU READ

MAIN IDEA

Despite major victories in the fight for civil rights, protesters and activists faced challenges and even violence in the early 1960s.

READING FOCUS

- What laws were passed to protect African Americans' civil rights?
- Why did the civil rights movement expand north?
- What sorts of violence did civil rights workers face?

KEY TERMS AND PEOPLE

Civil Rights Act of 1964
Voting Rights Act of 1965
de facto discrimination
Ralph Abernathy
Operation Breadbasket
Fannie Lou Hamer

BUILDING BACKGROUND

The early years of the civil rights movement were productive, with activists winning many victories that helped secure equality for African Americans. Over time, however, advances slowed. As people grew dissatisfied with the movement's progress, they began applying new tactics, and the nature of the movement changed. ▪

Civil Rights Laws

After the civil rights victories of the 1950s and early 1960s—desegregation in public schools, the Freedom Rides, the triumphs of Martin Luther King Jr.—equal rights for African Americans seemed likely. Two laws passed in the mid-1960s, the Civil Rights Act and the Voting Rights Act, seemed to confirm that likelihood.

Civil Rights Act of 1964

The **Civil Rights Act of 1964** was a major victory in the fight for African Americans' rights. Signed into law on July 2, 1964, the act outlawed discrimination against any individual "because of such individual's race, color, religion, sex, or national origin."

The Civil Rights Act was first proposed by President John F. Kennedy. Kennedy had not been an active civil rights supporter while a senator, but once in the White House, he pointed out the severe injustices faced by black Americans.

HISTORY'S VOICES

"One hundred years of delay have passed since President Lincoln freed the slaves, yet their heirs, their grandsons, are not fully free. They are not yet freed from the bonds of injustice. They are not yet freed from social and economic oppression. And this Nation, for all its hopes and all its boasts, will not be fully free until all its citizens are free."

—John F. Kennedy, Civil Rights Address, June 11, 1963

The passage of new civil rights legislation became one of Kennedy's top priorities, and he sent a bill to Congress. Its passage was delayed by southern senators who opposed the bill's goals, however, and Kennedy was assassinated before he succeeded in getting his bill passed. After Kennedy's death, his successor, Lyndon Johnson, continued to press for the Civil Rights Act. Finally, after months of fighting, the bill passed.

KEY FACTS

1. Underline a description of the terms of the Civil Rights Act. In the space below, explain why this law was so important in African American history.

_____

_____

_____

_____

_____

_____

VIRTUAL FIELDTRIP
Go online to experience a virtual field trip to key sites from the later civil rights movement.

go.hrw.com
Chapter Activity
Keyword: SAAH CH11

AFRICAN AMERICAN VOTER REGISTRATION IN THE SOUTH

■ Eligible African Americans registered   □ Eligible African Americans unregistered

1960

29.1% 70.9%

1971

41.4% 58.6%

Source: *Historical Statistics of Black America*

Skills FOCUS **INTERPRETING GRAPHS**

2. Interpret By what percentage did African American voter registration increase between 1960 and 1971?

_____

_____

✔ **Reading Check**

3. Identify Cause and Effect
Why were the Civil Rights Act and Voting Rights Act passed?

_____

_____

_____

_____

ACADEMIC VOCABULARY

4. Use the context, or surrounding words in the sentence, to write a definition of **conspiring**.

_____

_____

Voting Rights Act of 1965

Even after the passage of the Civil Rights Act, few black southerners could vote due to unfair election laws and practices. Without the vote, black citizens could not expect much progress toward equal rights. As a result, thousands of activists, supported and encouraged by U.S. Attorney General Robert Kennedy, took on the issue of voter rights.

In 1965 Martin Luther King Jr. led a massive voter registration campaign in Alabama. Along with John Lewis, head of SNCC, he organized a march from Selma to Montgomery, the state capital, demanding the right to register to vote. At the edge of Selma, Alabama state troopers, many on horseback, attacked King and 1,500 marchers, firing tear gas at them and beating them with clubs. Television cameras captured the episode, sending graphic images to a shocked nation. The television coverage so moved liberal whites and northern blacks that thousands of them rushed to Alabama to join the protest.

The violence stirred President Johnson and Congress to action. Passed in 1965, the **Voting Rights Act of 1965** outlawed literacy tests and other means used to keep black voters from the polls. The bill also gave the federal government the power to send officials into the South to oversee elections and guarantee their fairness. Over the next four years, the number of black southern voters more than doubled. ✔

Expanding the Movement North

Despite the guarantees of the Civil Rights Act and the Voting Rights Act, however, segregation continued to a certain degree. Though it was formally prohibited by law, racism continued in practice. In fact, the passage of the Civil Rights Act actually increased racist feelings in some places where racism had not been very strong before. Some white residents in these places felt that the government was trying to dictate how they lived, and they strongly resented that effort.

New Racism in the North

Much of the increased racial tension that followed the passage of the Civil Rights Act appeared in the North. Many northern cities found ways to keep up a sort of **de facto discrimination**, or discrimination not supported by laws but continued in practice. For example, an investigation by the Chicago Freedom Movement suggested that real estate agents were conspiring to keep black citizens from purchasing good homes. The investigators found that if two couples of equal income, wealth, social background, and family size—one white and one black—applied to move into the same neighborhood, the white family would almost invariably be approved while the black family would be denied. Appalled by the results, members of the movement began to picket the offices of racist realtors.

The Chicago Campaign

In response to this new racism, Martin Luther King Jr. and others decided to take the civil rights movement north. In 1966 King, accompanied by his closest adviser and fellow minister **Ralph Abernathy,** moved to a poor Chicago neighborhood to see what life was like for its black residents. What they learned amazed and saddened them. King later reported that he received worse treatment in Chicago than he had ever gotten in the South. The marches he and Abernathy led were met by screaming opponents who threw bottles at the marchers. King even received death threats. Meeting with city leaders, King and Abernathy were promised that changes would be made in Chicago's laws and policies. However, no real change came to the city.

Eventually, King and Abernathy left Chicago to return to the South. However, they did not abandon their plans to fight for civil rights in the North. When they left Chicago, they left behind an office of **Operation Breadbasket,** an organization they helped create that was dedicated to improving the economic lives of black Americans. The man responsible for running the Chicago office was a young preacher named Jesse Jackson, about whom you will read more in the next chapter. ✔

✔ **Reading Check**
5. Make Generalizations
What was the result of King's and Abernathy's Chicago Campaign?

_____

_____

_____

_____

_____

Protesters Face Violence

Partially as a result of the successes of the civil rights movement, some of its opponents began to use violence. Fearing that African Americans would obtain full and equal rights under the law, some extremely bigoted segregationists decided to take drastic measures.

Freedom Summer

You have already read how state and local officials tried to stop the march from Selma to Montgomery in 1965. Even before Selma, however, violence had been common. Murder and scare tactics had broken out in 1964 during a Mississippi voter registration drive called the Freedom Summer.

The Freedom Summer was organized by students and activists who gathered in Mississippi in 1964 to register new black voters. Among them was a Mississippi woman named **Fannie Lou Hamer,** an outspoken advocate of voting rights. A devout Christian, Hamer was famous for inspiring her fellow activists by singing Christian hymns like "This Little Light of Mine." In addition to working for voter rights, Hamer fought to win black representation in the Mississippi Democratic Party. She helped found a new branch of the party, the Mississippi Freedom Democratic Party, and even ran for Congress, though she was not allowed to participate in the party's state convention. Inspired by Hamer and others, activists flocked to Mississippi.

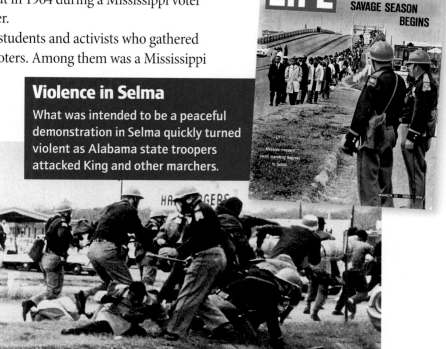

Violence in Selma
What was intended to be a peaceful demonstration in Selma quickly turned violent as Alabama state troopers attacked King and other marchers.

LIFE
Civil rights face-off at Selma **THE SAVAGE SEASON BEGINS**

▲ **In his funeral procession, Martin Luther King Jr.'s casket was drawn by mules to symbolize his efforts to help the poor.**

However, the presence of so many civil rights activists disturbed many locals, some of whom turned to violence to try to make the activists leave. These resisters burned or bombed 37 black churches in Mississippi during the Freedom Summer, and police arrested 1,000 people for taking part in demonstrations. In addition, three civil rights workers were killed near Philadelphia, Mississippi. They were a black man, James E. Chaney, and two white men, Andrew Goodman and Michael Schwerner.

In the end, though, attempts to frighten the civil rights movement out of Mississippi failed, and thousands more activists flocked to the state. In fact, the efforts of the Freedom Summer campaign were in large part responsible for the passage of the Voting Rights Act.

King Is Assassinated

As the most visible leader of the civil rights movement, Martin Luther King Jr. quickly became a target for the movement's opponents. King had already received threats against his life and recognized the danger he faced, but he continued to escalate his efforts for peace and freedom. For example, he called for an end to the Vietnam War, organizing an antiwar march to the United Nations in 1967.

In 1968, King traveled to Memphis, Tennessee, to support a strike by that city's sanitation workers. On the evening of April 4, while standing with friends on the balcony of the Lorraine Motel, Martin Luther King Jr. was shot and killed by a sniper. His assassination shocked people around the country. As news of the killing spread, riots broke out in more than 100 cities.

The man accused of King's assassination, James Earl Ray, was quickly arrested. While in custody, he confessed to the crime and was tried and sentenced to 99 years in prison. Later, however, Ray recanted, or withdrew, his confession, claiming that he had been framed by a conspiracy of anti-King plotters. Ray's recantation had no effect, and he stayed in prison, despite protests from civil rights activists, including Coretta Scott King, who wanted further investigation of the assassination. The investigation never happened, though, and Ray died in prison in 1998. ✔

✔ **Reading Check**
6. Summarize Against whom did some civil rights opponents turn violent in the early 1960s?

_____

_____

_____

_____

_____

SECTION 1 ASSESSMENT

go.hrw.com
Online Quiz
Keyword: SAAH HP11

Reviewing Ideas, Terms, and People

7. Identify What rights did the Civil Rights Act of 1964 and the Voting Rights Act of 1965 guarantee?

_____

_____

8. Explain Why did racism become an issue in the North after 1964?

_____

_____

9. Elaborate Why do you think riots followed news of the assassination of Martin Luther King Jr.?

_____

_____

Examining Consequences

One lesson we learn from the study of history is that almost nothing happens without consequences. Sometimes the consequences are good, as when passage of a law ends an unfair practice. Other times, the consequences are bad, as when bad economic policies lead to a crippling depression. Use the chart below to identify key events of the later civil rights movement and their consequences, both positive and negative. An example has been provided for you.

Event	Consequences	
	Positive	**Negative**
Passage of the Civil Rights Act	Officially ended discrimination	Stirred up resentment in some parts of the country

ASSESS YOUR KNOWLEDGE

1. Describe How did the civil rights movement lead to more freedom for black Americans?

_____

_____

2. Evaluate What do you consider the greatest achievement of the later civil rights era? Why?

_____

_____

Growing Militancy

1. **TAKING NOTES** As you read this section, use a graphic organizer like the one below to take notes on dissatisfaction with the civil rights movement, new directions the movement took, and Muslim activists. Use the **Reading Focus** questions on the next page to help guide your note taking.

2. As you read the section, underline or highlight definitions and descriptions of each of the **Key Terms and People** listed on the next page.

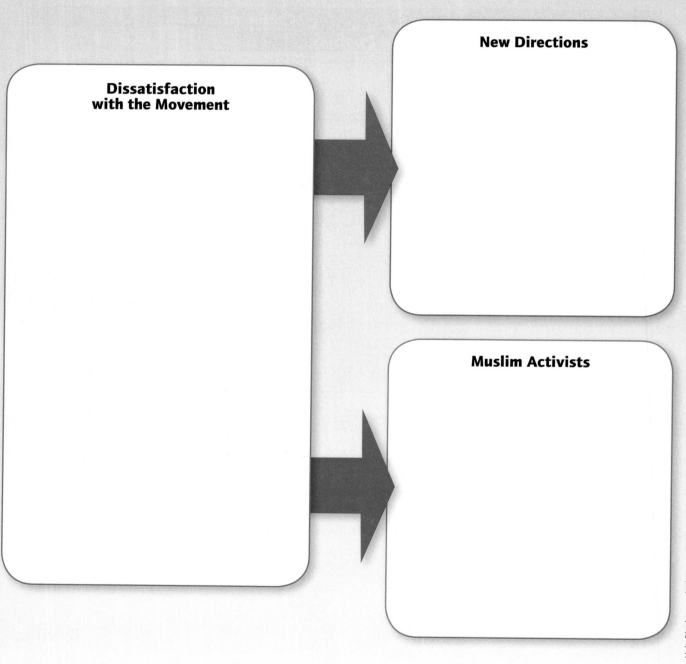

Dissatisfaction with the Movement

New Directions

Muslim Activists

2 Growing Militancy

BEFORE YOU READ

MAIN IDEA

Impatience with the slowness of change led many African American activists to seek out more militant forms of protest against discrimination and segregation.

READING FOCUS

- Why did some young black activists grow dissatisfied with the civil rights movement?
- In what new directions did the civil rights movement grow in the mid-to-late 1960s?
- What Muslim organizations and individuals were influential in the civil rights movement?

KEY TERMS AND PEOPLE

Black Power
Stokely Carmichael
Black Panther Party
Nation of Islam
Elijah Muhammad
Malcolm X
Louis Farrakhan

BUILDING BACKGROUND

Though the civil rights movement of the 1960s made progress toward equality for all Americans, that progress was slow. Tired of waiting for their rights to be recognized, some activists sought out new means of protest and persuasion. ■

Dissatisfaction within the Movement

By the late 1960s, a gulf had arisen between younger civil rights leaders and their older counterparts. Some younger leaders charged that the older leaders were selling out to the white power structure and becoming "Uncle Toms," a disparaging name—taken from Harriet Beecher Stowe's antislavery novel of the 1850s, *Uncle Tom's Cabin*—for black people who allied themselves with those in power. What had happened to change prevailing views of the civil rights movement?

Causes of Dissatisfaction

One cause of dissatisfaction was that black people were disappointed at the slow gains the civil rights movement was making. Many public facilities and schools, for example, were still segregated even though laws outlawing segregation had been passed. In addition, many southern states continued to uphold discriminatory laws.

A second reason for increased dissatisfaction was that the gains of the civil rights movement had not improved conditions in many urban black neighborhoods. While some middle-class African Americans had begun to benefit from recent civil rights legislation, unemployment and job discrimination continued to plague most working-class black communities. While some people had managed to start small businesses and gain a degree of economic independence, most black laborers still had little power in their workplaces or were still searching for steady employment. Many people felt that nonviolent protest was unlikely to change things for the better.

Another cause of dissatisfaction was unhappiness with American involvement in the Vietnam War. Many activists felt that the government was spending too much money on affairs halfway around the world and not enough on domestic problems. Their position was not new; in fact, Martin Luther King Jr. had said the same thing. However, these dissatisfied activists felt the time had come to take a firmer stand.

KEY FACTS

1. List causes and effects of dissatisfaction by many within the civil rights movement.

Causes

Effects

When racial tension led to riots in Watts in 1966, it took the involvement of the National Guard to restore order.

The Watts Riots

In 1965 the tension building in working-class black neighborhoods exploded into violence. In August of that year, the worst race riots in the country since World War II erupted in the overwhelmingly black Watts neighborhood of Los Angeles. The riots, also called the Watts Rebellion, began when a 21-year-old black man, Marquette Frye, was arrested for alleged reckless driving. A small crowd gathered around the arrest site, including Frye's brother and mother, both of whom protested his arrest. All three members of the Frye family were taken into custody. Soon afterward, large-scale rioting began in the streets of Watts.

Tension in Watts had been simmering for a long time. Unemployment in the area was high, and some residents openly distrusted the Los Angeles police. Only about 2 percent of the police officers assigned to patrol Watts were themselves black. The arrest of the Frye family was the trigger that turned that tension into violence.

Thousands of Watts residents took to the streets in protest. The protesters took their anger out first on the police and then on business owners. Many businesses were looted and burned during the riots. The fracas lasted several days. It resulted in the destruction of property worth more than $35 million and the deaths of at least 34 people. The rioting did not stop until the governor of California called in the National Guard to surround Watts and restore peace to the neighborhood.

Later Riots

Following Watts, riots broke out in working-class neighborhoods in other American cities. By 1968 American cities had witnessed hundreds of riots, some of which caused enormous damage and loss of life. In Chicago in 1966, for example, a three-day riot began when police shut off fire hydrants that black children had opened to cool down with. The appearance of the police sent black protesters into the streets, where they attacked police cars and looted stores.

Another huge riot followed in Detroit in 1967. It began with a police raid on a bar on 12th Street, so the event is sometimes known as the 12th Street Riot. Like in Watts, racial tension was running high in Detroit, where black and white workers labored alongside each other in auto plants but did not get along outside of work. The raid on the bar and subsequent arrest of everyone inside sparked five days of violence and looting. By the time the National Guard and the Army managed to quell the riot, 43 people were dead, 467 injured, over 7,200 arrested, and more than 2,000 buildings burned.

The worst, however, was yet to come. In April 1968, after news of Martin Luther King Jr.'s assassination spread, so did a wave of urban riots more violent than America had ever seen. The violence lasted a week. The most serious disturbances took place in Baltimore, Chicago, and Washington, D.C. In all, 46 people died in the rioting, and at least 2,600 more were injured. ✔

✔ Reading Check

2. Summarize What led to the outbreak of violence in Watts and other communities?

_____

_____

_____

_____

New Directions

The riots in Watts and other cities transformed the civil rights movement. A number of young black activists, believing that nonviolence was not successfully bringing about change in the country, decided to turn to more militant means of winning their goals.

Not all African American activists became extremists—most continued to work for equal rights in the same ways that their predecessors had. For a growing number of activists, however, violence seemed to be a new tool in the fight for their rights.

Resurgence of Black Nationalism

Before the 1960s, civil rights activism had focused mainly on the goal of integration. Older activists wanted blacks and other people of color to have the right to participate in civic life with their white neighbors, if they so desired. But some younger activists, frustrated with slow progress and inspired in part by the creation of new African nations that rejected European imperialism, began to think of themselves as residents of a nation within a nation. They wanted to control their own future in the United States by creating their own political parties, economic enterprises, and cultural standards. This effort to create a distinct African American community within the United States was a resurgence of Marcus Garvey's call for black nationalism.

Black Power

A new aspect of black nationalism, the **Black Power** movement, called for economic and political empowerment for black people. Supporters of Black Power did not believe in integration. They thought that black Americans should live in their own communities under their own laws and governments.

Black Power's chief spokesperson in the early 1960s was a young activist named **Stokely Carmichael.** Carmichael had been fighting for civil rights for many years as a member of CORE and the SNCC. In 1966 he was involved in the March Against Fear, a protest against racism. The march had been begun by James Meredith, who set out to walk from Memphis to Jackson, Mississippi. Soon after he started, however, Meredith was shot and wounded. When they heard the news, other civil rights leaders, including Martin Luther King Jr. and Stokely Carmichael, headed to Memphis to lead the march themselves.

When the marchers reached Greenwood, Mississippi, Carmichael and some other leaders were arrested. After he was released more than 40 days later, Carmichael made a speech calling for the rise of Black Power. He declared, "We've been saying freedom for six years. What we're going to start saying now is black power."

Carmichael, Fannie Lou Hamer, and other radical SNCC and CORE members began seeking new means for achieving their goals. Inspired by militant activists, they began to consider themselves urban guerrillas and armed themselves with surplus army weapons and homemade explosives. More and more SNCC members followed Carmichael's militant example, and the group became more aggressive.

The Black Panthers

In 1966 a group of young black working-class students led by Huey Newton and Bobby Seale formed the **Black Panther Party** in Oakland, California. Its original mission was to patrol Oakland's black neighborhoods and protect residents from police brutality.

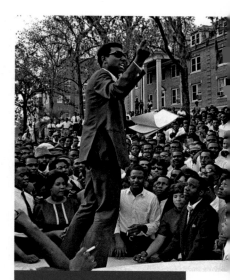

Black Power spokesperson Stokely Carmichael addresses students at Florida A&M University, a historically black college, in 1967.

INFO TO KNOW
In 1969 Stokely Carmichael moved to Guinea in West Africa to support the growth of African governments. He later changed his name to Kwame Turé in honor of two African leaders.

HISTORICAL DOCUMENT
Go online to read historical documents from the **black nationalist movement**.

go.hrw.com
Chapter Activity
Keyword: SAAH CH11

✔ **Reading Check**
3. Draw Conclusions Why do you think the Black Panthers worried some government officials?

_____

_____

_____

_____

Over time, however, the Black Panthers changed into a socialist group. Group members supported causes ranging from full black employment and housing to the exemption of black Americans from military service, the release of all black prisoners from jail, and the payment of reparations to the descendants of slaves. Some Panthers also began to call for their own land and for total self-determination.

Wearing black berets and black leather jackets, the Black Panthers trained in military tactics. Their actions attracted many young African Americans, and at its height, the Black Panther party had some 2,000 members and operated in major cities across the United States.

In many of those cities, violent conflict broke out between well-armed Panthers and local police. Shootouts between Panthers and police were reported in Los Angeles, New York, and Chicago. After one such incident, Huey Newton was arrested for the murder of a police officer. Partly as a result of this violence, agents from the FBI's Counter Intelligence Program (COINTELPRO) stepped in to weaken the Black Panthers and other militant black organizations. As a result, the party began to splinter.

Though the Black Panthers remained active through the 1970s, the group eventually fell apart. Many black Americans objected to the group's military tactics. Some Panther leaders tried to shift the group's focus to more traditional politics, but the Black Panthers had essentially broken up by the early 1980s. ✔

PRIMARY SOURCES

The Black Panthers' Ten-Point Plan

First published in 1966, the Ten-Point Plan expressed the basic goals of the Black Panther Party. As the name suggests, the goals were organized around 10 key points, which are listed below. Some portions of the 10 points were edited and republished in 1972.

1. We want freedom. We want power to determine the destiny of our Black Community.

2. We want full employment for our people.

3. We want an end to the robbery by the white man of our Black Community.

4. We want decent housing, fit for shelter of human beings.

5. We want education for our people that exposes the true nature of this decadent American society. We want education that teaches us our true history and our role in the present-day society.

6. We want all black men to be exempt from military service.

7. We want an immediate end to police brutality and murder of black people.

8. We want freedom for all black men held in federal, state, county, and city prisons and jails.

9. We want all black people when brought to trial to be tried in court by a jury of their peer group of people from their black communities, as defined by the Constitution of the United States.

10. We want land, bread, housing, education, clothing, justice, and peace. And as our major political objective, a United Nations–supervised plebiscite to be held throughout the black colony in which only black colonial subjects will be allowed to participate for the purpose of determining the will of black people as to their national destiny.

Skills FOCUS ANALYZING PRIMARY SOURCES

4. Contrast How do the goals of the Black Panthers differ from those of earlier civil rights groups?

_____

_____

Muslim Activists

Religion and the push for civil rights often went hand in hand. Many activists were deeply spiritual individuals whose personal beliefs shaped their opinions and actions. For example, Martin Luther King Jr. was a Baptist minister, and his strong Christian beliefs shaped his commitment to equality and human rights.

Likewise, African American Muslims have been active in the fight for civil rights. Muslims practice Islam, the religion based on the teachings of the eighth-century Prophet Muhammad. Beginning in the early-to-mid-1900s, thousands of African Americans converted to Islam. In the 1960s, African American Muslims were among the most vocal supporters of equal rights.

The Nation of Islam

Among the most active Muslim groups in the United States has been the **Nation of Islam**, or Black Muslims. This group can be traced back to the 1930s to a black salesman from Detroit named Fard Muhammad who taught his own form of Islam. Among his earliest followers was a young man named Elijah Poole, who changed his name to **Elijah Muhammad** and became the leader of the Nation of Islam when Fard Muhammad died in 1934.

Under Elijah Muhammad, the Nation of Islam's main principles were reminiscent of Marcus Garvey's self-help program. He taught that believers should work to create a nation within this nation, separating from their white counterparts and forming independent educational, religious, and business organizations. One key figure in spreading this message was a controversial young minister named **Malcolm X**, who was at one point a noted leader of the Nation of Islam. Eventually, however, Elijah Muhammad and Malcolm X parted ways, and the younger man left the organization to start his own group.

After Elijah Muhammad died in 1975, leadership of the Nation of Islam fell to his son, Warith Deen Muhammad. Before long, however, a conflict over philosophies led to a split in the Nation of Islam. Led by an energetic young minister named **Louis Farrakhan,** a significant percentage of the original Nation of Islam's membership broke away to form a new organization, which was also called the Nation of Islam. (The group that remained under Warith Deen Muhammad was renamed the American Society of Muslims.) Under Farrakhan, the movement continued to grow, drawing attention even from many non-Muslims. However, many of Farrakhan's speeches were criticized as controversial, containing comments that some people alleged were antiwhite or anti-Jewish.

Malcolm X

Once the national spokesman for the Nation of Islam, Malcolm X was one of the most prominent of all American civil rights activists. While still a member of the Nation of Islam, he had gained national acclaim. He founded mosques in Boston, Philadelphia, Harlem, and other cities and won many converts with his speeches, writings, and television and radio appearances.

INFO TO KNOW
Islam was first brought to America by slaves from Muslim regions of Africa, but most slaves were converted to Christianity and the religion essentially disappeared from the continent. It was re-introduced on a large scale in the early 1900s by immigrants.

Elijah Muhammad, leader of the Nation of Islam, was a firm supporter of black nationalism.

Malcolm X
1925–1965

The man known to history as Malcolm X was born Malcolm Little in Omaha, Nebraska, in 1925. At age 20, Little was arrested for robbery and sent to prison, where he became a follower of Elijah Muhammad and converted to Islam. Soon afterward, he dropped his last name, which he considered a symbol of his family's former slavery, and adopted the name Malcolm X.

After leaving the Nation of Islam, Malcolm X went on a hajj to Mecca, a duty of all Muslims. The experience changed many of his views. Before, he had been a supporter of black nationalism, but now he began to believe that black people and white people could live together in peace. As a sign of his changed attitudes, he changed his name once more, calling himself El-Hajj Malik El-Shabazz.

5. Make Inferences Why do you think Malcolm X changed his name twice during his lifetime?

_____

_____

In 1963 a disagreement over issues between him and Elijah Muhammad led Malcolm X to leave the Nation of Islam to found his own group, the Muslim Mosque, Inc.

Malcolm X was vocal in his criticism of the civil rights movement, which he considered ineffective and unfocused. He called loudly for militant action against white oppressors. As a result, his words could often stir up great controversy. He called on black Americans to fight for their rights "by any means necessary," even if it meant the use of violence against their oppressors.

Preferring black pride and separatism to equality and integration, Malcolm X traveled around the country—and throughout Africa—on speaking tours. During these tours, he warned white Americans that many blacks were no longer content to be treated poorly, as they once had been.

✔ Reading Check
6. Make Generalizations What was the general goal of black Muslim activists?

_____

_____

_____

_____

HISTORY'S VOICES

"Our people, 22,000,000 African Americans, are fed up with America's hypocritical democracy and today we care nothing about the odds that are against us . . . Our people are increasingly developing the opinion that we have nothing to lose but the chains of segregation and the chains of second-class citizenship."

—Malcolm X, Address to Militant Labor Forum, April 8, 1964

His speeches attracted many followers, but they also generated angry responses from those who did not agree with him. On February 21, 1965, he was shot to death at a rally of his supporters in Harlem. His killers were three members of the Nation of Islam who disagreed with his approach toward civil rights. ✔

SECTION 2 ASSESSMENT

go.hrw.com
Online Quiz
Keyword: SAAH HP11

Reviewing Ideas, Terms, and People

7. Describe What was the message delivered by Malcolm X to African Americans?

_____

_____

8. Compare and Contrast How did the Black Power movement differ from earlier civil rights approaches?

_____

_____

9. Develop How do you think growing militancy affected responses to the civil rights movement?

_____

_____

Planning a PowerPoint® Presentation

PowerPoint presentations can add interest and flair to presentations about historical subjects. By combining written information with sounds and animations, PowerPoint slides can help you keep an audience's attention while delivering valuable information.

Imagine that you have been asked to give a PowerPoint presentation about the civil rights movement in the late 1960s.

Choose a topic. Then, use the blank PowerPoint slides below to plan your presentation. On the slides, list the main points you will discuss and sketch any images that you would include. On the lines below each slide, describe any sounds or animations that you would use to add interest to your presentation.

Slide 1

Slide 2

Slide 3

Slide 4

Slide 5

Slide 6

Examining Differing Points of View

Understand the Skill

History is made by people, and people do not all think alike. Disagreements and conflicts between people and groups are what lead to change, such as the changes that occurred in the civil rights movement in the late 1960s. By identifying and examining the differing points of view of the people involved in those disagreements and conflicts, we can better understand the forces that shape our history.

Learn the Skill

Read the documents on this page and the next. Then use the strategies that accompany each document to learn how to examine differing points of view.

Step 1 To determine the first author's point of view, first examine his background. *For what were Gaither and his companions arrested?*

_____

_____

_____

Step 2 Use the selection to determine the author's opinion and perspective. *What form of protest is Gaither encouraging in this passage? Why does he think it is effective?*

_____

_____

_____

_____

_____

"Eight Friendship Junior College students and I served 30 days on the York County road gang for the 'crime' of sitting-in at McCrory's [segregated] lunch counter in Rock Hill, South Carolina. While hundreds of students have been jailed since the start of the sit-in movement, we were the first to be committed to a road gang, which is the present-day version of the dreaded southern chain gang.

We could have paid $100 fines, or we could have posted $200 bail each and gone out pending appeal. Instead, we chose to be jailed-in. All nine of us felt that this would strengthen the impact of our protest. Furthermore, instead of the city being $900 richer for the injustice it had committed, it would have to pay the expense of boarding and feeding us for 30 days . . .

[After 30 days] we were set free and walked in a group to the Friendship campus. Our 30 days on the road gang were over, but not our struggle to end lunch counter discrimination in Rock Hill.

As Clarence Graham expressed it at our first major press conference after getting out: 'If requesting first class citizenship in the south is to be regarded as a crime, then I will gladly go back to jail again. . .'

These students are determined to carry on the nonviolent action campaign until Rock Hill's lunch counters desegregate. Our jail-in has strengthened—not weakened—that determination. Unfortunately, I cannot stay with them. CORE field secretaries have to cover considerable territory and I will be dispatched elsewhere. For me, Rock Hill was my second jail-in. My first was in Miami, Florida, in August when seven of us at CORE's Interracial Action Institute remained 10 days in jail rather than accept bail. The Rock Hill experience has fortified my conviction in the effectiveness of jail-ins in cases of unjust arrests."

—Thomas Gaither, *Jailed-In*, 1961

"Now it is over. America has had chance after chance to show that it really meant 'that all men are endowed with certain inalienable rights.' America has had precious chances in this decade to make it come true. Now it is over. The days of singing freedom songs and the days of combating bullets and billy clubs with Love . . .

At one time black people desperately wanted to be American, to communicate with whites, to live in the Beloved Community. Now that is irrelevant. They know that it can't be until whites want it to be and it is obvious now that whites don't want it . . .

For [some black people] it simply means the white man no longer exists. He is not to be lived with and he is not to be destroyed. He is simply to be ignored, because the time has come for the black man to control the things which effect his life. Like the Irish control Boston, the black man will control Harlem. For so long the black man lived his life in reaction to whites. Now he will live it only within the framework of his own blackness and his blackness links him with the Indians of Peru, the miner in Bolivia, the African and the freedom fighters of Vietnam. What they fight for is what the American black man fights for—the right to govern his own life."

—Julius Lester, *Sing Out!*, 1966

Step 3 Compare the second author's attitudes and opinions to the first author's. *Do you think Lester would have supported Gaither's protests? Why or why not?*

_____

_____

_____

Step 4 Look for specific words and phrases that show differences between the two authors' points of view. *What does "the white man no longer exists" mean? How does it show Lester's opinion is different from Gaither's?*

_____

_____

_____

_____

_____

_____

_____

APPLY THE SKILL

1. Analyze Which of the two writers quoted on these pages represents the earlier ideals of the civil rights movement? How can you tell?

_____

_____

2. Compare and Contrast What goals do Gaither and Lester share? How do their approaches toward those goals differ?

_____

_____

3. Generalize How do these two documents reflect the changes that occurred in the civil rights movement in the late 1960s?

_____

_____

Arts and Culture in the Civil Rights Era

1. **TAKING NOTES** As you read this section, use a graphic organizer like the one below to take notes on black culture, literature, and the performing arts during the civil rights era. Use the **Reading Focus** questions on the next page to help guide your note taking.

2. As you read the section, underline or highlight definitions and descriptions of each of the **Key Terms and People** listed on the next page.

Black Culture in the 1960s

Literature

The Performing Arts

Arts and Culture in the Civil Rights Era

BEFORE YOU READ

MAIN IDEA

The sense of African heritage and pride generated by the civil rights movement found expression in the arts and culture of the era.

READING FOCUS

- How did the civil rights movement lead to changes in black culture?
- How was the quest for civil rights reflected in literature?
- What achievements were made by African Americans in the performing arts during the civil rights era?

KEY TERMS AND PEOPLE

kente
Muhammad Ali
Arthur Ashe
Wilma Rudolph
James Baldwin
Amiri Baraka
soul music
Motown Records

BUILDING BACKGROUND

In the 1960s black culture surged onto the American scene amid the raised fists of Black Panthers and cries of "Black Power!" The political philosophy of black nationalism inspired changes in many people's lifestyles, as African-inspired wardrobes and hairdos became popular. Meanwhile, dynamic writers and artists worked hard to describe the African American experience. ◼

Black Culture in the 1960s

The upsurge of black nationalistic feeling that swept through African American communities in the 1960s inspired a number of changes in African American culture during that period. People paid more attention to their history, heritage, and culture. The slogan "Black is beautiful" became popular, signifying the new pride many African Americans took in themselves.

Style and Clothing

Styles changed as a result of this new pride. For example, many African Americans grew Afros, a type of hairstyle in which the hair extends around the head. Because it requires tightly curled, kinky hair—a hair type common among African Americans—the Afro became a symbol of black pride to many people.

With the success of newly independent African nations like Guinea and Ghana, many African Americans became interested in African-inspired clothing. For example, many began to use kente cloth in their garments. **Kente** is a colorfully dyed, hand-woven fabric that originated in Ghana in West Africa as early as the 1000s. The dashiki, a loose, tunic-like garment inspired by African fashions, became quite popular among African Americans. Some scholars refer to these types of changes, in which people alter how they dress or behave to reflect pride in their culture, as cultural nationalism.

Another expression of cultural nationalism was the creation of a new African American holiday, Kwanzaa, in 1966. It was created by Maulana Karenga, a professor from California, as a way for black Americans to feel connected to their African roots.

▼ **Many African Americans in the 1960s wore Afros and African inspired clothing as symbols of their cultural pride.**

Education

Along with changes in how people dressed came a new interest in learning more about their past. The 1960s saw a dramatic increase in the demand for the teaching of black history and culture. At colleges and universities across the country, students and professors organized courses on African and African American history. Courses on African American literature, music, and art also appeared in college catalogs. In 1969 Harvard University established the country's first program in African American studies, which was followed later that same year by one at Stanford University. These two groundbreaking programs provided a model for similar programs that soon popped up on campuses throughout the United States.

Sports

As part of the cultural nationalism of the 1960s, black Americans took great pride in the accomplishments of their peers. Among the most prominent black figures of the day were several world-class athletes who broke racial barriers to achieve greatness.

Probably the most prominent of the new black sports stars who burst on the scene in the 1960s was boxer **Muhammad Ali.** Born Cassius Clay in 1942, he came to international attention when he won a gold medal in light heavyweight boxing at the Olympic Games in Rome in 1960. He then turned pro and, just four years later, won the heavyweight boxing championship, knocking out Sonny Liston. He successfully defended his title through 1967 and regained it twice, in 1974 and 1978.

Ali was as famous outside the ring as he was in it. He took the name Muhammad Ali in 1964 when he joined the Nation of Islam. In 1966 he was drafted by the Army to fight in Vietnam, but as a conscientious objector, he refused to fight. For this stand he became a hero to the antiwar movement as well as to many African Americans.

Another groundbreaking black sports star of the era was **Arthur Ashe.** In 1968 Ashe became the first black man to win a major professional tennis tournament, the U.S. Open—actually the first ever U.S. Open. The previous year, Ashe had won the last ever amateur U.S. Championships, itself a Grand Slam tournament but not a professional contest. Besides being a star athlete, Ashe was an outspoken opponent of racial prejudice. He was particularly vocal in his criticism of South Africa's apartheid policies.

ACADEMIC VOCABULARY

1. Use the context, or surrounding words in the sentence, to write a definition of **prominent**.

_____

_____

_____

It was not only in professional athletics that black athletes made strides, though. Track and field star **Wilma Rudolph** became the first American woman to win three Olympic gold medals in a single year in 1960. In 1966 the college basketball team from Texas Western College won the NCAA championship, the first team with an all-black starting lineup ever to do so. About 10 years earlier, the college—now the University of Texas at El Paso—had been the first college in the South to allow black players onto its sports teams.

Two African American Olympic athletes made international news in 1968 for expressing their black pride. During a medal ceremony at the Mexico City games in 1968, sprinters Tommie Smith and John Carlos raised their fists high—a symbol of black power—as a protest against continued racism in the United States. For their protest, both men were banned from all future Olympic competitions. ✔

Literature

Throughout history, dynamic times have inspired great works from writers and poets. The civil rights era was no exception. During the 1960s playwrights, novelists, and short story writers wove political messages into their creative works. In addition, many civil rights leaders were also influential writers. Among their major works were the *Autobiography of Malcolm X* by Alex Haley; *Soul on Ice* by Eldridge Cleaver, a leader of the Black Panthers; *Manchild in the Promised Land* by Claude Brown; and *Coming of Age in Mississippi* by Anne Moody.

James Baldwin

The works of **James Baldwin,** who burst upon the literary scene in the 1950s, probably best represent the writing of the civil rights era. Baldwin's novels deal with the dilemmas of black people in America. His first novel, *Go Tell It on the Mountain*, was completed in 1953. After its success, he went on to write several more novels, including *Another Country*, *Giovanni's Room*, and *Notes of a Native Son*.

Baldwin also published two collections of essays, *The Fire Next Time* (1963) and *No Name in the Street* (1972), which gained wide acclaim for their passion. In the essays, Baldwin lamented the status of African Americans.

HISTORY'S VOICES

"To be an Afro-American, or an American black, is to be in the situation, intolerably exaggerated, of all those who have ever found themselves part of a civilization which they could in no wise honorably defend—which they were compelled, indeed, endlessly, to attack and condemn—and who yet spoke out of the most passionate love, hoping to make the kingdom new, to make it honorable and worthy of life."

—James Baldwin, *No Name in the Street*, 1972

The Black Arts Movement

The Black Arts movement was an attempt by some African American writers of the 1960s and 1970s to promote social change through their writings. This movement has been called the literary equivalent of the Black Power movement, because the writers of the movement stressed many of the same themes as political activists.

✔ **Reading Check**
2. Define What is cultural nationalism?

Novelist and essayist James Baldwin was an outspoken and passionate defender of civil rights.

Skills FOCUS **IDENTIFYING POINTS OF VIEW**

3. How does Baldwin say African Americans feel about the United States?

The Black Arts movement was founded by essayist and playwright LeRoi Jones, who later changed his name to **Amiri Baraka.** Jones published his first book, *Preface to a Twenty-Volume Suicide Note*, in 1961. But it was with his 1964 play, *The Dutchman*, that he won wide acclaim, because of the play's brutally honest portrayal of racial problems in America. Baraka called on his fellow African Americans to become artists and creators to help define black culture.

> **HISTORY'S VOICES**
>
> "The Black artist . . . is desperately needed to change the images his people identify with, by asserting Black feeling, Black mind, Black judgment. The Black intellectual . . . is needed to change the interpretation of facts toward the Black Man's best interests, instead of merely tagging along reciting white judgments of the world."
>
> —Amiri Baraka, "The Legacy of Malcolm X, and the Coming of the Black Nation," 1965

Many young black poets, writers, and thinkers heeded Baraka's call and joined the Black Arts movement. Poets Nikki Giovanni and Sonia Sanchez, for example, provided determined voices for many black women. Novelist Ishmael Reed wrote moving novels that addressed injustices faced by African Americans. Playwrights Ed Bullins and Larry Neal brought their protests to the stage in cities across the country. ✔

The Performing Arts

Even before the civil rights movement, African Americans had helped shape America's cultural landscape. During the movement, as new opportunities opened to black performers, more and more African Americans helped entertain the country.

Film and Television

Several African American actors gained national fame for roles they played in the 1960s. James Earl Jones, for example, won Broadway's cherished Tony Award for best male performance in 1968 for his performance in the play *The Great White Hope*. In 1965 actor Sidney Poitier became the first black man to win an Oscar for his role in *Lilies of The Field*. Actress Cicely Tyson, who later won several prestigious acting awards, first came into the public eye for her role in *The Heart Is a Lonely Hunter*.

The Birth of Soul

Performing at such venues as the Apollo Theater in Harlem, artists like Aretha Franklin and Stevie Wonder brought soul to national attention.

In addition, Nichelle Nichols and Eartha Kitt became famous for their roles on popular television series. Nichols, one of the stars of *Star Trek*, was one of the first African American women to play a major role in a prime-time television series, while Kitt had a recurring role on the series *Batman* and a successful music career.

Music and Dance

Black singers also left their mark on the arts scene. African American diva Leontyne Price became one of the most celebrated opera singers in the world, starring in such productions as *Aida* and *Antony and Cleopatra*. Controversial nightclub singer Nina Simone put her career on the line many times to popularize songs that dealt with the African American struggle. Folk and blues singer Odetta helped shape the folk music scene that became popular with students in the 1960s. And gospel legend Mahalia Jackson brought popular Christian hymns to the attention of a whole new audience.

But it is probably for a new style of music that African American performers of the 1960s are best remembered. This era saw the birth of **soul music,** which blended elements of the blues and gospel into a completely new sound. Like the literature of the period, soul music often included commentaries on society. Born in clubs like Harlem's Apollo Theater, a popular venue for black performers, soul gradually spread through the United States. Among its major performers were James Brown, who called himself the "godfather of soul" and Aretha Franklin, the Queen of Soul, whose recordings brought the new style into the public limelight.

Soul really became a sensation, however, with the help of a new record label, **Motown Records,** based in Detroit. Founded by producer Berry Gordy, Motown was the home of such popular artists as Stevie Wonder, Diana Ross and the Supremes, the Temptations, Gladys Knight and the Pips, and Marvin Gaye.

In the world of dance, choreographer Katherine Dunham was the first person to put ethnic Caribbean and African dances on the concert stage. Dancers Arthur Mitchell, who founded The Dance Theater of Harlem, and Alvin Ailey, who established the Alvin Ailey American Dance Theater, both demonstrated the talent of African Americans on the modern dance stage. ✔

KEY FACTS

5. What made soul music different from earlier styles?

✔ **Reading Check**

6. Explain How did African American performers help shape America's cultural identity?

SECTION 3 ASSESSMENT

go.hrw.com
Online Quiz
Keyword: SAAH HP11

Reviewing Ideas, Terms, and People

7. Identify What new hairstyles and clothing styles became popular among African Americans in the 1960s? Why?

8. Summarize What role did African American writers play in the civil rights movement?

9. Elaborate How did Muhammad Ali and Arthur Ashe help inspire black pride?

Writing an Arts Analysis

Works of art, whether they be literary, visual, or performed, can make powerful and influential statements about the times in which they were created. Such is the case with many artistic works of the civil rights era, which both exposed injustices in American society and praised the achievements of black Americans. Choose one of the works of art mentioned in this section or another work from this era and conduct outside research about it. Your chosen work can be a book, a poem, a song, a painting, a sculpture, or any other type of art. In the space below, write a short analysis of your chosen work, explaining what the artist's purpose was in creating it and how it reflects the attitudes and ideals of the civil rights movement.

Title: _____

Type of Work: _____

Artist: _____

Analysis: _____

_____

_____

_____

_____

_____

_____

_____

_____

_____

_____

_____

_____

_____

_____

_____

_____

_____

_____

_____

Creating a Poster

The late 1960s saw a tremendous upsurge in black pride and changes in style and fashion that reflected that upsurge. Many black Americans adopted the slogan "Black is beautiful" as an expression of their newfound cultural pride. In the space below, create a poster that reflects the spirit of the black pride movement. You may wish to compose a slogan of your own to summarize the contents of your poster. Below the poster, write a brief explanation of the elements you have included and how they apply to black pride.

ASSESS YOUR KNOWLEDGE

1. Summarize How does your poster reflect the ideals and attitudes of black pride as expressed in the 1960s?

_____

_____

The Movement Continues

CHAPTER SUMMARY

SECTION 1 Victories and Violence

- The Civil Rights Act of 1964 and Voting Rights Act of 1965 protected the rights of African Americans.
- Resentment with civil rights legislation led to increased racism in the North and an expansion of the civil rights movement.
- Opponents of civil rights increasingly grew violent and attacked activists who campaigned on behalf of African Americans.

SECTION 2 Growing Militancy

- Frustration with slow progress and growing racial tension led some civil rights activists to turn militant in the late 1960s.
- An increase in black nationalism led to the creation of the Black Power movement and groups like the Black Panthers.
- Muslim activists, including the Nation of Islam and Malcolm X, supported the principles of black nationalism.

SECTION 3 Arts and Culture in the Civil Rights Era

- Changes in personal styles and in the teaching of African American subjects in the 1960s reflected an increasing pride in African American heritage, inspired in part by the accomplishments of prominent black athletes.
- Much of the literature of the civil rights period was intended to further social change.
- African Americans excelled in the performing arts, making great leaps forward in acting, music, and dance.

Online Resources

Visit **go.hrw.com** for review and enrichment activities related to this chapter.

go.hrw.com
Chapter Home Page
Keyword: SAAH CH11

Quiz and Review

ONLINE QUIZ
Take a practice quiz for each section in this chapter.

CHAPTER REVIEW
Use the online Chapter Review to help you prepare for the chapter test.

Activities

HISTORICAL DOCUMENTS
Read and explore key documents that shaped African American history.

VIRTUAL FIELD TRIP
Take a virtual field trip to experience key sites from African American history.

VOICES OF HISTORY
Experience African American history and culture through recordings of key people and documents.

Partner

CONNECTING TO OUR PAST
Examine artifacts from **Howard University's Moorland-Spingarn Research Center** that bring to life the study of African American history.

MOORLAND SPINGARN RESEARCH CENTER

CHAPTER 12
1965–1990

A Time of TRANSITION

The 1960s and 1970s witnessed the rise of powerful African American politicans. One of the leading black politicians was Barbara Jordan from Texas, who here is addressing the 1988 Democratic National Convention.

EXPRESSING YOUR OPINION

The years following the end of the civil rights movement were a time of great transition for African Americans. Think about periods of transition in your own life. Write a letter to a friend in which you discuss how these experiences have influenced your life.

Making Political Gains

1. **TAKING NOTES** Use a graphic organizer like this one to take notes on the rise of African American politicians, affirmative action, the conservative era, and the reaction to conservatism. Use the **Reading Focus** questions on the next page to help guide your note taking.

2. As you read the section, underline or highlight definitions and descriptions of each of the **Key Terms and People** listed on the next page.

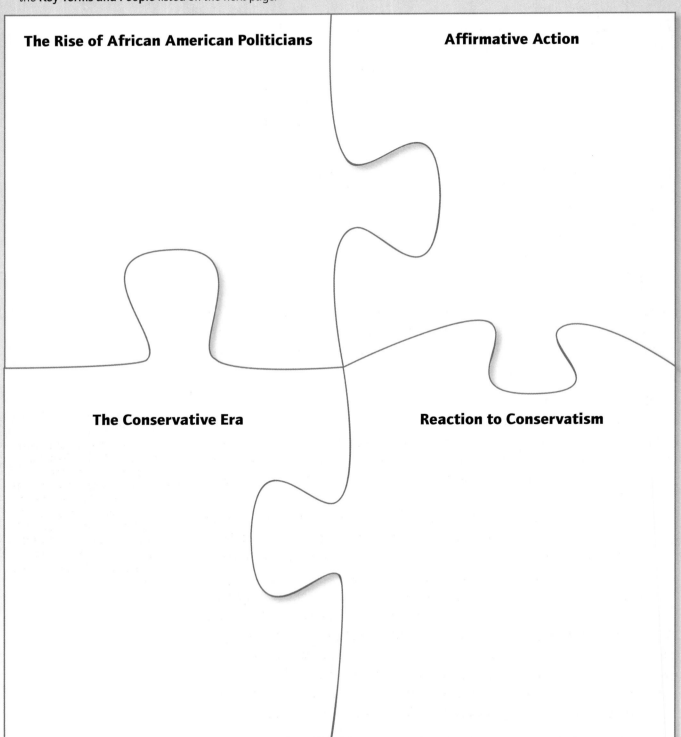

The Rise of African American Politicians

Affirmative Action

The Conservative Era

Reaction to Conservatism

BEFORE YOU READ

MAIN IDEA

In the 1970s and 1980s more black Americans became involved in the political process.

READING FOCUS

• What were some of the key political gains made by African Americans in the 1970s and 1980s?

• What are the arguments for and against affirmative action?

• What policies did conservative leaders support?

• How did the black community respond to conservatism?

KEY TERMS AND PEOPLE

Shirley Chisholm
Congressional Black Caucus
National Black Political Convention
affirmative action
Colin Powell
Clarence Thomas
Jesse Jackson
Rainbow Coalition

BUILDING BACKGROUND

Thanks to the successes of the civil rights movement of the 1950s and 1960s, black Americans made great strides toward full equality. The 1970s and 1980s proved to be a time of transition as African Americans tested their new political strength. During this period, blacks rose to power and took on key economic and social issues. ■

The Rise of African American Politicians

African Americans made great strides during the 1950s and 1960s. Encouraged by successes, many black Americans began entering political life. By the late 1960s and early 1970s African Americans had entered mainstream politics on both the local and national levels.

Entering the Political World

Inspired by gains during the civil rights movement of the 1960s, black Americans began entering the political field in the mid-1960s. President Lyndon Johnson led the way with appointments of African Americans to several high-ranking positions in his administration, including Thurgood Marshall as U.S. Supreme Court justice and Patricia Roberts Harris as a U.S. ambassador.

By the late 1960s the number of black politicians at all levels of government was on the rise. In 1966 Republican Edward W. Brooke of Massachusetts became the first African American elected to the U.S. Senate since the Reconstruction era. By the end of the 1960s several blacks had been elected to the U.S. Congress, including New York's **Shirley Chisholm**, the first African American woman elected to Congress.

In 1969 nine African American members of the House of Representatives joined together to form an organization to represent and unite black members of Congress. The organization, now called the **Congressional Black Caucus**, is dedicated to advancing issues of concern to the African American community. Although open to members of all political parties, the group primarily represents the interests of Democrats. In 2007 the Congressional Black Caucus boasted 43 members.

INFO TO KNOW

Patricia Roberts Harris made history in 1969 when she became the first African American woman to serve as ambassador. She later went on to serve in the cabinet of President Jimmy Carter, first as secretary of housing and urban development and later as secretary of health, education, and welfare.

FACES OF HISTORY

Shirley CHISHOLM
1924–2005

Politician Shirley Chisholm was a trailblazer. In the 1960s and 1970s she made history as the first black woman to serve in Congress and to seek the presidency of the United States.

The daughter of Caribbean immigrants, Chisholm was born in Brooklyn, New York. She worked as an educator before entering politics. In 1964 Chisholm won election to the New York State Assembly, and in 1968 she became the first African American woman elected to the U.S. Congress. During her 14 years in Congress, Chisholm was a champion of rights for minorities and women. She was a fierce opponent of the war in Vietnam and an advocate for poor people.

In 1972 Chisholm made headlines when she sought the Democratic nomination for the presidency. According to Chisholm, she ran for the presidency "despite hopeless odds, to demonstrate the sheer will and refusal to accept the status quo."

1. Explain What made Chisholm a trailblazer?

_____

_____

_____

HISTORICAL DOCUMENT
Go online to read a historical document relating to the Gary Convention.

go.hrw.com
Chapter Activity
Keyword: SAAH CH12

✔ Reading Check
2. Draw Conclusions Why did some people believe that social and economic improvements could come only with political strength?

_____

_____

_____

_____

The Gary Convention

Several thousand African Americans met in Gary, Indiana, in 1972 at the **National Black Political Convention**. Among those present at the meeting were politicians, social activists, and students. Black social and political leaders, such as Jesse Jackson and Louis Farrakhan, also attended. The goal of the convention was to identify ways to address key issues among the black community. Despite disagreements, delegates drafted a formal platform, known as the National Black Political Agenda, that focused on problems such as health care, housing, and the economy.

One key point of the agenda was to encourage African Americans to seek political office. Many black leaders believed that social and economic improvement for African Americans could come only with political strength. Soon, African Americans were entering the political world in growing numbers.

Black Political Leaders

Thanks in part to the National Black Political Convention, a number of black politicians rose to prominence on both the national and local political scenes during the 1970s and 1980s. From local sheriffs to U.S. senators, black politicians were determined to make a difference.

Among the leading black politicians was Virginia's Douglas Wilder. In 1969 Wilder won election to Virginia's state senate, where he served for 16 years. He later served as the state's lieutenant governor before his successful run for governor in 1989. Wilder's election made him the first elected black governor in U.S. history.

Another leading African American politician was Barbara Jordan of Texas, who served in the U.S. House of Representatives from 1973 to 1979. As a legislator, Jordan encouraged Americans to work together for the common good.

HISTORY'S VOICES

"We are a people in a quandary [confusion] about the present and in search of our future. We are a people in search of a national community. [W]e are . . . not only trying to solve the problems of the moment—inflation, unemployment—but on a larger scale, we are attempting to fulfill the promise of America. We are attempting to fulfill our national purpose, to create and sustain a society in which all of us are equal."

—Barbara Jordan, Democratic National Convention Keynote Address, July 1976

In addition to her other contributions, Jordan drew national attention for her role in congressional hearings on the impeachment of President Richard Nixon. ✔

Affirmative Action

One of the key issues that African American politicians dealt with was affirmative action. **Affirmative action** is the policy of giving special consideration to women and nonwhites in order to correct years of discrimination. Affirmative action actively promotes the admittance of minorities to schools or the workplace. The goal of affirmative action policies is to help correct the underrepresentation of women and minorities in certain occupations and educational institutions.

The idea of affirmative action dates back to the 1940s when, under President Franklin Roosevelt, the federal government prohibited defense companies hired by the government from discriminating against job seekers on the basis of "race, creed, color,

Affirmative Action

Controversy still surrounds the issue of affirmative action. These students are marching in favor of a University of Michigan policy of considering race as a factor in admissions.

or national origin." The Civil Rights Act of 1964 expanded the prohibition to cover all companies. In 1965 President Lyndon Johnson established the policy of affirmative action when he issued an executive order requiring companies with low levels of minorities to take steps to increase minority representation. In 1967 affirmative action was extended to include women. Increasingly, companies and government agencies established hiring goals to meet the requirements of affirmative action. In addition, many schools created programs in which a certain number of spots were set aside for minority applicants.

Over the years, supporters of affirmative action have argued that it is necessary to improve job and educational opportunities for women and minorities. To many Americans, affirmative action is a way to level the playing field after years of discrimination. Another argument in favor of affirmative action is that it enhances diversity in schools and in the workplace.

Affirmative action has also drawn much criticism. Opponents argue that affirmative action promotes the selection of candidates based on race rather than merit. Another argument against affirmative action is that it promotes "reverse discrimination," in which non-minorities are placed at a disadvantage.

Opponents of affirmative action have had some success challenging the policy in federal courts. In 1978 the U.S. Supreme Court ruled in *Regents of the University of California* v. *Bakke* that so-called set-aside programs were unconstitutional. At the same time, however, the Court ruled that race can be considered as a factor in admissions decisions. Althouh the *Bakke* decision changed some elements of affirmative action, it did not settle the issue altogether. Affirmative action has continued to be a hotly contested issue. ✔

ACADEMIC VOCABULARY

3. Use the context, or surrounding words in the sentence, to write a definition of **prohibition**.

_____

_____

_____

✔ Reading Check

4. Recall What is the goal of affirmative action?

_____

_____

_____

_____

_____

_____

Clarence Thomas is just the second African American to sit on the highest court in the land. As a member of the U.S. Supreme Court, Thomas is one of the nation's leading conservative figures.

Thomas, who grew up in Georgia, graduated from Yale Law School in 1974 before beginning his career in government. In the 1980s he served as assistant secretary for civil rights in the U.S. Department of Education and, later, as chairman of the Equal Employment Opportunity Commission. In both posts, Thomas made clear his opposition to affirmative action, claiming that minorities should succeed on their own merit. In 1991 President George H. W. Bush appointed Thomas to fill the Supreme Court seat vacated by Thurgood Marshall. In his years on the Court, Thomas has proven himself to be not only a steadfast conservative, but also a leading member of the Supreme Court.

5. Identify What is Thomas's view of affirmative action?

_____

_____

The Conservative Era

In the late 1970s the United States was on the verge of a new political era. A growing conservative ideology was beginning to take hold among many Americans. The election of Republican Ronald Reagan in 1980 kicked off the start of a conservative era in U.S. politics.

The Reagan Years

Led by Ronald Reagan, U.S. conservatives focused on restoring national prosperity and strength. They called for a return to smaller government, lower taxes, and conservative moral values. At the same time, they generally opposed liberal social and racial policies. Conservatives called for an end to affirmative action, gun control, and huge federal budgets.

One of the key items on the conservative agenda was to reduce government spending. To do so, conservative leaders made dramatic cuts to the federal budget. Big spending on social health and welfare programs, they argued, had to stop. Budget cuts meant that fewer Americans were enrolled in federal programs such as food stamps, student loans, and unemployment compensation.

Black Conservatives

One result of the conservative movement was the rise of a new group of conservative black politicians. Many black Americans were attracted to conservative views. In the 1980s and 1990s several black conservatives gained political power. One of the leading black conservative politicians in the 1980s was Alan Keyes. Trained as a diplomat, Keyes served a number of years in the U.S. State Department. In 1983 President Reagan appointed him U.S. ambassador to the United Nations. Since then, Keyes has become one of the leading conservative black activists. **Colin Powell** was another Reagan appointee. In the late 1980s Powell served as national security adviser to President Reagan. President George H. W. Bush appointed Powell Chairman of the Joint Chiefs of Staff, the highest-ranking military position in the United States. A four-star general, Powell was the highest-ranking African American to ever serve in the U.S. military.

A number of other black leaders emerged during the conservative era. One of the best-known figures was **Clarence Thomas**. Appointed in 1991 by President George H. W. Bush, Thomas became only the second African American to sit on the U.S. Supreme Court. U.S. Representative J. C. Watts of Oklahoma was another leading black conservative. Watts, a Republican, rose to one of the highest leadership positions in Congress during the 1990s. Condoleezza Rice is yet another conservative African American politician. She served as a special adviser on national security to President George H. W. Bush during his administration.

INFO TO KNOW
Thomas's appointment to the Supreme Court created intense controversy when a former staff member made accusations of sexual harrassment against him.

Black conservatives still play a prominent role in politics today. For example, President George W. Bush appointed Colin Powell secretary of state in 2001, the first African American to hold that position. In 2005 Condoleezza Rice succeeded Powell as secretary of state.

In addition to high-ranking black government officials, there are also highly visible groups that represent conservative African Americans. For example, the National Leadership Network of Black Conservatives—known as Project 21—helps promote the views of black conservatives and actively speaks out on issues of concern to the black community. Another conservative political organization is the American Civil Rights Institute (ACRI). Headed by conservative black activist Ward Connerly, ACRI opposes affirmative action policies across the nation.

✔ **Reading Check**
6. Identify Cause and Effect What led to the rise of the conservative movement?

_____

_____

_____

_____

Reaction to Conservatism

Despite the growing number of African American conservatives, most black Americans did not embrace the new movement. Many African Americans believed that conservative economic and social programs hurt the black community. As a result, African Americans looked for new solutions.

Opposition to Conservative Politics

Not all Americans were happy with conservative politics. Many pointed to economic troubles and to cuts in social programs as reasons for their unhappiness. In the early 1980s an economic recession led to troubles for many Americans. Unemployment rates rose, homelessness increased in many cities, and spending cuts reduced the amount of money spent on housing and education. Conservative policies under President Reagan also led to cuts in key programs, such as food stamps, student loans, and unemployment compensation. As a result, poor African Americans were particularly hard hit by these policies.

▲ **Condoleezza Rice is one of many black conservatives to rise in the political world.**

Politics in the Conservative Era KEY FACTS

7. Use the space provided to identify the goals of the conservative movement and the reaction to conservativism.

Goals of Conservative Movement	Reactions to Conservatism

Jesse Jackson's Speech at the 1988 Democratic National Convention

Jesse Jackson made history in 1984 when he became the first black man to run for the Democratic nomination for president. In 1988 Jackson sought the nomination a second time. In his speech before the Democratic National Convention, Jackson emphasized his support of issues crucial to minorities and the working poor.

Skills FOCUS ANALYZING PRIMARY SOURCES

8. Draw Conclusions How does Jackson appeal to minorities and the working poor?

Every one of these funny labels they put on you, those of you who are watching this broadcast tonight in the projects, on the corners, I understand. Call you outcast, low down, you can't make it, you're nothing, you're from nobody, subclass, underclass; when you see Jesse Jackson, when my name goes in nomination, your name goes in nomination.

I was born in the slum, but the slum was not born in me. And it wasn't born in you, and you can make it.

Wherever you are tonight, you can make it. Hold your head high, stick your chest out. You can make it. It gets dark sometimes, but the morning comes. Don't you surrender. Suffering breeds character, character breeds faith. In the end faith will not disappoint.

You must not surrender. You may or may not get there but just know that you're qualified. And you hold on, hold out. We must never surrender. America will get better and better.

Keep hope alive!
Keep hope alive!
Keep hope alive!

Because many black Americans relied on these government programs, they were among those most negatively affected by conservative policies. By 1985, the unemployment rate for African Americans was about 15 percent, while unemployment for white Americans was slightly more than 5 percent. In addition, about 30 percent of African Americans lived below the poverty level compared with 11 percent of white citizens. African Americans were ready for a change.

Jesse Jackson Seeks the Presidency

The conservative shift in politics gave rise not only to black conservative politicians but also to liberal politicians who opposed conservative ideology. The leading liberal black politician of the 1980s was **Jesse Jackson**. A leader of the civil rights movement, Jesse Jackson had long been involved in activism and social reform movements. By the early 1980s he had entered mainstream politics. In 1983 Jackson organized a voter registration drive in Chicago that helped lead to the election of that city's first black mayor, Harold Washington. Later that same year, Jackson announced that he would seek the Democratic nomination for the presidency. It was a notable moment for African Americans. Jackson became the first black man to seek the presidential nomination of a major political party.

Jackson broke new ground with his 1984 presidential campaign. He traveled across the nation winning supporters along the way. Jackson was determined that black voters could make a difference. "Hands that picked cotton in 1884 will pick the President in 1984," he told crowds. Jackson used his popularity to convince African Americans to register to vote. Although he failed to win the nomination, he had earned significant support and energized black voters.

The Rainbow Coalition

Jackson used his run for the presidency in 1984 to speak out against the policies of the conservative Republican administration. One way in which he did this was by forming a "rainbow coalition" of young people, minorities, and poor Americans. Jackson's **Rainbow Coalition** aimed at uniting unsatisfied voters together to enact reform. The Rainbow Coalition reflected the diversity of the United States.

In 1988 Jackson once again sought the Democratic nomination. His Rainbow Coalition continued to gain strength, attracting farmers, blue-collar workers, and environmentalists, among others. With considerable support from both black and white voters across the United States, Jackson made a strong showing. He won 11 primaries and was even the front-runner for the nomination for a time. Despite his successes, Jackson finished second to eventual nominee Michael Dukakis. However, Jackson had engineered an amazing campaign. He was proof that African Americans had risen to new political heights. ✔

VIRTUAL FIELD TRIP
Go online to experience a virtual field trip to key sites relating to the rise of African American politicians.
go.hrw.com
Chapter Activity
Keyword: SAAH CH12

✔ **Reading Check**
9. Analyze Why did Jesse Jackson appeal to many voters?

_____

_____

_____

_____

_____

go.hrw.com
Online Quiz
Keyword: SAAH HP12

SECTION 1 ASSESSMENT

Reviewing Ideas, Terms, and People

10. Explain How did African Americans begin to rise to political power in the 1970s and 1980s?

_____

_____

_____

11. Draw Conclusions Why might conservatives be opposed to affirmative action?

_____

_____

12. Evaluate Do you think that the movement against conservativism was successful? Why or why not?

_____

_____

_____

Examining Continuity and Change

Historians often study the past looking for clues that indicate continuity and change. **Continuity** is the connectedness that exists over time. In history we see continuity in the connections or similarities that exist between ideas, beliefs, and events across time. For example, people across time have used technology to make life easier. Historians also examine the **change** that takes place over time. They look for explanations of why nations expand and shrink or why people's attitudes change. Examining continuity and change is an important part of understanding history.

Learn the Skill

Use the strategies below to examine continuity and change.

1787	U.S. Constitution declares that slaves count as three-fifths of a person for purposes of representation.
early 1800s	Free blacks have the right to vote in some states.
1830s	Many states restrict voting rights for free blacks.
1868	Fourteenth Amendment grants citizenship to all people born or naturalized in the United States.
1870	Fifteenth Amendment guarantees U.S. citizens the right to vote regardless of race, color, or previous condition of servitude.
1870s	African Americans serve in political offices in large numbers.
1890	Jim Crow laws restrict voting rights in the South.
1965	Voting Rights Act of 1965 eliminates restrictions on voter registration.
1966	Edward W. Brooke becomes the first African American elected to the U.S. Senate since Reconstruction.
1972	Shirley Chisholm seeks the Democratic presidential nomination.
1984, 1988	Jesse Jackson seeks the Democratic presidential nomination.
2001	Colin Powell is appointed secretary of state.

Step 1 Identify the topic and the time span. *What is the topic of the chart? What time periods does it cover?*

Step 2 Examine changes that have taken place across time. *Circle information in the text that indicates change over time.*

Step 3 Look for connections that exist across time. *Underline information in the text that indicates continuity, or connections, across time.*

APPLY THE SKILL

Summarize How has African American political representation exhibited both continuity and change over time?

Preparing for an Oral History

Imagine that you are a historian during the 1970s and 1980s, a time when African Americans are beginning to enter the political world in large numbers. You decide to interview a rising national black politician for an oral history. An oral history is a recorded interview that seeks personal memories and experiences from a subject with firsthand knowledge of a particular period.

Review the section and identify an African American politician from the period that you would like to interview for an oral history. Then use the library, Internet, or other sources to conduct research on that person. Carefully consider what questions you could ask that would give you a better understanding of your subject, his or her background, and his or her memories of political life. Use the space provided to prepare for your oral history interview.

Oral History Preparation Form

What historical information or problem would you like to address in the interview?

_____

_____

_____

What specific person would be an ideal subject to address the problem above?

_____

_____

Why is the person you selected a good choice to address the topic you identified?

_____

_____

_____

Write at least 5 questions or specific topics you would like to address in the interview.

_____

_____

_____

_____

_____

_____

ASSESS YOUR KNOWLEDGE

1. Identify What kinds of information do you hope to obtain from your subject?

_____

_____

2. Draw Conclusions Why might oral histories be useful tools for historians?

_____

_____

As You Read

The African Connection

1. **TAKING NOTES** Use a graphic organizer like this one to take notes on African nationalism, apartheid in South Africa, and the struggle against apartheid. Use the **Reading Focus** questions on the next page to help guide your note taking.

2. As you read the section, underline or highlight definitions and descriptions of each of the **Key Terms and People** listed on the next page.

African Nationalism

African American Activists Take on Apartheid

South African Apartheid

BEFORE YOU READ

MAIN IDEA

After 1940 major changes came to Africa as former colonies demanded independence and South Africans sought to end years of racial division.

READING FOCUS

- How did nationalism bring about changes in Africa?
- What was apartheid, and how did it shape life in South Africa?
- What led activists around the world to protest apartheid, and what was the result of their protests?

KEY TERMS AND PEOPLE

Kwame Nkrumah
apartheid
African National Congress (ANC)
Nelson Mandela
Desmond Tutu
sanctions

BUILDING BACKGROUND

While African Americans activists were protesting for equal rights and making gains in U.S. politics, their counterparts in Africa were demanding their independence from European empires. In the 1950s and 1960s a wave of nationalism led to independence for many African nations. In the years that followed, African nations focused on rebuilding from decades of colonial rule. ■

African Nationalism

In the 1940s African nationalism was on the rise. Tired of years of imperialism, many Africans began to demand their freedom from European powers. Young African activists led the nationalist movement. Many were inspired by Pan-Africanism, the movement to unite people of African heritage in the struggle for freedom.

Among the first West African colonies to gain its independence was the Gold Coast, a British colony. In 1947 **Kwame Nkrumah** became the leader of the Gold Coast nationalist movement. Nkrumah, who was strongly influenced by Pan-African activists W. E. B. Du Bois and Marcus Garvey, used strikes and demonstrations to protest British rule. In 1951 British leaders finally agreed to hold national elections. The elections were a huge victory for Nkrumah's Convention People's Party. Britain eventually granted the colony full independence in 1957, and Nkrumah became the first prime minister of the new nation, which was renamed Ghana.

In some African countries, wars were fought for independence. For example, in Kenya nationalists led a rebellion against British control when white settlers rejected the idea of African self-rule. The rebellion served to convince the British to begin planning for independence. In 1963 nationalist leader Jomo Kenyatta became the first prime minister of Kenya and a year later became president. In North Africa, Algeria gained its independence from France in 1962 after a long and bloody war. In the 1970s Guinea-Bissau, Mozambique, and Angola each won their independence from Portugal after years of war.

By the 1980s most African nations had won their independence. As European powers withdrew, they left African nations with the task of building new governments and rebuilding their economies. Several countries faced the added difficulties of ethnic conflict and civil war. ✔

INFO TO KNOW

Kwame Nkrumah attended college in the United States in the 1930s and 1940s. While in the United States, he was especially interested in Pan-Africanism and black nationalism. In 1945 he organized the Fifth Pan-African Congress in England.

✔ Reading Check

1. Identify What methods did some African countries use to achieve independence?

_____

_____

_____

2. Use the graphic organizer below to identify the beginnings of apartheid, opposition to apartheid, and how apartheid came to an end.

Beginning of Apartheid

Opposition to Apartheid

End of Apartheid

Apartheid in South Africa

One of the countries most torn by ethnic conflict was South Africa. Originally a Dutch and, later, a British colony, South Africa had long been ruled by white descendants of European settlers. Nonwhite South Africans had almost no voice in the government, despite the fact that they outnumbered their white neighbors by a large margin. In fact, nonwhite South Africans (including black Africans and many South Asians) made up about 75 percent of the country's population. Long-standing customs and laws passed by the white government ensured that members of different races stayed separate and that nonwhite citizens owned little land.

The Beginning of Apartheid

In 1948 a new political party rose to power in South Africa. Called the National Party, it set in place a system that fully segregated South African society. This system of legal segregation was known as **apartheid**, which means "apartness" in Afrikaans. (Derived from Dutch, Afrikaans is widely spoken in South Africa.)

Under apartheid, the rights of nonwhite South Africans were curtailed even more than they had been. Many black citizens were forced to move into regions set aside by the government as "homelands." The original plan was that these homelands would develop and grow and eventually be granted independence. In fact, however, the homelands were located in the most remote and barren parts of the country, and the people who lived in them remained poor and dependent on South Africa.

Nonwhite South Africans who were not moved to homelands suffered under apartheid as well. They were forced to live in townships on the outskirts of whites-only cities, often little more than slums. Anyone caught in the wrong area or out after curfew could be arrested. In addition, nonwhite citizens could work only in certain jobs and had few educational opportunities.

Opposition to Apartheid

Angry and frustrated with their lack of rights, black South Africans banded together to fight apartheid. Many joined the **African National Congress (ANC)**, an organization that had been founded in 1912 to fight for equal rights. Among the most vocal leaders of the ANC's fight against apartheid was lawyer **Nelson Mandela**.

In the 1950s the ANC launched a program of nonviolent protest similar to that of the early civil rights movement in the United States. ANC members openly violated apartheid laws by, for example, sitting in whites-only waiting rooms and boycotting government programs. Though nonviolent, their protests angered the South African government. Many leaders of the ANC, including Mandela, were arrested and imprisoned, though they were eventually acquitted.

In 1960 the nonviolent protest against apartheid ended with the Sharpeville Massacre. At a peaceful demonstration in Sharpeville, a town near Johannesburg, police fired into a crowd of protesters, killing nearly 70 people and wounding more than 180 others. Soon afterward, the government disbanded the ANC. These actions drew worldwide attention and condemnation. They also convinced Mandela and other leaders of the ANC that the time for peaceful protest was over. From that point on, they believed, protests would have to be violent to be successful.

To carry out his violent protests, Mandela formed Umkhonto we Sizwe ("Spear of the Nation"), an underground militant branch of the ANC. This group was dedicated to sabotaging the unjust programs of the South African government. For his role in this sabotage, Mandela was arrested again in 1962 and sentenced to five years in prison. Soon afterward, his sentence was increased to imprisonment for life.

Despite the disbanding of the ANC and Mandela's arrest, protests against apartheid continued. The ANC continued to operate, working mainly from bases outside South Africa. In Mandela's absence, new leaders of the anti-apartheid movement emerged. Among them was Archbishop **Desmond Tutu**, who favored a peaceful end to apartheid. As one of the country's leading religious figures, Tutu worked tirelessly to win equal rights for all citizens. Another leader was Steven Biko, a medical student turned activist. Founder of the Black Consciousness movement, which encouraged black Africans to be proud of their heritage, Biko spoke out angrily and often against apartheid. His vocal protests drew the attention of South African officials, and he was banned and arrested. Biko died while in prison. ✔

African American Activists Take On Apartheid

As black South Africans struggled to end years of discrimination and racism, activists in the United States joined in their struggle. Protesters against apartheid spoke out in the U.S. Congress and in the international press, eventually helping bring an end to South Africa's unjust racial policies.

Slow Beginnings

At first, the fight against apartheid was slow to spread beyond South Africa. In the early 1960s the United States and Western European nations were South Africa's main trading partners, buying more than 60 percent of the country's exports. Thus, they were not eager to suspend trade with the South African government.

Some international organizations, on the other hand, jumped into the fight against apartheid quickly. In 1963, for example, the United Nations voted to ban arms sales to South Africa. The World Health Organization along with other technical organizations ousted South Africa from their ranks. South Africa was also excluded from the Olympic Games. But it would take nearly 25 more years of pressure and persuasion before the international community could force any true measures on South Africa.

▼ **American supporters of Nelson Mandela cheer for the anti-apartheid leader as he tours the United States in 1990.**

International Protests

Though U.S. leaders were leery about breaking off trade with South Africa, many Americans did not share those feelings. In cities nationwide they protested loudly against apartheid.

Archbishop Desmond Tutu and Nelson Mandela were among the most prominent opponents of apartheid.

Eventually, public opinion and the continuing injustice of apartheid led European and U.S. lawmakers to take steps against the South African government. In 1985 both the United Kingdom and the United States leveled **sanctions**, penalties intended to force a country to change its policies, against South Africa. Many companies began a policy of divestment, or refusing to do business, toward South Africa.

The End of Apartheid

Facing international protests, the South African government began to dismantle the apartheid system in 1989. Newly elected president F. W. de Klerk lifted a long-standing ban on anti-apartheid rallies and restored the legal status of the ANC. In addition, he ordered the release of Nelson Mandela after 27 years of imprisonment. Mandela toured the world, urging that sanctions stay in place until "the total elimination of apartheid and the extension of the vote to all [South African] people." Speaking before the U.S. Congress, Mandela recalled the inspiration that freedom fighters in South Africa had gained from their study of American history.

HISTORY'S VOICES

"We could not have made an acquaintance through literature with human giants such as George Washington, Abraham Lincoln, and Thomas Jefferson and not been moved to act as they were moved to act. We could not have heard of and admired John Brown, Sojourner Truth, Frederick Douglass, W. E. B. Du Bois, Marcus Garvey, and Martin Luther King, Jr., and not be moved to act as they were moved to act. We could not have known of your Declaration of Independence and not elected to join in the struggle to guarantee the people life, liberty, and the pursuit of happiness."

—Nelson Mandela, Address to Joint Session of Congress, June 26, 1990

The dismantling of apartheid continued. In 1991 the South African government repealed all of its apartheid laws. Three years later, the country held its first all-races elections. The ANC won the majority of seats in the election and Nelson Mandela became South Africa's first black president. For their work in ending apartheid, Mandela and de Klerk shared the 1993 Nobel Peace Prize. ✔

Reading Check

4. Explain How did the United States help bring an end to apartheid in South Africa?

_____

_____

_____

_____

SECTION 2 ASSESSMENT

go.hrw.com
Online Quiz
Keyword: SAAH HP12

Reviewing Ideas, Terms, and People

5. Identify Who were some of the leaders in South Africa's fight against apartheid?

_____

_____

6. Compare and Contrast How was apartheid in South Africa similar to Jim Crow laws in the United States? How were they different?

_____

_____

7. Elaborate How did American civil rights leaders help bring change to Africa?

_____

_____

Creating a Political Cartoon

As you have read, African American politicians and activists helped lead the U.S. outcry for an end to apartheid in South Africa. They used a variety of methods, including marches, protests, and petitions, to help persuade the U.S. Congress to enact sanctions against the South African government. In the space provided, create a political cartoon that expresses support for U.S. sanctions against the government of South Africa. Be sure to include symbols and captions to make your point and images that capture your audience's attention.

ASSESS YOUR KNOWLEDGE

1. **Explain** In what ways does your political cartoon make your point clear?

_____

_____

2. **Summarize** What symbols do you use in your political cartoon? Why did you select them?

_____

_____

As You Read

Economic and Social Challenges

1. **TAKING NOTES** Use a graphic organizer like this one to take notes on urban poverty and social issues. Use the **Reading Focus** questions on the next page to help guide your note taking.

2. As you read the section, underline or highlight definitions and descriptions of each of the **Key Terms** listed on the next page.

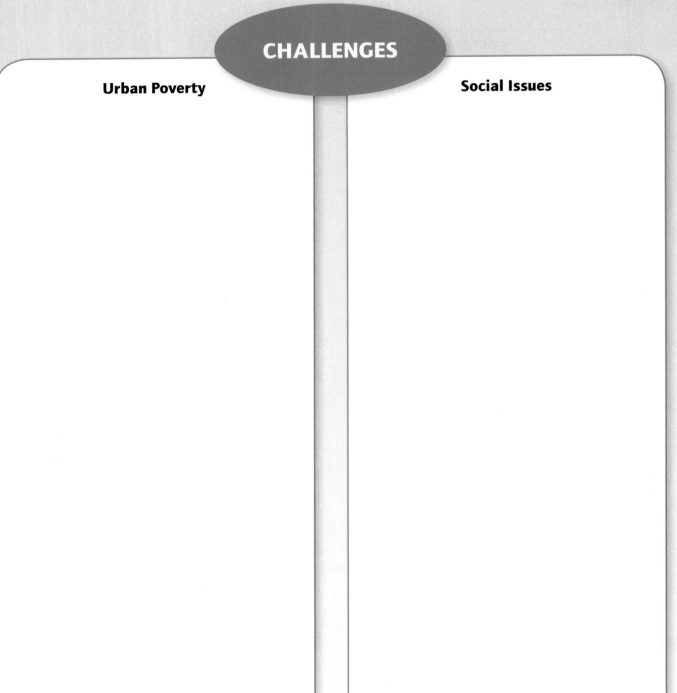

CHALLENGES

Urban Poverty

Social Issues

SECTION 3 Economic and Social Challenges

BEFORE YOU READ

MAIN IDEA

During the last part of the twentieth century, African Americans addressed a variety of economic and social issues.

READING FOCUS

- What steps did Americans take to address the issue of urban poverty?
- What social challenges did African Americans experience?

KEY TERMS

inner cities
Moynihan Report
Family Assistance
  Plan (FAP)
school busing

BUILDING BACKGROUND

The 1970s and 1980s saw dramatic improvements in equal rights and political opportunities for African Americans. However, difficulties still loomed large for many African Americans as they attempted to deal with economic and social issues. ◼

Urban Poverty

As black political leaders were gaining political power during the 1970s and activists were taking on South African apartheid in the 1980s, other leaders turned their attention to economic and social issues affecting the black community in the United States. Chief among their concerns were growing poverty rates for many black urban residents and a report on the black family.

Poverty and the Inner City

As you have learned, African Americans moved to northern cities in great numbers in the first half of the 1900s. Attracted by the availability of jobs and opportunities for better lives, black Americans flocked to inner-city neighborhoods. **Inner cities** are older neighborhoods located near the center of large urban areas. At times, these areas thrived. More often, however, conditions were poor. Most inner cities faced overcrowded conditions, deteriorating housing, and sometimes, racial tensions. Many white city dwellers began leaving cities to move to the suburbs. Soon, inner-city neighborhoods were dominated by African Americans and other minorities.

By the 1970s inner-city urban neighborhoods were in serious decline. Factories began moving out of cities. Economic troubles forced many businesses to close. Jobs in the inner city became more scarce, and unemployment skyrocketed. Poverty and crime rates in the inner city were on the rise. In addition, gains from the civil rights movement of the 1960s had allowed middle-income blacks to leave for the suburbs. As a result, city governments collected less in taxes and inner-city neighborhoods soon became rundown. For many black Americans in the inner cities, poverty became difficult to escape.

Skills FOCUS EXAMINING CONTINUITY AND CHANGE

1. How have economic conditions in the inner city changed over time?

_____

_____

_____

_____

_____

_____

Daniel Patrick Moynihan attempted to address issues of inner city poverty in his 1965 report.

The Moynihan Report

In 1965 the findings of a government study of poverty in inner cities triggered intense debate. In the mid-1960s Daniel Patrick Moynihan, the assistant secretary of labor in the Johnson administration, issued a report titled "The Negro Family: The Call to National Action." The study, which became known as the **Moynihan Report**, attempted to identify the causes of economic troubles among many inner-city black Americans. Moynihan concluded that much of the poverty facing black inner-city residents was the result of the decline of traditional two-parent families. According to the report, nearly 25 percent of black families were headed by women, almost double the rate for white families. The black family, Moynihan claimed, was in crisis.

HISTORY'S VOICES

"At the heart of the deterioration of the fabric of Negro society is the deterioration of the Negro family. It is the fundamental source of the weakness of the Negro community at the present time."

—Daniel Patrick Moynihan, "The Negro Family: The Call to National Action," 1965

The report theorized that the growing number of single-parent families had a negative effect on inner-city African American society. Because most single-parent households earned less than did two-parent households, poverty levels among black Americans were increasing. In addition, the number of single mothers receiving government aid was on the rise. The Moynihan Report also claimed that social problems such as juvenile delinquency, rising drop-out rates, and drug addiction could in part be traced to the decline in traditional two-parent families. Moynihan argued that a unified national effort was necessary to address the problems before the situation in U.S. inner cities became dire.

Response to the Moynihan Report

INFO TO KNOW
In recent years, many scholars and government experts have changed their opinions of the Moynihan Report. The report's findings, they claim, turned out to be accurate predictions of the problems still plaguing U.S. inner cities.

The Moynihan Report generated intense controversy, and Americans were divided over Moynihan's conclusions. President Lyndon Johnson and others supported the report. In a speech at Howard University, Johnson called on black students and the government to work to strengthen the black family. Supporters contended that strengthening black families could help lessen inner-city poverty and reliance on government aid.

In general, however, reaction to the report was negative. Many Americans were outraged at the study's findings. Some critics believed that the Moynihan Report only fueled stereotypes about poor black families. Others argued that the economic and social troubles of African Americans were not the result of changes in family structure but, rather, years of discrimination. Still other critics charged Moynihan with racism and with "blaming the victim." Leaders of the African American community, such as James Farmer of CORE and activist Bayard Rustin, opposed Moynihan's findings. Within months, the report had been rejected.

The Family Assistance Plan

In 1969 Daniel Patrick Moynihan once again undertook efforts to aid poor families. As a member of President Richard Nixon's administration, Moynihan helped draft the **Family Assistance Plan (FAP)**, a program that would have paid poor families a guaranteed annual income of $1,600 provided that they work or attend job training.

One goal of FAP was to eliminate costly, bureaucratic welfare programs such as food stamps and Medicaid. Nixon claimed that FAP was "a method for putting people back to work, reducing the welfare rolls, and expanding the payrolls of the Nation."

African American leaders generally supported the plan in the hopes that the annual income and job training would help pull some poor black Americans out of poverty. The plan had many critics, however. Some feared the program would be too expensive. Others believed the income proposed by the government was not enough to provide for families. As a result of the opposition, the plan failed to pass both houses of Congress ✔

Social Issues

Black Americans in the 1970s and 1980s faced social challenges in addition to economic ones. Among the top concerns facing African Americans were the issues of school busing and education.

School Busing

Despite the 1954 U.S. Supreme Court ruling in *Brown* v. *Board of Education*, many U.S. schools continued to be segregated in the late 1960s and early 1970s. With pressure from the federal government, the majority of schools in the South had integrated by the late 1960s—although questions remained over the integration of students in classes and school-related activities. In the North many urban schools remained largely segregated as a result of de facto segregation. Years of housing discrimination had led to the development of segregated neighborhoods and schools.

In the mid-1960s many segregated urban schools came under pressure to integrate. In 1968 in Berkeley, California, officials implemented a plan of **school busing** to desegregate schools by transporting students from one part of the city to another.

✔ **Reading Check**

2. Analyze What arguments did opponents of the Moynihan Report put forth?

_____

_____

_____

_____

_____

KEY FACTS

3. Underline or highlight the reasons why school busing was implemented.

School Busing Controversy

Busing was used by many districts across the nation to integrate public schools. Forced busing, however, created conflicts like this protest in Boston in 1974.

▲ **Schools and libraries, like this one in Miami, Florida, have started programs to improve performance by inner-city students.**

Soon, the federal courts began ordering some schools to implement school busing as a solution to segregation. In many cities, busing met fierce opposition when some parents objected to having their students bused across long distances to sometimes dangerous neighborhoods. In the early 1970s court-ordered busing in Boston, Massachusetts, led to two weeks of sometimes violent protests. Despite opposition, school busing remained in place in many cities through the 1980s.

Educational Opportunities

Another important social issue in the black community was education. Many leaders hoped to improve educational opportunities for young African Americans, especially those in the inner city. In 1964 the federal government began the Head Start program as an effort to improve conditions among the nation's poor citizens. The main focus of the program is to help preschool-age children from low-income families prepare to start school. Since 1964 the program has enrolled more than 23 million students. As you have learned, the 1960s also saw the beginning of affirmative action policies in higher education. As a result of affirmative action, higher education became more accessible for many young African Americans.

In the 1980s a report on the nation's public schools again focused attention on education. In 1983 the National Commission on Excellence in Education issued a report titled "A Nation at Risk." In the report, the commission found that schools in the United States were in serious decline. As a result, educators and government officials began looking for ways to improve education. Many programs were aimed at students who were less likely to complete their education. These students were often from the nation's impoverished inner cities, were members of minority groups, or were learning English. Since the late 1980s schools, government agencies, and other organizations have focused on helping these students. Many schools now feature programs that offer mentoring and tutoring, as well as other programs to help keep students in school. ✔

✔ Reading Check

4. Explain What social challenges faced African Americans, and how were they addressed?

_____

_____

_____

_____

_____

_____

_____

SECTION 3 ASSESSMENT

go.hrw.com
Online Quiz
Keyword: SAAH HP12

Reviewing Ideas, Terms, and People

5. Identify What economic and social challenges did the black community face in the last part of the twentieth century?

_____

_____

6. Summarize How would the Family Assistance Plan have helped poor families?

_____

_____

7. Develop What solution might you offer to help solve the problem of urban poverty in U.S. inner cities?

_____

_____

_____

Creating a Graph

Historians often use statistics to understand the past. Graphs and charts often help us to better understand the statistics and to make comparisons. Use the statistics below to create a graph that compares data among groups. Remember to use specific labels to indicate the data you are representing in the graph.

Percentage of African American families below the poverty level:

1970—32.2%, 1980—31.1%, 1990—31.0%, 2000—21.2%, 2005—23.8%

Percentage of Hispanic families below the poverty level:

1980—25.1%, 1990—26.9%, 2000—20.3%, 2005—20.6%

Percentage of white families below the poverty level:

1970—7.8%, 1980—7.4%, 1990—7.0%, 2000—5.5%, 2005—6.0%

Source: U. S. Census Bureau

Title: _____

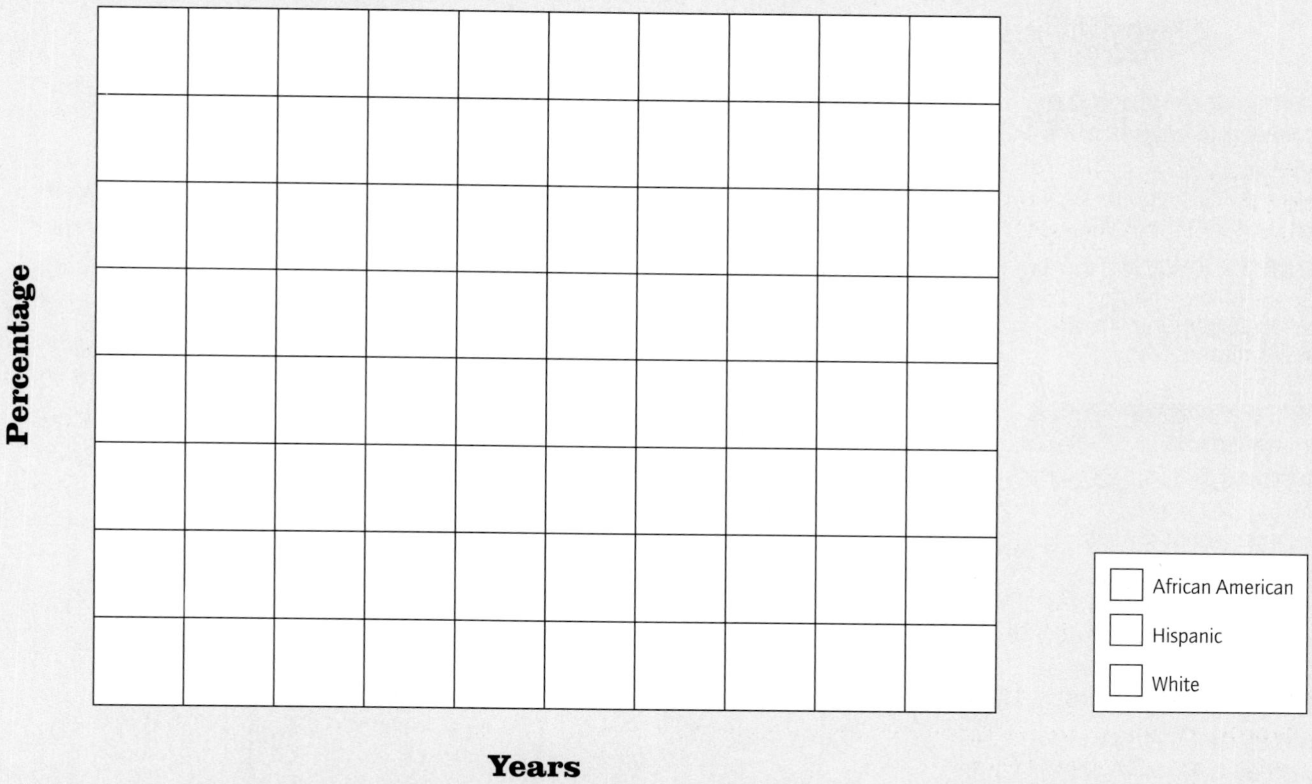

Percentage

Years

☐ African American

☐ Hispanic

☐ White

ASSESS YOUR KNOWLEDGE

1. **Interpret** What does the information in your graph tell you about poverty levels in the United States?

_____

_____

2. **Elaborate** Why might it be important to compare the data in the graph?

_____

_____

MOORLAND SPINGARN RESEARCH CENTER

A Time of Transition

CHAPTER SUMMARY

SECTION 1   Making Political Gains

- African Americans entered politics in growing numbers in the 1970s and 1980s.
- Affirmative action became a key issue in the 1970s.
- Some African American leaders promoted conservative politics in the 1980s and 1990s.
- Many African Americans opposed changes brought about during the conservative era.

SECTION 2   The African Connection

- The rise of nationalist movements in Africa following World War II led to independence for most African countries.
- The South African government's policy of racial segregation led to opposition and violence.
- International protests eventually led to the end of apartheid in South Africa.

SECTION 3   Economic and Social Challenges

- In the 1960s and 1970s government officials focused on ways to address poverty in U.S. inner cities.
- Continuing desegregation and improving education were among the key social issues facing African Americans in the 1970s and 1980s.

African Americans

in MODERN AMERICA

NBA legend Willis Reed and other NBA staff participate in a Habitat for Humanity home build in New Orleans in January 2007.

EXPRESSING YOUR OPINION

Based on what you have learned in this course, write a paragraph describing what you think the United States might be like in 10 years.

As You Read

Social and Cultural Life

1. **TAKING NOTES** Use a graphic organizer like this one to take notes on Afrocentrism, recent immigrants from Africa, and modern African American culture. Use the **Reading Focus** questions on the next page to help guide your note taking.

2. As you read the section, underline or highlight definitions and descriptions of each of the **Key Terms and People** listed on the next page.

Afrocentrism

New Immigrants

Modern African American Culture

SECTION 1 Social and Cultural Life

BEFORE YOU READ

MAIN IDEA

African Americans remain a strong presence in the cultural life of the United States.

READING FOCUS

- What is Afrocentrism, and what has been its impact?
- What are some characteristics of recently arrived African immigrants?
- What are some highlights of modern African American culture?

KEY TERMS AND PEOPLE

Afrocentrism
Kwanzaa
Maulana Karenga
racial stereotyping
hip-hop
Toni Morrison
Maya Angelou

BUILDING BACKGROUND

In the years following the civil rights movement, African Americans have taken on an increasingly significant role in the nation's public life. In turn, trends in national politics and American culture have influenced African American culture. ◾

Afrocentrism

Alienated by the cultural conservatism of the 1980s, some African Americans began to take a more separatist approach. Influenced by earlier black nationalist movements, such as Pan-Africanism, this movement became known as **Afrocentrism**. Though its origins can be traced back to the early 1900s, Afrocentrism gained momentum in the United States in the 1960s.

Afrocentrists promote a shift toward a more Africa-centered view of world history. They reject the traditional and widely accepted Eurocentric view in which the accomplishments of Europeans are emphasized and discussed more than those of other cultures. Afrocentrists argue that the contributions of indigenous African peoples have long been neglected in the study of world history and cultures. They believe that greater emphasis should be put on Africa's contributions to the development of world civilizations, as well as in the study of world history.

Afrocentrism places a lot of emphasis on learning about the past, but it also advocates preserving contemporary African American language, food, music, and dance. One such cultural tradition is **Kwanzaa**, a nonreligious and nonpolitical holiday celebrated from December 26 to January 1. In 1966 **Maulana Karenga** created Kwanzaa to introduce and reinforce core African family and community values. Karenga modeled the holiday after the traditional harvest festivals of African societies.

The Afrocentrist movement has been credited with improving the self-image of many black Americans and with revealing aspects of African history that had long been ignored in public education. However, some scholars have criticized Afrocentrism for distorting aspects of African history and of **racial stereotyping**, which means making judgments, usually negative, about people on the basis of their race or physical appearance alone. Some critics say that by promoting separatism, Afrocentrism is, in effect, promoting racism. Today Afrocentrism's popularity has faded, though its influence is still felt in some intellectual and cultural circles. ✔

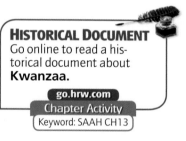

HISTORICAL DOCUMENT
Go online to read a historical document about **Kwanzaa**.

go.hrw.com
Chapter Activity
Keyword: SAAH CH13

✔ **Reading Check**
1. Recall What is Afrocentrism?

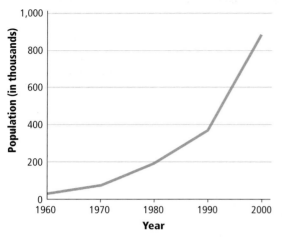
New Immigrants

In the past, the term African American generally meant black people born in the United States. Today, however, the term encompasses other groups, including Africans who have immigrated to the United States. Other groups of black immigrants include those from Latin America and the Caribbean. More Africans have migrated voluntarily during the past 30 years than were transported during all the years of the Atlantic slave trade combined.

Leaving Africa

Crises within Africa are one reason for increased U.S. immigration rates. Those crises include high unemployment rates, drought and famine, government corruption, civil wars, and genocide. Of the approximately 50,000 Africans that immigrate legally to the United States each year, the majority are from sub-Saharan Africa. Most of these immigrants arrive from Nigeria, Ghana, and Ethiopia. According to some activists, because of illegal immigration, the African population in the United States may be even larger than reported.

Changes in immigration law have also contributed to the recent increase in newcomers from Africa. In 1993 Congress instituted the Diversity Visa Lottery, a program aimed at increasing the number of immigrants from countries with low rates of immigration to the United States. Today most Africans come to the United States by way of this program. In 2003 the diversity visa accounted for about one-third of immigrant visas awarded to Africans.

A New Life in the United States

African immigrants are often highly educated and familiar with urban life. They work in a wide range of occupations. Many recent immigrants choose to live in major cities, such as Washington, D.C. and New York City, where sizable African communities already exist. Not all recent immigrants move to large cities, however. Increasing numbers of African immigrants are moving to smaller cities in less densely populated regions, such as the Midwest. Moving to areas in which friends or family members live allows newcomers a support network, as well as increased job opportunities. In many cities, the effects of the increasing number of immigrants are visible through the growing number of African-centered businesses and places of worship.

Some new African immigrants are very successful and have vigorously pushed for employment and entrepreneurial opportunities, causing concern and resentment among some native-born African Americans. As a result, the relationship between recent black immigrants and some African Americans has at times been tense. ✔

Modern African American Culture

Modern African American culture reflects black history, black life, and black attitudes. Cultural products of black America—books, music, television shows, movies—educate people not just in this country but around the world.

Skills FOCUS INTERPRETING GRAPHS

2. Between which years did the most dramatic increase of African immigrants occur?

_____

_____

✔ **Reading Check**

3. Explain Why are many Africans moving to the United States?

_____

_____

_____

_____

Hip-Hop Culture

One of the most popular African American cultural products is **hip-hop**. Hip-hop refers to a cultural movement that began among youth, primarily African American and Latino, in the South Bronx in the late 1970s. For many, hip-hop has since become synonymous with rap music, though the terms do not have the same meaning. Rap is spoken verse, often improvised, over a rhythmic beat.

Hip-hop culture—including rap, break dancing, and graffiti art—emerged as a way to counteract the deteriorating urban landscape of the South Bronx. Construction projects had gradually destroyed a number of Bronx apartment buildings and businesses, and many people were out of work. Hip-hop was a new aesthetic system that placed value on art and self-respect and allowed youth a creative outlet to discuss the social conditions around them.

Hip-hop has influences from many musical genres, but perhaps the most significant modern influence on hip-hop is the Jamaican style of *toasting*, or talking over a rhythm or beat. Though the modern style developed in Jamaica in the 1960s, toasting is an oral tradition whose roots can be traced back to the griots of West Africa.

By the mid-1980s different subsets of hip-hop had developed, such as gangsta rap or jazz rap. Some African Americans criticized gangsta rap artists because their lyrics often glorified the gang subculture. Jazz rap, a fusion of hip-hop and jazz, is known for its intellectual lyrics that often deal with Afrocentric, social, or political themes.

The influence of the hip-hop movement continues to spread around the world. Today both hip-hop and rap are widely accepted by mainstream audiences across the globe and have enjoyed huge commercial success.

Hip-Hop Nation

The Smithsonian's National Museum of American History began collecting objects in 2006 for an exhibit entitled "Hip-Hop Won't Stop: The Beats, The Rhyme, The Life." Hip-hop pioneers Grandmaster Flash (below) and MC Lyte were among the first to donate artifacts. Artists like LL Cool J (right) often use their fame to raise support for a cause.

"Lady Freedom Among Us"

Poet Rita Dove read this poem in 1993 at a ceremony honoring the 200th anniversary of the U.S. Capitol and the return of the repaired "Freedom" statue to the Capitol dome. As you read this excerpt, think about what Lady Freedom might mean to Dove.

consider her drenched gaze   her shining brow
she who has brought mercy back into the streets
and will not retire politely to the potter's field

having assumed the thick skin of this town
its gritted exhaust its sunscorch and blear
she rests in her weathered plumage
bigboned   resolute

don't think you can forget her
don't even try
she's not going to budge

no choice but to grant her space
crown her with sky
for she is one of the many
and she is each of us

Skills FOCUS ANALYZING PRIMARY SOURCES

6. Points of View What does Dove mean when she writes that "she is one of the many / and she is each of us"?

_____

_____

VIRTUAL FIELD TRIP
Go online to experience key sites relating to modern African American life.
go.hrw.com
Chapter Activity
Keyword: SAAH CH13

African American Writers

The number of internationally acclaimed African American writers has increased dramatically over the last few decades. A leading light in the crowded field of successful black writers is **Toni Morrison**. In 1988 she received the Pulitzer Prize for her novel *Beloved*, which focuses on a former slave who is haunted by the ghost of her murdered child. Morrison received the Nobel Prize in literature in 1993.

In 2004 Edward P. Jones won a Pulitzer Prize in fiction for *The Known World*, which deals with issues surrounding slave ownership by both free black and white families in pre-Civil War Virginia. Jones showed the destructive power of slavery for both the slaveholder and the slave. His most recent work, *All Aunt Hagar's Children*, is a collection of short stories that examines issues related to the modern urban African American working class.

Maya Angelou was San Francisco's first black streetcar conductor before she gained literary fame. Angelou achieved national recognition with her autobiography, *I Know Why the Caged Bird Sings*. In this book she dicusses the racism she encountered growing up with her grandmother in a small, segregated Arkansas town. Today Angelou is perhaps best known for her poetry. During Bill Clinton's presidential inauguration in 1993, Angelou read her poem "On the Pulse of Morning," which she had written for the occasion.

Rita Dove is another acclaimed poet. She received a Pulitzer Prize for her collection of poems *Thomas and Beulah* and was named this country's poet laureate in 1993. She was the first African American, and at 40, the youngest person ever, to be appointed to the post.

Of the contemporary African American playwrights whose works have been produced on Broadway and other venues, August Wilson may be the most successful. He received Pulitzer Prizes for two of his plays, *Fences* and *The Piano Lesson*. Anna Deaveare Smith is another distinguished playwright. She is perhaps best known for her plays *Fires in the Mirror: Crown Heights, Brooklyn, and Other Identities* and *Twilight: Los Angeles 1992*, both of which examine race riots and the events surrounding them. Smith was a nominated finalist for the 1993 Pulitzer Prize in drama for *Fires in the Mirror*. In 1996 she was awarded a MacArthur Fellowship, informally known as a "genius grant." Her work continues to receive critical acclaim.

African American Entertainers

Black entertainers in television and film have attracted large audiences. One recent sign of that achievement was on display at the 2001 Academy Awards. African Americans Halle Berry and Denzel Washington won Oscars for best actress and best actor, respectively. It was the first time a black woman had won the prestigious award.

In the late 1980s Oprah Winfrey became the first woman in history to own and produce her own talk show, *The Oprah Winfrey Show*. After its national syndication, the show became the highest-rated television talk show in the United States and has earned several Emmy Awards. Winfrey's media empire does not end there. Her other enterprises include acting, publishing, and philanthropy. In 2007, *Forbes Magazine* declared Winfrey the richest woman in show business.

Spike Lee is a successful African American film director, producer, writer, and actor. Lee is known for dealing with controversial social issues, and his films often depict tense racial situations. For example, in *Do the Right Thing* (1989) Lee examined the causes of a race riot. He also won praise for his 1992 film, *Malcolm X*, a biography of the popular and controversial black nationalist leader.

INFO TO KNOW
Oprah's Angel Network helps establish scholarships and schools, builds youth centers and homes, and supports women's shelters. Since its creation in 1998, the charity has raised more than $50 million.

African American Athletes

Accomplished athletes include Michael Jordan, who played basketball for the Chicago Bulls, and Tiger Woods, a professional golfer. Jordan won six NBA championships while obtaining numerous successful sponsorships. Woods is one of the most dominant professional golfers of his era, arguably of all time.

Black women, including Florence Griffith Joyner and Jackie Joyner-Kersee, became record setters in track and field events. Two African American sisters, Venus and Serena Williams, have both had tremendous success in the traditionally white-dominated sport of tennis.

In recent years, African Americans have made gradual gains toward assuming more leadership roles in the sports industry. Though the majority of leadership positions at both the professional and collegiate level are still held by white men, the number of African Americans in coaching, management, and behind-the-scenes positions such as agents and corporate executives, continues to increase. ✔

✔ Reading Check
7. Identify What themes are common to works of some contemporary black authors and entertainers?

SECTION 1 ASSESSMENT

go.hrw.com
Online Quiz
Keyword: SAAH HP13

Reviewing Ideas, Terms, and People

8. Identify What do Rita Dove, Toni Morrison, and Maya Angelou have in common?

9. Explain How has immigration from Africa to the United States changed in recent years? Why?

10. Elaborate Why would some black authors and entertainers choose to deal with controversial subject matter?

Designing a Web Site

The social and cultural life of African Americans today is becoming more familiar to most Americans. Use the space below to design a Web site that explores this social and cultural life. Use the first blank screen to design a home page with interesting links. Use the second blank screen to design a Web page that informs the viewer of a particular aspect of modern African American social or cultural life.

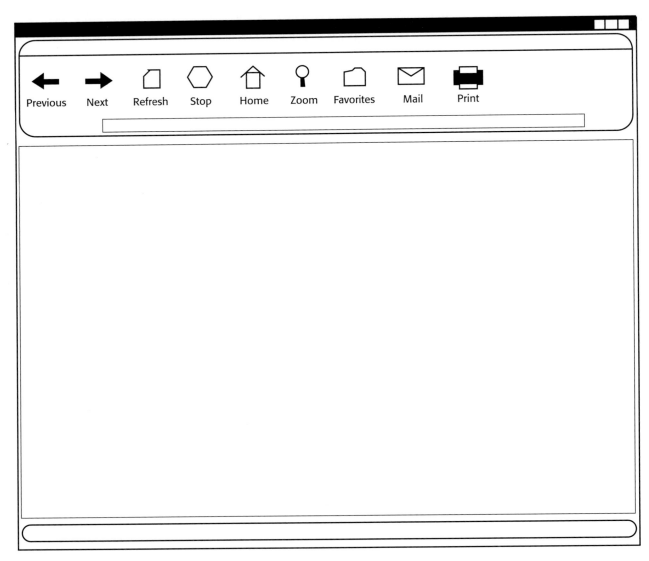

Think about Web sites that you frequent and that you like. Review the items below to help you design your Web pages. Before you begin, it might be helpful to create an outline or a mini-site map.

Audience: What is the purpose of the Web site? Who is the audience?

Navigation: How will you organize your site? Think about what will be easiest for the user.

Appearance: Will the design be consistent for each of your pages? Where will you place the text and images? What fonts and colors will you use?

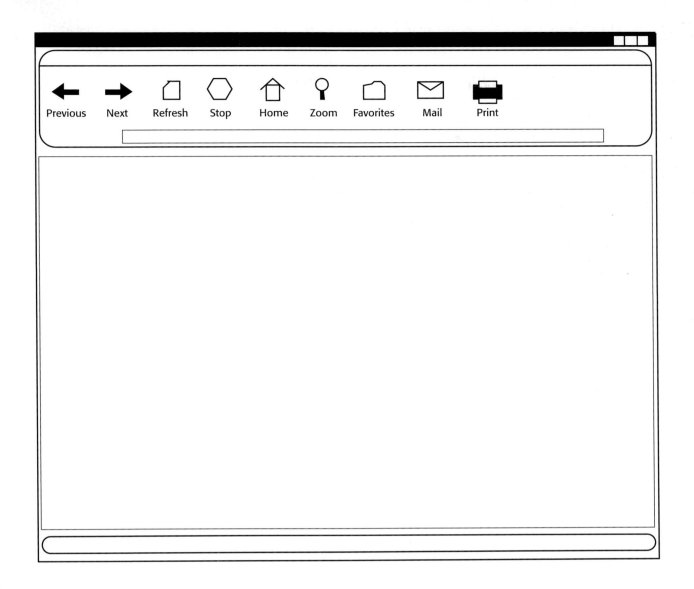

Previous Next Refresh Stop Home Zoom Favorites Mail Print

ASSESS YOUR KNOWLEDGE

1. Explain Which items did you include as links on your home page? Why?

_____

_____

_____

2. Elaborate How is the item on your second Web page important to African American social and cultural life?

_____

_____

_____

As You Read

Activism Today

1. **TAKING NOTES** Use a graphic organizer like this one to take notes on how African Americans are fighting discrimination today and on how Hurricane Katrina affected African Americans. Use the **Reading Focus** questions on the next page to help guide your note taking.

2. As you read the section, underline or highlight definitions and descriptions of each of the **Key Terms and People** listed on the next page.

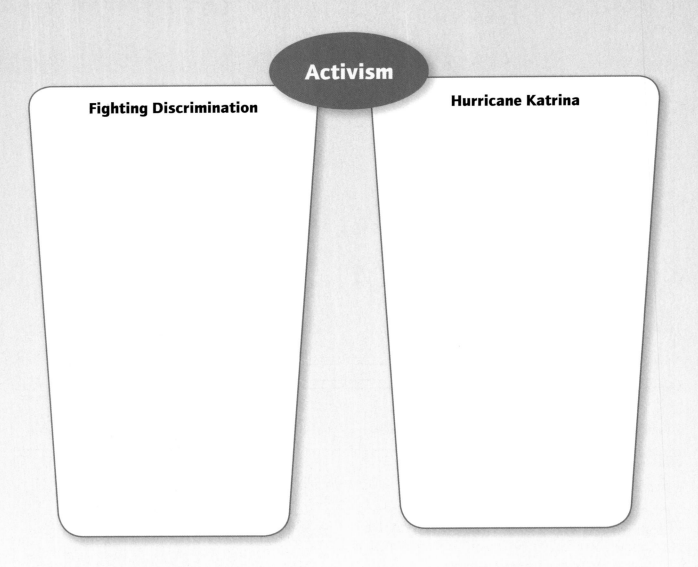

Activism

Fighting Discrimination

Hurricane Katrina

Activism Today

BEFORE YOU READ

MAIN IDEA

African Americans have been active in fighting racial inequalities and discrimination that persist in the United States, such as in the areas of justice and federal support.

READING FOCUS

- How have activists continued to fight racial discrimination since 1990, and what have their efforts accomplished?

- How did Hurricane Katrina reveal racial inequalities, and how did African Americans work to address those inequalities?

KEY TERMS AND PEOPLE

Million Man March
Coretta Scott King
Rodney King
racial profiling
Hurricane Katrina

BUILDING BACKGROUND

During the 1970s and 1980s African Americans made major political and economic gains. With those gains, black leaders and politicians have worked to reduce crime and poverty within their communities and to address racial inequalities. Although African Americans made notable improvements, many racial inequalities remained. For this reason, black activists have continued to work for full equality for African Americans. ■

Fighting Discrimination

Segregation is no longer legal, but African Americans still face discrimination in the United States. For example, white and black Americans are often treated differently by the criminal justice system and social programs such as welfare. By pledging to fight this continued injustice, today's black leaders are picking up where the civil rights movement of the 1960s and 1970s left off.

Million Man March

Some black leaders today are fighting discrimination by promoting activism within the black community. In the mid-1990s Louis Farrakhan, head of the Nation of Islam, helped organize the **Million Man March**. Held on October 16, 1995, this march in Washington, D.C. was promoted as a day of unity, spiritual renewal, and protest by and for black men. Women were not allowed to attend. Estimates on the total attendance vary widely, but between 670,000 and 1 million black men attended the monumental event.

After the march, crowds gathered to hear black leaders such as Jesse Jackson and Rosa Parks speak. The speakers urged black men to take personal responsibility for improving the lives of African Americans. Attendees were encouraged to become more active in politics and in their communities and to help register African Americans to vote. In addition, some speakers criticized the social policies of the Republicans in power at the time.

▼ African American men from around the country gathered to attend the Million Man March.

▲ **Coretta Scott King** remained an active supporter of civil rights until her death in 2006.

The Million Man March received mixed reactions from blacks and whites alike. Some criticized the involvement of Louis Farrakhan, who has been accused of being antiwhite, anti-Semitic, and sexist. Others criticized the organizers for limiting the march to men. Nonetheless, the Million Man March made important gains. Proponents claim that, in the months after the march, about 1.5 million black men registered to vote. The march also gave rise to similar events, such as the Million Woman March, held by black women in 1997. Attendance estimates for this women-only event range from 300,000 to 1 million. In 2005 a coalition of African American leaders called the Millions More March to celebrate the tenth anniversary of the Million Man March.

Coretta Scott King

Another modern black leader who has led the fight against discrimination is **Coretta Scott King**, the widow of Martin Luther King Jr. After her husband's assassination she continued to play an important role in social activism. In 1968 she founded the Martin Luther King Jr. Center for Nonviolent Social Change, commonly known as the King Center, in Atlanta, Georgia. The center and its staff are dedicated to teaching the world about Martin Luther King Jr.'s life, goals, and activism. Coretta Scott King and the King Center were also influential in having her husband's birthday made a national holiday in 1986. We now celebrate Martin Luther King Jr. Day each year on January 15.

Coretta Scott King continued to speak out against discrimination and injustice around the world until her death in January 2006. Among the causes she supported were ending South Africa's apartheid regime and gaining equal rights for other underrepresented groups, such as women.

African Americans Seek Justice

KEY FACTS

1. Underline reasons why relations between African Americans and law enforcement are often strained.

In recent decades, black activists have also fought racial discrimination in law enforcement and criminal justice. Throughout history, African Americans have witnessed inequality in all stages of the justice system, from arrests to sentencing. On average, black men in the United States are imprisoned more often and for longer terms than are white men. In addition, African Americans convicted of murder receive the death penalty more often than white murderers, regardless of the victim's race. By the mid-1990s, nearly one in three black men between 20 and 29 was under some form of criminal justice supervision.

Events of the 1980s and 1990s further hurt relations between African Americans and law enforcement. In several well-publicized cases, police officers were accused of using excessive force against African Americans. One highly publicized case occurred in 1991 when **Rodney King**, a black motorist, was pulled over after a high-speed chase. Four Los Angeles Police Department officers, claiming that King resisted arrest, used batons to beat him. A bystander captured the violence on videotape, and his footage was aired repeatedly on news media outlets nationwide. Americans were outraged. The situation worsened in 1992 when a mostly white jury acquitted the officers. Furious, many African Americans claimed that the beating and the verdict were the result of racial prejudice. Outrage over the verdict led to violent rioting in the Los Angeles area. The riots, which lasted three days, resulted in more than 50 deaths, at least 2,000 injuries, and approximately $1 billion in property damage. This made them one of the most costly riots in American history.

VIRTUAL FIELD TRIP
Go online to experience a virtual field trip to key sites in **recent activism**.

go.hrw.com
Chapter Activity
Keyword: SAAH CH13

The riots brought the racial tension that existed in many parts of the country into nationwide focus. In response, Los Angeles and many other communities made changes that have helped build trust between the black community and law enforcement. For example, police departments increased the number of African American officers on the streets and in positions of authority. Departments also shifted their focus to community policing, in which officers work with a community to prevent crime instead of just reacting to crimes that have already happened. More civilian watchdog groups began to monitor police and to ensure that complaints of excessive force were fully investigated.

During the 1990s activists also opposed the widespread use of **racial profiling**, which is a system that uses race, among other factors, to determine which people are likely to commit certain types of crime. Many citizens claimed that police used racial profiling as an excuse to target African Americans far more than other groups. In particular, the black community accused law enforcement of stopping and searching cars simply because their drivers were black. Despite denials from police, most Americans today believe that racial profiling against black Americans occurs and that it is wrong.

In the 1990s a scandal in New Jersey brought national attention to the use of racial profiling. At that time black motorists complained they were being pulled over on the New Jersey Turnpike solely because they were African American. New Jersey state troopers eventually admitted the claim was true. After national protests erupted, the state's police force adopted a new policy not based on race. Shortly after this event, at least 30 states enacted laws prohibiting racial profiling or requiring data collection on police stops. Such reforms have improved the chance that African Americans will receive equal justice. Until reforms are fully implemented, however, African American males in particular still face challenges in receiving fair or equal treatment. ✔

Hurricane Katrina

In August 2005 a natural disaster led many Americans to question the government's attitudes toward African Americans. On August 29, Americans watched in horror as **Hurricane Katrina** struck the coast of the Gulf of Mexico. The massive hurricane was the third-strongest on record to strike land in the United States and the most devastating natural disaster in the history of the United States. Katrina left a path of death and destruction across Alabama, Florida, Louisiana, and Mississippi. Many felt that the situation was made worse by the slow response of some government agencies to the destruction. Many African Americans protested that the government's inadequate response was due to discrimination against poor black communities.

✔ **Reading Check**
2. Analyze What issues have black activists and other leaders addressed to reduce racial discrimination in the justice system?

Katrina's Legacy
Hurricane Katrina left much of New Orleans underwater. Thousands of residents had to be rescued by boat from flooded homes and hotels.

Skills FOCUS ANALYZING VISUALS

3. Interpret Based on this photo, why might rescue efforts in New Orleans have been slower than usual?

▲ **Oprah Winfrey speaks with a Hurricane Katrina evacuee sheltered in the Astrodome in Houston, Texas, in September 2005.**

Damage along the Gulf Coast

Hurricane Katrina left destruction all along the Gulf Coast. In some places, whole communities were destroyed by the storm's fierce winds and heavy rains. However, the worst damage of all was suffered by the city of New Orleans, Louisiana. Heavy rains broke some of the city's levees—earth and concrete walls to hold back the Mississippi River and seawater. Because much of New Orleans lies below sea level, floodwaters poured through the breached levees, submerging some 80 percent of New Orleans beneath a mix of water, raw sewage, and chemicals.

The flooding of New Orleans left many residents stranded on rooftops, along highways, and in emergency shelters, often for days with little or no food and water. Some New Orleans residents who were unable to evacuate the city found refuge in the Louisiana Superdome. Large-scale looting broke out, and the military was called in to restore order. Early news reports reported hundreds of horrific crimes in New Orleans, but many were later proved to be untrue.

The human suffering that resulted from Hurricane Katrina was immense. More than 1,500 people died—most of them residents of New Orleans—and hundreds of thousands of people lost their homes and sources of livelihood. Damage estimates reached as high as $80 billion. To make matters worse, a second hurricane, Hurricane Rita, struck Louisiana and Texas just weeks later, adding to the destruction.

Response and Protest

The federal response to the horrors of Hurricane Katrina were led by the Federal Emergency Management Agency (FEMA), which is part of the U.S. Department of Homeland Security. FEMA officials assisted local and state agencies in their relief efforts after the storm. Workers from FEMA and other government agencies helped evacuate disaster victims to other states, mainly across the southern United States.

INFO TO KNOW
There were 67,719 FEMA, Department of Defense, and Coast Guard personnel supporting relief efforts during the height of the Hurricane Katrina response.

Many aspects of the Hurricane Katrina response were successful. For example, the Coast Guard was praised for its rescue efforts. Within two weeks, the Coast Guard had rescued more than 24,000 people in peril and assisted with the evacuation of more than 9,000 hospital patients and workers. Volunteers from organizations such as the Citizen Corps and the American Red Cross also assisted with relief efforts. Individuals donated their time, too, often traveling from other states to help.

However, the extent of the disaster and suffering overwhelmed some government agencies, including FEMA, which drew criticism from across the country. Some people thought that the response of agencies at all levels—federal, state, and local—had been slow, inadequate, and poorly organized. The response revealed problems in the U.S. government's emergency management system and level of preparedness. Many local New Orleans officials, who were predominantly African American, were also held responsible for the poor response to the crisis in that city. Among the African American officials who shared blame for the response was mayor Ray Nagin.

Criticism against the government was particularly heated because many of the areas most devastated by the hurricane, such as the Lower Ninth Ward in New Orleans, were largely populated by poor African Americans. Some observers have claimed that issues of race and class contributed to the poor response. Jesse Jackson spoke for many of these observers when he said, "Many black people feel that their race, their property conditions and their voting patterns have been a factor in the response." This observation seemed to be supported by statements from national officials that could be read to imply bias against blacks and poor New Orleanians.

In addition, some African Americans claimed that media coverage after the hurricane depicted New Orleans as a crime-ridden city that needed military intervention to restore order. They complained that African Americans in Louisiana were shown as a dangerous, impoverished class of people undeserving of aid.

Recovery

Recovery from Hurricane Katrina has been slow and will take several years. In New Orleans, for example, only about half of the 1 million residents evacuated had returned a year later. Of those who had returned, many were still living in temporary housing while they tried to rebuild. Furthermore, some poorer areas of the city still did not have electricity and sewage service. Parts of the Ninth Ward remained abandoned like a ghost town. In addition, some victims of the storm had not yet received relief money from government agencies and were still living in temporary FEMA or FEMA-subsidized housing. Some people that had flood insurance on their homes often found the money was not enough to cover all the costs of rebuilding.

Some people have blamed the slowness of recovery after Katrina on the government's desire to prevent certain racial or social classes from returning to the Gulf Coast region. William Quigley, a Katrina evacuee and law professor at Loyola University in New Orleans, concluded, "There is not a sign outside of New Orleans saying, 'If you are poor, sick, elderly, disabled, a child or African-American, you cannot return,' but there might as well be."

On the other hand, some evacuees do not want to return. Nearly half of those who settled in Texas, for example, have no plans to return to Louisiana. Even outside of New Orleans, however, many Katrina evacuees were still struggling to survive without jobs and on household incomes of less than $500 a month. ✔

Skills FOCUS EVALUATING SOURCES

4. What opinion does underlined the source express about response to Hurricane Katrina?

✔ **Reading Check**
5. Explain Why do some claim that the inadequate response to Katrina was due to race or class prejudices?

SECTION 2 ASSESSMENT

go.hrw.com
Online Quiz
Keyword: SAAH HP13

Reviewing Ideas, Terms, and People

6. Recall What are ways in which some contemporary activists have worked to fight discrimination?

7. Explain What were some of the effects of Hurricane Katrina on New Orleans?

8. Develop Why do you think that many federal agencies were slow to respond to the destruction caused by Hurricane Katrina?

Evaluating Sources

Understand the Skill

Historians must constantly evaluate sources to determine their credibility. Credible sources help historians produce an accurate and reliable historical account. Historians use several criteria for evaluating sources.

- They consider the author or producer of a source.
- They think about where, when, and why a source was created.
- They assess the level of bias in a source.
- They acknowledge that sources are more reliable if the author was close in time and place to a given event.

Learn the Skill

Use the strategies at right to evaluate sources.

> In 1965, Los Angeles and other urban areas exploded for a brief second and everyone got concerned. Those of us who live in these neighborhoods today are watching them *implode* all of the time. The violence and the criminalization make people eat each other up. Most of what is proposed in response are Band-Aid solutions—build more jails, put more police on the street. That is working at the problem from the back end.
>
> What is central now is the need for economic access; the political process has been opened—there are no formal barriers to voting, for example—but economic access, taking advantage of new technologies and economic opportunity, demands as much effort as political struggle required in the 1960s.
>
> –civil rights activist Robert P. Moses, *Radical Equations: Civil Rights from Mississippi to the Algebra Project*, 2001

Step 1 Identify and learn the background of the author of the source. *Who wrote this source?*

_____

_____

_____

_____

Step 2 Examine the content of the source. *What does this source tell you about African American activism today?*

_____

_____

_____

Step 3 Determine whether the source was meant to be public or private. *Who is the author addressing in this source?*

_____

_____

_____

APPLY THE SKILL

1. Draw Conclusions Do you think this source is reliable? Why or why not?

_____

_____

2. Evaluating Sources Why would this source be useful to current students?

_____

_____

Conducting an Interview

Activists today continue to fight economic and political discrimination in the United States. In the space below, write five questions that you would like to ask a modern activist. Include the name of the activist on the first line.

Modern Activist: _____

Question 1: _____

_____

_____

Question 2: _____

_____

_____

Question 3: _____

_____

_____

Question 4: _____

_____

_____

Question 5: _____

_____

_____

ASSESS YOUR KNOWLEDGE

1. **Express** Why is the activist you chose an important figure in the modern United States?

   _____

   _____

2. **Describe** Which question do you think is the most important one to ask the activist you have chosen? Why?

   _____

   _____

Looking to the Future

1. **TAKING NOTES** Use a graphic organizer like this one to take notes on African American leaders for today and on the ways that African Americans are ensuring the legacy of their achievements for tomorrow. Use the **Reading Focus** questions on the next page to help guide your note taking.

2. As you read the section, underline or highlight definitions and descriptions of each of the **Key Terms and People** listed on the next page.

The Future

Leaders for Today

Ensuring the Legacy

BEFORE YOU READ

MAIN IDEA

The future holds great promise for African Americans, but challenges remain. Strong leaders help point the way to a bright future.

READING FOCUS

- Who are some of the African Americans in leadership positions today?
- What are some of the challenges and opportunities facing African Americans today?

KEY TERMS AND PEOPLE

Condoleezza Rice
Barack Obama
resegregation
Third Great Migration
environmental racism

BUILDING BACKGROUND

You have read how Africans first came to America hundreds of years ago. Since then, African Americans have fought for and achieved dignity, education, and success, often against daunting odds. What does the future hold? ■

Leaders for Today

More opportunities exist now than ever before for African Americans. As they set their sights on lifelong achievement, African American youth can look to notable figures in government, business, and other fields to guide them.

Many of today's most visible black leaders are in the political world. Among them is **Condoleezza Rice**, who served as national security adviser during the first administration of George W. Bush. Rice later replaced Colin Powell as U.S. secretary of state. Political adviser Donna Brazile is another influential black leader. She became the first African American to direct a major presidential campaign when she headed Vice President Al Gore's 2000 run for the presidency.

Recently African Americans have also increased their presence in elected offices. In 2000 there were more than 9,000 black elected officials in the United States. Among recent leaders was Carol Moseley Braun of Illinois. In 1993 Braun became the first black woman elected to the U.S. Senate and in 2004 she sought the Democratic nomination for president. **Barack Obama** is another well-known black politician. Representing Illinois in the U.S. Senate, Obama is only the fifth black American senator. At the state level Deval Patrick made history in 2006 when he became the first black governor of Massachusetts. Patrick is only the second African American elected governor since Reconstruction.

Many of today's black leaders are working to improve the black community. Organizations such as the National Urban League strive to strengthen and empower black communities through leadership and educational programs. Other groups are working to improve education, health care, and the criminal justice system. Opportunities to take action in political, economic, and cultural arenas are endless. Past leaders have provided a strong foundation on which to build. It is up to the leaders of tomorrow to continue their legacy. ✔

✔ Reading Check

1. Explain In what areas are some black leaders making an impact today?

_____

_____

_____

_____

_____

Ensuring the Legacy

Black activism did not end with the achievements of the civil rights era. Though there remain areas in which progress can be made, African Americans of all ages and walks of life are working to improve life in the United States and around the world.

Educational Challenges

Today's African American leaders continue to emphasize that education is the key to real progress. They point out that an achievement gap remains between white and black students. As a group, black students have higher dropout rates and lower scores on standardized tests than do white students.

African Americans also face challenges in higher education. The percentage of African Americans who attend college is disproportionately lower than that of other Americans. About 13 percent of African Americans enrolled in colleges attend historically black colleges and universities (HBCUs). In 2001 more than one-fifth of all bachelor's degrees awarded to blacks were from HBCUs. In the past few decades, however, black enrollment at HBCUs has declined.

INFO TO KNOW
More than half of all African American professionals are graduates of HBCUs.

More than 50 years after the U.S. Supreme Court ruling in *Brown* v. *Board of Education*, many schoolchildren are increasingly separated according to race. In some areas, schools that had been integrated years ago are now either mostly black or mostly white, a situation that some people call **resegregation**. As large numbers of white and middle class black families moved to the suburbs, the tax base of many urban school districts declined. As a result, inner-city schools often lack adequate funding, which creates obstacles to effective education.

Debates continue over the effects of single-parent households on high black student dropout rates. Some scholars have suggested that single-parent households may have a more difficult time providing full educational and health opportunities for youth. In working-class neighborhoods around the country, however, one can find informal networks of friends and families that pool their resources in order to help ensure their youth have a greater chance of staying in school.

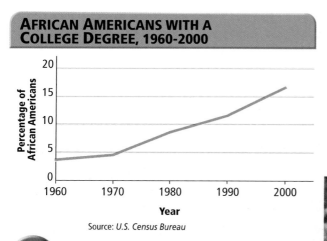

AFRICAN AMERICANS WITH A COLLEGE DEGREE, 1960-2000

Source: *U.S. Census Bureau*

Skills FOCUS INTERPRETING GRAPHS

2. About what percentage of African Americans had college degrees in 1960 and in 2000?

_____

_____

African American Population

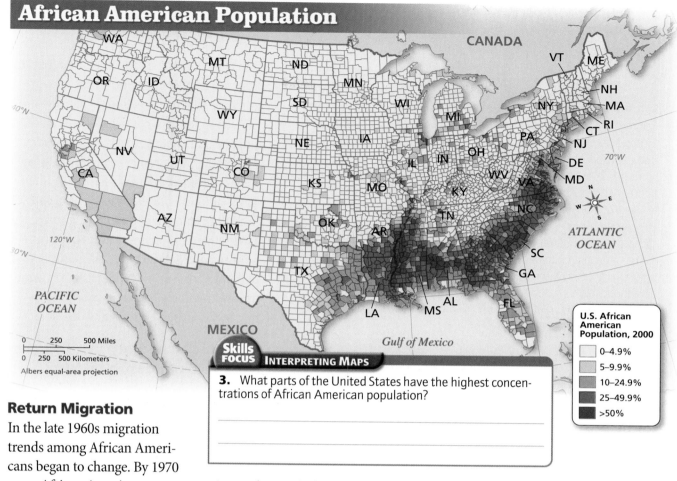

U.S. African American Population, 2000

☐	0–4.9%
☐	5–9.9%
☐	10–24.9%
☐	25–49.9%
☐	>50%

Skills FOCUS INTERPRETING MAPS

3. What parts of the United States have the highest concentrations of African American population?

Return Migration

In the late 1960s migration trends among African Americans began to change. By 1970 more African Americans were returning to the South than leaving it, a situation sometimes referred to as the **Third Great Migration**. Many blacks moved south out of a feeling of family duty or responsibility. For example, some black Americans who had left the South in the 1940s and 1950s returned later to care for elderly parents.

Many Northern-born blacks also migrated to the South. Some had a desire to return to their roots or heritage, though many came for greater job opportunities. Many companies had moved their manufacturing operations to the South for various reasons such as cheaper land, government incentives, and a more temperate climate.

This trend continues today. By 2000 some 7 million African Americans had returned to former slave states. Although room for improvement remains, the South offers some distinct lifestyle advantages over the North, including lower crime rates and a lower cost of living. Many people see the return of African Americans to the South as a sign of great progress.

INFO TO KNOW
In February 2007 Virginia legislators passed a resolution officially apologizing for the state's role in the slave trade. Virginia is the first state to do so. The resolution also expresses regret for the exploitation of Native Americans by European settlers.

Societal Challenges

African Americans today still face societal challenges such as equal access to jobs and education. Affirmative action programs designed to address this issue face growing resistance today, mainly among white Americans. Many opponents contend that affirmative action policies require that decisions are based on race or gender rather than merit. In 1996 voters in California approved Proposition 209, an amendment that banned the use of racial preferences in decisions such as university admissions.

Barack Obama does not have the background one might expect of an up-and-coming political figure. Born to a white American mother and a Kenyan father, Obama was raised in Hawaii and Indonesia. In 1991 he graduated from Harvard Law School and later began his political career in the Illinois Senate.

In July 2004 Obama came to national attention with his keynote address at the Democratic National Convention. He drew praise for his view of a government: "[P]eople don't expect government to solve all their problems. But they sense, deep in their bones, that with just a slight change in priorities, we can make sure that every child in America has a decent shot at life, and that the doors of opportunity remain open to all." In 2004 he was elected to the U.S. Senate, and in 2007 he announced his run for the Democratic nomination for president.

4. Evaluate What do you think of Obama's view of government?

_____

_____

✔ **Reading Check**

5. Recall What are some obstacles to equality that African Americans still face?

_____

_____

_____

_____

In 2003 the Supreme Court upheld a policy of the University of Michigan Law School which used race as a factor in its admissions process. In the same year, however, the Court struck down the university's undergraduate affirmative action policy. Affirmative action remains a much-debated issue and one that continues to stir controversy.

Another important societal issue today is that of **environmental racism**, the intentional or unintentional practice of racial bias in dealing with environmental concerns. Environmental racism includes targeting minority and low-income communities for pollution sites and excluding minority community members from regulatory bodies that make such environmental decisions.

A Promising Future

Though challenges remain, the future is bright and full of promise for today's youth. By looking to positive black role models, such as Barack Obama and others, young people can begin to see how their actions can make a difference in their communities and in the world.

The African American community is dynamic and diverse. Regardless of their political or religious views, cultural heritage, or socioeconomic status, African Americans have the responsibility and the privilege of working together to improve the quality of life for generations to come. From modern times back to our country's infancy, there are many courageous figures that will continue to inspire African Americans to greatness in the twenty-first century and beyond. ✔

SECTION 3 ASSESSMENT

go.hrw.com
Online Quiz
Keyword: SAAH HP13

Reviewing Ideas, Terms, and People

6. Recall Who are some modern African American leaders in public service?

_____

_____

7. Analyze How is the Third Great Migration different from the original Great Migration?

_____

_____

8. Elaborate How can today's youth continue the legacy of progress established by past generations of African Americans?

_____

_____

Creating a Time Capsule

The future cannot be predicted, but looking at the past can help us understand the changes that will come. In the space below, create a list of items that you would include in a time capsule to be opened in 30 years. Be sure to include items that will help explain to future citizens what life is like today.

Time Capsule to Be Opened in Year _____

Items to Be Included _____

_____

_____

_____

_____

_____

_____

_____

_____

_____

_____

_____

_____

_____

_____

_____

ASSESS YOUR KNOWLEDGE

1. **Explain** How will the contents of your time capsule show future citizens what life is like for African Americans today?

_____

_____

_____

2. **Elaborate** If you could include only one of your items in a classroom time capsule, which one would you choose? Why?

_____

_____

_____

Quiz and Review

ONLINE QUIZ
Take a practice quiz for each section in this chapter.

CHAPTER REVIEW
Use the online Chapter Review to help you prepare for the chapter test.

Activities

HISTORICAL DOCUMENTS
Read and explore key documents that shaped African American history.

VIRTUAL FIELD TRIP
Take a virtual field trip to experience key sites from African American history.

VOICES OF HISTORY
Experience African American history and culture through recordings of key people and documents.

Partner

CONNECTING TO OUR PAST
Examine artifacts from **Howard University's Moorland-Spingarn Research Center** that bring to life the study of African American history.

African Americans in Modern America

CHAPTER SUMMARY

SECTION 1   Social and Cultural Life

- Afrocentrism is a separatist black nationalist movement that rejects the traditional Eurocentric view of world history.
- Many recent African immigrants are highly educated and familiar with urban life and tend to live in large cities.
- African Americans have contributed much to contemporary culture.

SECTION 2   Activism Today

- Activists have continued to fight racial discrimination by promoting community participation.
- Emergency response to Hurricane Katrina revealed some racial inequalities that many Americans are attempting to address.

SECTION 3   Looking to the Future

- The number of African Americans in leadership positions continues to grow.
- African Americans have made significant strides toward racial equality and social justice in the last few decades, though some challenges still remain.

Reference Section

Biographical Dictionary

A

Aaron, Henry "Hank" (1901–1971) African American athlete, he holds several Major League Baseball records, including most career home runs.

Abbott, Robert S. (1870–1940) African American journalist and publisher, he founded the influential black newspaper the *Chicago Defender* in 1905. (p. 194)

Abernathy, Ralph (1926–1990) Martin Luther King Jr.'s closest advisor and successor as head of the SCLC. He led the Poor People's Campaign after King's death. (p. 281)

Ailey, Alvin (1931–1989) African American dancer and choreographer, he founded the Alvin Ailey American Dance Theater. (p. 299)

Ali, Muhammad (1942–) African American athlete and civil rights activist, he is one of the most successful boxers of all time, winning the world heavyweight boxing championship three times. (p. 296)

Allen, Richard (1760–1831) Former slave who founded the first church for African Americans in the United States. His church was the foundation for the African Methodist Episcopal (AME) Church. (p. 73)

Anderson, Marian (1897–1993) Singer who fought discrimination in the 1930s, Eleanor Roosevelt arranged for her to perform on the steps of the Lincoln Memorial in 1939. (p. 245)

Angelou, Maya (1928–) African American poet, author, and actress, she is known for her autobiography *I Know Why the Caged Bird Sings* and her collection of poetry *Just Give Me a Cool Drink of Water 'Fore I Die*. (p. 332)

Armistead, James (c. 1760–1830) A former slave who served as a spy in the Continental Army; he provided information that helped American forces defeat the British at the Battle of Yorktown in 1781. (p. 61)

Armstrong, Louis (1901–1971) Jazz musician during the Harlem Renaissance, he was a talented trumpeter and singer who influenced later musicians. (p. 220)

Ashe, Arthur (1943–1993) African American athlete, he was the first black man to win a major professional tennis tournament, the U.S. Open. (p. 296)

Attucks, Crispus (c. 1723–1770) An African American sailor and former slave; one of five colonists killed during the Boston Massacre of March 5, 1770. (p. 58)

B

Baldwin, James (1924–1987) Black author of the civil rights era, his works include the novels *Go Tell It On the Mountain* and *Notes of a Native Son*, and the essay collections *The Fire Next Time and No Name in the Street*. (p. 297)

Banneker, Benjamin (1731–1806) African American inventor, mathematician, astronomer, and writer; he was hired to help survey land for the city of Washington, D.C. (p. 75)

Baraka, Amiri (1934–) American poet, essayist, playwright, and activist born LeRoi Jones, he founded the Black Arts movement. His works include *Preface to a Twenty-Volume Suicide Note* and the play *The Dutchman*. (p. 298)

Basie, William "Count" (1904–1984) African American composer and musician, he was one of the most influential bandleaders in the 1930s and 1940s. (p. 246)

Bearden, Romare (1911–1988) African American artist known for his oil paintings, cartoons, and collages.

Beckwourth, James (1798–1866?) African American explorer and mountain man who spent time in the unsettled western United States. (p. 92)

Benezet, Anthony (1713–1784) White Protestant leader from Philadelphia who wrote several pamphlets opposing slavery; he set up a school to educate the children of slaves. (p. 66)

Berry, Chuck (1826–) African American musician and composer, one of the pioneers of rock 'n' roll.

Berry, Halle (1966–) American actress and model, she was the first African American woman to win the Oscar for best actress in 2002, for her role in *Monster's Ball*. (p. 333)

Bethune, Mary McLeod (1875–1955) Educator and civic leader, she was the first African American woman to head a federal agency, the Division of Negro Affairs of the National Youth Administration. (p. 230)

Biko, Steven (1946–1977) South African anti-apartheid activist, founder of the Black Consciousness Movement. Biko was murdered by South African police while in their custody. (p. 317)

Bluford, Guion (1942-) U.S. Air Force colonel and astronaut, he became the first African American in space in 1983.

Booth, John Wilkes (1838–1865) Actor and Confederate supporter who assassinated Abraham Lincoln in 1865. (p. 140)

Bouchet, Edward Alexander (1852-1918) African American physicist, he was the first African American to receive a Ph.D from an American university. He was awarded the degree by Yale University in 1876.

Bowser, Mary Elizabeth (c. 1840–unknown) Former slave who served as a Union spy in the home of Confederate President Jefferson Davis during the Civil War. (p. 122)

Bradley, Benjamin (c. 1830-?) African American slave and inventor who devised a steam engine to be used on warships, he was not allowed to patent his invention because he was a slave.

Braun, Carol Moseley (1947-) American politician and lawyer, she became the first black woman elected to the U.S. Senate in 1992. Braun was also the first black senator from the Democratic Party. (p. 345)

Brazile, Donna (1959-) African American political consultant and campaign manager for Al Gore's run for the presidency in 2000, she was the first African American to head a major presidential campaign. (p. 345)

Brooke, Edward W. (1919-) African American politician, he served as U.S. Senator from Massachusetts from 1967 to 1979. (p. 305)

Brooks, Gwendolyn (1917–2000) American poet, in 1950 she became the first African American poet to win a Pulitzer Prize for her book *Annie Allen*. (p. 247)

Brown, Claude (1937–2002) African American author, his works include *Manchild in the Promised Land* and *The Children of Ham*. (p. 297)

Brown, Henry "Box" (1815–c. 1864) African American who escaped slavery in Virginia by folding himself into a box and having himself mailed to a free state. (p. 98)

Brown, James (1933–2006) Singer and composer who helped popularize soul and funk music. His best-known songs include "Please, Please, Please," "Papa's Got a Brand New Bag," and "I Got You (I Feel Good)." (p. 299)

Brown, John (1800–1859) Militant white abolitionist who organized a slave revolt and raid on a federal arsenal at Harpers Ferry, Virginia. (p. 108)

Bruce, Blanche K. (c. 1841–1898) Founder of the first elementary school for blacks in Kansas, he later moved to Mississippi and was elected to the Senate. (p. 151)

Bullard, Eugene Jacques (1894–1961) First black fighter pilot, he fought in World War I. (p. 203)

Bullins, Ed (1935–) African American playwright and political activist, he was a member of the Black Panther Party and joined the Black Arts movement in the 1960s. His plays include *Clara's Old Man, The Theme Is Blackness*, and *The Fabulous Miss Marie*, which won an Obie award in 1971. (p. 298)

Bunche, Ralph (1904–1971) African American diplomat and United Nations adviser, he became the first black man to win the Nobel Peace Prize in 1950 for his role in negotiating a peace treaty in the Arab-Israeli War of 1948. (p. 274)

Bush, George Washington (1790?–1863) African American soldier and pioneer, he served during War of 1812 and led settlers along the Oregon Trail to Washington. (p. 92)

Calloway, Cab (1907–1994) African American singer and bandleader popular during the jazz age and the swing era and a master of the scat musical style, he is best known for his hits "Minnie the Moocher" and "St James Infirmary Blues." (p. 246)

Carlos, John (1945–) African American track and field star who drew international criticism by raising his fist in a black power salute from the medal platform at the 1968 Olympic Games in Mexico City. (p. 297)

Carmichael, Stokely (1941–1998) American civil rights activist, he was an important leader of the Black Power movement in the 1960s. (p. 287)

Carney, William H. (1840–1904?) A sergeant in the 54th Massachusetts Infantry who was awarded the Congressional Medal of Honor for his bravery in battle during the Civil War. (p. 121)

Carson, Benjamin S. (1951–) African American neurosurgeon, he became the leader of the pediatric neurosurgery group at Johns Hopkins Hospital in Maryland at age 33. (p. 345)

Carver, George Washington (c. 1864–1943) African American scientist and educator, he developed more than 400 products that could be made from peanuts, soybeans, and sweet potatoes. (p. 195)

Chesnutt, Charles Waddell (1858–1932) African American author, he wrote three novels: *The House Behind the Cedars, The Marrow of Tradition*, and *The Colonel's Dream*. (p. 193)

Chisholm, Shirley (1924-2005) First black woman to serve in the U.S. Congress, she was elected in 1968. In 1972 she became the first black woman to seek the Democratic party's nomination for president. (p. 305)

Cinque, Joseph (c. 1873-c. 1879) Slave who led the successful mutiny aboard the Spanish slave ship *Amistad*. Cinque and his shipmates were tried in the United States where they were judged to be free and allowed to return to Africa. (p. 96)

Cleaver, Eldridge (1935–1998) American civil rights leader and author, he was one of the leaders of the Black Panther Party. He is known for a collection of essays, *Soul on Ice*, which influenced the black power movement. (p. 297)

Coffin, Levi (1798–1877) American abolitionist and Underground Railroad conductor, he is believed to have helped more than 2,000 slaves reach freedom. (p. 98)

Coltrane, John (1926–1967) African American musician and composer, he helped shaped the sound of modern jazz. His important albums include *Giant Steps, My Favorite Things, Blue Train*, and *A Love Supreme*.

Connerly, Ward (1939-) Conservative black activist and opponent of affirmative action, he served on the University of California Board of Regents and founded the American Civil Rights Institute. (p. 309)

Cooke, Sam (1931–1964) African American singer, composer, and entrepreneur who helped transform gospel and rhythm blues style into soul music. His hit songs include "You Send Me," "Chain Gang," "Another Saturday Night," "Wonderful World," and "A Change Is Gonna Come,"

Cosby, Bill (1937–) American comedian and actor, he was the first black actor to star as the lead in a dramatic television series, *I Spy*. His other shows include *The Cosby Show, Cosby*, and *Fat Albert and the Cosby Kids*. Cosby has also supported numerous charities that provide educational opportunities to American children.

Cuffe, Paul (1759–1817) Freeborn African American who became a successful shipping merchant; he built schools for black children and attempted to use his wealth to take free blacks to Africa to live. (p. 67)

D

Daley, Phyllis Mae (unknown) African American nurse, during World War II she became the first black woman to serve in the U.S. Navy Nurse Corps. (p. 238)

Davis, Angela (1944–) African American professor, civil rights activist, and Communist, she was put on trial for the murder of a federal judge in 1970. Acquitted in a well-publicized trial, Davis became a vocal critic of racial and gender prejudice.

Davis, Benjamin O. (1877–1970) American Army officer and educator, he served with distinction during World War I and World War II, and became the first African American to be promoted to the rank of general. (p. 237)

Davis, Benjamin O., Jr. (1912–2002) The son of General Benjamin O. Davis, he was the commander of the Tuskegee Airmen during World War II. In 1965 became the first African American brigadier general in the U.S. Air Force. (p. 238)

Davis, Miles (1926–1991) African American musician and composer, he was instrumental in the development of several different styles of jazz. His albums include *Kind of Blue, Milestones, Miles Ahead,* and *Sketches of Spain.*

de Klerk, F. W. (1936–) South African president who helped dismantle that country's apartheid system in the 1980s. (p. 318)

Delany, Martin R. (1812–1885) African American abolitionist, physician, and officer in the Civil War; he was an early supporter of colonization. (p. 107)

DePriest, Oscar (1871–1951) African American politician and businessman, he was elected to the U.S. House of Representatives from Illinois in 1928, the first black congressman elected in the twentieth century. (p. 229)

Douglas, Aaron (1898–1979) Harlem Renaissance painter, among the first to experiment with modernism and to use African symbols in his art. He has been called the father of African American art. (p. 221)

Douglass, Frederick (1817–1895) Former slave, abolitionist, and writer, he published his autobiography, *The Narrative of the Life of Frederick Douglass,* and founded the abolitionist newspaper, the *North Star.* (p. 106)

Dove, Rita (1952–) American poet, the second African American to win the Pulitzer Prize, for *Thomas and Beulah.* She was the first African American and the youngest person to be named U.S. Poet Laureate. (p. 332)

Drew, Charles (1904-1950) African American physician and scientist noted for his research on blood plasma and for establishing the first blood bank.

Dunham, Katherine (1909–2006) African American dancer and choreographer, she was the first person to put ethnic Caribbean and African dances on stage. (p. 299)

Durham, James (1762–c. 1802) First African American doctor in the United States; he set up a successful medical practice in Philadelphia. (p. 75)

Du Bois, W. E. B. (1868–1963) African American educator, editor, and writer, he led the Niagara Movement, calling for economic and educational equality for African Americans. He helped found the NAACP. (p. 177)

Dunbar, Paul Laurence (1872–1906) African American poet, his works include poetry collections *Oak and Ivy, Majors and Minors,* and *Lyrics of Lowly Life,* and the novels *The Uncalled* and *The Sport of the Gods.* (p. 193)

Dunbar Nelson, Alice Moore (1875–1935) African American poet and civil rights advocate, wife of Paul Laurence Dunbar, her published works include *Violets and Other Tales* and *The Goodness of St. Rocque and Other Stories.* (p. 193)

Du Sable, Jean Baptiste Point (c. 1750–1818) Haitian-born merchant and trader, he founded the frontier settlement that became Chicago, Illinois. (p. 43)

E

Eckford, Elizabeth (1941–) One of the Little Rock Nine, a group of African American students who desegregated Central High School in Arkansas. (p. 256)

Ellington, Edward "Duke" (1899–1974) African American composer and musician, he led one of the country's most popular jazz bands from the 1920s to the 1970s. His most famous compositions include "Mood Indigo," "Sophisticated Lady," "Down Beat," and "Black, Brown, and Beige." (p. 245)

Elliott, Robert B. (1842–1884) African American attorney elected to Congress in 1870, he resigned his seat in 1874 to serve as the South Carolina speaker of the house. (p. 150)

Ellison, Ralph (1913–1994) African American writer, his novel *Invisible Man* won the National Book Award in 1953. Other works include the novel *Juneteenth.* (p. 247)

Ellison, William (1790–1861) former slave, successful South Carolina businessperson, and slave owner . (p. 90)

Equiano, Olaudah (c. 1750–1797) Enslaved African who was freed, became an abolitionist, and wrote *The Interesting Narrative of the Life of Olaudah Equiano.* (p. 35)

Estevanico (c. 1503–1539) North African slave who accompanied Spanish expeditions in the Americas; known for his explorations of the southwestern United States. (p. 42)

Evers, Medgar (1925–1963) Head of the National Association for the Advancement of Colored People (NAACP) in Mississippi, he was shot and killed in front of his home in 1963 by a member of the Ku Klux Klan. (p. 273)

Farmer, James (1920–1999) American civil rights leader and one of the founders of the Congress of Racial Equality (CORE). He later served as assistant secretary of Health, Education, and Welfare under President Nixon. (p. 269)

Farrakhan, Louis (1933–1975) American religious leader and head of the Nation of Islam. He organized the Million Man March in 1995. (p. 289)

Fauset, Crystal Bird (1894–1965) African American politician, the first black woman to serve in a state legislature. (p. 239)

Fauset, Jessie Redmon (1882–1961) Female writer of the Harlem Renaissance. (p. 219)

Fields, Mary (1832–1914) Former slave who moved west and ran a stagecoach line through the Montana Territory in the late 1890s. (p. 187)

Fletcher, Benjamin (1890–1949) Black labor leader who was jailed for organizing unions in the 1910s. (p. 213)

Flipper, Henry O. (1856–1940) First black cadet to graduate from the United States Military Academy at West Point. (p. 166)

Forbes, George (unknown) African American publisher, he co-founded the *Guardian* newspaper in 1901. (p. 194)

Forten, Charlotte (c. 1817–1885) African American teacher and abolitionist who became a volunteer teacher for African Americans during the Civil War. (p. 133)

Forten, James (1766–1842) African American abolitionist and entrepreneur, he attempted to use his wealth to start a shipping line to take blacks to Africa. (p. 98)

Franklin, Aretha (1942–) African American musician known as "the queen of soul" and one of the most popular singers of the 1960s and 1970s. Her hits include "Respect," "Chain of Fools," "(You Make Me Feel Like) A Natural Woman," "Think," and "Freeway of Love." (p. 299)

Gabriel Prosser (c. 1776–1800) Slave who led the first major slave rebellion in the United States. (p. 95)

Gaines, Lloyd (c. 1913–1939) Civil rights activist, he filed a lawsuit after being denied admission to law school at University of Missouri on the basis of his race. (p. 254)

Gandhi, Mohandas (1869–1948) Leader of India's struggle for independence, he taught nonviolent resistance, which was later practiced by many U.S. civil rights leaders. (p. 264)

Garrison, William Lloyd (1806–1879) White American journalist and reformer; he published *The Liberator* and helped found the American Anti-Slavery Society. (p. 107)

Garnet, Henry Highland (1815–1882) Former slave and African American minister and abolitionist, he urged slaves to fight for their freedom. (p. 106)

Garvey, Marcus (1887–1940) Founder of the black nationalism movement and the Universal Negro Improvement Association. A staunch supporter of relocation to Africa, Garvey also encouraged pride in African heritage. (p. 212)

Gaye, Marvin (1939–1984) One of the most successful singers with Motown Records, his hits included "How Sweet It Is (To Be Loved By You)," "Ain't No Mountain High Enough" and "Heard It Through the Grapevine." (p. 299)

Gillespie, John Birks "Dizzy" (1917–1993) African American musician, composer, and bandleader, he helped shape American jazz. His best-known works include "Salt Peanuts," "Groovin' High," and "Manteca."

Giovanni, Nikki (1943–) African American poet, her works include the poetry collections *Black Feeling, Black Talk* and *Re: Creation*. (p. 298)

Glover, Savion (1973–) African American dancer, choreographer, and tap dancer, he has appeared in several successful Broadway musicals.

Goode, Sarah (1850-?) Former slave and inventor, she became the first African American woman to receive a patent in 1885.

Gordy, Berry (1932–) African American record producer and entrepreneur, he founded Motown Records. He produced hits by such artists as Smokey Robinson, Diana Ross and the Supremes, the Four Tops, the Temptations, Marvin Gaye, Stevie Wonder, and the Jackson 5. (p. 299)

Graham, Shirley (1907–1977) Composer, playwright, and biographer, her 1932 work *Tom-Tom* may be the first opera written by an African American woman. (p. 246)

Green, Ernest (1941–) One of the Little Rock Nine, he later served as assistant secretary of Housing and Urban Affairs under President Jimmy Carter. (p. 256)

Griffith-Joyner, Florence (1959–1998) African American athlete, she won numerous medals in track and field events during the 1988 Olympics. (p. 333)

Griggs, Sutton E. (1872–1933) African American minister and author, he wrote more than a dozen books, including *The Hindered Hand* and *Imperium in Imperio*. (p. 193)

H

Haley, Alex (1921–1992) African American novelist, he wrote the *Autobiography of Malcolm X* and *Roots: The Saga of an American Family*. (p. 297)

Hall, Primus (1756–1842) African American educator; he allowed black children to be taught in his Boston home and later built a school for African Americans. (p. 73)

Hamer, Fannie Lou (1917–1977) American civil rights activist, she was a prominent member of the Mississippi Freedom Democratic Party. (p. 281)

Handy, W. C. (1873–1958) Southern musician and composer who was the first to publish the blues, he is considered the father of that musical form. (p. 210)

Harper, Frances Ellen Watkins (1825–1911) Poet and abolitionist, she worked with the Underground Railroad and Pennsylvania Abolition Society. (p. 193)

Harris, Patricia Roberts (1924-1985) First African American ambassador and first black woman appointed to the cabinet, serving as secretary of housing and urban development and secretary of health, education, and welfare in the Carter administration. (p. 305)

Haynes, Lemuel (1754–1833) Revolutionary war hero, writer, and pastor; he was perhaps the first African American to serve as a minister in a white church. (p. 73

Height, Dorothy (1912-) African American educator and activist who campaigned for the rights of African Americans and women as a member of the National Council of Negro Women and the Young Women's Christian Association.

Hemings, Sally (1773–1835) A slave owned by Thomas Jefferson who served as maid and lady-in-waiting to Jefferson's daughters. (p. 60)

Hendrix, Jimi (1942–1970) African American musician and composer, one of the most influential guitarists in the history of rock 'n' roll.

Henson, Matthew (1866–1955) African American explorer, he was the chief guide and translator with the expedition that reached the North Pole in 1909. (p. 196)

Holiday, Billie (1915–1959) African American singer, considered one of the greatest female jazz singers of all time. Her hits include "Summertime," "God Bless the Child," and the anti-lynching ballad, "Strange Fruit."(p. 246)

Horne, Lena (1917–) Singer and actress, she was the first African American actor to sign a long-term contract with a major studio. She refused to play the subservient roles usually reserved for black actresses. (p. 246)

Horton, George Moses (c. 1797–c. 1883) African American poet, his first collection of poems, *The Hope of Liberty*, was published in 1829. (p. 85)

Houston, Charles Hamilton (1895–1950) African American attorney and civil rights activist, he led the NAACP's fight against segregated schools in the 1930s. (p. 254)

Hughes, Langston (1902–1967) Poet, essayist, and playwright of the Harlem Renaissance, he focused on black life and culture in the United States. (p. 218)

Hurston, Zora Neale (1891–1960) Novelist, story writer, and folklorist of the Harlem Renaissance, she wrote *Of Mules and Men* and *Their Eyes Were Watching God*. (p. 219)

Jackson, Jesse (1941–) American civil rights leader, minister, and politician; he became famous for his work on behalf of the poor and mounted campaigns for the Democratic presidential nomination in 1984 and 1988. (p. 310)

Jackson, Mahalia (1912–1972) African American singer and civil rights activist, she was one of the most popular gospel singers of all time. (p. 299)

Jemison, Mae (1956–) African American astronaut, scientist, and physician, she became the first black woman in space in 1992.

Jemison, T. J. (1918–) American pastor, he helped organize a protest and boycott in 1953 that eased segregation on buses in Baton Rouge, Louisiana. (p. 261)

Jennings, Thomas (1791-1859) African American inventor, he was the first black American to receive a patent.

Johnson, Andrew (1808–1875) American politician and the seventeenth president of the United States upon the assassination of Abraham Lincoln, he was impeached for his unpopular ideas about Reconstruction. (p. 140)

Johnson, Henry (1897–1929) World War I soldier, he fought with the 369th Infantry and was awarded France's Croix de Guerre. (p. 205)

Johnson, Jack (1878–1946) African American athlete, became the first black world heavyweight boxing champion in 1908, a title he held until 1915. (p. 244)

Johnson, James Weldon (1871–1938) Songwriter, poet, and activist of the Harlem Renaissance. He is most famous for the song "Lift Every Voice and Sing" and for the book of poems *God's Trombones*. (p. 219)

Johnson, Lyndon B. (1908–1973) Thirty-sixth president of the United States, became president after the assassination of John Kennedy. Johnson led the nation through the civil rights movement, signing many antidiscrimination bills into law. (p. 279)

Johnson, William H. (1901–1970) Artist of the Harlem Renaissance known for landscapes and scenes of daily life among African Americans. (p. 221)

Jones, Edward (unknown) African American clergyman; he was one of the first two blacks to graduate from a college in the United States when he received his degree from Amherst College in Massachusetts in 1826. (p. 73)

Jones, Edward P. (1951–) African American author, he won the Pulitzer Prize in 2004 for his novel *The Known World*. (p. 332)

Jones, James Earl (1931–) Award-winning African American actor, he appeared in the films *Field of Dreams, The Hunt for Red October,* and as the voice of Darth Vader in *Star Wars*. (p. 298)

Jones, Loïs Mailou (1905–1998) Famed painter of the Harlem Renaissance. (p. 221)

Joplin, Scott (1868–1917) African American musician and composer, he is credited with developing ragtime. His best-known compositions include "The Entertainer," "Maple Leaf Rag" and the opera "Treemonisha."

Jordan, Barbara (1936-1996) Politician from Texas; she served in the Texas Senate from 1966 to 1972 and was elected to the House of Representatives in 1972, the first black woman elected to Congress from the South. (p. 306)

Jordan, Michael (1963–) African American athlete, one of the greatest basketball players of all time. He led the Chicago Bulls to six National Basketball Association (NBA) championships and set many records in the sport. (p. 333)

Joyner-Kersee, Jackie (1962–) African American athlete, she won multiple gold and silver medals in track and field events during Olympic games during the 1980s and 1990s. (p. 333)

Julian, Percy L. (1899–1975) African American scientist and the first black chemist elected to the National Academy of Sciences with patents for many medicines.

Karenga, Maulana (1941–) American educator and author, he created Kwanzaa in 1966. (p. 329)

Keckley, Elizabeth (c. 1818–1907) African American dressmaker and confidante to Mary Todd Lincoln, she wrote the memoir *Behind the Scenes*. (p. 192)

Kennedy, John F. (1917–1963) Thirty-fifth president of the United States, he was the youngest person and the first Roman Catholic elected president. He had proposed the Civil Rights Act but was assassinated before the bill could be passed. (p. 279)

Kennedy, Robert (1925–1968) American politician, he was attorney general during his brother President Kennedy's presidency and worked toward desegregation. He was assassinated during his bid for the 1968 Democratic presidential nomination. (p. 270)

Kenyatta, Jomo (c. 1893-1978) African nationalist and political leader; he helped Kenya achieve independence from British control and became its first president. (p. 315)

Keyes, Alan (1950-) American diplomat and conservative activist; served as U.S. ambassador to the United Nations from 1983 to 1985. (p. 308)

King, Coretta Scott (1927–2006) American civil rights leader and wife of Martin Luther King Jr. After his murder in 1968, she remained active and founded the Center for Nonviolent Social Change, more commonly known as the King Center. (p. 338)

King, Martin Luther, Jr. (1929–1968) American minister, writer, and civil rights leader, he was a celebrated and charismatic advocate of civil rights for African Americans in the 1950s and 1960s. (p. 263)

King, Rodney (1965–) African American whose beating by four white Los Angeles police officers was captured on videotape and broadcast across the country. In 1992, the officers were acquitted, sparking a series of riots in Los Angeles. (p. 338)

Kitt, Eartha (1927–) African American actress and singer, she is best known for singing the hit song "Santa Baby" and for appearing on the TV series *Batman*. (p. 299)

Knight, Gladys (1944–) African American singer with the group Gladys Knight and the Pips. Their hit songs include "Heard It Through the Grapevine," "Neither One of Us (Wants to Be the First to Say Goodbye)," and "Midnight Train to Georgia." (p. 299)

Larsen, Nella (1891–1964) Female writer of the Harlem Renaissance. (p. 219)

Latimer, Lewis (1848–1928) African American inventor who worked on the telephone and the light bulb. (p. 195)

Lawrence, Jacob (1917–2000) American artist who drew upon African American history as subjects for paintings, prints and murals. He is best known for his series of paintings, *The Migration of the Negro*. (p. 247)

Lawson, James (1928–) African American minister and civil rights leader, he taught nonviolence to members of the civil rights movement in the United States. (p. 264)

Lee, Spike (1957–) American filmmaker who wrote, directed, produced, and acted in movies that deal with the African American experience, including *Do the Right Thing, Malcolm X, 4 Little Girls,* and *When the Levees Broke*. (p. 332)

Lewis, John (1940–) American politician and civil rights activist who became head of the Student Nonviolent Coordination Committee (SNCC). He was elected to Congress in 1986. (p. 280)

Lincoln, Abraham (1809–1865) Sixteenth president of the United States, he issued the Emancipation Proclamation in 1863. (p. 116)

Locke, Alain (1886–1954) Howard University professor who encouraged black artists to connect to their heritage and helped inspire the Harlem Renaissance. (p. 217)

Long, Jefferson (1836–1900) First African American from Georgia to serve in the House of Representatives. (p. 152)

Louis, Joe (1914–1981) African American boxer, world heavyweight champion from 1937 to 1949. Considered one of the greatest heavyweight boxers of all time. (p. 244)

Love, Nat (1854–1921) Former slave who moved west and gained fame as a cowboy, champion rider, and marksman, earning the nickname "Deadwood Dick." (p. 186)

Lynch, John R. (1847–1939) Former slave who was elected to the Mississippi state legislature in 1869, eventually becoming speaker of the house. (p. 151)

Malcolm X (1925–1965) Militant African American civil rights leader who spoke in support of black separatism, black pride, and the use of violence for self-protection. (p. 289)

Mandela, Nelson (1918-) South African anti-apartheid activist; he helped end apartheid and became the first black president of South Africa. (p. 316)

Mansa Musa (died c. 1332) Mali's greatest and most famous ruler, he was a devout Muslim. He made a famous pilgrimage to Mecca that helped spread Mali's fame to the rest of the world. (p. 10)

Marsalis, Wynton (1961–) African American musician, composer, and educator, known for his recordings of both jazz and classical music.

Marshall, Thurgood (1908–1993) First African American U.S. Supreme Court Justice, he first rose to prominence by arguing *Brown* v. *Board of Education*. (p. 254)

Mason, Bridget "Biddy" (1818-1891) Former slave and entrepreneur who became one of the first African Americans to purchase land in Los Angeles.

Matzeliger, Jan Ernst (1852–1889) African American inventor, he developed a machine that automated the shoemaking process. (p. 194)

McCoy, Elijah (c. 1843–1929) African American inventor, he patented a machine that automatically lubricated the steam engines of trains and later adapted the device to be used in factory machines. (p. 195)

McKay, Claude (1890–1948) Militant writer of the Harlem Renaissance, he wrote the poem "If We Must Die" and the novel *Home to Harlem*. (p. 219)

McDaniel, Hattie (1895–1952) American actor, she was the first African American to win an Academy Award for her role in *Gone With the Wind*. (p. 246)

Meredith, James (1933–) Civil rights activist who entered the University of Mississippi after being denied admission because of his race, leading to violent riots. (p. 271)

Miller, Doris "Dorie" (1919–1943) Sailor who was the first African American awarded the Navy Cross for his bravery during the attack on Pearl Harbor in 1941. (p. 236)

Miller, May (1899–1995) African American playwright, her works often addressed racial issues. Miller's works include *Scratches, Stragglers in the Dust*, and *Nails and Thorns*. (p. 246)

Mitchell, Arthur (1934–) American dancer and choreographer, he founded the Dance Theater of Harlem, the first African American ballet company. (p. 299)

Monk, Thelonious (1917–1982) Jazz musician and composer, one of the founders of bebop. His works include "'Round Midnight," "Blue Monk," and "Misterioso."

Moody, Anne (1940–) African American author and civil rights activist, she wrote the autobiography *Coming of Age in Mississippi*. (p. 297)

Moore, Harry T. (1905–1951) African American educator and activist who sought equal pay for black teachers in Florida; he was killed due to his activism. (p. 254)

Morgan, Garrett (1877-1963) African American inventor who devised an early form of traffic light and an early form of the gas mask.

Morris, Robert (1823–1882) One of the nation's first African American attorneys, he filed an unsuccessful segregation suit against the city of Boston in 1849. (p. 254)

Morrison, Toni (1931–) African American author, she won the Pulitzer Prize for *Beloved* in 1988 and the Nobel Prize for Literature in 1993. Her other novels include *The Bluest Eye, Song of Solomon, Paradise*, and *Love*. (p. 332)

Moses, Robert (1935–) African American civil rights activist, he was one of the leaders of the Student Nonviolent Coordinating Committee (SNCC) who organized voting registration drives in the south during the 1960s. (p. 271)

Moynihan, Daniel Patrick (1927-2003) U. S. Senator and author of the controversial report, "The Negro Family: The Case for National Action." (p. 322)

Muhammad, Elijah (1897–1975) American religious leader, he led the Nation of Islam following the death of Fard Muhammad. (p. 288)

Muhammad, Fard (c. 1877–1934) Founder of the Nation of Islam. (p. 288)

Myers, Isaac (1835–1891) Black labor leader, he organized the Colored National Labor Union in 1869. (p. 181)

Nash, Diane (1938–) Civil rights activist and a founder of the SNCC, she helped organize a series of sit-ins at stores and bus terminals in the South in the 1960s. (p. 264)

Neal, Larry (1937–1981) black playwright, he co-founded the Black Arts Repertory Theatre/School. (p. 298)

Newton, Huey P. (1942–1989) American civil rights activist and founder of the Black Panther Party. (p. 288)

Nichols, Nichelle (1932–) American actress, she was one of the first African American women to play a major role in a prime time television series, *Star Trek*. (p. 299)

Nkrumah, Kwame (1909-1972) African nationalist leader and statesman; he was the first president of Ghana. (p. 315)

Northrup, Solomon (1808-c. 1893) Former slave and abolitionist who wrote about his experiences in *Twelve Years a Slave*. (p. 91)

Obama, Barack (1961–) African American political leader and author elected to the Senate from Illinois in 2004, he announced his run for the presidency in 2007. (p. 345)

Odetta (1930–) African American musician who helped popularize blues and folk music during the 1950s and 1960s. (p. 299)

O'Neil, Buck (1911–2006) A star of baseball's Negro Leagues, he became the first African American coach in Major League Baseball in 1962.

Owens, Jesse (1913–1980) Black track and field star, he won four gold medals at the 1936 Olympic Games. (p. 244)

Paige, Satchel (1906–1982) African American athlete, he was one of the best players in baseball's Negro Leagues.

Parker, Charlie (1920–1955) Musician and composer, he helped create bebop. His compositions include "Yardbird Suite," "Anthropology," and "Confirmation."

Parker, William (1822-?) Escaped slave who founded the Christiana black self protection group in Christiana, Pennsylvania. Parker fled to Canada after members of his group killed a white slave trader. (p. 114)

Parks, Gordon (1912-2006) African American photographer and director, he is best known for his photo essays in *Life* magazine and for the 1971 film *Shaft*.

Parks, Rosa (1913–2005) African American civil rights activist, she was arrested in 1955 for refusing to give her bus seat to a white man. (p. 262)

Parsons, Richard D. (1973–) African American business leader, he is chairman and chief executive officer of Time Warner, Inc.

Patrick, Deval (1956–) American political leader, he became the first black governor of Massachusetts in 2006 and the second black governor in U.S. history. (p. 345)

Patterson, Frederick (1901-1988) African American scientist and educator, he served as president of Tuskegee University and created the United Negro College Fund. (p. 243)

Pickett, Bill (c. 1860–1932) African American cowboy, the inventor of the rodeo sport of steer wrestling. (p. 186)

Pinchback, P. B. S. (1837–1921) Black delegate at the Louisiana convention during Reconstruction, he became a state senator, lieutenant governor, and governor. (p. 150)

Plessy, Homer (1863–1925) American civil rights activist, in 1891 he challenged Louisiana's segregation laws by boarding a streetcar reserved for whites. (p. 167)

Poitier, Sidney (1927–) African American actor and civil rights activist, the first black man to win an Oscar for his role in the *Lilies of the Field*. Other films include *A Raisin in the Sun* and *Guess Who's Coming to Dinner*. (p. 298)

Powell, Colin (1937-) Chairman of the Joint Chiefs of Staff and a four-star general; served as secretary of state from 2001 to 2005. (p. 306)

Price, Leontyne (1927–) African American opera singer, one of the most celebrated sopranos in the world. (p. 299)

Rainey, Gertrude Pridgett "Ma" (1882–1939) African American blues singer popular during the 1920s. (p. 333)

Rainey, Joseph (1832–1887) Former slave who was elected to the U.S. House of Representatives in 1870, the first black man to serve in that body. (p. 152)

Randolph, A. Philip (1889–1979) African American labor leader whose work prompted President Franklin Roosevelt to issue the Fair Employment Act in 1941. (p. 231)

Ray, James Earl (1928–1998) Confessed assassin of Martin Luther King Jr., he later recanted his confession. He died in prison in 1998. (p. 282)

Reed, Ishmael (1938–) African American author, his works include *The Free-Lance Pallbearers, Mumbo-Jumbo*, and *The Last Days of Louisiana Red*. (p. 298)

Revels, Hiram (1822–1901) American clergyman, educator, and politician, he became the first African American in the U.S. Senate. (p. 151)

Reyes, Francisco (unknown) Black settler who served as mayor of Los Angeles from 1793 to 1795. (p. 92)

Rice, Condoleezza (1954–) American political leader, she was the first black woman to be named national security advisor in 2001 and secretary of state in 2005. (p. 345)

Rillieux, Norbert (1806-1894) African American scientist and former slave who developed a process vital to the refining of sugar.

Roberts, Needham (unknown) World War I soldier, he fought with the 369th Infantry and was awarded France's Croix de Guerre. (p. 205)

Robeson, Paul (1898–1976) African American actor, singer, and activist, he won acclaim for his roles in *Othello, All God's Chillun Got Wings*, and *Emperor Jones*. (p. 246)

Robinson, Bill "Bojangles" (1878–1949) Tap dancer and vaudeville star who became one of the first black stars on Broadway and in Hollywood. (p. 221)

Robinson, Jackie (1919–1972) American baseball player, he was the first black player in the major leagues. (p. 257)

Roosevelt, Eleanor (1884–1962) Author, diplomat, humanitarian, and First Lady of Franklin D. Roosevelt, she supported much New Deal legislation aimed at young people and minorities. (p. 245)

Roosevelt, Franklin Delano (1882–1945) Thirty-second president of the United States, he led the country through the Great Depression and World War II and passed laws to help black Americans. He served four terms, more than any other president. (p. 229)

Rosenwald, Julius (1862-1932) American business leader and philanthropist, he donated millions of dollars to open schools for black students across the country in the early 1900s.

Ross, Diana (1944–) African American singer and actress, a member of the Supremes. Her hits include "Baby Love," "Stop! In the Name of Love," and "Love Child." (p. 299)

Rudolph, Wilma (1940–1994) African American athlete, she was the first American woman to win three Olympic gold medals in a single year at the 1960 Summer Olympics. (p. 297)

Rush, Benjamin (1745–1813) American statesman and one of the signers of the Declaration of Independence; he was a prominent figure in the antislavery fight. (p. 66)

Russwurm, John B. (1799–1851) African American writer and publisher; he was one of the first two blacks to graduate from college in the United States. (p. 73)

Rustin, Bayard (1912–1987) African American civil rights leader, he was one of the founders of the Congress of Racial Equality (CORE). (p. 265)

Salem, Peter (1750–1816) African American soldier who served in the Continental Army; he fought in the Battle of Bunker Hill in 1775. (p. 61)

Sanchez, Sonia (1934–) African American poet and author, her works include *Homegirls and Handgrenades* and the play *Black Cats and Uneasy Landings*. (p. 298)

Savage, Augusta (1892–1962) Sculptor of the Harlem Renaissance, known for portraits of black leaders. (p. 221)

Scott, Dred (1795?–1858) Slave who sued for freedom, but was eventually rejected by the Supreme Court. (p. 115)

Scott, Emmett J. (1873–1957) Former secretary to Booker T. Washington who served as special assistant to the Secretary of War during World War I. (p. 202)

Seale, Bobby (1937–) Founder of the Black Panthers, he was also one of the Chicago Eight, a group of Vietnam War protestors accused of inciting riots at the 1968 Democratic National Convention in Chicago. (p. 288)

Simone, Nina (1933–2003) African American jazz singer who often used her music to address social issues and protest the treatment of blacks. (p. 299)

Singleton, Benjamin "Pap" (c. 1809–1892) Former slave who led the Exodus of 1879 to the West. (p. 185)

Smalls, Robert (1839–1915) Former slave and steamboat pilot who captured the Confederate warship *Planter* during the Civil War. (p. 121)

Smith, Anna Deavere (1950–) African American actor and playwright; she wrote *Fires in the Mirror*. (p. 332)

Smith, Bessie (1892–1937) African American singer, she was one of the most popular and highest paid blues singers of the 1920s and 1930s. (p. 220)

Smith, J. W. (1850–1876) First African American to attend the United States Military Academy at West Point, he was expelled under suspicious circumstances. (p. 166)

Smith, Tommie (1944–) African American track and field star who drew international criticism by raising his fist in a black power salute from the medal platform at the 1968 Olympic Games in Mexico City. (p. 297)

Stevens, Thaddeus (1792–1868) Radical Republican leader of the House of Representatives during Reconstruction, he supported equality for African Americans. (p. 143)

Stowe, Harriet Beecher (1811–1896) American author and abolitionist, she wrote the famous antislavery novel, *Uncle Tom's Cabin*. (p. 108)

Sumner, Charles (1811–1874) Massachusetts senator and Radical Republican leader during Reconstruction; he was vocal in his opposition to slavery and support for equal rights. (p. 143)

Sweat, Heman (1912–1982) African American civil rights activist, he was the plaintiff in the Supreme Court case of *Sweatt* v. *Painter*. (p. 255)

Taylor, Susie King (1848–1912) African American nurse, teacher, and author who taught many African Americans during and after the Civil War. (p. 122)

Terrell, Mary Church (1863–1954) African American civil rights activist and author, she published her autobiography, *A Colored Woman in a White World*, in 1940. (p. 176)

Terry, Lucy (1730–1821) First known African American poet, she was also the first African American woman to argue a case before the U.S. Supreme Court. (p. 74)

Thomas, Clarence (1948–) Former chairman of the U.S. Equal Employment Opportunity Commission, he became the second black Supreme Court justice in 1991. (p. 306)

Till, Emmett (1941–1955) African American teenager murdered for whistling at a white woman. (p. 258)

Trotter, Monroe (1872–1934) African American activist newspaper publisher, he co-founded the *Guardian*. (p. 191)

Truth, Sojourner (c. 1797–1883) American evangelist and reformer, she became a speaker for abolition and women's suffrage. (p. 107)

Tubman, Harriet (c. 1820–1913) American abolitionist, the most famous Underground Railroad conductor. (p. 98)

Turner, Nat (1800–1831) American slave leader who led the most violent slave revolt in U.S. history. (p. 96)

Tutu, Desmond (1931–) South African bishop and apartheid activist; he won the Nobel Peace Prize in 1984. (p. 317)

Tyson, Cicely (1933–) African American actress, she won acclaim for her roles in the movies *Sounder*, *The Autobiography of Miss Jane Pittman*, *The Oldest Living Confederate Widow Tells All*, and *Roots*. (p. 299)

Tyson, Neil deGrasse (1958–) Astrophysicist and director of the Hayden Planetarium at the American Museum of National History in New York City.

Valiente, Juan (c. 1505–1553) African slave who participated in the Spanish conquest of South America. He played a role in founding the city of Santiago, Chile. (p. 43)

VanDerZee, James (1886–1983) Photographer of the Harlem Renaissance, best known for his portraits of prominent African Americans. (p. 221)

Vesey, Denmark (c. 1767–1822) A former slave who organized a slave revolt in South Carolina in 1822. (p. 96)

Walker, A'Lelia (1885-1931) African American business leader, she was a patron of the arts during the Harlem Renaissance. She was the daughter of Madame C. J. Walker, the cosmetics tycoon.

Walker, David (1785–1830) African American merchant and abolitionist, he published the controversial pamphlet, *Appeal to the Colored Citizens of the World*. (p. 106)

Walker, Edwin G. (1831–1901) Black politician elected to the Massachusetts House of Representatives in 1866, becoming the nation's first black legislator.

Walker, Kara (1969–) African American artist celebrated for representations of race and gender in her works.

Walker, Maggie Lena (1865–1934) A successful African American businesswoman, she was the country's first black female bank president. (p. 194)

Walker, Quock (1753–c. 1812) An escaped slave who brought a lawsuit against his former owner, which eventually led to slavery being outlawed in Massachusetts. (p. 66)

Walker, Sarah Breedlove "Madame C. J." (1867–1919) African American entrepreneur and benefactor, she was the first black woman to become a millionaire. (p. 194)

Waller, Fats (1904–1943) Jazz pianist and singer of the Harlem Renaissance, perhaps best known for the song "Ain't Misbehavin." (p. 220)

Wanton, George H, (1866–1940) African American soldier, he was awarded the Medal of Honor for his service during the Spanish-American War. (p. 188)

Washington, Booker T. (1856–1915) African American educator and civil rights leader, he founded the Tuskegee Institute. (p. 176)

Washington, Denzel (1954–) African American actor and director, he has won Academy Awards for his roles in *Glory* and *Training Day*. (p. 332)

Washington, Harold (1922-1987) Black politician, he represented Illinois in the U.S. House of Representatives and was the first black mayor of Chicago. (p. 311)

Watts, J. C. (1957-) Conservative Republican politician from Oklahoma, he served in the U.S. House of Representatives from 1995 to 2003. (p. 308)

Wells-Barnett, Ida (1862–1931) African American journalist and anti-lynching activist, she was part owner and editor of the *Memphis Free Speech*. (p. 169)

Wheatley, Phillis (c. 1753–1754) Poet and slave, the first African American to have her work published. (p. 74)

White, George Henry (1852–1918) American statesman, he was the first African American to serve in Congress after Reconstruction. (p. 169)

Wilder, Douglas (1931) First African American elected governor of a U.S. state, he served as governor of Virginia from 1990 to 1994. (p. 306)

Williams, Daniel Hale (1858–1931) African American surgeon, he performed the first successful heart operation in the world in 1893. (p. 196)

Williams, Serena (1981–) African American athlete and sister of Venus Williams, she is one of the most successful female tennis players of all time. (p. 332)

Williams, Venus (1980–) African American athlete and sister of Serena Williams, she is one of the most successful female tennis players of all time. (p. 332)

Wilson, August (1945–2005) African American playwright, he won Pulitzer Prizes for his plays *Fences* and *The Piano Lesson*. (p. 333)

Winfrey, Oprah (1954–) Actress, talk show host, entrepreneur, and philanthropist, she was the first woman in history to own and produce her own talk show. (p. 332)

Wonder, Stevie (1950–) African American singer, songwriter, and record-producer. He is an award-winning musician and popular Motown recording artist. (p. 299)

Woods, Granville T. (1856–1910) African American inventor, he developed an automatic air brake system for trains that significantly improved railroad safety. (p. 195)

Woods, Tiger (1975–) African American athlete, he is one of the top golfers of all time. (p. 332)

Woodson, Carter (1875-1950) African American historian and author, he helped establish the academic field of African American Studies. He led the first campaign to set aside a Black History Week each year.

Wright, Richard (1908–1960) African American writer, his best-selling novels *Native Son* and *Black Boy* dealt with racism in American society. (p. 247)

York (c. 1770–c. 1832) African American slave who accompanied the Lewis and Clark expedition. (p. 92)

BIOGRAPHICAL DICTIONARY

Glossary

A

abolition movement the individuals and groups that opposed slavery and their activities to end it (p. 106)

affirmative action a policy of giving special consideration in hiring and school admissions to women and nonwhites in order to correct years of discrimination (p. 307)

African diaspora the scattering of people of African descent throughout the Americas and the world that resulted from the forced migrations of Africans away from their homelands in Africa (p. 36)

African National Congress (ANC) an organization founded in 1912 to press the South African government for equal rights for the country's nonwhite citizens (p. 316)

Afrocentrism a view of the world and history emphasizing Africa and developments coming from African cultures as central (p. 329)

age-sets social groupings of those close in age and usually of the same gender who share strong bonds and common experiences (p. 13)

Amistad mutiny an 1839 revolt of African captives aboard a Spanish slave ship that led to a series of trials in the United States and eventual freedom for the captives (p. 96)

amnesty usually referring to a formal or official act of forgiveness or pardon (p. 139)

animism the belief that belief that bodies of water, animals, trees, and other natural objects have spirits (p. 13)

antebellum period a period in U.S. history that lasted from after the War of 1812 to just before the outbreak of the Civil War (p. 83)

antislavery societies groups that supported and actively worked for the elimination of slavery (p. 65)

assembly line a manufacturing system in which one step is performed at each stop as the product moves along (p. 227)

Atlanta Compromise a philosophy given in a speech by Booker T. Washington that economic improvement of African Americans would lead to their later gains in political rights (p. 176)

Atlantic slave trade the transportation of captured Africans across the Atlantic Ocean for sale into slavery primarily in the New World (p. 29)

B

Bantu migrations a series of migrations over the course of about 2,500 years of various Bantu speaking people from west and central Africa south and across the African continent (p. 20)

Battle of the Bulge the final major push by Germany during World War II; it succeeded in breaking through Allied lines and temporarily stopped the Allied advance (p. 236)

Black Cabinet a term used to describe a group of both informal and appointed African American advisors to President Franklin D. Roosevelt (p.230)

Black Codes local and state laws adopted in the South during Reconstruction that greatly limited the rights of African Americans (p. 141)

black nationalism an ideology in favor or black self-government as well as social separation from whites. (p. 212)

Black Panther Party a group founded in 1966, inspired by the idea of Black Power, that provided aid to black neighborhoods; often thought of radical or militant black civil rights organization (p. 287)

Black Power an African American social movement that advocated black pride, unity, and self-reliance to address injustice (p. 287)

blues a form of music that originated in the Mississippi Delta and spread north during the Great Migration; it combines instrumental rhythms and expressive lyrics to convey emotions (p. 210)

border states located between the North and the Confederacy, these strategically important states of Kentucky, Missouri, Maryland, and Delaware sided with the Union during the Civil War (p. 122)

Boston Massacre event that became a symbol of the American Revolution after British soldiers fired into a crowd and killed five Boston patriots who were among those who had thrown snowballs at the soldiers (p. 58)

boycott to reject or avoid products or dealing with someone or some group, usually used to show disapproval or to force changes in policies or actions (p. 58)

Brown v. Board of Education the Supreme Court case in which the justices unanimously decided that segregation in public schools was unconstitutional (p. 255)

buffalo soldiers a term given to all African American army regiments serving mostly in the West after the Civil War (p. 187)

C

cash crops agricultural products that are produced primarily for profit (p. 39)

Civil Rights Act of 1866 a law passed during Reconstruction that gave African Americans rights equal to those of white Americans (p. 143)

Civil Rights Act of 1957 civil rights legislation passed under the Eisenhower administration that gave the federal government certain powers meant to ensure African American voting rights (p. 271)

Civil Rights Act of 1964 a law passed during the Johnson administration that authorized federal action against racial, ethnic or gender discrimination in employment and public places (p. 279)

colonization movement the plan to resettle African Americans in colonies in Africa (p. 99)

Compromise of 1850 an agreement by Congress that bridged the differences between the pro-slavery and antislavery representatives, giving slaveholders more power to capture escaped slaves, while allowing California to join the U.S. as a free state and ending slave trading in Washington, D.C. (p. 113)

conductor a person who coordinated the escape of slaves in the Underground Railroad (p. 92)

Confederate States of America also commonly called the Confederacy, the government of the eleven states whose withdrawal from the United States started the Civil War (p. 116)

Congress of Racial Equality (CORE) an early and nonviolent action organization in the American civil rights movement (p. 269)

Congressional Black Caucus an organization of African American members of the U.S. Congress that is dedicated to promoting issues of concern to the black community (p. 305)

contrabands escaped slaves (p. 120)

cotton belt large expanse of cotton-producing lands that stretched from the southeastern states across the Gulf Coast states into Texas (p. 82)

cotton gin a machine that changed the cotton production industry in the late eighteenth century by removing seeds from raw cotton fibers about 50 times faster than a worker could do by hand (p. 81)

creole a language that arises from contact between two other languages and has features of both, such as Gullah (p. 71)

D

D-Day Invasion a major military offensive considered a turning point in World War II when Allied forces landed in Europe on the beaches of Normandy in Northern France on June 6, 1944 to take on German soldiers and liberate Europe (p. 236)

Declaration of Independence document written in 1776 announcing the colonies' freedom from British control and guaranteeing certain rights to all colonial citizens (p. 59)

de facto discrimination discrimination not supported by laws, but commonly practiced (p. 280)

de facto segregation a separation of different groups that is not legally sanctioned, but is practiced informally (p. 323)

discrimination prejudice towards an entire group often resulting in unfair treatment of those people judged to be different or inferior from those in the majority or in power (p. 107)

domestication a process that takes plants and animals from a wild state to one under human control (p. 3)

domestic slave trade the sale, exchange and relocation of slaves within the United States (p. 83)

***Dred Scott* decision** (1857) a U.S. Supreme Court ruling that African Americans were not U.S. citizens, that the Missouri Compromise's restriction on slavery was unconstitutional, and that Congress did not have the right to ban slavery in any federal territory (p. 115)

E

emancipation freeing of the slaves (p. 66)

Emancipation Proclamation Abraham Lincoln's order freeing all the slaves in rebel territory (p. 124)

Enforcement Acts group of laws passed by Congress in 1870 and 1871 that banned the activities of groups like the Ku Klux Klan; empowered the army and courts to capture and punish KKK members (p. 158)

environmental racism actions and non-actions on the subject of pollution and the environment that harm certain racial groups more than others (p. 348)

Exodus of 1879 a mass movement of African Americans who travelled west to Kansas in 1879 seeking more freedom and economic improvement (p. 185)

Exodusters a term given to those African Americans who took part in the Exodus of 1879 (p. 185)

extended family a family unit consisting of parents and children that includes relatives such as grandparents, uncles, aunts, and cousins and that might live together in one household (p. 13)

Fifteenth Amendment the 1870 addition to the Constitution that guaranteed the vote to all U.S. males without reference to racial or social background (p. 145)

54th Massachusetts Infantry one of the first all black Civil War regiments formed after Congress approved recruitment of black soldiers (p. 121)

First Louisiana Native Guards an all black Civil War regiment, also called the *Corps d'Afrique*, that gained control of New Orleans for the Union forces (p. 121)

folklore traditional customs, sayings, stories, or other forms of art (p. 219)

Fourteenth Amendment a law added to the Constitution in 1868 giving citizenship to anyone born in, or accepted as a citizen into, the United States and guaranteeing all citizens equal protection under the law (p. 144)

free blacks African Americans who during colonial times either had never been slaves or had gained their freedom (p. 67)

Freedmen's Bureau a Reconstruction agency that provided emergency relief to poor people throughout the South and that also assisted the African Americans adjust to their new lives (p. 133)

Freedom Rides CORE's idea for nonviolent form of protest intended to challenge segregation in which blacks and whites took bus trips together through the deep south (p. 270)

French and Indian War part of a much larger European conflict that France and Great Britain fought from 1754 through 1763 over territories in North America (p. 57)

Fugitive Slave Act laws passed by Congress intended to ensure the return of runaway slaves (p. 113)

GI Bill an act that provided education and economic support for veterans returning from World War II (p.243)

grandfather clause a law added to the constitutions of many Southern states, stating that a man could vote if he, his father, or his grandfather had been eligible to vote before January 1, 1867 (p.158)

Great Depression a slowdown and decline in the national and worldwide economy that began around 1929, lasted for more than a decade and brought about widespread unemployment and poverty (p. 228)

Great Migration the trend during the second decade of the twentieth century when hundreds of thousands African Americans left the South for greater opportunities in northern cities (p. 210)

griots the traditional storytellers of West Africa who were charged with remembering and telling of history (p. 13)

Harlem a neighborhood in northern Manhattan in New York City that became the home of large numbers of blacks during the Great Migration, and that retains its African American cultural identity to this day (p. 217)

Harlem Renaissance the flourishing of African American cultural, social and artistic activities and developments centered in Harlem during the early decades of the twentieth century (p. 217)

hieroglyphics ancient Egyptian writing system using pictures and symbols (p. 4)

hip-hop a predominantly urban cultural movement popular especially among young African Americans and Latinos; it encompasses music, clothing styles, dance, and art. (p. 331)

historically black colleges and universities (HBCUs) accredited institutions of higher education founded before 1964 to educate black Americans (p. 191)

hominid two-legged, erect form of humans including their extinct relatives (p. 3)

Hurricane Katrina one of the strongest, deadliest and costliest storms to hit the United States, it battered the Gulf Coast in the late summer of 2005, laying waste to large parts of New Orleans and Mississippi as well as doing widespread damage in Alabama and Florida (p. 339)

imperialism taking over control or influence of smaller and weaker countries by a stronger, larger country (p. 201)

indentured servant a servant who agrees to work for a specific period of time, usually in exchange for passage to the place of employment, room and board (p. 52)

indigo term used for both the plant used to make a dark-blue dye and the name of the dye or color (p. 49)

Industrial Revolution a period of dramatic social and economic change in the western world during the late eighteenth century when machines replaced many areas of human production (p. 81)

inner cities neighborhoods located in older, central areas of urban regions; they tend to struggle with poverty, poor living conditions, and racial tensions (p. 321)

integration equal acceptance and incorporation of all in a community or society; assimilation (p. 165)

island hopping a strategy used by the Allies against Japan during World War II in which military forces captured one strategically important island after another and used each as a base to launch an attack on the next (p. 217)

jazz an African American musical form that developed in New Orleans, Louisiana, that blends several different styles of music (p. 221)

Jim Crow Era a period following Reconstruction during which laws and customs that enforced segregation developed (p. 165)

Juneteenth annual holiday in Texas that celebrates when news of the Emancipation Proclamation had arrived for the first time in Galveston, Texas on June 19, 1865 (p. 125)

K

Kansas-Nebraska Act the congressional law that set up the Kansas and Nebraska territories and opened these lands to settlers (p. 114)

kente brightly colored, patterned, usually hand-woven ceremonial cloth of Ghana (p. 295)

Ku Klux Klan a private group that believed in the superiority of the white race and opposed Reconstruction by terrorizing its Union representatives, freed blacks and anyone they thought supported blacks or Reconstruction (p. 157)

Kwanzaa a modern, non-religious, seven day African American cultural festival held from December 26 to January 1 created in 1966 to promote traditional family and community values (p. 329)

L

Little Rock Nine refers to nine African American students caught up in a conflict with the Arkansas governor who prevented their attendance to an all white Little Rock high school (p. 256)

Louisiana Purchase the largest single purchase of territory in U.S. history; made in 1803 it extended to the West and doubled the size of the United States (p. 92)

lynchings murders, usually by hanging, often by a mob, often directed at a person accused of a crime or offense without reason and without a trial (p. 170)

M

manual labor unskilled physical work done by hand (p. 25)

manumission the formal or legal freeing of a slave by his or her owner (p. 27)

March on Washington or, in full, the March on Washington for Jobs and Freedom, was a huge integrated demonstration in August 1963, the first of its size in Washington, D.C. and a key event in the civil rights movement (p. 273)

Maroons a term that developed in the 17th century to describe fugitive slaves in the Americas (p. 40)

Meroë a center of trade and the capital of the ancient kingdom of Kush (p. 6)

middle colonies Delaware, New Jersey, New York and Pennsylvania when they were part of colonial America before it became the United States of America (p. 51)

Middle Passage the long, forced transatlantic trip from West Africa to the Americas endured by captured Africans aboard slave ships (p. 34)

Million Man March a march organized by the Nation of Islam and held in Washington, D.C. in 1995 to protest inequality and to display social harmony and participation among black men (p. 337)

Missouri Compromise an agreement between pro-slavery and antislavery divisions in the U.S. Congress that determined the slavery issue in Maine and Missouri and where slavery could or could not be extended in areas that had been part of the Louisiana Purchase (p. 111)

Motown Records a popular record label based in Detroit, Michigan; it featured African American artists (p. 299)

Montgomery bus boycott 1955 boycott organized in Montgomery, Alabama, in which blacks protested unequal treatment by refusing to use the city's buses (p. 262)

 N

Nation of Islam also known as the Black Muslim movement, it was originally an African American separatist organization that promoted self-improvement for blacks through the religious principles of Islam (p. 289)

National Association for the Advancement of Colored People (NAACP) a civil rights organization formed by W.E.B. Du Bois, other members of the Niagara Movement and white reformers (p. 180)

National Black Political Convention a 1972 gathering of black politicians, activists, and educators that developed an agenda of political, social, and educational issues of importance to the black community (p. 306)

National Urban League a contemporary organization originally formed as the National League on Urban Conditions Among Negroes in 1911 to consolidate economic development among African Americans (p. 179)

Navigation Acts a series of laws created by the British government for Great Britain's economic benefit controlling all shipping commerce into or out of the American colonies (p. 57)

New Deal a term used to describe the sweeping reform programs put into action under President Franklin D. Roosevelt (p.210)

New England colonies northernmost colonies including Connecticut, Massachusetts, New Hampshire and Rhode Island; a term that in modern times includes Maine and Vermont (p. 53)

neutral not taking or supporting any side, usually in regard to war or disagreement (p. 202)

Niagara Movement a civil rights organization started by W.E.B. Du Bois and others that led to the creation of the National Association for the Advancement of Colored People (p. 178)

Nubia meaning "land of the blacks" to the Egyptians, it was located along the Nile, south of Egypt (p. 5)

O

Operation Breadbasket an organization started by Martin Luther King Jr.'s Southern Christian Leadership Conference in 1962 that took action to advance the economic status of African Americans (p. 281)

oral history a narrative of the past often passed from one generation to the next (p. 12)

overseer someone who watches over or supervises while someone else works (p. 39)

 P

Pan-Africanism the idea of uniting all African nations or all people of African heritage to work together for a common goal (p. 201)

pharaoh a powerful ruler of ancient Egypt, often thought to be a god (p. 4)

plantation large farm specializing in a single crop (p. 29)

Plessy v. *Ferguson* a Supreme Court case that found in favor of a Louisiana statute and ruled that segregation was legal if it was "separate but equal" (p. 167)

poll tax a tax that must be paid in order to vote (p. 158)

popular sovereignty the idea that government is for and by people, and during the Civil War the opinion of abolitionists that citizens living in the territories should be free of government interference (p. 113)

Progressive movement a late nineteenth century and early twentieth century movement for social change (p. 175)

R

racial profiling characterizing a person based solely on race as a suspect likely to commit or to have committed a crime (p. 339)

racial stereotyping forming and often acting on a usually negative opinion about an entire group of people based on their race (p. 329)

Radical Republicans a small but influential group of anti-slavery Republicans in Congress during the Civil War and Reconstruction who took strict and unforgiving positions toward the states that had joined the Confederacy (p. 143)

Rainbow Coalition organization founded by Jesse Jackson to unite and represent the interests of various under-represented groups in U.S. politics (p. 311)

Reconstruction a period of 12 years following the Civil War when the Confederate States were rebuilt and once again included with the rest of the United States (p. 131)

Reconstruction Acts laws passed by Congress over President Johnson's veto that set out specific conditions under which Confederate states could be readmitted to the Union (p. 144)

Redeemer governments a term given to Southern state governments that sought to overturn or undo Reconstruction reforms (p. 156)

Red Summer a violent period of race riots during 1919 (p. 210)

Republican Party a new political party organized in 1854 by those who were antislavery and opposed the Kansas-Nebraska Act (p. 116)

resegregation returning to a separation of the races after desegregation has already been accomplished (p. 346)

Revolutionary War the battle for freedom by the colonies in North America against Great Britain from 1775 to 1783 that led to the independence of the colonies and the formation of the United States of America (p. 59)

school busing a program designed to solve the issue of segregated schools by transporting white and black students from one area to another (p. 323)

scribe someone who records or copies information in written form (p. 5)

Second Great Migration the mass movement of African Americans from southern states to western and northern states which took place following World War II (p. 243)

sectionalism clash of interests between people of different regions (p. 111)

segregation keeping groups separate based on their differences (p. 165)

sharecropping a new system that developed after the Civil War when a farmer who could not afford his own land would work for someone else in exchange for use of the land, the necessary supplies to farm it and a portion of the owner's crop (p. 159)

sit-in a form of nonviolent protest in which people occupy a place, often a seat, such as in a restaurant, and refuse to leave; used by the civil rights movement to achieve equal treatment (p. 265)

slaver a ship used to transport slaves (p. 35)

Slaughterhouse Cases a group of lawsuits over Louisiana statutes affecting the meatpacking industry that reached the Supreme Court as a single case about the Fourteenth Amendment (p. 167)

soul music a style of music originated by African Americans that combines elements of gospel music along with rhythm and blues (p. 299)

Southern Christian Leadership Conference (SCLC) a civil rights organization formed to unite and thereby strengthen the efforts of several smaller groups (p. 264)

southern colonies Georgia, Maryland, North Carolina, South Carolina, and Virginia when they were part of colonial North America before the founding of the United States (p. 49)

Southern Homestead Act a mostly ineffective law passed by Congress during Reconstruction, and later repealed, meant to provide southerners, both black and white, with farm land (p. 135)

Spanish-American War a brief war in 1898 between the United States and Spain which helped Cuba win independence (p. 188)

spirituals a kind of religious song, usually associated with African Americans and often with themes from the Bible (p. 85)

Student Nonviolent Coordinating Committee (SNCC) a civil rights nonviolent action organization formed and led by black college students (p. 266)

sub-Saharan Africa the area and countries of the African continent below the southern edge of the Sahara (p. 9)

Swahili an East African coastal people and their common language, widely spread by traders, that combined elements of Bantu and Arabic (p. 19)

Sweatt v. Painter 1950 Supreme Court case that overturned the policy that had prevented blacks from attending University of Texas Law School first at all and later as "separate but equal" (p. 255)

swing a type of jazz particularly popular during the 1930s; it featured complicated, carefully planned orchestrations (p. 245)

Ten-Percent Plan a Reconstruction plan of President Lincoln's in which any former Confederate state could rejoin the Union and set up a new state government if ten percent of its citizens who had voted in the presidential election of 1860 swore their loyalty to the Union, and if the state outlawed slavery (p. 139)

tenant farming evolved out of sharecropping when a farmer was successful enough that he could afford to rent the land from the owner, choose which crops to grow and earn the profit (p. 160)

Thirteenth Amendment an addition to the Constitution that in 1865 outlawed slavery anywhere in the United States (p. 131)

Third Great Migration the migration of African Americans from northern cities to the South that took place in the last part of the twentieth century (p. 347)

Three-Fifths Compromise an agreement reached during the 1787 drafting of the U.S. Constitution between representatives of pro-slavery states and antislavery states that counted a slave as three-fifths of a person to set both taxation and a state's representation in Congress based on population (p. 68)

369th Infantry an all black infantry regiment of World War I also known as the Harlem Hellfighters (p. 204)

triangular trade any of many routes of three-way trade involving captured West Africans sold into slavery in exchange for commodities in or from Europe and the New World (p. 33)

Tuskegee Airmen an all African American division of combat pilots who trained at the Tuskegee Institute and served in World War II (p. 238)

Underground Railroad a network of people who helped enslaved people escape to free states in the North (p. 97)

United Negro College Fund a charitable organization created in 1944 to support higher education for African Americans (p. 244)

vaudeville a type of entertainment popular at the turn of the century which featured acting, music, and comedy (p. 221)

Voting Rights Act of 1965 a law that increased voting access for blacks by outlawing obstacles such as literacy tests and allowing federal involvement to enforce black voter rights (p. 280)

Wade-Davis Bill a Radical Republican plan voted into law by Congress but vetoed by President Lincoln that would have set extremely strict conditions by which Confederate states could rejoin the Union (p. 140)

white supremacy a belief that white people are better than people of other races, often including the view that therefore they should rule over the others (p. 156)

World War II a war fought from 1939 to 1945 across Europe, Asia and Africa between the Allied Forces consisting mainly of Great Britain, France, Russia and the United States against the Axis powers mostly made up of Germany, Italy and Japan (p. 235)

NOTES

In the space below, list any additional terms, people, or places from *Holt African American History* or your own research that you consider noteworthy or significant.

GLOSSARY

Index

sources, 215; distinguishing fact from opinion, 147; evaluating sources, 342; examining continuity and change, 312; examining differing points of view, 292–293; interpreting graphs, 189; interpreting maps, 7; interpreting political cartoons, 259; interpreting time lines, 63; interpreting visuals, 86–87; making comparisons, 241

Songhai, *10m*, 11–12

soul music, 299

Souls of the Black Folks, The (Du Bois), 178, *178q*

South Africa, in: apartheid, 316–318

South Carolina: emergence of black political leaders, 150; readmitted to the Union, 145; secession of, 116; slaves in colony, 49

Southern Christian Leadership Conference (SCLC): Albany Movement, 272; Birmingham campaign, 273; formation of, 264

southern colonies: plantation system, 49–50; slave revolts, 51; slaves on smaller southern farms, 51

Southern Homestead Act, 135

Southern University, *191c*

Spain: slave trade, *28c*, 33

Spanish-American War, 188

Spelman College, 191

spirituals, 85

sports: 1930s and 1940s, 244; and civil rights era, *277p*, 296–297, *296p*; breaking color line in baseball, *257p*, 257–258, 296–297; modern America, 332

St. Louis: Great Migration and, *210c*, *210m*

stage. *See* theater and film.

Stamp Act, 58

Stevens, Thaddeus, 143, 159

St. Philip's College, *191c*

stock market, 228

Stowe, Harriet Beecher, 108, 285

Student Nonviolent Coordinating Committee (SNCC): Black power movement, 287; voter registration drive, 271; formation of, 266; Freedom Rides, 270; March on Selma, 280

sub-Saharan Africa, 9–13, 17–20

Sugar Act, 58

Sumner, Charles, 143, 159, 254

Sumter, Fort, 119

Sunni Ali, 11

Suppression of the African Slave Trade to the United States of America, 1638-1870, The (Du Bois), 178

Supreme Court: 66, 348; black justices on, 254, 308; *Brown v. Board of Education*, 255–256, 323; *Buchanan v. Warley*, 180; *Dred Scott* decision, 115; *Gaines v. Canada*, 254; *Guinn v. United States*, 180; *McLaurin v. Oklahoma State Regents*, 255; *Moore v. Dempsey*, 180; *Plessy v. Ferguson*, 167–168; *Regents of the University of California v. Bakke*, 307; Slaughterhouse Cases, 167; *Sweatt v. Painter*, 255

Supremes, 299

Swahili, *18m*, 19

Sweatt, Heman, 255

Sweatt v. *Painter*, 255

swing era, 245–246

Taney, Roger, 115

Tappan, Arthur and Lewis, 108

Taylor, Susie King, 122, 133, *133q*

television, 298–299, 332

Temptations, 299

tenant farmers, 158–159

Tennessee: civil rights movement in, 264, 265–266, 282; HBCUs, *191c*; readmitted to the Union, 145; secession of, 119

Tennessee State University, *191c*

Terrell, Mary Church, 176

Terry, Lucy, 74

Texas: HBCUs, *191c*; Hurricane Rita, 340; integration of higher education, 255; readmission of, 157; secession of, 116

Texas Western College, *296p*, 297

theater and film: 1930s–1950s, 246; civil rights era, 298–299; in modern America, 332–333; Harlem Renaissance, 221

Their Eyes Were Watching God (Hurston), 219

Third Great Migration, 347

Thirteenth Amendment, 131

Thomas, Clarence, 308, *308p*

Thomas and Beulah (Dove), 333

Three-Fifths Compromise, 68

369th Infantry, 204–205, *204p*, *205p*

Till, Emmett, 258, *258p*

Timbuktu, *10m*, 11

time lines, 63, 101, 117

Tom-Tom (Graham), 246

trade. *See* also domestic slave trade, slave trade: ancient East Africa, 17–18; ancient Ghana, 9–10; ancient Kush, 6; ancient Songhai, 12; Great Zimbabwe, 20

Treaty of Paris, 61

triangular trade, *32m*, 33, *37m*

Trowbridge, J. T., 134, *134q*

Truman, Harry S, 237, 253; ending segregation in military, 244, *244q*, 253

Truth, Sojourner, 107, 122, *122p*

Tubman, Harriet: fighting Fugitive Slave Act, 113; life of, 98, *98p*; as Union spy, 122

Turé, Kwame, 287

Turner, Benjamin, *150p*

Turner, Nat, 96, *96p*

Tuskegee Airmen, 238, *238p*

Tuskegee Institute, *175p*, 177, 191, 196, 237, 238, 243

Tutu, Desmond, 317, *318p*

Tyson, Cicely, 298

Umkonto we Sizwe ("Spear of the Nation"), 317

"Uncle Toms", 285

Uncle Tom's Cabin (Stowe), 108, 285

Underground Railroad, *97m*, *97p*, 97–98, 113

unemployment: see also employment; after World War I, 211; during Great Depression, 228–231; during 1970s and 1980s, 308–309; and Watts riots, 286

Union army: African American soldiers, 120–121; black military spies, 122; Emancipation Proclamation, 123–125

unions: after World War I, 211, 213; during Great Depression, 231; during Progressive Era, 180–181; during World War II, 239

United Nations, 282, 317

United Negro College Fund (UNCF), 244

Universal Negro Improvement Association (UNIA), 212–213

Valiente, Juan, 43

VanDerZee, James, 221

Van Vechten, Carl, 246

Veracruz, Mexico, 41

Vesey, Denmark, 96

Vietnam War: dissatisfaction with civil rights movement and, 282, 285

Villard, Oswald Garrison, 180

Virginia: 306, 347; secession of, 119; slaves in colony, 49, 51

vocational education, 176

Voting Rights Act of 1965, 280

voting rights: among free blacks, 91; during Jim Crow era, 168–169; during Reconstruction, 144–145, 149–150, 160; Civil Rights Act of 1957, 271; Fifteenth Amendment, 145, *145p*; Populist movement, 169; registration drives, 271, 280, *280c*, 281, *281p*, 282; Voting Rights Act of 1965, 280

Wade-Davis Bill, 140

Waklimi, 18

Walker, David, 106, *106q*

Walker, Madame C. J., 194, *194p*

Walker, Maggie Lena, 194

Walker, Quock, 66

Wallace, George, 272

Waller, Fats, 220

Walls, Josiah, *150p*

Wanton, George H., 188

Warren, Earl, 255, *255q*

Washington, Booker T.: 176, *176p*, 212; Tuskegee Institute, 177

Washington, D. C.: Great Migration and, *210c*, *210m*; March on Washington, 273–274; Million Man March, 337; race riots in, 211, 286

Washington, Denzel, 332

Washington, George, 60, 74

Washington, Harold, 310

Washingtonians, The, 245

Watts, J. C., 308

Watts Riots, 286, *286p*

Weld, Theodore, 108

Wells-Barnett, Ida, 169, *169p*, 176

West Africa, *1p*, *12p*; culture, *7m*, *10m*, 12–13; arts, 13; ancient, 9–13; modern, 315; religion, 13; Songhai, 11–12; village and family life, 13

West Point, 166

Westward movement, 92, 185–188; black communities in, 186; black cowhands, 186–187; buffalo soldiers, 187–188; Exodusters, 185; Louisiana Purchase, 92

Wheatley, John, 74

Wheatley, Phillis, *74p*, 75

White, George Henry, 169, *169q*

Credits and Acknowledgments

Grateful acknowledgement is made to the following sources for permission to reproduce copyrighted material: